Praise for Marianne Ra
Winning Scholarships for
and The Scholarship Worksho

D1110354

"Nothing has proved more valuable than information gleaned from your book and your workshop. The scholarship success I have experienced, I owe to you. . . . You showed my family unbelievable opportunity!"

> —Brooke Brandon, Ragins/Braswell National Scholarship winner and attendee of Marianne Ragins's teleclass, *The Scholarship Class for High School Students*. Brooke won 26 scholarships and grants totaling $133,316. Brooke's brother, Barrett, also won over $45,000 in scholarships and grants.

"Marianne Ragins has been presenting The Scholarship Workshop to our youth and parents for years. Her enthusiasm, passion, and depth of knowledge in the area of obtaining scholarships for college education has not only encouraged and inspired first-time college students but also those students in pursuit of other advanced degrees. Marianne's presentations are precise and well organized. Her passion for educating others comes across every time she presents. The clarity of her presentations makes an overwhelming process a manageable and achievable goal for all who attend. The Scholarship Workshop is a MUST for anyone seeking to continue their educational endeavors."

> —Reverend Yalonda Blizzard, Mount Zion Baptist Church, workshop sponsor

"Marianne Ragins's Scholarship Workshops are phenomenal! Ms. Ragins has a wealth of knowledge and experience that is unparalleled. For the past three years, the U.S. Virgin Islands College Access Challenge Grant Program has included and plans to continue The Scholarship Workshop as part of our program activities. Through her workshops and presentations, Marianne provides valuable insights, information, strategies, and support that achieve successful results. Based on the feedback received from students, parents, and educators that have attended The Scholarship Workshop here in the Virgin Islands, everyone agrees that Marianne Ragins has perfected the art of the scholarship search."

> —Denise Lake, Educational Outreach Coordinator, College Access Challenge Grant Program

"Ms. Ragins is a powerful and passionate presenter who has tremendous knowledge and expertise regarding the college scholarship search and application process. She has provided the keynote address for our annual College Scholarship Conference for five consecutive years, and each year I continue to be impressed by her dynamic and comprehensive presentation. She has the unique ability to engage audiences of all ages and backgrounds, including traditional-age students, adult learners, parents, and professional educators. Folks leave her workshop empowered and inspired to execute the scholarship search and application process by using the practical strategies she shares. Ms. Ragins is a superb speaker and a consummate professional. She does not disappoint!"

—Dr. Debra Bright, Chair, College Scholarship
Conference, Montgomery College

"I received the Terry Winters Scholarship ($40,000) to attend the Corcoran College of Art + Design. The scholarship is for artistic talent and academic achievement. I am a nontraditional student (wife and mother returning to school). I learned so much during your lecture about finding scholarships, putting together the best application, and the importance of the supplementary materials. If your teachings could work for me, it will work for any student! Anyhow, thank you once again!! I traveled all the way from Baltimore for your Reston workshop . . . and it was the best thing I could have ever done!"

—Dara Brown, workshop attendee

"I would like you to know what a difference your book, *Winning Scholarships for College: An Insider's Guide*, has made to me and my son. After reading your advice, we began to collect data about college and financial aid. Greg (my son) was beginning his junior year last fall when we found out about a scholarship sponsored by a local celebrity. . . . Due to the preparation you recommended, we were ready to send in all of the necessary information by the deadline. In December, Greg was awarded $2,500 to be used at the college of his choice. That same month, using the same carefully prepared information, he was given a $3,500 grant."

—Mrs. Rebecca Rymer Baker

"Marianne Ragins is an example to everyone that if you try hard enough and put forth the effort you can accomplish anything."

—Thomas B. Murphy, former speaker of the House
of Representatives

"Some of the main things I learned at the workshop (weekend boot camp) was how to really sell yourself and all that you do in a positive light, and not to downplay anything you have done in your community, school, or wherever. After attending your workshop (weekend), it really opened my eyes to all the financial aid that is available to students and motivated me to apply to all scholarships, big or small, because knowing that I could possibly go to school for free just by applying for these scholarships pushed me to apply without constraint."

—Nisha Hodge, workshop attendee. Nisha attended
The Scholarship Workshop Weekend Boot Camp
which is also based on the book, *Winning
Scholarships for College*. Nisha used the knowledge
gained at the boot camp to compete against 24,000
other students and win the Gates Millennium
Scholarship, which will fully pay for her education.

"My son Marcus was accepted to a private university that cost $15,000 per year in tuition alone. The university did not offer any type of scholarship to him. After learning of this, Marcus and I started preparing and organizing information based on Marianne Ragins's book, *Winning Scholarships for College: An Insider's Guide*, and her workshop. Using this information, we were able to get enough scholarship money to pay for his entire tuition bill."

—Francine Robinson, parent and workshop attendee

"I was waitlisted at the University of Oklahoma whose automatic admission this year was 1170 on the SAT. I scored 1140. I did not meet their waitlist qualifications. . . . Based on what I learned from you [Marianne Ragins] I took the initiative to include with my application, my résumé, three reference letters, and a personal statement of why I wanted to attend their university. The admissions director later told me my application stood out. He earmarked my application, placing me number one on their waitlist because of my application presentation and its focus on community involvement. In fact, he chose me and ten other out-of-state students out of 4,000 applicants for the President's Leadership Class even when I was still on the waitlist. If I had not sent in the additional materials, my community involvement would not have been recognized and I would have been denied admission. Because of your advice, I not only have admission to the college where I really wanted to go, I also have the privilege to serve and learn from the president of the university in his leadership class, along with a $13,500 scholarship. . . . I watched my brother and sister who were ranked number one in their high school class achieve great scholarship success from following your advice. . . . I really didn't think I could qualify for anything with a bottom–50 percent class rank. . . . But I presented my platform of what I could do well . . . followed your advice . . . and was rewarded immensely for my achievements. . . . You challenged me that there was something out there for everyone. There really is."

> —Blair Shelton Brandon, Ragins/Braswell National Scholarship winner and attendee of Marianne Ragins's teleclass. Blair also won 15 other scholarships and grants totaling $112,400 for her first year of college.

"Marianne's presentation is both relevant and engaging. Both the parents and the students in the audience could relate to her material. By using her own personal stories, Marianne Ragins managed to encourage and motivate students to pursue their goals of going to college. I saw many parents and students taking notes during her presentation. Her use of visuals kept the attention of the audience well. Out of the families that attended the session, 98 percent stated their desire to see our organization sponsor Marianne again as a speaker in the future."

> —D. Fiavi, Program Liaison, Fairfax County Schools College Partnership Program

"My fraternity has been sponsoring a Financial Aid Forum for parents for over 25 years. In the five years that Marianne has been participating in that event, the timely and invaluable information she provides has made her the most popular portion of the forum, consistently high-rated by attendees. Marianne's Scholarship Workshop helps lift the fog on financing a college education and gives families a practical road map to making that education attainable."

—Rufus Little III, Kappa Alpha Psi Fraternity, Inc.,
Guide Right Program for Students

"Attending The Scholarship Workshop changed my whole perspective of obtaining money for college. Before, I felt helpless and less than prepared. But everything that Ms. Ragins said was easily understood and encouraged me to try. I learned how to use the Internet, libraries, and outside sources to find scholarships. One of the best things Ms. Ragins taught was essay-writing techniques. I have used her methods on all nineteen of my scholarship applications and three college applications. I was accepted into all three schools, and each gave me several scholarships and grants. The Scholarship Workshop helped me to be confident enough to pursue my dreams and left me with no question unanswered. Ms. Ragins helped me to succeed and I learned more than I thought I could."

—Jennifer Dorsey, workshop attendee

"The first edition of the book [1994] was an extremely important tool I used to get scholarships in high school. I [wanted] the new edition of the book in order to refresh my ideas and research techniques."

—Ophelia Groomes, *Winning Scholarships for College*
reader

"Marianne Ragins's presentation of The Scholarship Workshop offered students extensive guidance through every possible means of obtaining a scholarship. . . . Ragins revealed a staggering list of places where students can look for a scholarship. . . . I never imagined there could be so many resources to search."

—Kathryn Burke, workshop attendee

"The Scholarship Workshop gave me some practical research methods for scholarship searching as well as a wealth of nostalgia! I remember searching frantically for scholarships as a graduating senior from high school and this workshop would have done wonders for me back then. . . . The most important part of the workshop for me was the special session for students planning to attend graduate school. I did not even know what fellowships and stipends were before this session."

—Jennifer Herman, workshop attendee

"While I knew you could find information at the local library, knowing which books had the most accurate and legitimate scholarships was out of my field of expertise. By giving specific book titles and offering books at the seminar such as *Winning Scholarships for College*, it gave me an idea of what types of scholarships I could be looking for. . . . I also found it interesting and amusing that there were scholarships based on specific things such as being left-handed. . . . Another area I truly appreciated were the sample forms provided for essay formats. The outline broke down clearly the how-to and how-not-to of essay writing. . . . I felt I invested my time wisely by coming to the seminar."

—Susan Smith, workshop attendee

"The information the workshop offered was by far the most valuable resource I have used. . . . I would like to thank you for instilling the confidence to express myself openly as to who I am and what I hope to achieve. . . . You were inspirational."

—Jamie Luketic, workshop attendee

"The most important aspect of the workshop for me was the section on writing essays and typing a résumé of student activities. Ever since I attended the workshop . . . I have been writing essays with a lot of energy and confidence."

—Kimberly Saffold, workshop attendee

"I attended The Scholarship Workshop because I was amazed by Ms. Ragins's accomplishments and fame, which inspired me to acquire scholarships to help fund my education. . . . Important aspects of the workshop were scholarship research processes, organizational skills, and essay-writing techniques. . . . I learned to explore libraries, the Internet, and outside sources. Through my research, I discovered and applied for many scholarships for which I met the criteria."

> —Mia Armstrong, Ragins/Braswell National Scholarship winner. Mia also won two other scholarships.

"The workshop was needed and informative. It gave me a lot of inspiration because it helped me to realize that if I have the determination to achieve something I will."

> —Kimberly Duhart, Ragins/Braswell National Scholarship winner. Kimberly also won four additional scholarships and grants for her first year of college.

"I have received many positive comments regarding the workshop as a whole and your presentation specifically. I'm sure many of the participants walked away inspired and energized to start their own scholarship search."

> —Dawn Sinclair Dixon, director, Access, workshop sponsor

"Entire workshop—every aspect—was incredible. Most beneficial."

> —Gerald Ann Smith, workshop attendee

"Information presented was easily understood; relevancy and hands-on experience as well as the how-to portion were the most valuable of the workshop."

> —Mary Rivera, workshop attendee

"The most important aspect of The Scholarship Workshop was the encouragement given by Ms. Ragins to keep applying for scholarships. I have applied for seventeen scholarships and have been inspired by her strategies to create—and send along with my applications—a résumé. Because of this I have already been offered a part-time job at a bank. I sent them my scholarship application along with my résumé, and they called and asked if I would be interested in working part-time for them."

> —Adrienne Hickox, Ragins/Braswell National
> Scholarship winner. Adrienne also won three other
> scholarships and grants for her first year of college.

"Dear Ms. Ragins, I wanted to tell you thank you for coming to speak at Northeastern University. The seminar was excellent. . . . Thanks to you Ms. Ragins, I will be starting a part-time schedule in the fall."

> —Lisa Jean Martin, workshop attendee

"Thank you for speaking to us in Tuscambia. You did a great job. I really appreciate your presentation because you are the first person to tell it like it is, nothing held back. It is refreshing to hear a speaker who really knows what they are talking about. . . . You made a difference."

> —Charles Wickwire, workshop attendee

"Dear Ms. Ragins, I just wanted you to know how helpful your scholarship workshop has been to me. It is a wonderful program which has enlightened my knowledge about how and where to apply for scholarships."

> —Jorida Cokee, workshop attendee

"My prayers were answered when you came to Charleston, South Carolina, to present The Scholarship Workshop to parents and students. You really did get the attention of the audience. I have received phone calls from teachers, parents, and students about when the next workshop will be held. I think you have presented a workshop so unique that now parents will be able to assist their children in applying for various scholarships."

> —Eva Middleton Lance, director, COP Educational
> Center, and workshop sponsor

"Many of the students in our program who have read your book have commented on how well the book and the information in it have guided them through their college application process. It also teaches individuals how to keep track of their community service and volunteer work, which are so valuable but often overlooked. I highly recommend this book to all students pursuing college and also to those already in college."

—Frances L. Thompson, director, Health Careers
Opportunity Program, Boston, Massachusetts, and
Winning Scholarships for College reader

WINNING
SCHOLARSHIPS
FOR COLLEGE

WINNING
SCHOLARSHIPS
FOR COLLEGE

AN INSIDER'S GUIDE

FOURTH EDITION

Marianne Ragins

A Holt Paperback
Henry Holt and Company
New York

Holt Paperbacks
Henry Holt and Company, LLC
Publishers since 1866
175 Fifth Avenue
New York, New York 10010
www.henryholt.com

A Holt Paperback® and ® are registered trademarks of Henry Holt and Company, LLC.

Copyright © 1994, 1999, 2004, and 2013 by Marianne Ragins
All rights reserved.

Reading any edition of *Winning Scholarships for College* does not guarantee the finding or winning of any scholarship, fellowship, award, or other opportunity. Neither the author, the publisher, nor any entity associated with *Winning Scholarships for College* assumes any liability for errors, omissions, or inaccuracies. Inclusion in *Winning Scholarships for College* of any website, publication, company, or program does not imply endorsement by the author, the publisher, or any other associated entity.

Library of Congress Cataloging-in-Publication Data

Ragins, Marianne.
    Winning scholarships for college : an insider's guide / Marianne Ragins.—Fourth edition.

    Includes index.
    ISBN 978-0-8050-9947-8 (papercover)—ISBN 978-0-8050-9994-2 (electronic book)   1. Scholarships—United States.   2. Student aid—United States.   I. Title.
    LB2338.R27 2013
    378.30973—dc23   2013012603

Henry Holt books are available for special promotions and premiums. For details contact: Director, Special Markets.

First Edition 1994
Second Edition 1999
Third Edition 2004
Fourth Edition 2013

Designed by Meryl Sussman Levavi

Printed in the United States of America

10 9 8 7 6 5 4 3 2 1

To my grandmother, Ella Braswell;

my father, Otis J. Ragins Sr.;

and my cousin, Gloria Solomon,

who can only see my achievements from up above—

this book is dedicated to your memory.

I shall be telling this with a sigh

Somewhere ages and ages hence:

Two roads diverged in a wood, and I—

I took the one less traveled by,

And that has made all the difference.

—ROBERT FROST,
"The Road Not Taken"

CONTENTS

WINNING
SCHOLARSHIPS
FOR COLLEGE

INTRODUCTION

If you have picked this book out of the hundreds of choices in the bookstore, online, or the library, it means you want to attend a college or university and you need money to do so. By choosing *Winning Scholarships for College* you are well on your way to achieving both of those goals. I know because that's the situation I was in as I neared my graduation from high school. I decided to do something about it, and my efforts have since become history. By the first semester of my freshman year in college I had accumulated more than $400,000 in scholarships and monetary awards. In the process of winning these scholarships I gained national attention. Letters began to pour in from all corners of the United States. They all wanted to know: "How did you do it?" In response, I wrote a book, and you are now reading the latest version, the fourth edition.

Congratulations! You have just taken the first step on the road to winning scholarships for college!

Winning Scholarships for College is intended for students of all ages and all circumstances. Whether you are in middle or high school, returning to college, currently enrolled in college, a person with disabilities, or planning to study abroad, this guide will show you how to secure funds for college. It is designed to help a student locate scholarships in any area of the country, since scholarship programs differ from region to region, state to state, and community to community. For instance, the information available in the Southeast, the state of Georgia, or the communities of Macon may not be available elsewhere. In addition, this book offers advice on how to make the best choices when you get scholarship offers from more than one college or university. It suggests ideas on how to look for the best scholarship package, which often includes not only tuition and room and board but also "sweeteners" such as personal-expense stipends. This book will take you beyond any obstacles you might face in your scholarship search. Once you finish it, you will have an excellent understanding of how to secure money to finance your education.

Although there are several hundred books on the market about winning scholarships, there is only one like this. Nearly everything written in this book is based on personal experience. As a scholarship recipient I have experienced the disappointment of rejection, the weariness of constant research, the anxiety of interviews, the joy and satisfaction of extracurricular activities, the tedium of applications, and the frustration and triumph of writing (or attempting to write) "perfect" essays. This list, which represents much of the scholarship process, is by no means complete. That is why I have designed this book to make the scholarship process much easier for *you*. This book is not only about scholarships, it is about *how you win* scholarships. By reading this book and using my winning strategies, you too can experience the joy of success as you attain goals far beyond your expectations.

The initiative and zeal I displayed by going after scholarship money in high school ensured that I never had to worry about undergraduate college expenses. You can be a carefree college student just like I was. By reading *Winning Scholarships for College* and employing the strategies I perfected, coupled with your own initiative and zeal, you will have an unbeatable combination for scholarship success.

As well as leaving your mind free to concentrate on your studies, wouldn't it take a load off your parents' minds and pockets to know your college education is completely paid for? It did for mine. My mother felt as if she was in heaven when she read the letters of award that continually came in the mail. She was extremely proud of her baby girl. She also knew that as the letters quickly began to fill up the scrapbook she started that she would not have to pay one cent toward my college education. Guess what? She didn't. And even after I completed graduate school, she still hasn't. In my arrangement with the university I attended for my undergraduate degree, Florida Agricultural and Mechanical University, I got enough spending money to handle all of my personal expenses and still had money for Burger King (my favorite), the movies, clothes, music, and most anything else I desired. The only expense my mother incurred for my college education was the postage on the packages she sent me from home. Also, while attending graduate school at George Washington University, the costs for my tuition and fees were taken care of by the tuition reimbursement plan of my employer.

Throughout this book you will find a quotation as a prelude to each chapter. These quotations are meant to set the overall tone for the chapter, stimulate positive insight, and give you material for essays. The excerpt from the poem by Robert Frost at the beginning of this book contains words that I have used as my guiding light for most of my life, including in my search for scholarship money. I saw my quest to find scholarships to attend college as a long journey on a road previously untraveled. I have always taken paths that at the time seemed to be strewn with uncertainty, yet those paths have led to the greatest rewards.

Believe it or not, scholarship success can happen for you as well. All it takes is SDP: Self-motivation, Determination, and Persistence. This book outlines my strategies for success and the role that SDP played in my scholarship search. As you begin your personal scholarship journey, remember this: The only place where *success* comes before *work* is in the dictionary. My equation for success: Work + SDP = Success. My successful equation totaled well over $400,000. What will yours total?

It worked for me. It can work for you. Good luck!

Join our mailing list for important updates to available scholarships and other helpful information you can use for your scholarship quest. Visit http://www.scholarshipworkshop.com to join or scan our QR code. You can also text "SCHOLARSHIP INFO" to 22828.

1

COLLEGE COSTS

What we obtain too cheap, we esteem too lightly;
It is dearness only that gives everything its value.

—Thomas Paine

Before you begin your search for scholarship money, it's a good idea to get a handle on how much a college education is going to cost you over the next four years or more. The cost of tuition at most colleges has been steadily escalating for years. Currently a college education can cost anywhere from $55,000 for four years of tuition at a public institution to more than $100,000 for four years at a private institution. For many students, who now take five or six years to graduate versus the traditional four years, that cost rises to nearly $60,000 at a public college or university and more than $140,000 at a private college or university. At the school I attended in pursuit of my MBA, George Washington University in Washington, D.C., tuition and fees alone for one year of full-time study, twelve credit hours on a semester system, were $21,435. They've since risen to over $29,000 per year. At the time I attended, without considering a yearly percentage increase in tuition and fees, which is common, the cost of a four-year college education at George Washington University was $85,740. Now it's well over $100,000 to attend for four years.

Although the cost estimates above may scare you, be aware that the estimates are based on national averages and that there are many institutions that cost considerably less. You should also be aware that even though an institution may seem to be completely out of your price range, it can still be affordable. Why? Because choosing institutions with higher price tags results in your having more financial need and may actually qualify you for more aid. One factor that goes into determining your need is the cost of attendance at the school you plan to attend. Your need is determined by looking at the estimated total cost per year of attending a school and then subtracting your Expected Family Contribution (EFC) from it. This means you will have more financial need for schools costing more to attend, such as private colleges and universities, and thus may be awarded more money in your financial aid package. For more information on financial aid packages, read chapter 5, "Financial Aid Forms and Help from the Government with College Expenses."

The following table is based on the average expenses for the academic year 2013–2014 for a full-time student enrolled in a four-year college or university. The table that follows it is an estimate of expenses during the next four years. For estimated costs extending beyond the next four years, visit http://www.scholarshipworkshop.com.

The amounts listed in these tables are estimates. Actual amounts could be more or less, less, one hopes. "Room" refers to the cost of staying in dormitory or campus housing without the benefit of meals. In the commuter estimate, it is assumed you are living with your parents. If this is not

TABLE 1

	Public College/ University (In-State)	Public College/ University (Out-of-State)	Public College/ University Commuter Students	Private College/ University	Private College/ University Commuter Students
Tuition and Fees	$8,700	$13,500	$8,700	$38,100	$38,100
Room	$7,200	$7,200	N/A	$8,450	N/A
Board	$4,860	$4,860	$4,860	$5,620	$5,620
Books and Supplies	$1,720	$1,720	$1,720	$1,720	$1,720
Miscellaneous and Personal Expenses	$3,200	$3,200	$3,200	$3,200	$3,200
Transportation	$1,530	$1,530	$2,250	$1,550	$2,250
Estimated Total Per Year	$27,210	$32,010	$20,730	$58,640	$50,890

Estimated Average Expenses for Academic Year 2013–2014 for a Full-Time Student in a Four-Year College or University.

TABLE 2

Public College/University (In-State)				
	2014–2015	2015–2016	2016–2017	2017–2018
Tuition and Fees	$9,310	$9,960	$10,660	$11,400
Room	$7,700	$8,240	$8,820	$9,440
Board	$5,200	$5,560	$5,950	$6,370
Books and Supplies	$1,840	$1,970	$2,110	$2,260
Miscellaneous and Personal Expenses	$3,420	$3,660	$3,920	$4,190
Transportation	$1,640	$1,750	$1,870	$2,050
Estimated Total	$29,110	$31,140	$33,330	$35,710

TABLE 3

Public College/University (Out-Of-State)				
	2014–2015	2015–2016	2016–2017	2017–2018
Tuition and Fees	$14,450	$15,460	$16,540	$17,700
Room	$7,700	$8,240	$8,820	$9,450
Board	$5,200	$5,560	$5,950	$6,370
Books and Supplies	$1,840	$1,970	$2,110	$2,260
Miscellaneous and Personal Expenses	$3,420	$3,660	$3,920	$4,190
Transportation	$1,640	$1,750	$1,870	$2,050
Estimated Total	$34,250	$36,640	$39,210	$42,020

the case and you are living in an off-campus apartment, your expenses will be more than those shown for a student living on-campus (your rent is not likely to be less than zero). "Board" is the amount you will need for meals from the college or university cafeteria.

For a better assessment of your college/university expenses, look at the websites and catalogs of the various schools you are interested in and use the information you find to calculate a more realistic estimate. In addition to using the Internet, you can also call the admissions office and ask about the cost of tuition, related fees, and room and board for a year. Personal, transportation, and miscellaneous expenses are variable costs that depend primarily upon your needs. Do not inquire about these items. The amounts listed in the preceding table should suffice if you cannot reach an estimate

TABLE 4

Public College/University (Commuter Students)				
	2014–2015	2015–2016	2016–2017	2017–2018
Tuition and Fees	$9,310	$9,960	$10,660	$11,400
Room	N/A	N/A	N/A	N/A
Board	$5,200	$5,560	$5,950	$6,370
Books and Supplies	$1,840	$1,970	$2,110	$2,260
Miscellaneous and Personal Expenses	$3,420	$3,660	$3,920	$4,190
Transportation	$2,410	$2,580	$2,760	$2,960
Estimated Total	$22,180	$23,730	$25,400	$27,180

TABLE 5

Private College/University				
	2014–2015	2015–2016	2016–2017	2017–2018
Tuition and Fees	$40,770	$43,620	$46,670	$49,900
Room	$9,040	$9,670	$10,350	$11,100
Board	$6,010	$6,430	$6,880	$7,360
Books and Supplies	$1,840	$1,970	$2,110	$2,260
Miscellaneous and Personal Expenses	$3,420	$3,660	$3,920	$4,190
Transportation	$1,660	$1,780	$1,900	$2,050
Estimated Total	$62,740	$67,130	$71,830	$76,860

on your own. The cost of books also varies, but most institutions should be able to give you a general average. For specific costs and expenses at thousands of colleges throughout the United States, refer to the College Board website, http://www.collegeboard.org, and search for "college costs."

One important way to keep your college costs under control is to make sure you are following a four-year plan to complete your undergraduate degree. Try to get as much information as possible about your intended major before you declare one. Also, you should declare your major no later than the end of your freshman year, even if you feel you have more time. This minimizes your risk of taking unnecessary classes. Changing majors or declaring your major late can cost you a lot of extra money because it might

TABLE 6

Private College/University (Commuter Students)				
	2014–2015	2015–2016	2016–2017	2017–2018
Tuition and Fees	$40,770	$43,620	$46,670	$49,900
Room	N/A	N/A	N/A	N/A
Board	$6,010	$6,430	$6,880	$7,360
Books and Supplies	$1,840	$1,970	$2,110	$2,260
Miscellaneous and Personal Expenses	$3,420	$3,660	$3,920	$4,190
Transportation	$2,410	$2,580	$2,760	$2,960
Estimated Total	$54,450	$58,260	$62,340	$66,670

result in staying at college for a fifth or even sixth year. You can avoid this by making decisions as soon as possible based on good information.

You may also be able to minimize your college costs by taking advanced placement courses in high school. If you do well in these courses, take the advanced placement exam and score in the acceptable range, it could save you hundreds and possibly thousands of dollars because you won't have to take the course or pay for it when you get to college. You should find out whether the institutions you are applying to charge by the course or by the semester.

Understanding how much money you will actually need for the education you seek can help to add extra zeal and determination to your search. Now that you know what college or graduate school can cost, read the next three chapters, which extensively cover research techniques to help you secure the money to cover the costs.

2

THE SCHOLARSHIP SEARCH: DISCOVERING HIDDEN TREASURES

> Books are the quietest and most constant of
> friends; they are the most accessible and wisest of
> counselors, and the most patient of teachers.
>
> —Charles Eliot

Many scholarship opportunities are available throughout the country. In fact, thousands of scholarship dollars may go unclaimed each year because students are not aware they exist. This book shows you how to find those dollars. It lists programs and addresses uncovered during my own scholarship search as well as many others in Appendix A. Yet the addresses I supply should not be used as a substitute for doing your own research. It is most important to know what is available in the state and city in which you live, because what's available in one state or city may not be available in another. Also, be knowledgeable of the various sources of financial aid available throughout the United States. If you have no idea of the scholarships offered each year simply because you don't look for them, then you can't expect to win any of them. Thorough research will reveal many of the opportunities available to you, and without the benefit of extensive research on your part, scholarship dollars that could have been awarded to you will either go unused or go to others who have done their research. Good research, as well as attentive ears and eyes, will be crucial to winning scholarships. Numerous opportunities are waiting for you, but it's your job to discover them.

When is the best time to start your scholarship search?

Most important tip: Do not wait until spring of your senior year. Start as soon as senior year begins if you haven't started before!

Start researching scholarships early in your high school career since there are some you can win even as a freshman, sophomore, or junior. For those that require you to be a senior, review applications early and look carefully at them. Doing so can help you see areas the scholarship programs emphasize. It could be grades, certain extracurricular activities, test scores, or community service. Or they may focus entirely on the essay.

See if you can get information about past essay questions and winners. If the essay questions only change slightly each year, you can begin to work on your answers years ahead of time. If they focus more on community service, that's an area you can also work on by starting to participate and help out in your community.

If you've gotten beyond the ninth or tenth grades, you should start intensive scholarship research during your eleventh-grade year. Many of the largest scholarship programs have deadlines early in the school year, such as October or November. If you're a senior who hasn't already started your search, this time frame could make you frantic. So, researching and getting applications before your senior year begins will give you time to focus on submitting an outstanding application and more time to enjoy all the fun of being a senior.

Here are some terms and facts to make your search easier and less confusing:

- A *scholarship* is money given to a student that does not have to be repaid. Scholarships are given for a variety of reasons: academic achievement, leadership potential, community involvement, financial need, hobbies, affiliations, personal characteristics, and special talents. Scholarships that are not based on financial need are usually called *merit based* or *non-need* scholarships. Some scholarships may require a service commitment, such as those funded by the military and some government agencies. Read chapter 14, "Scholarships and Awards for Community Service, Volunteering, and Work," for more information.
- A *grant* is also financial aid that does not have to be repaid. The most popular grants issued are federal and include the Pell Grant and the Supplemental Educational Opportunity Grant, both of which are awarded by the federal government and issued through academic

institutions. Most government grants are based primarily on need. However, many grants are awarded for other reasons.

- An *award* is also financial aid that does not have to be repaid. Awards and/or prizes are sometimes given to you in exchange for your winning some type of contest or competition.
- A *loan* is the only form of financial aid that you must repay, although some scholarships or grants, as previously discussed, may require you to work for a few years after you graduate as a type of repayment.
- A *fellowship* is designed to support individuals who want to obtain a graduate or doctoral degree. The fellowship may include a tuition waiver or payment of tuition and fees. The fellowship may also provide a housing allowance and include a personal expense stipend.

THE LIBRARY

The library can be the most important resource for a potential scholarship winner. Not only is it a quiet and comfortable place to concentrate, but it contains vast amounts of information vital to your scholarship search. In addition, the library has friendly librarians who will be more than happy to help you find any information you require. It will save you time if you talk to them first about where to find information on various scholarships and other types of monetary aid. These materials—particularly the latest volumes— may be in one central college reference area at the library. You should look for books, catalogs, directories, pamphlets, and brochures on scholarships. These guides will include numerous college profiles, listing basic facts about colleges and universities: number of students enrolled, majors with the highest enrollment, percentage of financial need met, minority enrollment, website and e-mail addresses, physical addresses, telephone numbers, types of scholarships and monetary awards, and application requirements. You will find these in scholarship directories such as *The Scholarship Book*, the *Ultimate Scholarship Book*, and *Peterson's Scholarships, Grants and Prizes*. You will find material on government programs, too.

If the library does not have the information you are seeking or does not have a large quantity of material on scholarships and financial aid, ask when it might be getting books on the subject. The librarian should be able to help you, or you can visit your local bookstore.

Another important way to conduct research for your scholarship journey is to use the Internet. Not only can you access certain public libraries online, you can also find loads of information about scholarships as well. See chapter 3, "Using the Internet and Social Media in Your Scholarship Search," for more information.

THE SCHOLARSHIP RESEARCH QUESTIONNAIRE

The questions that follow will help narrow down your particular needs and attributes. Your answers, when combined with the information you find at the library, will pinpoint special areas you should look into for potential college dollars. For example, certain colleges and universities give scholarships to the children of their alumni. Likewise, some churches, fraternities, and other organizations give scholarships and monetary aid to children of their members.

These questions are also necessary because some scholarship guides or sections of directories are only for minorities. Others deal specifically with children or close relatives of war veterans or are directed specifically toward

Feeling a little lost trying to use a scholarship directory?

Here's how to use a scholarship directory and how the scholarship research questionnaire can help you. For example:

"I am a student whose parents were in the military. I participate in several extracurricular activities like the Beta Club. I also do a lot of community service. I live in Chicago, Illinois, where I am a member of the Presbyterian Church. I want to study engineering."

If this student is you, look through the following short list of sections usually found in directories such as *The Ultimate Scholarship Book* to target scholarships you may be eligible to apply for and win.

- *Extracurricular Activity Section*—for scholarships associated with activities like the Beta Club, an organization that offers the National Beta Club Scholarship.
- *Community Service Section*—for scholarships or awards that focus on community service (e.g., Prudential Spirit of Community Award).
- *City of Residence Section*—to find scholarships specifically for students who live in Chicago.
- *Military Section*—to find scholarships for the children of military parents
- *Religious Affiliation Section*—for scholarships benefiting members of the Presbyterian Church.
- *Field of Study Engineering Section*—for scholarships to study engineering.

women. Still others cover scholarships for unusual hobbies or specific areas of interest. As you read these questions, place a checkmark beside those types of scholarships that apply to you so you know what types of directories to find and the sections of those directories you should review. For any question below with an answer that pinpoints a possible opportunity for you, do an Internet search for that specific type of scholarship or organization using the techniques in chapter 3. To find Web and Facebook pages, Twitter accounts, or YouTube channels, conduct advanced Internet searches for local organizations of the type your answers to the questions below reveal.

1. Where would you like to attend college? In what region? In what state?

Look in guides and directories to find the colleges or universities that match your response to this question. Guides such as *Peterson's Four-Year Colleges* as well as its website, http://www.petersons.com, will help you find schools in the regions or states you favor. Just about all colleges and universities have scholarships and aid available only to individuals who actually attend their institution. For example, I won the Bellingrath & Hyde Scholarship at Rhodes College located in Memphis, Tennessee. This scholarship was specific to this institution and could only be used for my studies there.

Don't forget to look for wives' clubs, teachers' organizations, and panhellenic associations in your area

If you're a child or a dependent of military personnel, you may be eligible to win a scholarship from clubs such as the Naval Officers' Spouses' Club (http://www.noscdc.com) or the Army Officers' Wives' Club (http://www.aowcgwa.org). If this applies to you and one of these organizations is in your area, give them a call.

Or, if you're thinking of a teaching career, organizations in your area similar to the Virginia Council of Teachers of Mathematics may sponsor a scholarship. This council sponsors a scholarship to students planning a teaching career in mathematics.

Panhellenic associations may also offer scholarships in your area. Consult chapter 3, "Using the Internet and Social Media in Your Scholarship Search," to learn how to find Panhellenic or other associations with available scholarships.

2. Would you settle for a college other than one of your initial choices if it offers you a scholarship and if its credentials are just as good?

If you answer yes to this question, you should look at all college profiles, regardless of location, for schools that have large scholarship programs. You can usually find this information in the financial aid section of each college profile. You should also visit a site such as http://www.meritaid.com for scholarships and awards associated with specific colleges and universities.

3. What are your hobbies?

There are many scholarships for people who have particular hobbies. Books with extensive scholarship listings will have special sections dealing with these types of scholarships. Look for these special sections during your scholarship search. Some scholarship directories will title this section as extracurricular activities. An example of a scholarship or award that focuses on your hobbies would be the *National Make It Yourself with Wool Competition* (http://www.makeitwithwool.com—they are also on Facebook), in which a $2,000 scholarship and various other awards are given to winning students who sew, knit, or crochet a garment made of at least 60 percent wool. If you sew, knit, or crochet (activities I did as a 4-H Club member), you may have an opportunity.

4. If you are currently employed, where do you work?

Contact the personnel or human resources office of your employer to inquire about scholarship opportunities and tuition reimbursement programs. If your company does not have a personnel office, speak with the general manager about the possibility of scholarship opportunities, or contact the company's general headquarters to learn if such opportunities exist. Many companies offer tuition reimbursement programs as an employee benefit. In tuition reimbursement, the employee initially pays the cost of tuition and fees for the courses taken in college or graduate school. Once the courses are completed and a satisfactory grade has been earned by the employee, the company/employer will then reimburse all or part of the tuition and fees initially paid by the employee. Some companies pay these costs upfront. As a student working at Wendy's Old-Fashioned Hamburgers in high school, I was eligible for a Wendy's scholarship which I applied for and won. See chapter 28, "Making Choices: You've Won an Award . . . Now What Do You Do?," for a copy of my award letter.

5. Where do your parents currently work?

Ask your parents to contact their company personnel or human resources department to inquire if there are scholarships available to the children of employees. If the company does not have a personnel office, your parent should speak with the general manager about the possibility of scholarship opportunities or contact the company's general headquarters. Scholarship directories also list companies that sponsor scholarship programs for the children of their employees. You can also check books or online directories such as *The Foundation Directory*, usually available in your local library, to learn whether your parent's company has a foundation set up to disburse scholarship money to the children of their employees or for other purposes. For example, Johnson Controls, Inc., maintains the Johnson Controls Foundation that offers scholarships to its employees' children.

6. Do you belong to a religious organization; for example, a church or synagogue?

Many religious organizations give scholarships not only to members of their congregations but to nonmembers as well. Some of them stipulate that the recipients of their scholarships must attend a college or university established to operate under the edicts of their denominational faith, such as a Presbyterian college or university. An example of this type of scholarship would be the National Presbyterian College Scholarship (http://www.presbyterianmission.org) offered to superior high school seniors who are members of the Presbyterian Church and are planning to attend a college related to the Presbyterian Church (U.S.A). Contact churches and religious organizations to inquire about scholarships such as these. You can also look in scholarship directories for the sections based on religious affiliations. In addition, speak with the minister of the church that either you and/or your parents attend. Most churches are more than willing to establish a small scholarship fund for their students. For instance, the church I was a member of in Macon, Georgia, Stubbs Chapel Baptist Church, gave me a small scholarship to attend college and also gave me money every year while I was enrolled.

7. Are you a child or close relative of a war veteran? If so, in which war and in what branch of service did your relative serve?

Numerous scholarships are available for children and close relatives of veterans who served in specific wars, such as World War II. Books with extensive scholarship listings will have special sections dealing with these types of scholarships. The sections may be titled "Armed Forces" or "Military." You will need to know the branch of the Armed Forces in which your relative served to find scholarships that apply specifically to you. Examples of these scholarships are those offered by the Seventh Corps Desert Storm Veterans Association (DSVA; http://www.desertstormvets.org) for those who served in Operation Desert Storm, their spouses, and their children; or the Military Benefit Association, which provides scholarships to its members who serve in the military (http://www.militarybenefit .org). The Fisher House Foundation's website (http://www.militaryscholar .org) is another resource for scholarship information associated with the military. See chapter 27, "Scholarships and Funding for the Military and Their Family," for more information.

8. Are you a veteran or a disabled veteran?

Scholarship and financial assistance is available to most disabled veterans, especially from the government. If you are a disabled veteran, contact the Federal Student Aid Information Center (800-433-3243), visit Student Aid.gov (see chapter 3 for Twitter, Facebook, and YouTube information) to inquire about scholarship opportunities, or call the Department of Veterans Affairs (800-827-1000; http://www.va.gov or http://www.gibill.va.gov). You may find governmental organizations with programs that pay for tuition, fees, books, and equipment of veterans disabled during active duty and honorably discharged. To find financial aid such as this, look in the "Military Disabled" or "Armed Forces" sections of the scholarship guides. Also make sure to look at chapter 27 in this book.

9. Are you legally blind or do you have any other disabilities?

Students who are legally blind or in some other way disabled can usually receive scholarships and financial aid assistance from many sources, especially the government. During your search, look for directories that have special sections dealing with scholarships for the disabled. The American

Council of the Blind (http://www.acb.org) currently offers scholarships to students who are legally blind. See chapter 22, "Scholarships for Disabled Students."

10. Are you related to someone with a disability or who is a survivor of a disease?

There are scholarships for children of disabled parents such as the Through the Looking Glass (http://www.lookingglass.org) organization, as well as scholarships for survivors of certain diseases such as cancer. Currently the Dr. Angela Grant Memorial Scholarship Fund awards scholarships to cancer survivors or those within the immediate family of a cancer survivor (http://www.drangelagrantscholarship.org). This is an area where an advanced search, as outlined in chapter 3, could be helpful to you in finding college aid specific to your situation, disease, or disability. And see chapter 22 on scholarships for the disabled.

11. Are you a member of a minority group? If so, to which ethnic group do you belong?

Most scholarship directories have sections listing numerous minority scholarships. During your search you may also find books that deal exclusively with scholarship opportunities for minorities. As an example, the Bill and Melinda Gates Foundation offers the Gates Millennium Scholarship (http://www.gmsp.org) to minority students only. See chapter 17, "Scholarships for Minorities: What's the Difference in a Minority Scholarship Hunt?"

12. For minority groups other than African American, can you trace your lineage? (For example, Samoan, Japanese, Native American, etc.)

Many programs have scholarships strictly for minorities of a certain descent. To win these scholarships you may be required to prove your lineage. Look for scholarships such as these if you fall into this category. An example of this type of scholarship would be the scholarships offered by the Welsh Society of Philadelphia to students of Welsh descent (http://www.philadelphiawelsh.org). To be eligible to receive this scholarship, applicants must prove their lineage and enroll in a college within 100 miles of Philadelphia.

13. Are you or your parents a member of a union, trade group, or association?

If you or your parents are members of a union, trade group, or association, you may be eligible to win scholarships such as the E. C. Hallbeck Memorial Scholarship offered by the American Postal Workers Union (http://www .apwu.org) to high school seniors who are dependents of active or deceased members of the union. Or consider the scholarship program from Union Plus (http://www.unionplus.org), an organization established by the AFL-CIO to provide consumer benefits to members and retirees of participating labor unions.

Did you know that the company from which you or your parents buy electricity may offer scholarships?

In the Virginia area, the Northern Virginia Electric Cooperative (NOVEC) offers scholarships to students who live in their service area. For many years, the Southern Maryland Electric Cooperative (SMECO) has offered scholarships to high school seniors who lived and attended school in the utility's service territory.

There are thousands of electric cooperatives in the United States, many of whom belong to the National Rural Electric Cooperative Association. Visit http:// www.nreca.org to see if there's an electric cooperative in your area offering a scholarship. Or you can do an advanced Internet search (see chapter 3) to find one in your region.

---

14. What are you strongly interested in studying at college?

Scholarships are available to students interested in a particular major. If you are certain of your intended major, look for directories and scholarship opportunities in that area. For students interested in the field of health care, for example, the Tylenol Scholarship program (http://www.scholarship .tylenol.com; this program is also on Facebook) is available, or consider reviewing scholarships offered by the American Medical Association Foundation (http://www.ama-assn.org). The scholarships don't just stop at health care or medicine—you can find other associations for scholarships in other fields. Use a scholarship directory or do an advanced Internet search (as explained in chapter 3) to find scholarships related to your current or future major.

15. Are you a member of a fraternity or sorority?

Many sororities and fraternities sponsor scholarships. For instance, members of Theta Delta Chi can apply for scholarships, and the Alpha Kappa Alpha Sorority, Inc., Educational Advancement Foundation also offers several scholarships, including some that are open to nonmembers. As you look through scholarship directories, look for scholarships sponsored by a fraternity or sorority. If you are unable to discover any, write or call the national chapter of your organization, or visit its website, Facebook, or other social media platforms to uncover opportunities. In fact, local sororities and fraternities will often contact me to help them advertise a scholarship program that may be suffering from a low application rate.

16. Are your parents members of a fraternity or sorority?

Some sororities and fraternities sponsor scholarships for the children of their members. As you look through scholarship directories, look for scholarships sponsored by your parents' fraternity or sorority. If you are unable to discover any, write to the national chapters of the organizations or visit their website, Facebook, or other social media platforms, if available. You can also do an advanced Internet search, as explained in chapter 3.

17. Are your parents alumni of a college or university?

Many colleges and universities offer scholarships to the children of their alumni. Contact the college or university they attended to inquire about scholarship opportunities that may be available to you.

18. Where do you live? Have you checked for community foundations in your area?

Numerous scholarships are offered by organizations and companies to students who live in a specific area, usually where the company or organization is located or does business. To find scholarships in this category, do an advanced Internet search (see chapter 3) to find community foundations, county websites, or school websites with scholarships specific to your area. Use search terms such as "scholarships" and the name of your county, city, or state to find scholarships in local areas. Also do the same for "scholarships" and the search words "community foundation" along with the name of your city, county, or state to uncover community foundations in your area. For example, the Community Foundation of Northern Virginia (http://www.novacf.org), the Berks County Community Foundation in Pennsylvania (http://www.bccf.org), and the Community Foundation of Central Georgia (http://www.cfcga.org) are all examples of community-based foundations that serve a specific community or a group of communities within a specific region.

19. What are your extracurricular activities?

Activities such as participation in Distributive Education Club of America (DECA; http://www.deca.org), Future Business Leaders of America (FBLA; http://www.fbla-pbl.org), the National Honor Society (NHS; http://www.nhs.us), and Junior Achievement (http://www.ja.org) may allow you to become eligible for scholarships from these organizations. For example, high school seniors who are members of DECA are eligible for renewable Harry A. Applegate Scholarships, for use in pursuing business education.

The books you'll find on scholarships, grants, and other types of monetary aid usually list in alphabetical order the names of various programs, Web and e-mail addresses, telephone numbers, special requirements, and deadlines. As you look through these books, deciding which programs apply to you, you should begin recording this information. Or, as you visit websites and social media pages you find, start bookmarking your favorites in your browser, downloading applications, and organizing them. See chapter 6 for tips on getting organized.

RESEARCH CHECKLIST FOR YOUR LIBRARY VISIT

1. Be certain you understand and remember the key terms and facts explained in the beginning of the chapter.
2. Have you conducted your research in the library? Ask the librarians at the reference desk for the latest references they have available for colleges, financial aid, and scholarships.
3. Look for catalogs, books, directories, pamphlets, brochures, and guides.
4. Pinpoint the special areas outlined in the Scholarship Research Questionnaire.

Why should you use the Internet PLUS books and directories?

The Internet is awesome in helping to make your search more comprehensive, especially in searching a vast amount of information in a relatively short amount of time. But consider these reasons why your search should go beyond the Internet:

- Using the Internet-based college or scholarship search engines exclusively could cause you to miss out on many local scholarship opportunities.
- Even though information can be updated more quickly on the Internet, it can still be outdated.
- Reading a book or directory helps you control and understand your search, which could actually help you maximize your opportunities.
- You can browse through a book at any time. For the Internet you need access to a computer or tablet.
- When using computerized services you are at the mercy of the system you're using. Information you find may or may not be relevant, even if in your favorite search engine.

GETTING INFORMATION ON COLLEGES

In addition to collecting books about scholarships and monetary aid, gather books on colleges and universities in general. There you will find common facts on colleges as well as information on financial aid. Colleges that give large quantities of non-need aid usually have huge scholarship programs. After reading the preliminary information about the institutions you are interested in attending, record their addresses. A sample college profile with preliminary information may contain the following:

- *General information* provides a brief overview of the college. It describes the type of institution it is, such as a four-year or two-year institution, and also gives the location and the date it was founded.
- *Academic information* describes academic components of the college, including the faculty-to-student ratio, the number of volumes the library contains, and majors with the highest enrollment.
- *Costs or expenses* categorizes the costs associated with attending the college. For example, tuition and room and board are listed separately.
- *Financial aid* deals with the amount of financial aid the college offers the average student and the percentage of financial need that is met by the college.

- *Admissions information or requirements* gives details about the application process and lists documents required for acceptance consideration.
- *Transfer admissions* outlines the requirements for a transfer student to be admitted to the college.
- *Entrance difficulty* describes the difficulty involved in gaining admittance to the college.
- *Further information* gives the address, name, and title of a person whom you can contact for more information about the college and the programs it offers.

If you prefer to use the Internet to find much of this information, visit http://www.collegeboard.org. Remember, it is important to read explanatory chapters at the beginning of the directory, guide, or book to completely understand how the information inside is organized.

If the library in your hometown keeps pamphlets and brochures in its vertical files, look at them. You may find current information on local scholarship programs or colleges that have large financial aid programs. Before you leave the library, take the time to catalog your information in some specific order. It saves time later, especially if you do it according to deadlines. Chapter 6, "Getting Organized," contains more information about cataloging and how to keep track of all the material you have gathered.

The next step in the scholarship search process is the local telephone book. Use it to locate and record the contact information and addresses for all the major businesses in your area. Some companies may fund scholarships of which the general public may not be aware. Also, look for clubs, sororities, and fraternities, on local and national levels, because they usually offer scholarships. Find the contact information for the chamber of commerce, too, if there is one in your area. The chamber of commerce may have knowledge of scholarships sponsored by local businesses. You can use the Internet to help you with this process but not replace it. Conduct an advanced Internet search to find these types of organizations. (See chapter 3, "Using the Internet and Social Media in Your Scholarship Search.")

The organizations listed below may or may not sponsor awards in your area, but this list is a starting point and it should lead you in the right direction. Some of these organizations may have national scholarship programs administered by their office headquarters, but many may also have scholarships that they award separately on a local basis.

Sample List of Sponsoring Organizations

American Legion	Masons
American Red Cross	National Association for the
Boy Scouts/Girl Scouts of America	Advancement of Colored People
Daughters of the American	(NAACP)
Revolution	National Exchange Clubs
Daughters of the Confederacy	National Honor Society
Circle K	Optimist International
Elks Club	Urban League
Jaycees	Rotary Club
Junior League	Ruritan
Kiwanis International	Soroptimist International
Knights of Columbus	YMCA/YWCA
Lions Club	Veterans of Foreign Wars

Write to the trust departments of all your local banks. Sometimes banks and other financial institutions have trusts set up by patrons to administer scholarships to deserving students who meet specific qualifications. The American State Bank & Trust Company in North Dakota is an example of a bank with trust services that include scholarships. Check banks in your area for others. Credit unions may also offer scholarships to members or students in the community. The Robins Federal Credit Union of Georgia announced a scholarship program in 1998 that each year offers several scholarships to children of its members. You should contact the credit unions and banks in your area to inquire about scholarships and if you are eligible to apply for them. This is also another area where an advanced Internet search (as explained in chapter 3) would be helpful.

Local radio and television stations may also offer scholarships or internships (usually unpaid) to students in the community interested in going to college. Stations may also advertise scholarship programs and be able to supply you with information about them. You should call and ask for the producer who works on education-related segments to inquire about scholarships or scholarship experts in your area.

If, for instance, you are interested in becoming a teacher, visit the website of your local board of education and inquire about special scholarships for high school graduates who would like to become educators. There are scholarships of this type in many areas. Contact your state financial aid agency, discussed in chapter 5, and review its website for special teaching-related college financial aid and scholarships. This may apply to those in the medical field as well.

You should also read newspapers and magazines for information written or advertised about scholarships. *USA Today*, a nationally circulated newspaper, frequently publishes information on college and financial aid issues. Magazines such as *Money, Ebony*, and *Essence* often include articles about the financial aid process and other college-related issues. *U.S. News & World Report* as well as other popular magazines have special issues devoted to their readers' pursuit of higher education.

After you've done all your research, the next step is drafting two business letters, one that applies only to colleges and another that applies only to independent organizations sponsoring scholarships. (Independent scholarships can be used at any institution subject to the sponsor's requirements, whereas college-sponsored scholarships are for that institution only.) Avoid misspelled names, incorrect titles, and incomplete addresses by calling organizations to ensure the accuracy of your information or using the Internet to confirm information. You may need to use these letters for organizations that require a written request to obtain an application. You should be able to use the Internet and social media to access much of the information you might need or want, although it is nice, much easier, and actually a little exciting to have a glossy brochure to read and browse through for the colleges and universities that interest you.

Sample College/University Letter

500 Scholarship Street°
Opportunity, Georgia 00000

October 16, 2025

Name of Admissions Director
Director of Admissions
Name of the college/university
City, State Zip Code

Dear *Name of Admissions Director*:
The time is rapidly approaching for me to choose a college. I am currently a *senior* at *Anytown High School* and will be entering college in the

---

°NOTE: Items in italics can be changed to suit your specific letter.

fall of the *year 2026*. I am interested in *Anytown College* as a possible choice. Therefore, I would like to request a catalog and applications for admission and financial aid to help me become more familiar with *Anytown College* and the requirements needed to apply. I am also interested in reviewing any brochures about your institution, especially those relating to *internships, pre-professional programs, and financial aid*. I appreciate your assistance.

Sincerely yours,
Your signature
Your name, typed

Sample Private Scholarship Inquiry Letter

This letter can be used for companies, churches, sororities, and other private organizations that do not have an e-mail address or a Web-based contact system.

500 Scholarship Street
Opportunity, Georgia 00000

October 16, 2025

Example Association
Name of Scholarship Program
P.O. Box XXXX
Arlington, Virginia 22219

To whom it may concern:

I would like to receive more information about the scholarship(s) and/or award(s) administered by your organization that are listed in various resource materials and/or on the Internet. I would also like to receive an application as well as notification of special guidelines, deadlines, or other pertinent information, if any. Please send this information as soon as possible.

If you need any further information from me, my number is *(912) 555-1212* and my e-mail address is *tmgfs@aol.com.*

Thank you for your assistance,
Your signature
Your name, typed

If a Snail Mail Letter Is Necessary

Sending letters to organizations and colleges and universities can be an important, sometimes necessary step in your scholarship search to get the information or applications you need. The information you request and subsequently receive is essential to your success for two crucial reasons: (1) it lists the requirements governing the scholarship or financial aid; and (2) it includes applications. The listing of requirements helps you to determine whether you are eligible to apply and also helps determine whether you *will* apply. In all cases you should have a positive attitude. However, be wary of scholarship programs that specifically state their scholarships are only for students interested in a certain area of study, such as engineering or graphic arts. If you are unsure of your intended major, then applying for a scholarship of this type may not be wise only because if you change your major later, you could lose the scholarship. In addition to sending applications and stating requirements, many colleges and universities usually include brochures concerned with meeting the costs of attending in their correspondence. These brochures list programs that are financially responsive to the needs of prospective students.

Once you have prepared your letters, mail them to every address on your list. To save time when sending inquiry letters to scholarship programs listed in this book or the scholarship directories you're using, you may want to send a self-addressed, stamped postcard with your initial inquiry letter. This could get you a faster response. To do this, go to Office Depot or Staples and get a box of Avery laser postcards that you can run through your printer for a typed professional appearance. Include a reference to this postcard in your inquiry letter and ask the recipient to use it. For example, after the line in your letter that states, "Please send this information as soon as possible," you can add this sentence: "I have included a self-addressed, stamped postcard. If possible, please use it so I can receive an immediate response after you receive this letter." An example postcard is shown below.

Sample Self-Addressed Stamped Postcard (SASP)

Items in italics should be changed for each scholarship program.

Front of postcard

Marianne Ragins
P.O. Box 176
Centreville, Virginia 20122

> *National Scholarship Competitions of America*
> *Program Office*
> *Annual Audio Essay Contest*
> *122 Opportunity Street*
> *Scholarship, VA 00000*

Back of postcard

Our organization, *National Scholarship Competitions of America*

___ Does not offer scholarships to students in your area

___ No longer offers scholarships or awards to students

___ Will send complete details about our program, including an application by _____

___ Requires that you contact your counselor for an application and details about our program

___ Requires that you access our website or Facebook page at _____ for more information and/or an application

___ Requires that you send a self-addressed stamped envelope (No. 10, 6×9-inch, 9×12-inch) for complete details.

Ideally you should mail your inquiry letters simultaneously, because then it is easier to keep track of responses. Make a note of the date you send them out. For some organizations you may have to follow up your letter with a phone call or another letter if they do not respond to your initial letter within six weeks. Also, visit the website of Federal Student Aid Information Center at http://studentaid.ed.gov or call (800) 4-FED-AID for information on all federally funded programs. (Refer to chapter 5 for more information on federal aid.) Many scholarship services charge $25, $35, even as much as $200 to uncover scholarship sources that can be found at this website free of charge. Some services that guarantee they will locate at least six or eight scholarship sources merely send addresses gleaned from the U.S. Department of Education. If you decide to use a scholarship service, try to find out as much as you can about it by consulting the Better Business Bureau and the information below to get the most for your money.

COMPUTERIZED SCHOLARSHIP SEARCH SERVICES

Before you decide to use a computerized scholarship search service that charges a fee, investigate the many computerized scholarship search services that are free on the Internet. Some of those are FastWeb, Scholarships.com, Zinch.com, and CollegeNET MACH25. You can find the Web addresses for these free search services in chapter 3 or you can access their links through The Scholarship Workshop, at http://www.scholarshipwork shop.com.

Important Questions to Ask Computerized Scholarship Services That Charge Fees

1. How often do you update your database?
2. What is the success rate for students who utilize your services?
3. How long will it take you to send me a listing? How will I receive this listing? For example, via e-mail in a spreadsheet, on a disc or flash drive, in a letter, or via a website.
4. Will the listing be sent in time for me to meet the deadlines of the scholarships and programs?
5. What percentage of your information is composed of well-known, federally funded programs such as the Pell Grant?
6. Will your list contain loans as scholarship sources?
7. Will your list be tailored to fit me? For example, if I am an international student, will the list contain addresses of programs that are only for U.S. citizens?

If you decide to use a computerized scholarship search that costs you money, send your information in very early, ideally in the fall of your junior year. Often these services send information late, so avoid that problem by contacting them as early as possible. If you are a senior in high school and are looking for scholarship information it may be too late for you to use a computerized scholarship search, and your money could be wasted. It may take more energy, but I think you can do an excellent job on your own to find scholarship search sources that do not charge.

SCHOLARSHIPS SWEEPSTAKES AND LOTTERIES

Often companies will offer the chance to win cash prizes and scholarships to those who enter their name and contact information in an online sweepstakes. For example, WellsFargo has conducted the CollegeSTEPS Sweepstakes, which offers $100,000 yearly in scholarship awards to students.

A few search services have drawings similar to sweepstakes; they may actually want to obtain your information for marketing purposes but in return provide you with a chance to win a scholarship. The primary goal of many companies that offer sweepstakes is to get people interested in buying or using their products as they try to win the sweepstakes. In doing so, some offer you a chance to win money for college or other purposes. In fact, at one time a website offered the chance to win free scholarships all day, every day, just for visiting the site frequently.

Although these sweepstakes and online lotteries are based entirely on luck and the probability of winning can be low, if you have the time and the willpower not to be pulled into buying what you see (you may be bombarded with ads), go for it. But be careful about the information you give and the sites you visit. If it sounds fishy, check out the section, "Places to Check Scholarship Offers Too Good to Be True" later in this chapter.

SCHOLARSHIP PROGRAMS INCORPORATING SOCIAL MEDIA, TEXTING, AND BLOGGING INTO THE SELECTION PROCESS

WyzAnt, a tutoring service, has been offering an annual college scholarship essay contest where high school and college students can win up to $10,000 in scholarship money. To enter, students complete an entry form and an essay in 300 words or less describing how they will use their education to make an impact on others. After you complete your essay, you promote it via e-mail and social media to contact friends and family to get votes for it. Finalists will be determined by popular vote. Tutors from

WyzAnt will then review the finalists' essays to determine the winners for scholarships worth $10,000, $3,000, and $2,000. Visit http://www.wyzant .com (see Scholarships section on the website).

DoSomething.org is a nonprofit for young people focused on social change for causes such as bullying, homelessness, and cancer. They have several scholarship programs available and some of them require texting to win scholarships ranging from $2,000 to $5,000. Several are open to U.S. and Canadian citizens 25 and under and do not require a minimum GPA. Visit http://www.dosomething.org (see Scholarships section on the website).

Collegescholarships.org also has a blogging scholarship for students who maintain a blog. They award $1,000 annually. See http://www.college scholarships.org/our-scholarships/blogging.htm.

These types of scholarship programs may also be savvy marketing techniques for the companies to promote themselves or certain causes. For some, you may need to share information about yourself, encourage others to visit specific websites or read about certain issues, and potentially have numerous marketing efforts directed your way. Just make sure you don't share personal identifying information such as Social Security numbers or bank account numbers. And if you're wondering about a giveaway, see "Places to Check out Scholarship Offers Too Good to Be True" later in this chapter. Also note that many of these types of scholarships may be here today and gone tomorrow.

SCHOLARSHIP SCAMS

Since college costs have been escalating higher and higher every year, there are millions of students and parents who are trying to lessen the cost of their total bill by searching for scholarships. We live in an economy where an easy fix or a promise to reduce the time it takes to do something is a surefire way for people to make money. The scholarship scam artist looks for just the type of person who is trying to reduce the time spent searching for scholarship programs. The following are some typical comments made by scam artists to innocent people in search of scholarship money.

This scholarship requires a handling fee.

A few scholarship programs may ask for a small fee of $5 or less to cover the costs of mailing application materials to you and other administrative costs. To combat this, some scholarship programs may ask that you send an SASE of a certain size to offset the costs of mailing. If a program wants more than this I would be wary of entering, unless it's an artistic competition that may have larger entrance fees. To be safe contact the Better Business Bureau and your guidance counselor or career center director to find out if the scholarship program is legitimate. Most scholarship programs, particularly large ones, do not require either a self-addressed stamped envelope or a handling fee.

We'll do all the work for this scholarship.

All scholarship programs require that you do some type of work, most often some type of essay or entry. When you hear comments like this, remember that all scholarships require you to do something.

You can't get this information anywhere else.

Particularly if the service is touting that it is the only source for a listing of scholarships, more than likely you can get the information in many places for free. Check out:

- The U.S. Department of Education Website (http://www.ed.gov)
- Free computerized scholarship searches such as FastWeb (http://www.fastweb.com)
- The FinAid Website (http://www.finaid.org)
- Books such as *Winning Scholarships for College* or http://www.scholarshipworkshop.com
- Directories such as *The Scholarship Book*, *Peterson's Scholarships, Grants and Prizes*, or *The Ultimate Scholarship Book*
- Your counselor or career center director
- Your library
- The college or university you plan to attend
- Social media platforms such as Facebook, Twitter, YouTube, and more

We need your credit card number or bank account number to hold this scholarship for you.

Never give your or your parents' credit card or bank number to hold a scholarship. Scholarships are free money. I applied for many scholarships during my search and was never asked, so it would be unusual if you were asked for this information. If I had been, I would have refused to supply it and reported the organization to the Federal Trade Commission.

You have been selected by a "National Foundation" to receive a scholarship, or you have won a scholarship contest when you have never actually applied for the scholarship nor entered the contest.

To win a scholarship from a program you never applied to is virtually unheard of, and if you are told you have won, check out the program by contacting the sources above to see if it is listed anywhere. If it's mentioned in a Web-based source other than that of the federal government, you should not automatically assume it is legitimate. Make sure to contact other sources as well. To be doubly safe, you and your parents should contact the sources in the next section, "Places to Check Scholarship Offers That Seem Too Good to Be True."

We guarantee we'll find at least ten scholarships.

This is a typical line used by many fraudulent scholarship search services. They may also guarantee five or six or some other number. Often the scholarships they are referring to are loan programs, which are not scholarships, or you're ineligible for the scholarships, or you receive the information too late to apply. Some search services may even have you call a 900-number to get more information, which can be costly and net few results. Refer to the section in this chapter on computerized scholarship search services for more information.

You are eligible to receive a free scholarship and financial aid package. Please call us to schedule your appointment at XYZ Hotel to pick it up.

Usually when you go to pick up your free package at the hotel, you and your parents are subjected to high-pressure sales methods (sometimes about costly insurance programs) meant to make you spend hundreds or thousands of dollars to help you with your scholarship search. The help you receive is something you can usually get from a counselor or by reading a book.

Please attend our free financial aid seminar.

Once again this offer may be an enticement to get you in so you and your parents can be subjected to high-pressure sales methods (sometimes about costly insurance programs) meant to make you spend hundreds or thousands of dollars. The help you receive is something you can usually get from a counselor or by reading a book. Very little information is provided about finding or winning scholarships or getting college financial aid without great cost to you.

We can help you complete the Free Application for Federal Student Aid (FAFSA). The cost is . . .

There is an amazing of array of sources offered by the federal government at no cost to you to help you complete the FAFSA. And actually filing the FAFSA after you complete it is also free. Visit any of the following sources to get additional help:

- Website: http://www.fafsa.ed.gov or www.fafsa4caster.ed.gov
- Facebook: https://www.facebook.com/FederalStudentAid
- Twitter: @FAFSA
- YouTube: http://www.youtube.com/user/federalStudentAid
- Phone: (800) 4-FED-AID (433-3243)

PLACES TO CHECK SCHOLARSHIP OFFERS TOO GOOD TO BE TRUE

Consult with your counselor or career center director about what seem to be national scholarship scams. In addition, you can also refer to the following sources.

FEDERAL TRADE COMMISSION

600 Pennsylvania Avenue NW
Washington, DC 20580
(877) FTC-HELP (382-4357) or (202) 326-2222
http://www.ftc.gov

COUNCIL OF BETTER BUSINESS BUREAUS

http://www.bbb.org (visit the website and input your zip code for
    local information)
3033 Wilson Boulevard, Suite 600
Arlington, VA 22201
(703) 276-0100
E-mail: info@mybbb.org

COLLEGE FAIRS

To gather additional information about colleges and their available
scholarships, attend college fairs where representatives from hundreds of
colleges and universities distribute information and talk to prospective
students and their parents. Attending these fairs will also help you get a
feel for a college or university by talking to student or faculty representatives. If your intention is to enroll in a popular university, the number of
people visiting each booth will let you know just how popular it is. The
fairs are held in most major cities across the nation during the course of the
year, and they usually begin in September. Contact your guidance counselor about dates and locations. College fairs are often held in shopping
malls, so you can call the events coordinator of the local mall or malls for
the dates of future college fairs in your area. You can also visit the National
Association for College Admission Counseling (NACAC) website at http://
www.nacac.com for a list of upcoming college fairs. Most fairs are huge
and are held at civic and convention centers.

Before Visiting a College Fair

- Get a list of college fair participants before the fair. Write down the
  colleges you want to get more information about and speak with the
  representatives. If you haven't already, research each college you plan
  to visit by looking at books such as *Peterson's Guide to Four-Year
  Colleges* or visiting their websites. For websites providing information
  about colleges, visit http://www.petersons.com or http://www.college
  board.org.
- Based on your research and your special interests, write down questions to ask admission representatives in a small notebook that will be

easy to flip through or put them in the Notes section of your smart-phone or other portable electronic device. If you're looking at several different schools and need to decide among them, ask the same questions at each table you visit. Please note that at some fairs, particularly the small ones that may be held in a gymnasium or a local community center, the representatives you speak with may be alumni from the university or college and not actually recruiters from the school. If the answers to your questions don't seem as thorough as you would like, ask if the representative is from the college or is an alumnus from the area. If an alumnus, ask for the e-mail address of one of the school recruiters so you can get more thorough answers later if you need them.

- To prepare for the fair, put your notebook with your questions and list of colleges and something to write with inside a lightweight back-pack or tote bag to hold all of the brochures and pamphlets you'll probably be collecting at the fair. You may also want to include a small Post-it pad so you can put pertinent information like an e-mail address or phone number directly on a pamphlet or brochure. In some cases, you may scan a Quick Response Code (QR) code to have additional information sent to you or have your information scanned for the college or university's mailing-list database. If your time at the fair is limited and you want to get to as many colleges and universities on your list as possible, print computer labels that have your name, address, phone number, e-mail address, name of your high school, year of graduation, intended major(s), and other special information that you want the representatives to know about you, such as your GPA (3.0 or above), SAT scores (1700 or above) or the fact that you're a debate team member, student council president, or champion swimmer. Since some college representatives ask you to fill out college information cards, you can quickly move on after you've asked your questions by putting a label on the card instead of writing the same information at every table you go to. You may be tempted to skip filling out these cards or providing your information in some other manner, but there are a few good reasons for completing them:
  - Some colleges or universities follow up with students by inviting them on preview trips or visits to the college or university.
  - Some colleges or universities, particularly those that ask for your GPA or SAT scores, use the cards to give on the spot scholarships.

- Others periodically send or e-mail information that may be of interest to particular students as it becomes available.

At the Fair

- Once you get to the fair, get a map to find out where the tables or booths of the colleges you want to visit are located and decide the quickest route to them. For small fairs, this probably won't be necessary. For large and heavily advertised fairs like some of those held in malls or convention centers, you definitely need a plan to make sure you don't get lost among all of the booths and miss out on visiting the schools that are high on your list.
- As you leave a table and before you visit the next one, write down the answers you received to your questions and your impressions of the college or university.
- If information sessions on the admissions process or financial aid are scheduled make sure you know the times for those. You'll want to set aside time to attend these as well, since financial aid is important to you.
- If you have time after visiting the colleges on your list and attending some of the information sessions, browse. You may find some colleges and universities have intriguing opportunities that you'll want to explore more.

After Visiting the College Fair

- Look through all your brochures and the notes you took at the fair. You may find some colleges and universities have large scholarship competitions you'll want to enter. Based on the information you read and the notes you wrote about each school you visited, you may decide to visit the website, take a virtual tour, interact with the school using social media, or actually visit the college or university.

Questions You Should Ask at College Fairs

1. Are you a representative directly from the college or university or an alumni member from the local area? (For small fairs, those at the table may be alumni and as such may not have the most accurate and up-to-date statistics for a particular college or university. If this is the case, ask for an e-mail address or phone number of someone at

the university to ask questions, in cases where alumni may not be entirely certain of the answers.)

2. What percentage of students attending your college receive scholarships and financial aid?
3. What percentage of the scholarships is based on financial need?
4. What percentage of the scholarships is based on merit?
5. What is the name of the financial aid director? If necessary, how would I contact the director?
6. Does the institution conduct a large scholarship competition? If so, how many levels are there?
7. What is the deadline for the application for admission?
8. What is the deadline for the application for financial aid and scholarships? What is the scholarship application process? Is it online? Is it part of the admissions application?

CAMPUS VISITS

A campus visit is an effective method of obtaining an overall impression of a college or university. Many students have determined during a campus visit if they are genuinely interested in attending an institution. My campus visit certainly changed my mind. Before the recruiter from Florida A&M University contacted me, I really knew nothing about the school and had already decided to attend a university in New Orleans. I did not want to visit another school, simply because I had made my decision about where I was going to college and had no intention of changing my mind. However, after being convinced by my brother Dutch that I should visit, I went to the campus in July 1991 and before I left, Florida A&M had become my future alma mater.

As you can see, a campus visit is an effective decision-making tool. It can give you a chance to absorb the academic atmosphere by talking with faculty members and students, walking around the campus, sitting in on classes, eating in the dining halls, sleeping in the dormitories, and wandering around the surrounding city. Not only does a visit give you a chance to assess the college or university, but it also gives university officials a chance to view you as a prospective student. During campus visits you are given chances to ask questions about the curriculum, possible majors, academic resources, computer availability, Internet and wireless access, classrooms using interactive whiteboards, online classes, employment statistics for graduates, and library hours. You can also ask students about the social and extracurricular activities at the college.

Arranging a campus visit is usually done through the admissions office. One-day or overnight visits are available. Alumni associations in your city may also put together preview trips. If possible, plan to make your visit when the school is in regular session; for example, in the fall or spring. This way you can be assured of getting a realistic view of the college. Most colleges will plan activities for student visitors and will allow you to attend classes. Remember, if it is a weekend designated for prospective students to visit, you are likely to see the most positive aspects of the school. While this type of visit is informative and lots of fun, try to arrange another visit so that you can see what the institution is really like.

Scholarship Research Checklist

1. Have you exhausted the resources of the public library? For example, have you looked in all scholarship directories such as *Peterson's Guide to Scholarships, Grants and Prizes* and *The Ultimate Scholarship Book*, the vertical files of pamphlets and brochures, magazines, books, and college catalogs? For the most recent directories, you may need to browse in a local bookstore. Have you gone through the Scholarship Research Questionnaire in this chapter and checked off all sources of funds that may apply to you and your situation?
2. Have you looked in general college guides such as *Peterson's Guide to Four-Year Colleges*?
3. Have you looked in the telephone book for local private organizations such as fraternities, sororities, and clubs? Have you done an advanced Internet search for these?
4. Have you contacted local and national associations and clubs? Have you done an advanced Internet search for these?
5. Have you contacted local radio and television stations?
6. Have you contacted your area's chamber of commerce?
7. Have you talked with your guidance counselor or career center director about college fairs in your area, or attended one?
8. Have you spoken with your guidance counselor or career center director about scholarships or financial aid opportunities, including those from local organizations?
9. Have you visited a nearby college campus?

10. Have you contacted the banks in your area about trust funds, scholarships, and awards? Have you done an advanced Internet search for these?
11. Have you contacted your local board of education and state financial aid agency to inquire about special scholarships for students who would like to become teachers or health care professionals and other scholarships as well?
12. Have you used the Internet and social media to find sources of monetary aid?

IMPORTANT NOTE FOR USING REFERENCE BOOKS FOR SCHOLARSHIP INFORMATION

Many organizations that offer scholarships move frequently. Even though mail you send to them can be forwarded from the old address, the postal service will only forward mail to the new address for one year. If you use scholarship directories that are more than a year old, then you will probably have letters returned from organizations that have moved and whose mail can no longer be forwarded. You can avoid this by calling the organization first to update its address or searching for it on the Internet. Visit The Scholarship Workshop, http://www.scholarshipworkshop.com, for links to many of the organizations listed in this book and get updated addresses so that you can visit their websites directly.

INTERESTING PLACES FOR SCHOLARSHIP OPPORTUNITIES

Throughout your journey on the road to winning scholarships you must be alert to any information that can be used to find scholarship dollars. For example, while listening to the radio, watching television, reading, or talking to people, you may become aware of new scholarship opportunities. Although some of the programs below are still available, some are not. I include them only as encouragement to keep your eyes and ears open for scholarship opportunities until you receive notification that you've received enough funds to pay for your entire education or you have your bachelor's or graduate degree in your hands.

- As I was finishing the novel *The Vow* by Linda Lael Miller, I discovered a scholarship contest offered by the book's publisher, Pocket

Books, on the inside back cover. In this contest, three $5,000 scholarships were awarded. Applicants entered the contest by submitting a 500-word essay on the subject, "What Vow Have You Made to Further Your Education or Career."

- In *Ebony* magazine, I read about a contest sponsored by the cable channel HBO titled, "HBO Remembers *4 Little Girls*," in which four grand-prize winners received $5,000 scholarships. HBO also awarded two $2,500 scholarships. Students who entered the contest were required to express their feelings about the 1963 Birmingham bombing and racial intolerance. For those who were aware of this contest, the odds were pretty good since there were only 4,100 entries.

- As I listened to satellite radio on a sports channel in the car, I learned about the Dr. Pepper Million-Dollar Scholarship giveaway. By the way, I never tune in to sports channels voluntarily. But my ears perked up when I heard the words, "scholarship giveaway."

- While reading a magazine from the utility that supplies electricity to my house, I discovered the NOVEC scholarship program available to students in this service area.

- Through a search for another program on Facebook, I found numerous scholarship programs with Facebook pages that actually post information to help students prepare and win.

- As I was listening to a morning talk show, I learned of plans for the Gates Millennium Scholars Program, funded by the Bill and Melinda Gates Foundation. This was a year before the scholarship program was introduced.

3

USING THE INTERNET AND SOCIAL MEDIA IN YOUR SCHOLARSHIP SEARCH

Few things are impossible to diligence and skill.

—Samuel Johnson

When it comes to research, the Internet is a giant library of information, especially when researching college and scholarship information. The Web has a major advantage over traditional types of paper-based communication because Web pages can be instantly updated by organizations and educational institutions, thus giving them the ability to provide more accurate, up-to-date, and thorough information. In fact, most colleges and universities are now using their Web pages to attract students. In addition to creating apps that students can use on their smartphones to learn more about the university, some schools are embracing social media, from organizing private Facebook groups for prospective students to letting applicants augment their applications with YouTube videos.

Many college and university websites have realistic images of almost every area of their institution, and many allow you to take virtual campus tours. Using the Internet you can:

- Connect to college websites and take virtual campus tours in your own home.
- Perform extensive scholarship searches using free computerized databases and search engines.
- Visit scholarship program websites such as the Coca-Cola Scholars Foundation to find out more information. With most scholarship programs, such as this one, you can even apply online.

- Visit organizations such as the National Association of Secondary School Principals that administer or sponsor scholarships to find out more and how to win scholarships they sponsor or administer.
- Read financial aid information from a variety of sources, including the U.S. Department of Education.
- Take practice tests, such as the SAT, or view sample questions and tips from the SAT.
- Talk to college students and scholarship program administrators by sending e-mail, chatting online, or using social media.
- Submit college applications, financial aid applications such as the Free Application for Federal Student Aid (FAFSA), and other types of applications online.

An online college and scholarship search can save you a lot of time and can usually be done more quickly and easily than a paper-based search. When I began my scholarship search in the early 1990s, I spent several weeks in the library poring over directories. My advice for you, now that we have technology to make things easier, is to use the Internet as a way

Keys to organizing your Internet scholarship search

- Use computerized scholarship search engines such as FastWeb, Zinch.com, and Scholarships.com.
- Visit general websites for college and scholarship information, such as The Scholarship Workshop Online, FinAid.org, and the College Board.
- Use general search engines such as Yahoo! and Google for less well-known scholarship websites. Enter, search terms like "college scholarships" and "college financial aid."
- Conduct an advanced Internet search to find local scholarship opportunities.
- Use social media effectively. Some scholarship programs have Facebook pages and Twitter accounts.
- Search for magazine and news articles that may contain scholarship information.
- Go directly to scholarship organizations and foundations such as the Elks National Foundation and the Coca-Cola Scholars Foundation.
- Visit government websites such as the U.S. Department of Education.
- Connect to college and university Web pages to prepare for college visits and interviews or get more information about costs and financial aid.
- Use the Internet for required forms and testing information such as the FAFSA and the SAT.

to make your search as comprehensive as possible. One of the main reasons students do not apply for scholarships is that they don't know what is available. One of my primary goals for this book and the workshops I conduct is to help you find scholarships no matter where you live or your personal eligibility criteria. Once you find them, my next goal is to show you how to win them. This is why I caution that if you do research online, you should *not* skip any of the research methods discussed in chapter 2. The Internet does not have all of the information about scholarships to be found nor is all the information you find accurate. This means that you should still look at all the current paper-based scholarship directories you can find. Also, you should still call local organizations, banks, television stations, and radio stations. Utilize all the other methods discussed in chapter 2 so you leave no stone unturned. Much of the information on the Internet is from large or nationally oriented scholarship programs. If you rely on the Internet exclusively, or even scholarship directories whose focus is also national, you may miss out on opportunities closer to home. You should also note while doing your research online, particularly for scholarships and financial aid, that not every website has legitimate information or scholarships. (Read the information about scams in chapter 2.)

Following are the most popular and frequently used directories, databases, and search engines on the Internet. Using them, you should have a comprehensive listing of scholarship sources and information for college.

General Search Engines

Google http://www.google.com
Yahoo! http://www.yahoo.com
Bing http://www.bing.com
AOL Search http://search.aol.com

Ask! http://www.ask.com
Excite http://www.excite.com
WebCrawler http://www.webcrawler.com

When you use these search engines to find scholarships and financial aid information, enter keywords such as "financial aid," "scholarships," "college scholarships," "money for college," "education," "college aid," "grants," "fellowships," "admissions offices," "universities," "college applications," "merit scholarships," "academic scholarships," "minority scholarships," and so on. Use quotation marks around your entries to make sure you get more specific results. You can also conduct an advanced search as explained in the next paragraph.

To conduct an advanced search, go to a search engine such as Yahoo! On the main toolbar at the top of the page, look for *More* or Web. In the dropdown box that appears, choose *Advanced Search*. You should see options on the page that appear similar to the image below.

Show results with all of these words	macon	any part of the page ▼
the exact phrase	scholarships	any part of the page ▼
any of these words	georgia	any part of the page ▼
none of these words		any part of the page ▼

For example, the above advanced search was done specifically to find scholarships in the area of Macon, Georgia. You can use an advanced search such as this one or Boolean search logic (which the advanced search is based upon) to find scholarships in a specific county, city, state, or region. An advanced search can also be used to find specific types of scholarships such as for certain majors or for cancer survivors. Conducting an advanced search allows you to cut through the clutter of millions of Internet results that are sometimes loosely related to what you need, and gives you more targeted results.

COMPUTERIZED SCHOLARSHIP SEARCHES

You can also utilize search engines that are for scholarships only. I call them computerized scholarship search services. Some of the most popular are listed below. You can link to even more by visiting http://www.scholar shipworkshop.com.

Free Scholarship Search Services on the Internet

College Board Scholarship Search
http://apps.collegeboard.com/cbsearch_ss/welcome.jsp or
https://bigfuture.collegeboard.org/scholarship-search

College Answer
http://www.collegeanswer.com/paying/content/pay_free_money.jsp

Fastweb
http://www.fastweb.com
Facebook: https://www.facebook.com/PayingForSchool
Twitter: @PayingForSchool

Mach25 from CollegeNET
http://www.collegenet.com/mach25
Twitter: @CollegeNET

Meritaid.com
http://www.meritaid.com

Scholarships.com
http://www.scholarships.com
Facebook: https://www.facebook.com/scholarships.com.info
Twitter: @Scholarshipscom

UNCF Scholarship Search
http://www.uncf.org (see *For Students* section on website)
Twitter: @uncfscholarship

U.S. News & World Report Scholarship Searches
http://www.usnews.com/usnews/edu/dollars/tools/scholarship_search
  .htm

Zinch.com
http://www.zinch.com
Facebook: https://www.facebook.com/zinch
Twitter: @Zinch
YouTube: http://www.youtube.com/user/JoJoZinch

Use a service such as HighBeam Library Research (a paid service with a free trial period) or your public library website to search for magazine and newspaper articles on the Internet about scholarships. For example, if you lived in Fairfax County, Virginia, you could visit the library online at http://www.co.fairfax.va.us/library to use its databases, or you could download apps for your smartphone to search for magazine articles and other relevant information. Some magazines with previous scholarship and college money-related articles are *Money, Ebony,* and *U.S. News & World*

Report. You can also go directly to these magazine websites and perform a search on past articles using search terms such as "scholarships" and "financial aid." Most publications covering finance also publish articles about college aid.

To conduct searches for magazine and newspaper articles on the Internet visit http://www.highbeam.com. You can also use the Internet Public Library at http://www.ipl.org. Or you can conduct a search of articles relating to scholarships and financial aid by using Google Advanced News Archive Search (http://news.google.com/archivesearch/advanced_search).

You can also use Google Alerts (in Google, click on *More*, then *Even More* in the top menu bar) to get e-mail alerts for recent articles that have been written about scholarships, college, and financial aid. Or visit Yahoo!'s scholarship directory (see http://dir.yahoo.com, then click on *Education*, then click on *Financial Aid*, then click on *Scholarship Programs*) for links to numerous scholarship organizations.

Search for major companies and associations such as those listed in chapter 2 and explore their websites to see if they sponsor scholarship programs. For example, in a search for scholarships on Kohl's home page (http://www.kohls.com), you will find information for the Kohl's Cares Scholarship Program. When searching company home pages, use their search function and type "scholarships" in the keyword box. If this doesn't yield results, you can try visiting sections of the website with labels such as *About Us, Philanthropy, Corporate Giving*, or *Foundation*. Likewise, in a search of the National Association of Secondary School Principals, you will find information on scholarship programs they administer. To find more associations, consult the *Encyclopedia of Associations*, available in your local library. You can also visit the Internet Public Library (http://www.ipl.org) and go to the section for "Associations on the Net," which is organized by category. So if you're looking for associations that are affiliated with law, go directly to that section. When I did this, I saw the American Political Science Association website. I used their site's search engine to search for scholarships and immediately found an available graduate scholarship for students studying political science. To find organizations on the Web when you do not know a website address, you can go to Google or Yahoo! In the search box, type the name of the organization and put quotation marks around it to make your search specific, with more accurate results. If the organization is on the Web, the search should return an entry for it.

USING SOCIAL MEDIA TO FIND SCHOLARSHIPS AND COLLEGE AID

Increasingly, many organizations use Facebook pages, Twitter handles, YouTube videos, and other forms of social media to assist students with their college and college-funding search. If you want to determine if a program has a social media presence, use the search toolbar in Facebook (http://www .facebook.com) to find if a Facebook page is available. Just type in the name and see what comes up. YouTube (http://www.youtube.com) has a similar search toolbar to find a program. For Twitter (http://www.twitter.com), use Google and type in the program name along with the name Twitter to see if there is a handle for the program. When you review the listing of scholarship programs on the Internet later in this chapter, you see Twitter handles, Facebook pages, and YouTube channels listed as well. In some cases, the social media outlet may not directly relate to the scholarship program, so it was not included, or it may not have been available at the time of publication.

To get you started with Twitter, use these Twitter handles for sites that are helpful to students in search of college aid and college-related information:

@Scholarshipscom
@ScholAmerica
@FAFSA
@CollegeBoard
@CollegeNET

HOW CAN FACEBOOK, TWITTER, YOUTUBE, AND OTHER SOCIAL MEDIA HELP YOU?

Thorough research of a scholarship foundation, national foundation, or scholarship program can help you prepare to write scholarship essays, perfect your application, and get ready for interviews. If you have prior information about a program it could help you highlight certain personal qualities or activities you've been involved in that could sway the opinions of a scholarship committee in your favor. Students who have no knowledge of a program or a competition could have a tough time winning. Social media can help you keep a finger on the pulse of a program by keeping you aware of the events and news it considered important enough to broadcast on its social media platforms. Specifically, social media can help you in the following ways:

- If you "Like" certain pages for scholarship and college-related programs on Facebook, you may get alerts on scholarship application availability, deadlines, tips, and more.
- Following programs on Twitter can keep you aware of tips, deadline extensions, application availability, and announcements.
- Viewing YouTube videos can help you understand a program's mission, values, and goals, which can help you prepare for an essay or interview. Or, in the case of a competition, you may be able to view previous performances or submissions to help you prepare and perfect your own.

START YOUR INTERNET AND SOCIAL MEDIA SEARCH WITH THESE SCHOLARSHIP FUNDING AND COLLEGE INFORMATION SOURCES

To launch your scholarship search on the Internet, use the following listings to get more information about colleges, scholarships and financial aid, and other related advice. Please note that website links and programs change frequently. The list below is meant to give you a starting point with your Internet and social media research. Do not rely solely on this list and do not become frustrated if some of these sites are no longer available. It is important to do your own research, which I outline how to do throughout this book. For up-to-date listings with examples of available scholarships, visit http://www.scholarshipworkshop.com for new and updated listings since the publication of this book. You can also read *10 Steps for Using the Internet in Your Scholarship Search* or the eBook *Find and Win Scholarships Online: Strategies from a $400,000 Scholarship Winner*. These publications are updated yearly and, if necessary, twice yearly. Visit http://www.scholarshipworkshop.com for more information.

COLLEGE PREPARATION AND SELECTION

The College Board
http://www.collegeboard.com
http://socialmedia.collegeboard.org

Facebook: https://www.facebook.com/thecollegeboard
Twitter: @CollegeBoard
YouTube: http://www.youtube.com/collegeboard

Princeton Review
http://www.princetonreview.com
Facebook: https://www.facebook.com/ThePrincetonReview
Twitter: @ThePrincetonRev
YouTube: http://www.youtube.com/user/ThePrincetonReviewUS

CollegeNET
http://www.collegenet.com
Twitter: @CollegeNET

College Answer
https://www.collegeanswer.com
Facebook: https://www.facebook.com/SallieMae
Twitter: @SallieMae

US News Online: Education
http://www.usnews.com (click on Education)

Campus Tours
http://www.campustours.com

College Express
http://www.collegexpress.com
Twitter: @CollegeXpress

ALTERNATIVE EDUCATION RESOURCES

Yahoo! Alternative Education
http://www.yahoo.com/Education/Distance_Learning

MAJOR SCHOLARSHIP PROVIDERS AND COLLEGE INFORMATION SITES: INTERNET AND SOCIAL MEDIA REFERENCES

The College Board
http://www.collegeboard.com
http://socialmedia.collegeboard.org

Facebook: https://www.facebook.com/thecollegeboard
Twitter: @CollegeBoard
YouTube: http://www.youtube.com/collegeboard

College Answer
https://www.collegeanswer.com
Facebook: https://www.facebook.com/SallieMae
Twitter: @SallieMae

The Scholarship Workshop Online
http://www.scholarshipworkshop.com
Facebook: https://www.facebook.com/scholarshipworkshop
Twitter: @ScholarshipWork

FinAid—The SmartStudent Guide to Financial Aid
http://www.finaid.org

Peterson's Education Center
http://www.petersons.com
Facebook: https://www.facebook.com/petersons
Twitter: @Petersons

CORPORATE/ORGANIZATION SCHOLARSHIP AND AWARD WEBSITES

Buick Achievers Scholarship Program
http://www.buickachievers.com

Coca-Cola Scholars Foundation
http://www.coca-colascholars.org
Facebook: https://www.facebook.com/CocaColaScholarsFoundation
Twitter: @cokescholars
YouTube: http://www.youtube.com/user/CocaColaScholars/feed

Veterans of Foreign Wars of the United States
http://www.vfw.org (click on Community\Programs\VFW
   Scholarship Programs)

National Foundation for Advancement in the Arts
http://www.nfaa.org or http://www.youngarts.org
Facebook: https://www.facebook.com/YoungArtsFoundation

Twitter: @YoungArts
YouTube: http://www.youtube.com/user/YoungArtsNFAA
Pinterest: http://pinterest.com/youngartsnfaa

The DuPont Challenge
http://www.thechallenge.dupont.com
YouTube: http://www.youtube.com/user/TheDuPontChallenge

Intel Science Talent Search
http://www.societyforscience.org/sts
Facebook: https://www.facebook.com/societyforscience
YouTube: http://www.youtube.com/societyforscience

The Ayn Rand Institute
http://www.aynrand.org/contests
Facebook: https://www.facebook.com/aynrandessaycontest
Twitter: @aynrandnovels

Elks National Foundation
http://www.elks.org (click on Elks National Foundation\ENF
    Programs\Scholarships)
Facebook: https://www.facebook.com/ElksNationalFoundation
Twitter: https://twitter.com/ElksNtnlFndtn

The American Legion National High School Oratorical Contest
http://www.legion.org/oratorical
Facebook: https://www.facebook.com/americanlegionhq
YouTube: http://www.youtube.com/user/americanlegionHQ

SCHOLARSHIPS FOR THE DISABLED

National Center for Learning Disabilities: The Anne Ford and Allegra Ford Thomas Scholarship Award
http://www.ncld.org (click on About Us\Scholarships & Awards)
Facebook: https://www.facebook.com/LD.org
Twitter: @LDorg
Pinterest: http://pinterest.com/ncld/
YouTube: http://www.youtube.com/user/NCLD1401

National Federation of the Blind Scholarship Program
http://www.nfb.org (search for "Scholarships")
Facebook: https://www.facebook.com/
NationalFederationoftheBlind
Twitter: @NFB_voice
YouTube: http://www.youtube.com/user/NationsBlind

Through the Looking Glass—College Scholarships for Students of Parents with Disabilities
http://www.lookingglass.org (click on Services\National Services\Scholarships)

MINORITY SCHOLARSHIPS

The Jackie Robinson Foundation
http://www.jackierobinson.org
Twitter: @JRFoundation

League of United Latin American Citizens (LULAC) National Scholarship Fund
http://www.lnesc.org
Facebook: https://www.facebook.com/LNESC
Twitter: @LNESC

Hispanic Scholarship Fund
http://www.hsf.net
Facebook: https://www.facebook.com/HispanicScholarshipFund
Twitter: @HSFNews

Ron Brown Scholar Program
http://www.ronbrown.org
Facebook: https://www.facebook.com/ronbrownscholarprogram

GEM PhD Science Fellowship
http://www.gemfellowship.org

Consortium for Graduate Study in Management
http://www.cgsm.org
Facebook: https://www.facebook.com/cgsm.org
Twitter: @cgsm_mba

The PhD Project
http://www.phdproject.com
Facebook: https://www.facebook.com/thephdproject
Twitter: @ThePhDProject

Gates Millennium Scholars Program
http://www.gmsp.org

Hispanic College Fund
http://www.hispanicfund.org
Facebook: https://www.facebook.com/HispanicCollegeFund
Twitter: @hispanicfund

Presbyterian Church—Native American Education Grant
http://gamc.pcusa.org/ministries/financialaid or
http://www.presbyterianmission.org/ministries/financialaid/native
   -american-education-grant
Facebook: https://www.facebook.com/pcusa
Twitter: @Presbyterian

INTERNATIONAL AND STUDY ABROAD SCHOLARSHIPS

The Rotary Foundation
http://www.rotary.org (click on Students and Youth\Educational
   Programs)
Facebook: https://www.facebook.com/rotary
Twitter: @rotary
YouTube: http://www.youtube.com/user/RotaryInternational

International Education Financial Aid
http://www.IEFA.org
Facebook: https://www.facebook.com/internationalstudent
Twitter: @intstudent

EduPASS
http://www.edupass.org

EducationUSA
http://www.educationusa.info

https://www.facebook.com/EducationUSA
Twitter: @EdUSAupdates

Institute of International Education (IIE) Funding for U.S. Study

http://www.fundingusstudy.org
Facebook: https://www.facebook.com/IIEglobal
Twitter: @IIEglobal

Institute for the International Education of Students (IES)

http://www.iesabroad.org
Facebook: https://www.facebook.com/IESAbroad
Twitter: @IESAbroad
YouTube: http://www.youtube.com/iesabroad

ScholarshipsCanada

http://www.scholarshipscanada.com
Facebook: https://www.facebook.com/scholarshipscanada
Twitter: @ScholarshipsCA

StudentAwards

http://www.studentawards.com
Facebook: https://www.facebook.com/studentawards
Twitter: @studentawards

NONTRADITIONAL SCHOLARSHIPS

Soroptimist Women's Opportunity Awards

http://www.soroptimist.org
Twitter: @soroptimist

Executive Women International: Adult Students in Scholastic Transition (ASIST)

http://www.executivewomen.org
Twitter: @EWICorporate

College Fish

http://www.collegefish.org

Facebook: https://www.facebook.com/collegefish
Twitter: @CollegeFish_4yr

To find more Web addresses for various scholarship programs, refer to Appendix A. You can also visit http://www.scholarshipworkshop.com, or follow us on Facebook, http://www.facebook.com/scholarshipworkshop, or Twitter, @ScholarshipWork.

GOVERNMENT FUNDING, INFORMATION WEBSITES, AND SOCIAL MEDIA

Federal Student Aid and Free Application for Federal Student Aid (FAFSA)
http://www.fafsa.ed.gov or www.fafsa4caster.ed.gov
Facebook: https://www.facebook.com/FederalStudentAid
Twitter: @FAFSA
YouTube: http://www.youtube.com/user/federalStudentAid

The Student Guide
StudentAid.gov **or** http://studentaid.ed.gov/resources#funding
Facebook: https://www.facebook.com/FederalStudentAid
Twitter: @FAFSA
YouTube: http://www.youtube.com/user/federalStudentAid

IRS Tax Information and Benefits for Students
http://www.irs.gov/Individuals/Students

TEST REGISTRATION AND TEST PREPARATION WEBSITES AND SOCIAL MEDIA

Practice Test Questions for the ACT
http://www.act.org or http://www.actstudent.org
Facebook: https://www.facebook.com/theacttest
Twitter: @ACTStudent

Preparing for the SAT
http://www.collegeboard.com (click on SAT Practice)
http://socialmedia.collegeboard.org
Facebook: https://www.facebook.com/thecollegeboard
Twitter: @CollegeBoard
YouTube: http://www.youtube.com/collegeboard

4

THE LOCAL SCHOLARSHIP SEARCH:
FINDING SCHOLARSHIPS IN YOUR BACKYARD

A wise man will make more opportunities than he finds.

—Francis Bacon

As fall approaches and thoughts of college enter your and your parents' minds, many resources can aid you in answering an extremely important question: "How will we pay for it?" With very little effort, most students can usually get information in sources such as *The Scholarship Book* and *Peterson's Scholarships, Grants and Prizes* about the most well-known national scholarship programs, like the Coca-Cola Scholars Foundation Scholarship, the Horatio Alger Association Scholarship Program, or the Elks Most Valuable Student contest. Since these programs are so well known, thousands of students could be applying, making them highly competitive. On the other hand, many college hopefuls and their parents unintentionally ignore the gems in their own backyard. These are local scholarships and many of them have fewer than a hundred students applying. Sometimes as few as ten students apply since many of these programs have neither the time nor the resources to publicize their scholarships. Nor do the research departments for most of the big scholarship directories have time to find them, which is why they are not found in most large nationally focused directories.

If you are trying to find scholarships for college or funding for any level of higher education, you should be prepared to do a lot of research in three main areas: local, via the Internet, and at a library or bookstore. You may not realize that even though the Internet is easy to use and contains a wealth of information, the college scholarship search should extend beyond it. Why? Well, for starters, not all scholarships, particularly those that are smaller and available locally, can be found on the Internet. Not only that, since they are smaller, they could be easier to win since many students choose to ignore small scholarships in favor of larger ones.

After working with several small community-based scholarship programs, I know from experience the challenge that many have in getting students to apply. In fact, for the Ragins/Braswell National Scholarship, a scholarship I have sponsored since 1995 and for which thousands of students are eligible based on their attendance at a workshop or online scholarship class that I conduct, we have never received more than thirty applications. One reason: it's not heavily publicized.

I have also interviewed representatives of several community-based scholarship programs. Of those surveyed, none received more than fifteen scholarship applications. Even when the scholarship was open to those who were not affiliated with the organizations, many of the applications they did receive were from students who knew people who were members of the organization. And those members strongly urged the students to apply.

Also, in general scholarship searches on the Internet I have found postings from some organizations that plead for help in getting students to apply. Not only that, I periodically receive blanket e-mails from organizations reaching out to individuals and other affiliated organizations to help get the word out to students about their scholarship programs. Or organizations may ask to set up a table during one of The Scholarship Workshop presentations or even ask for time during a break in the workshop presentation to encourage students to apply for their publicly available scholarships. I once worked on the scholarship committee of a local scholarship program that was awarding four scholarships valued at $1,000 each. We got a total of five applicants. Imagine those odds! In addition, I currently work with a scholarship program that sometimes awards up to $5,000 to a single student, yet because the application rates are so low we often extend the deadline to give more students time to apply. "Like" The Scholarship Workshop on Facebook (http://www.facebook.com/scholarshipworkshop) to be notified about scholarship programs that desperately need more students to apply.

By sniffing out opportunities available in your own communities, state, or region, you can win several small scholarships, which just might buy you an entire year of tuition or a year of books. It might even be easier for you to win them because you are not competing against thousands of students throughout the country. Even though these scholarships may not be more than $2,500 or $1,000 (and sometimes less than that), they can definitely add up. So don't ignore them. Most important, if you've already prepared applications for larger scholarship programs, it will be easier to complete applications for local opportunities using a little cutting-and-pasting skill on your computer.

Let me run through a few tips to help you find and apply for these hidden gems:

- Visit your counselor or career center director. Since many local scholarship programs send information about their scholarships to high schools in the area, your counselor or career center director may have a list of scholarship opportunities or a school website containing links to scholarship programs. You can also call the local Board of Education or do an Internet search to see if it has a list as well. Some school systems do a wonderful job of maintaining online databases that list scholarship opportunities by date and even include a copy of the application online.
- Find community foundations in your area. Community foundations often administer scholarship programs that are specific to students within a certain county or region or even certain high schools. Use an advanced search to find community foundations in your city and state such as the example shown in the image below. For example, in the city of Arlington, Virginia, there is the Arlington Community Foundation, and the Berks County Community Foundation in Pennsylvania that offer scholarships. There are community foundations throughout the United States—there may be one in your community, too!
- Investigate the websites of local radio and television stations, newspapers, companies, banks, and social organizations to see if they offer aid to students in your community. And don't forget to visit your church or faith-based organization's website.

Advanced Search

Find Results	With **all** of the words	Arlington
	With the **exact phrase**	Community foundation
	With **at least one** of the words	Virginia

- Ask teachers and other administrators at your school. Some teachers may actually serve on scholarship committees or may know of someone who does. If that's the case, they can give you more information about the scholarship program or refer you to someone who can. They may also be able to give you the address, telephone number, website, or Facebook page for the sponsoring organization of a local scholarship program.

- Call local clubs and organizations, associations, sororities, fraternities, service clubs, companies, and banks. Look in the Yellow Pages of your phone book. For example, when looking under clubs you might find the Elks or the Kiwanis Club. Call and identify yourself and your purpose. You could say something like this, "Hello. My name is *Marianne Ragins* and I am a high school student at *Northeast High School* here in *Macon, Georgia*. I was wondering if your organization has scholarships or awards that are made available to students in the area?" If the answer is yes, then ask how you can get additional information and an application. You can also conduct an advanced Internet search for these types of clubs and organizations in your area, if you don't have or use a telephone book.

- Contact your local chamber of commerce. They may have a list of business members whose companies sponsor community-based scholarship opportunities. Visit the website if they have one.

- Call radio and television stations. Although most may not have a scholarship program available, some may have had guests on in the past who had been interviewed about college, scholarships, and financial aid. The guest may have left information with producers such as a telephone number, website address, Twitter handle, or Facebook information. When you call a station ask for the producer who works on education or college-financing segments.

TAKE NOTE—SPECIAL CONSIDERATIONS FOR LOCAL SCHOLARSHIPS

As you make your calls, talk to teachers and counselors and anyone else you think could be of help in your search for local scholarship opportunities. Also, be aware of situations that are unique to small and local scholarship programs.

- For some organizations that are small chapters of a larger national organization, you may not have a telephone number but only the address. If this is the case, do an Internet search to see if you can find any contact information or Web page for the local chapter. If you come up empty, then send an inquiry letter such as the one shown in chapter 2. Before mailing your inquiry letter, affix a label (1×2-inch) on the outside of your envelope, that is similar to the example below.

> **Information and Application REQUEST**
> Self-Addressed Stamped Envelope
> and Postcard Enclosed
> Please Open Immediately

This is helpful because some organizations assume that all mail received contains actual scholarship applications. Thus they may delay opening your request until it's time to review applications. If you are a senior, you may miss the deadline and become ineligible for the scholarship.

- Some organizations indicate a certain grade point average is required for eligibility. However, they may actually accept and evaluate applications from students based on the student's overall application. Refer to chapter 9, "Writing Your Scholarship Résumé—How to Stand Out and Why Grades Don't Mean Everything."

- Some organizations may ask for proof of financial need, a copy of your FAFSA, a certificate of financial eligibility, or a financial needs statement. Although many organizations don't actually have a specific way of evaluating one student's need versus another's, they may actually disqualify you if do not include the information requested. In some cases, they just want proof that you have completed the FAFSA or a written statement specifically stating why you need money for college. If this is requested on an application, call, e-mail, or write the organization immediately to find out what they need if you don't understand the request. Ask for an example. Never ignore requests made on an application. And, most important, even if an organization states that the award is based on need, you can still apply. You never know—your need, even though small, may still be greater than someone else's.

- Remember, just because an organization is small does not warrant that your application can be handwritten or in any way sloppily thrown together. Put together the best application you can for all opportunities that come your way, even those in your backyard.

5

FINANCIAL AID FORMS AND HELP FROM THE GOVERNMENT WITH COLLEGE EXPENSES

> Next in importance to freedom and justice is
> popular education, without which neither freedom
> nor justice can be permanently maintained.
>
> —James A. Garfield

Government assistance comes in a variety of forms. For instance, you can obtain grants and loans from the U.S. government, or you can get help as a taxpayer with certain tax credits for educational expenses. State governments also contribute to the students of their states by offering various types of aid programs ranging from tuition waivers to full scholarships.

For federal and some state assistance you will need to complete the Free Application for Federal Student Aid (FAFSA). The FAFSA will help most colleges and universities determine your financial aid package. The financial aid package usually contains some type of federal aid such as the Pell Grant, work-study, or a Direct or Plus Loan in addition to university scholarships. For some institutions, you will also need to complete the CSS—Financial Aid PROFILE (College Scholarship Service—Financial Aid PROFILE). You may also have to submit another financial aid form specific to the institution you are planning to attend to determine your aid package.

For information about the CSS PROFILE, visit http://www.college board.org. To get more information about federal financial aid forms, visit these websites and social media platforms:

Federal Student Aid and Free Application for Federal Student Aid (FAFSA)

http://www.fafsa.ed.gov or www.fafsa4caster.ed.gov
Facebook: https://www.facebook.com/FederalStudentAid
Twitter: @FAFSA
YouTube: http://www.youtube.com/user/federalStudentAid

The Student Guide

StudentAid.gov or http://studentaid.ed.gov/resources#funding
Facebook: https://www.facebook.com/FederalStudentAid
Twitter: @FAFSA
YouTube: http://www.youtube.com/user/federalStudentAid

IRS Tax Information and Benefits for Students

http://www.irs.gov/Individuals/Students

Now let's answer a few basic questions that will help you understand the financial aid process and how it works.

WHAT IS A FINANCIAL AID PACKAGE?

A financial aid package is the total amount of financial aid a student receives. For example, a package could consist of loans, grants, work-study (a job arranged for you on the college campus and funded by the federal government), and scholarships. The contents of a financial aid package are usually communicated to a student in a financial aid award letter similar to the one shown at the end of this section or in an online account established for a student who submits an online application.

HOW IS A FINANCIAL AID PACKAGE DETERMINED?

A financial aid package is determined primarily by the FAFSA and/or the CSS—Financial Aid PROFILE, and the financial aid committee/director at the universities or colleges to which you have applied. Both the FAFSA and the CSS—Financial Aid PROFILE are financial aid forms with several differences that help determine a student's total need. The FAFSA uses federal methodology to determine your need and the CSS—PROFILE uses institutional methodology and may be requested by some private colleges and universities.

WHAT IS MY FINANCIAL NEED?

Your financial need will be based on how much you and your parents can contribute to the total cost of your education at the college you have chosen. This amount plus the amount of outside aid you receive (such as scholarships that are not from the university or college you are applying to) is subtracted from the total cost of college attendance to obtain the total of your financial need. Your contributions will be based on your current income, assets, and so on. To get an estimate of your financial need and expected family contribution, and for an idea of how much federal financial aid you may be able to receive, visit the federal student aid information websites listed above.

Once need has been demonstrated and is sent to the college on your student aid report (SAR), the institution will determine your total financial aid package—the amount of your need they can meet. Some colleges and universities meet 100 percent of your need. Some don't even come close. It depends on the institution and the circumstances. Also keep in mind that if you have been awarded a financial aid award package by a specific college or university and you win an additional merit-based non-need scholarship award, your financial aid package at the school may be reduced. This is because it lowers your total need amount. For example, if your financial aid package at a school is for $15,000 per year and you win a scholarship for $5,000 a year, your award package may be reduced to $10,000 per year. If you win a need-based award, but have already received a financial aid package from a college or university meeting your total financial need you may be ineligible to receive this award even after you've won it, since the award amount can never be higher than your actual need. Some schools and organizations will allow you to use the additional monies toward books and personal expenses. When applying to schools, ask about their policies regarding this issue.

Now that we understand those concepts, let's explore the primary way your need and financial aid package is calculated—the financial aid forms.

THE FINANCIAL AID FORMS

There are two primary financial forms accepted by colleges and universities. The most common application is the FAFSA (Free Application for Federal Student Aid). If you are applying for any government aid, such as a Pell Grant or a SEOG grant, you will need to complete the FAFSA. This is one of your first steps in securing aid for college. Even if you are applying for merit-based scholarships, many colleges and universities will require you to either complete the FAFSA or the College Scholarship Service—Financial Aid PROFILE. There is a fee for using the CSS—Financial Aid PROFILE. You can get information about obtaining the FAFSA from your high school guidance office, from public libraries, or directly from the U.S. Department of Education. Completing the FAFSA online is also very easy and streamlined at http://www.fafsa.ed.gov. It's also free to complete and file. If you have any questions concerning how to obtain the FAFSA, call (800) 433-3243 or (800) 4FED-AID.

The FAFSA will determine your eligibility for the following federal financial aid programs:

- Pell Grant—Federal grant given to students who are enrolled full-time or part-time and have financial need; amount is determined by the depth of the student's need. As long as you attend an eligible school, there is no minimum grade point average or specific academic requirement. This grant is usually the first form of financial aid a student obtains. For this reason, many scholarship programs require you to fill out the FAFSA when applying for scholarships, especially if the scholarship is need- rather than merit-based. The Pell Grant may be paid directly to you or credited to your student account by your school. If your Pell Grant exceeds the balance on your account, the remainder may be distributed directly to you.
- Federal Supplemental Educational Opportunity Grant (SEOG)—Given in addition to the Pell, this grant is awarded to students who have extreme financial need. The amount is determined by the institution you attend. Most schools deplete their SEOG funds early, so it is imperative that you complete the FAFSA as soon as possible.
- Work-Study—A part-time job at the college or university you attend pays you money to offset your educational expenses.
- Loans—Various types of loans are available from the federal government. The William D. Ford Federal Direct Loan Program is the

TABLE 7

	Pell Grant	Federal Supplemental Educational Opportunity Grant (SEOG)
Summary of Popular Federal Grants		
Eligibility Requirements	• You must be pursuing your first undergraduate degree. • You must be a U.S. citizen or an eligible non-citizen. • You must have a high school diploma or GED. • Incarcerated students are ineligible. • You are ineligible if you owe a refund on a Title IV grant or are in default on a Title IV loan. • If you are male, you must be registered with the Selective Service.	• Undergraduate students who have exceptional financial need (the lowest Expected Family Contribution) are eligible. • Federal Pell Grant recipients receive priority but are not guaranteed a FSEOG.
Award Amounts	Up to $5,550. The actual amount of your award will be based on the cost of the school you currently attend, your estimated family contribution (EFC), and whether you are attending your school on a full- or part-time basis. Award amounts can change each year based on funding allotted by Congress.	Up to $4,000. The amount of the grant depends on the date you apply for aid or completed your FAFSA (based on your school's guidelines), your need, the SEOG funds your school has available, and the policies of your school's financial aid office.
How do I get an application?	This grant is determined by your FAFSA. Visit http://www.fafsa.ed.gov for an online version. Or call (800) 4FED-AID.	Contact your financial aid office. Many schools also base this grant on your FAFSA and the student aid report they receive.
When do I apply?	As soon as possible after January 1 of each school year. Make sure to meet your state and school deadlines.	Contact your financial aid office as soon as possible because these funds may be depleted early.

Alternative Ways of Paying off Education Loans

In addition to devoting a significant portion of your paycheck to pay off loans after you graduate, there are a few other ways to help you pay off your education loans:

- Join the Upromise.com savings program. With it you earn back a certain percentage from purchases you make at hundreds of retailers. The money you earn back is placed in a Upromise savings account. You can use the money you accumulate in this account to help pay off your education loans. Go to http://www.upromise.com for more information.
- Volunteer or agree to work in an underrepresented area. Consult chapter 14 for more information.

largest. For loans under this program, the U.S. Department of Education is your **lender**. Visit http://www.direct.ed.gov for additional information about any of these direct loans. Four types of Direct Loans are available from the federal government:

1. Direct Subsidized Loans—*the government pays the interest while you're in school at least half-time.* These loans are need based and made to eligible undergraduate students to help cover the costs of higher education at a college or career school. Your school determines the amount you can borrow, which cannot exceed your financial need. Visit http://www.direct.ed.gov or http://www.studentaid.ed.gov for current loan limits.

2. Direct Unsubsidized Loans—*you pay the interest while you're in school or it accrues and is added to the loan balance.* These are non–need based loans made to eligible undergraduate, graduate, and professional students. Your school determines the amount you can borrow. This amount may be based upon the cost of attendance and other financial aid you receive. Visit http://www.direct.ed.gov or http://www.studentaid.ed.gov for current loan limits.

3. Direct PLUS Loans—*made to parents of dependent undergraduate students and also graduate or professional students to help pay for education expenses not covered by other financial aid.* Visit www.direct.ed.gov or www.studentaid.ed.gov for current loan limits. The limit on a PLUS Loan is equal to your cost of attendance minus any other financial aid you receive. For example, if your cost of attendance is $10,000 and you receive $3,000 in other financial aid, your parents can borrow up to but no more than $7,000.

4. Direct Consolidation Loans—*a combination of all your eligible federal student loans into a single loan with a single loan servicer.*

- Perkins Loans—Students who show exceptional financial need and who are enrolled in a participating school are eligible to participate in this federal program. This is a school-based program where your school is the lender. With the Perkins Loan, you can borrow $5,500 each year for undergraduate study up to a maximum of $27,500. As a graduate student you can borrow $8,000 each year for graduate or professional study up to a maximum of $60,000. The maximum $40,000 includes amounts you borrowed as an undergraduate. So, if you borrowed the maximum amount of $27,500 for your undergraduate degree, you will only be able to borrow $32,500 as a graduate student. Visit http://www.studentaid.ed.gov for additional information.

Before You Borrow—Special Note for Parents and Students

Before signing the promissory note for a student or parent loan, please review chapter 34, "Understanding and Minimizing Student Loans If You Don't Win Enough Scholarship Money Initially." Most important, please think twice about attending a school that will leave you in significant debt. According to a recent article (http://www.credit.com), "The most recent Federal Reserve Bank of New York report indicates that roughly 17% of total student loans are more than 90 days past due." Ponder these questions before you promise to pay: Are there alternate schools that can meet your needs? If you choose a school that greatly exceeds your current and future budget, have you reviewed the school's job placement statistics for recent and past graduates? Have you explored the occupational prospects for the career path the school will start you on? Do you know the projected salary levels? For example, if you can get a job when you graduate, will your salary land you at the poverty level once you factor in your student loan payments? If your figures look promising, at least you've done some homework before incurring debt.

DETERMINING YOUR ELIGIBILITY FOR FEDERAL FINANCIAL AID

To be eligible for federal financial aid you must:

1. Be a U.S. citizen or an eligible non-citizen.
2. Have a valid Social Security number.
3. Be registered with the Selective Service if you are male and between the ages of 18 and 25.

4. Show financial need, except for some of the loan programs.
5. Have a high school diploma, a GED, pass a test approved by the U.S. Department of Education, meet other standards your state establishes that are approved by the U.S. Department of Education, or show that you completed a high school education in a homeschool setting approved under state law.
6. Be enrolled or accepted in an eligible program as a regular student and be working toward a degree or certificate.
7. Be making satisfactory academic progress.
8. Be enrolled at least half-time to be eligible for Direct Loan Program funds.
9. Sign a statement on the Free Application for Federal Student Aid (FAFSA) stating that you are not in default on a federal student loan and do not owe money on a federal student grant and you will use federal student aid only for educational purposes.

For more information on the requirements for federal financial aid programs, consult the Student Guide published by the U.S. Department of Education. Call (800) 4FED-AID or visit the website at http://www.studentaid.ed.gov to obtain it.

Basic Tips on Completing the FAFSA

File early. For federal student aid, state student aid, and institutional aid, you must file the FAFSA. Send your FAFSA in as soon as possible after January 1. To meet many college, university, and state deadlines, file it by mid-February.

Be Careful When Searching the Web for Help with Your FAFSA!

Various companies on the Internet have Web addresses that include FAFSA as part of their address. Many of these companies charge a fee for completing the FAFSA. But the FAFSA is free, and the Federal Student Aid website at http://www.studentaid.ed.gov or http://www.fafsa.ed.gov has plenty of information to assist you at no charge.

Be prepared. The FAFSA will ask for information from your and your parents' tax returns. If you gather the information you need early and acquire the FAFSA worksheet, then as soon as your parents receive their W-2 forms you can send it off. If eligible, early applications receive the money first, as is the case with the SEOG mentioned previously in this chapter. All applications should be submitted as soon as possible after January 1 of the year you plan to enter college but no later than June 30. Some states have specific cutoff dates for submitting the FAFSA and obtaining state-based funds. Call your state financial aid agency for more information. Or you can visit http://www.fafsa.ed.gov to look up your state's filing deadline. Also, some scholarships sponsored by private organizations may require a financial aid statement or a copy of your parents' W-2 forms if determination of winners is based partially or fully on need.

Use the following checklist to help you gather the information you'll need to fill out the FAFSA. You and your parents or guardians will need to gather the following materials:

- Current year's income tax return for you and your parents. If your tax returns are not completed, you can use an estimate. You can base this on your W-2 forms and other information.
- W-2 forms and any other record of income earned
- Records of untaxed income, such as welfare, Social Security, AFDC or ADC, and veterans' benefits
- Records of child support paid to or received by a former spouse
- Bank statements
- Brokerage statements
- Business and farm records (financial statements or corporate tax returns)
- For the self-employed, a record of income received and a record of IRS-deductible business expenses
- Records of stocks, bonds, and other investments
- Your driver's license and Social Security card

Before you fill out the FAFSA for submission, consider completing a FAFSA worksheet. See http://www.fafsa.ed.gov and search for "worksheet." Download a copy and practice filling it out.

Once you complete the actual FAFSA, download the completed form to your computer or flash drive along with all supporting documents used to fill it out so you will have a backup just in case something gets lost.

You can also submit a paper version of the FAFSA. To request a paper-based copy, call (800) 4-FED-AID (433-3243) or (319) 337-5665.

To receive financial aid for the following college year, a FAFSA renewal form must be filed after January 1 of that year—just as you did for your first FAFSA. The amount of your financial aid award may change each year. This could happen if the costs at the college or university you are attending increase or if your family's financial situation changes. Changes in your family situation—or your situation if you filed as an independent student— include reduced or increased salary, another child entering college, one of your parents starting college, a long-term illness, or a disability.

If a college you are applying to also requires the CSS—Financial Aid PROFILE, you can register and get additional information by visiting http://www.collegeboard.org or calling (305) 829-9793 or e-mailing help@ cssprofile.org. You should do this at least two to three weeks before the college or university has its earliest filing deadline. Unlike the FAFSA, there is a fee for the CSS—Profile, although waivers are available for those with low income.

Some colleges also have their own financial aid forms to complete in order to be considered for their private sources of funds. If this is required it should be listed in the application materials, the college catalog, or in other materials provided by the institution or on the website. Check with the financial aid office at the school to find out if they require one of these financial aid forms to be completed as well.

File all applications for financial aid as early as possible, well before required deadlines. For the FAFSA, complete and submit it as soon as possible after January 1, as previously mentioned. Make sure that when you file, you do it in time to meet college deadlines for filing the FAFSA, usually in February and early March. If it is necessary to submit the CSS—Financial Aid PROFILE for the colleges you are applying to, register for the PROFILE at least two to three weeks before the earliest financial aid or scholarship program deadline at the schools you have selected.

Assuming you used the online process, once you have completed the FAFSA, you will receive a Student Aid Report (SAR) within three to five days that reviews your information and contains your estimated family contribution (EFC) for the colleges you listed. Paper-based filings will take longer. Review the information in your SAR carefully. If you or your parents find errors, correct them online and submit your corrections, or if a paper submission, correct and send back using the address provided. Copies of your SAR are usually available to the colleges you included on your FAFSA within one to two days of submission, assuming it is complete. The financial aid administrator at each institution will determine from the SAR your financial aid award or package. You will usually receive this information in an award letter or the information will be shown in your student account. The package could consist of a Pell Grant, loans, work-study, or scholarships. A sample award letter is shown below.

Sample Financial Aid Award Letter

Many colleges and universities show this information in your online student account rather than as a letter.

Anytown University
Office of Financial Aid
Aid, Georgia 00001

To: Caroline F. Student   Student ID #
   P.O. Box 4000
   Raleigh, North Carolina 29333 March 15, 2025

On behalf of the Financial Aid Committee, I am pleased to inform you that your request for financial aid has been approved for the 2025–2026 academic year. Please read carefully the conditions listed below and the appropriate messages on the reverse side of this notice.

Approved:
$8,500.00	XYZ Alumni Scholars Scholarship
$5,000.00	NYS General Scholarship
$2,000.00	Federal College Work-Study
$1,500.00	Federal Perkins Loan
$17,000.00	Total Approved

Lynn Smith
Director of Financial Aid

Please read the following financial aid conditions carefully:

- All grants and loans will be credited directly to the student's account each term in the following manner: 37½% Fall; 25% Winter; 37½% Spring. College work-study eligibility is the amount a student may earn working on campus. The actual amount may depend on the number of hours worked. Students who work under the college work-study program will be paid bi-weekly.
- Academic scholarships are automatically renewed for students who maintain a cumulative 3.0 grade point average. All other scholarships require a minimum 2.0 for renewal unless otherwise specified.
- All grants, loans, and work eligibilities are awarded for one year, and you must reapply every year by completing an Anytown University financial aid application and the College Scholarship Service—Finan-

cial Aid PROFILE. Further information is available in the Financial Aid Office.

- Students are required to report all financial awards received from other sources. The Financial Aid Office will reevaluate the student's need for assistance and a revision in the award may be necessary.

_____ I accept the financial aid award and the conditions listed above.
_____ I reject the financial aid award listed above.

Please sign the white copy of this award notice and return it as soon as possible to the Financial Aid Office.

Signature: _____   Date: _____

If you have completed the PROFILE from the College Board, the data you submitted in the PROFILE is then reviewed using institutional methodology, which is more stringent than FAFSA (federal) methodology in counting the family's and student's assets as a basis for contribution to the student's college education. The college that has requested this report from the CSS then uses it to determine your financial aid award package, as discussed earlier. The CSS—Profile does not determine your eligibility for federal financial aid. It is used only to help determine institutional aid for the universities and colleges that request it.

Even though your family may have a six-figure income, don't assume you won't qualify for college financial aid. You should always try. Usually the more expensive the school, the greater your need. Even if your family may be asset-rich (savings bonds, investments, etc.) it could be debt-poor (credit card debt). Since the FAFSA and/or the CSS—Financial Aid PROFILE will recognize the assets (those in the student's name more so than the parents') but not the debt—thus not qualify you for as much aid—your family should use some of its assets to pay off consumer debt to help you qualify for more aid, assuming this strategy makes sense for you and your family. Do this by the end of your junior year in high school. In addition, since more of a student's income and savings are expected to be used for college expenses, use savings and investments in the name of the student to buy needed college items such as books, computer, desk, and possibly a car. Depleting assets in the student's name can also help you qualify for more financial aid. This should also be done by the junior year of high school. As the author of this book, I am not an expert on investments, or assets relating to finanical aid forms, so please consult a certified college-planning consultant or financial aid advisor for expert help in this area.

TAX ASSISTANCE FOR COLLEGE EXPENSES

The government also provides aid in the form of tax credits that can help ease the burden of college expenses. Some of the major tax credits and deductions are explained below.

The American Opportunity Tax Credit

This credit is a per-student, partially refundable tax credit. At least until 2017 and with hope beyond, students can claim up to $2,500 for expenses on tuition, fees, and educational materials in the first four years of post-secondary education. This credit is dependent upon your filing status and income level. See publication 970 at http://www.irs.gov or your tax professional for additional information. Low-income families who owe no tax may also be eligible to receive a credit refund of up to $1,000 for each qualifying student.

The Lifetime Learning Tax Credit

This tax credit focuses on adults who want to go back to school, change careers, or take a couple of courses to upgrade their skills. It is also applicable for students who are already in college such as juniors, seniors, graduate students, and professional degree students. Using the Lifetime Learning credit, a 20 percent tax credit can be taken for the first $10,000 of tuition and required fees paid each year. For example, a secretary, whose family has an adjusted gross income of $60,000, wants to attend a graduate program at a public university ($2,700 tuition). Her intention is to upgrade her skills and eventually get a management position. The secretary has been working and out of college for the past twelve years. If she uses the Lifetime Learning credit, her family's income taxes could be cut by as much as $540. The Lifetime Learning tax credit is available for tuition and required fees minus grants, scholarships, and other tax-free educational assistance. See publication 970 available at http://www.irs.gov or your tax professional for additional information.

Coverdell Education Savings Accounts

If you have a child under age 18, you can deposit $2,000 per year into a Coverdell Education Savings Account in his or her name. Earnings in the

Coverdell Education Savings Account will accumulate tax-free. If you withdraw the money in this account to pay for post-secondary tuition and required fees (less grants, scholarships, and other tax-free educational assistance), books, equipment, and eligible room and board expenses, no taxes will be due. Once your child reaches age 30, his or her Coverdell Education Savings Account must be closed or transferred to a younger member of the family.

Your ability as a taxpayer to contribute to a Coverdell Education Savings Account may be phased out based on your income level and filing status. See http://www.irs.gov, publication 970, or your tax professional for additional information.

Early Withdrawals from IRAs

Generally when you withdraw money from an IRA before you reach age 59½ you are subject to an additional 10 percent tax on the money withdrawn. However, if you use the withdrawal to pay the qualified higher education expenses of you, your spouse, or a dependent in that year, you will not owe the additional 10 percent tax. See http://www.irs.gov, publication 970, or your tax professional for additional information.

Tax-Free Interest for Education Savings Bonds and Employer-Provided Educational Assistance

Normally, interest earned on savings bonds and money provided by your employer to pay for your higher education is taxable. However, the interest earned on certain types of bonds that are cashed in and used for qualified higher-education expenses is not taxable. Your ability to take advantage of this deduction will depend upon your income level and marital status. Likewise, your employer can provide you with up to $5,250 each year for higher education without including this amount in your taxable income. See http://www.irs.gov, publication 970, or your tax professional for additional information.

Tuition and Fees Deduction

Up to $4,000 in college tuition and related fees can be deducted each year. The deduction is taken as an adjustment to income, which means you can use the deduction even if you don't itemize. Income limits do apply, however. Your ability to take advantage of this deduction will depend upon your income level and marital status. See http://www.irs.gov, publication 970, or your tax professional for additional information.

Qualified Tuition Plans (QTP) or 529 Plans

Qualified tuition plans can be either college savings accounts or prepaid tuition programs, established and maintained by your state or an eligible educational institution. These plans are frequently called 529 Savings Plans and 529 Prepaid Tuition Plans. The 529 Savings Plan allows your money to grow tax-free for future educational costs and can be withdrawn tax-free when used for qualified higher-education expenses. In contrast, 529 Prepaid Tuition Plans allow you to buy tuition credits or certificates for your son or daughter. Then when he or she is ready to attend college, the credits or certificates can be used as a waiver or as payment of college tuition. Refer to chapter 31, "For Parents Only: Saving for College," for more information about 529 plans. Consult your tax professional or financial advisor for more information.

Lowering the Overall Cost of Your Student Loan

If you are currently repaying student loans, you may be able to take a deduction for interest paid on your student loans. The deduction is available even if you do not itemize other deductions. The maximum deduction is $2,500. It is phased out for certain income levels. See http://www.irs.gov, publication 970, or your tax professional for additional information. The deduction is available for all loans taken to pay tuition or other qualified higher-education expenses.

For additional information about other tax assistance or deductions, visit the IRS website at http://www.irs.gov and read or download IRS Publication 970. You can also call (800) 4FED-AID.

FREQUENTLY USED TELEPHONE NUMBERS AND WEBSITES FOR FEDERAL GOVERNMENT AID

- To chat, e-mail (FederalStudentAidCustomerService@ed.gov), or call with questions about federal government aid, visit https://fafsa.ed.gov/contact.htm.

Contacting Your State Financial Agency Can Really Pay Off!

Even though it's not technically a state, Washington, D.C., is an excellent example of how your state can help you and/or your parents fund your education. If you lived in the District of Columbia for the past twelve months, you are eligible for the D.C. Tuition Assistance Grant Program (DC TAG). With this program you can attend any public institution in the nation as if you're a resident of the school's state. You pay their in-state tuition and the grant pays the difference between in-state and out-of-state tuition rate up to $10,000 a year for a maximum of six years or $50,000. TAG can also help you attend private colleges and universities in the metropolitan D.C. area and any historically black college or university (HBCU) in the nation by awarding you a $2,500 grant for a maximum of six years. This is for students 24 years of age and younger.

- General information requests—(800) 4FED-AID
- If outside the United States or you do not have access to 800 numbers— (319) 337-5665
- TDD number for hearing-impaired individuals—(800) 730-8913

Use any of these additional sources for information about federal government aid:

Federal Student Aid and Free Application for Federal Student Aid (FAFSA)
http://www.fafsa.ed.gov or www.fafsa4caster.ed.gov
Facebook: https://www.facebook.com/FederalStudentAid
Twitter: @FAFSA
YouTube: http://www.youtube.com/user/federalStudentAid

The Student Guide
http://studentAid.gov or http://studentaid.ed.gov/resources#funding
Facebook: https://www.facebook.com/FederalStudentAid
Twitter: @FAFSA
YouTube: http://www.youtube.com/user/federalStudentAid

IRS Tax Information and Benefits for Students
http://www.irs.gov/Individuals/Students

STATE FINANCIAL AID AGENCIES

Before you complete your search for government aid, make sure to contact and explore state financial aid agencies for money to attend college. Some states, such as Georgia, can be very generous. Students who are residents of Georgia and maintain a 3.0 GPA can automatically qualify for the Hope Scholarship (distinct from the HOPE tax credit), which helps to pay their tuition and fees to public colleges and universities in the State of Georgia. A listing of state agency contact information follows. When contacting the agency ask about the following items:

- If you are in the military, inquire about military waivers. States with military waivers may grant immediate residency status allowing you to pay reduced tuition rates even if you have just moved to the state. This may extend to dependents of active military parents as well.
- If you are thinking about attending a public college or university in another state, inquire about reciprocity. Some states will give reduced in-state tuition to students in other states with which they have reciprocity agreements. For example, certain western states belong to WICHE (http://www.wiche.edu), which is the Western Interstate Commission for Higher Education, established by the western states of Arkansas, Arizona, California, Colorado, Hawaii, Idaho, Montana, Nevada, New Mexico, North Dakota, Oregon, South Dakota, Utah, Washington, and Wyoming to promote resource sharing, collaboration, and cooperative planning among their higher education systems. States in WICHE may have reciprocity arrangements with other member states. WICHE states participate in the Western Undergraduate Exchange (WUE), which allows students to attend school in other WICHE states that belong to WUE at reduced tuition rates.
- If you are new to a state and want to attend school there at in-state tuition rates, ask about the requirements to gain in-state residency status, including the length of time and the documents required to be considered a resident of the state and qualify for reduced tuition rates. Although some states require 1 year residency, a driver's license, tax return, and/or vehicle registration, other states may require 3 years residency or a copy of a signed lease agreement. If you are planning to attend a public university or college, look at the table in chapter 1 on college costs and you will see that the difference between in-state and out-of-state tuition can be significant.

- Also ask about state-specific scholarships, grants, and other financial aid. If you're interested in teaching, make sure to inquire about the Paul Douglas Teacher Scholarship Program.

What Is a State Financial Aid Agency?

The term state financial aid agency applies to government organizations that administer state or federally funded aid. In some states, this may be the Board or Department of Education or it may be a separate Commission on Higher Education, Higher Education Assistance Authority, or Post-Secondary Education. Regardless of the name, the agency could be a great source for funding your education.

STATE FINANCIAL AID AGENCY CONTACT INFORMATION

Since website addresses change frequently, some of the websites listed below may be invalid. If you get an error message in your browser, try going to a search engine like Yahoo! or Google. Type the name of the financial aid agency into the search box, making sure to put quotation marks around it. This should bring up the new website. For example, if you are looking for the Alabama Commission on Higher Education, type in your search box, "Alabama Commission on Higher Education." In addition, many of these programs are on Facebook, Twitter, LinkedIn, and other social media platforms. Stay connected or follow them on your favorite social media outlet to stay aware of any new student aid developments for your state.

ALABAMA
Alabama Commission on Higher
 Education
100 N. Union Street
P.O. Box 302000
Montgomery, AL 36130-2000
(334) 242-1998;
 fax: (334) 242-0268
Website: http://www.ache.state.al.us

ALASKA
Alaska Commission on Post-
 Secondary Education and

Alaska Student Loan
 Corporation
P.O. Box 110505
Juneau, AK 99811-0505
(907) 465-2962, (800) 441-2962;
 fax: (907) 465-5316
E-mail: customer.service@alaska
 .gov
Website: http://acpe.alaska.gov

ARIZONA
Arizona Commission for Post-
 Secondary Education

2020 North Central Avenue, Suite 650
Phoenix, AZ 85004-4503
(602) 258-2435; fax: (602) 258-2483
Website: http://www.azhighered.gov

ARKANSAS
Arkansas Department of Higher
   Education
Four Capitol Mall, Room 403-A
Little Rock, AR 72201
(501) 682-4475
Website: http://www.arkansased.org

CALIFORNIA
California Student Aid Commission
P.O. Box 419027
Rancho Cordova, CA 95741-9027
(888) CA-GRANT (224-7268);
   fax: (916) 464-8002
E-mail: custsvcs@csac.ca.gov
Website: http://www.csac.ca.gov

COLORADO
Colorado Department of Higher
   Education
1560 Broadway, Suite 1600
Denver, CO 80202
(303) 866-2723; fax: (303) 866-4266
Website: http://www.highered
   .colorado.gov

CONNECTICUT
Connecticut Office of Higher
   Education
61 Woodland Street
Hartford, CT 06105-2326
(860) 947-1800, (800) 842-0229;
   fax: (860) 947-1310

E-mail: edinfo@ctohe.org
Website: http://www.ctohe.org

DELAWARE
Delaware Higher Education Office
401 Federal Street, Suite 2
Dover, DE 19901
(302) 735-4120, (800) 292-7935;
   fax: (302) 739-5894
Website: http://www.doe.k12.de.us
   (click on Students \ Higher
   Education) or http://www.doe
   .k12.de.us/infosuites/students
   _family/dheo/default.shtml

DISTRICT OF COLUMBIA
D.C. Office of the State
   Superintendent of Education
810 1st Street NE, 9th Floor
Washington, DC 20002
(202) 727-6436
Website: http://seo.dc.gov

FLORIDA
Florida Department of Education
Office of Student Financial
   Assistance
325 West Gaines Street, Suite 1314
Tallahassee, FL 32399-0400
(888) 827-2004
Email: osfa@fldoe.org
Website: http://www.floridastudent
   financialaid.org

GEORGIA
Georgia Student Finance
   Commission
State Loans and Grants Division
2082 East Exchange Place, Suite 200

Tucker, GA 30084
(800) 505-GSFC (4732);
    fax: (770) 724-9089
E-mail: gsfcinfo@gsfc.org
Website: http://www.gsfc.org

HAWAII
Hawaii State Board of Education
P.O. Box 2360
Honolulu, HI 96804
(808) 586-3334;
    fax: (808) 586-3433
E-mail: BOE_Hawaii@notes.k12
    .hi.us
Website: http://www.doe.k12.hi.us

IDAHO
Idaho State Board of Education
650 West State St.
P.O. Box 83720
Boise, ID 83720-0037
(208) 334-2270; fax: (208)334-2632
E-mail: board@osbe.idaho.gov
Website: http://www.boardofed
    .idaho.gov

ILLINOIS
Illinois Student Assistance
    Commission
1755 Lake Cook Road
Deerfield, IL 60015-5209
(800) 899-4722;
    fax: (847) 831-8549
Website: http://www.isac.org

INDIANA
Indiana Commission for Higher
    Education
Division of Student Financial Aid

W462 Indiana Government Center
    South
402 W. Washington Street
Indianapolis, IN 46204
(317) 232-2350, (888) 528-4719;
    fax: (317) 232-3260
E-mail: awards@sfa.che.in.gov
Website: http://www.in.gov/ssaci

IOWA
Iowa College Student Aid
    Commission
603 E. 12th Street, 5th Floor
Des Moines, IA 50319
(515) 725-3400, (877) 272-4456;
    fax: (515) 725-3401
Website: http://www.iowacollege
    aid.gov

KANSAS
Kansas Board of Regents
Student Financial Assistance
1000 SW Jackson Street, Suite
    520
Topeka, KS 66612-1368
(785) 296-3517, (785) 296-3421;
    fax: (785) 296-0983
Website: http://www.kansasregents
    .org

LOUISIANA
Louisiana Office of Student
    Financial Assistance
P.O. Box 91202
Baton Rouge, LA 70821-9202
(800) 259-5626;
    fax: (225) 208-1496
E-mail: custserv@osfa.la.gov
Website: http://www.osfa.la.gov

MAINE
Finance Authority of Maine
Maine Education Assistance
  Division
P.O. Box 949
5 Community Drive
Augusta, ME 04332-0949
(800) 228-3734;
  fax: (207) 623-0095
E-mail: education@famemaine
  .com
Website: http://www.famemaine
  .com

MARYLAND
Maryland Higher Education
  Commission
6 North Liberty Street
Baltimore, MD 21201
(410) 767-3300, (800) 974-0203;
  fax: (410) 332-0250
E-mail: osfamail@mhec.state
  .md.us
Website: http://www.mhec.state
  .md.us

MASSACHUSETTS
Massachusetts Office of Student
  Financial Assistance
454 Broadway, Suite 200
Revere, MA 02151
(617) 391-6070; fax: (617) 727-0667
E-mail: osfa@osfa.mass.edu
Website: http://www.osfa.mass.edu

MICHIGAN
Michigan Bureau of Student
  Financial Assistance
Office of Scholarships and Grants

P.O. Box 30462
Lansing, MI 48909-7962
(888) 447-2687; fax: (517) 241-5835
E-mail: osg@michigan.gov
Website: http://www.michigan.gov
  /mistudentaid

MINNESOTA
Minnesota Office of Higher
  Education
1450 Energy Park Drive, Suite 350
Saint Paul, MN 55108-5227
(651) 642-0567, (800) 657-3866;
  fax: (651) 642-0675
Website: http://www.ohe.state.mn
  .us

MISSISSIPPI
Mississippi Office of Student
  Financial Aid
3825 Ridgewood Road
Jackson, MS 39211-6453
(601) 432-6997, (800) 327-2980
  (toll free in Mississippi)
E-mail: sfa@mississippi.edu
Website: http://www.mississippi
  .edu

MISSOURI
Missouri Department of Higher
  Education
205 Jefferson Street
P.O. Box 1469
Jefferson City, MO 65102-1469
(573) 751-2361
(800) 473-6757;
  fax: (573) 751-6635
E-mail: info@dhe.mo.gov
Website: http://www.dhe.mo.gov

MONTANA
Montana Office of the
    Commissioner of Higher
    Education
2500 Broadway Street
P.O. Box 203201
Helena, MT 59620-3201
(406) 444-6570;
    fax: (406) 444-1469
Website: http://www.mus.edu/che

NEBRASKA
Nebraska Coordinating
    Commission for Postsecondary
    Education
140 N. Eighth Street, Suite 300
P.O. Box 95005
Lincoln. NE 68509-5005
(402) 471-2847; fax: (402) 471-2886
Website: http://www.ccpe.state
    .ne.us

NEVADA
Nevada Department of Education,
    Financial Aid
700 East 5th Street
Carson City, NV 89701
(775) 687-9200;
    fax: (775) 687-9101
Website: http://www.doe.nv.gov

NEW HAMPSHIRE
New Hampshire Higher Education
    Commission
101 Pleasant Street
Concord, NH 03301-3494
(603) 271-3494
Website: http://www.education.nh
    .gov/highered

NEW JERSEY
New Jersey Higher Education
    Student Assistance Authority
P.O. Box 540
Trenton, NJ 08625
(609) 584-4480, (800) 792-8670;
    fax: (609) 588-2228
Website: http://www.hesaa.org

NEW MEXICO
New Mexico Higher Education
    Department
2048 Galisteo Street
Santa Fe, NM 87505
(505) 476-8400;
    fax: (505) 476-8453
Website: http://hed.state.nm.us

NEW YORK
New York State Higher Education
    Services Corporation
99 Washington Avenue
Albany, NY 12255
(518) 473-1574, (888) 697-4372;
    fax: (518) 473-3749
Website: http://www.hesc.ny.gov

NORTH CAROLINA
North Carolina State Education
    Assistance Authority
P.O. Box 14103
Research Triangle Park, NC 27709
(919) 549-8614; fax: (919) 549-8481
E-mail: information@ncseaa.edu
Website: http://www.ncseaa.edu

NORTH DAKOTA
North Dakota University System
600 East Boulevard Avenue

Bismarck, ND 58505-0230
(701) 328-2960;
　fax: (701) 328-2961
E-mail: ndus.office@ndus.nodak.
　edu
Website: http://www.ndus.edu

OHIO
Ohio Board of Regents
25 South Front Street
Columbus, OH 43215
(614) 466-6000, (888) 833-1133;
　fax: (614) 466-5866
E-mail: hotline@regents.state
　.oh.us
Website: https://www.
　ohiohighered.org

OKLAHOMA
Oklahoma State Regents for
　Higher Education
655 Research Parkway, Suite 200
Oklahoma City, OK 73104
(405) 225-9100;
　fax: (405) 225-9230
E-mail:
　communicationsdepartment@
　osrhe.edu
Website: http://www.okhighered
　.org

OREGON
Oregon Student Assistance
　Commission
1500 Valley River Drive, Suite 100
Eugene, OR 97401
(541) 687-7400; fax: (541) 687-7414
Website: http://oregonstudentaid
　.gov

PENNSYLVANIA
Pennsylvania Higher Education
　Assistance Agency
1200 North Seventh Street
Harrisburg, PA 17102-1444
(800) 692-7392;
　fax: (717) 720-3786
Website: http://www.pheaa.org

RHODE ISLAND
Rhode Island Higher Education
　Assistance Authority
560 Jefferson Boulevard, Suite 100
Warwick, RI 02886
(401) 736-1100, (800) 922-9855;
　fax: (401) 732-3541
E-mail: info@riheaa.org
Website: http://www.riheaa.org

SOUTH CAROLINA
South Carolina Higher Education
　Tuition Grants Commission
800 Dutch Square Boulevard,
　Suite 260A
Columbia, SC 29210-7317
(803) 896-1120;
　fax: (803) 896-1126
E-mail: info@sctuitiongrants.org
Website: http://www.sctuition
　grants.com

SOUTH DAKOTA
South Dakota Board of Regents
306 East Capitol Avenue, Suite
　200
Pierre, SD 57501-2545
(605) 773-3455
E-mail: info@sdbor.edu
Website: http://www.sdbor.edu

TENNESSEE
Tennessee Higher Education
   Commission
404 James Robertson Parkway,
   Suite 1900
Nashville, TN 37243-0820
(615) 741-3605;
   fax: (615) 741-6230
Website: http://www.state.tn.us
   /thec

TEXAS
Texas Higher Education
   Coordinating Board
P.O. Box 12788, Capitol Station
Austin, TX 78711-2788
(512) 427-6101; fax: (512) 427-6127
Website: http://www.thecb.state
   .tx.us

UTAH
Utah Higher Education Assistance
   Authority
60 South 400 West
Salt Lake City, UT 84101
(801) 321-7294, (877) 336-7378;
   fax: (801) 366-8430
Website: http://www.uheaa.org

VERMONT
Vermont Student Assistance
   Corporation
Champlain Mill
P.O. Box 2000
Winooski, VT 05404-2601
(802) 655-9602;
   fax: (802) 654-3765
E-mail: info@vsac.org
Website: http://www.vsac.org

VIRGINIA
State Council of Higher Education
   for Virginia
James Monroe Building, 10th
   Floor
101 N. Fourteenth Street
Richmond, VA 23219
(804) 225-2600;
   fax: (804) 225-2604
E-mail: communications@schev
   .edu
Website: http://www.schev.edu

WASHINGTON
Washington Student Achievement
   Council
P.O. Box 43430
917 Lakeridge Way SW
Olympia, WA 98504-3430
(360) 753-7800
E-mail: info@wsac.wa.gov
Website: http://www.wsac.wa.gov

WEST VIRGINIA
West Virginia Higher Education
   Policy Commission
1018 Kanawha Boulevard East,
   Suite 700
Charleston, WV 25301
(304) 558-2101;
   fax: (304) 558-5719
Website: http://wvhepcnew.wvnet
   .edu

WISCONSIN
Higher Educational Aids Board
P.O. Box 7885
Madison, WI 53707-7885
(608) 267-2206; fax: (608) 267-2808

E-mail: HEABmail@wisconsin.gov
Website: http://www.heab.state.wi.us

WYOMING
Wyoming State Department of
   Education

2300 Capitol Avenue
Hathaway Building, 2nd Floor
Cheyenne, WY 82002
(307) 777-7690;
   fax: 307-777-6234
Website: http://edu.wyoming.gov

6

GETTING ORGANIZED

I should never have made my success in life
if I had not bestowed upon the least thing I have
ever undertaken, the same attention and care
that I have bestowed upon the greatest.

—Charles Dickens

Do you have enough applications and guides, etcetera., to fill an entire table and all of its chairs? I hope you do, because I did. (I had so much material my mother gave up on the idea of cleaning the room I occupied!) At this point, you should have catalogs, brochures, pamphlets, and applications not only for the colleges you're interested in but also for many that you're not. You should also have numerous scholarship applications for private organizations. If you don't, you soon will—if you followed the instructions in chapters 2, 3, and 4. When almost every available surface in your scholarship planning room is covered with material and your electronic files are starting to clutter up your browser's bookmarks folder or hog your hard drive, it's time to organize! Read this chapter carefully to avoid missing out on opportunities simply because you've lost sight of an application that may be hiding under a book or in some type of electronic storage. If you are not organized it may stay hidden—just until the deadline has passed. Since that is definitely not what you want, let's get organized.

Prepare paper file folders for each organization or college and put all relevant information into its corresponding file. If you have an available file cabinet, organize all the files according to deadline dates. If you do not have a file cabinet, a box will serve the purpose just as well. On each file folder write the deadline date in large, eye-catching print so that you can see them as you flip through.

Alternatively, or in addition to your hard-copy folders, make separate file folders on your computer for each scholarship application you download from the Internet. For example, create a folder called "Scholarship Applications." Then create subfolders in this folder for each application. An example would be a subfolder titled "XYZ Local Scholarship." In this folder you may have a downloaded copy of the application, a copy of the essay you are planning to submit, a recommendation letter, and other files specific to this application. Be aware that most applications you download from the Internet will probably be in an Adobe Acrobat Portable Document Format (PDF). Make sure you have a current copy of Adobe Acrobat Reader, available free on http://www.adobe.com, so you can view PDFs. You'll also want to print hard copies of each application to put in your hard-copy file folder box, so you can flip through them by deadline date.

As you organize your information and put it into files, there should be nothing you haven't read. It is essential to read everything sent to you in the mail or via e-mail. You can miss many opportunities if you do not take the time to carefully read all the information sent in correspondence packages. This is especially true for packages sent by college recruiters. Make sure your organization includes notes and brochures from college fairs and visits.

About one-third of the letters or e-mails sent to you by independently sponsored organizations may contain notices stating they are out of funds, or that their scholarships are only for children of their employees, or you are not in the specific region they are trying to reach. These special requirements should have been listed in the scholarship directories at the time of your initial research. Unfortunately, this information may not have been included because updates were not available at the time of publication. Some programs may ask for an application request in writing, or may require you to go through other channels to obtain an application. Many will refer you to an online site for additional information on the scholarship's application process.

Purchase a calendar, or be enterprising and make one large enough to record information under the dates. Some applications require special information, but many require the same information (see chapters 2 and 10). If you keep certain facts about yourself and your family members handy—for example, written on the inside cover of your calendar—it will take less time to complete an application. You should also use your calendar to post application deadlines, with reminder notes a week before the deadlines.

A Burning Question

When are most scholarship deadlines?

For the largest scholarship programs awarding the most money—for example, $20,000, $40,000, and up—the deadlines will occur early in your senior year. This means that you should be prepared to start submitting applications in October, November, and December of your senior year.

If you wait until March, April, May, or later, the scholarship amounts start to get smaller, and by the end of spring most deadlines will have passed except for some small community-based programs and online promotional scholarship giveaways and sweepstakes.

In addition to preparing background information and a recommendations reference list, you may need to take some photos if you do not have recent ones. Some scholarship programs like to see smiling faces in black-and-white, 2x3-inch photographs. These are usually for publicity purposes; in certain scholarship competitions a recent photograph will be requested.

For information that is repeatedly asked for on applications, consider a program such as ScholarSnapp to make the process of completing multiple applications a little easier. To get more information about Scholar-Snapp, visit http://scholarsnapp.org.

You can also use *The Scholarship Monthly Planning Calendar*, available at http://www.scholarshipworkshop.com, to ease the process of getting organized with important scholarships and their dates. Staying on track by keeping up with deadlines is key.

Devise an overall monthly scholarship plan that will help you quickly see the tasks you need to accomplish each month. Here for your reference are my four- and five-month scholarship plans from my search.

YOUR MONTHLY SCHOLARSHIP PLAN

Many of my scholarship deadlines fell during the months of October, November, and December. By the time I made a January-through-May plan (during the month of December), much of my work was already done—before I was actually required to complete and submit the applications. I kept notes and made charts like those previously mentioned primarily as a reminder for recommendations I needed to check on and essays I needed to revise. I decided not to apply to some of the organizations and institutions in the five-month plan, because by the middle of April my future was set.

A scholarship plan for January 1 to May 31 should look like the example on the following pages. Deadlines for turning in materials will be different for various scholarships. Therefore your plan may look very different from these examples. However, the months your scholarship search begins should closely parallel the following example.

FOUR-MONTH PLAN: SENIOR YEAR
SEPTEMBER 1–DECEMBER 31

September

1. Go to the library and conduct research. Gather addresses.
2. Search the Internet for additional information.
3. Draft two inquiry letters. Prepare one for colleges. Prepare one for private organizations.
4. Send letters or e-mails if necessary.
5. Find local organizations and chambers of commerce that may offer scholarships.
6. Talk to the high school counselor.
7. Register for the SAT and ACT.
8. Get ready to start submitting applications and entering competitions with early deadlines.

October

1. Organize all replies and applications received and found. Create reference files and put in folders.
2. Prepare résumé.
3. Prepare two basic essays describing future career goals and yourself.
4. Make a recommendations list of teachers, advisors, and employers.
5. Continue submitting applications and entering competitions.
6. Look for additional scholarships and college money opportunities.

November

1. Visit colleges.
2. Continue submitting applications and entering competitions.
3. Look for additional scholarships and college money opportunities.

December

1. Continue submitting applications and entering competitions.
2. Look for additional scholarships and college money opportunities.

FIVE-MONTH PLAN: SENIOR YEAR
JANUARY 1–MAY 31

Continue searching for national and local scholarship opportunities and contests throughout your senior year until you have received enough award letters and e-mails to ensure that your entire college education will be funded by scholarships and other free aid. Often students will receive one national scholarship which may be for $30,000 or $40,000 and stop their scholarship search. Even though a scholarship for this amount is wonderful, it still does not cover an entire education, particularly when the funds are divided among four or five years. Keep looking and applying until you don't need to anymore. And don't assume a win unless you've received a note in writing via e-mail or letter that you've won. You may have a good chance, but it's still a chance.

January

(List activities, forms, and applications you must complete this month.)

1. Complete the financial aid form. If I don't have a W-2, gather all other financial information needed to complete the application. Consider using http://www.fafsa4caster.ed.gov.
2. Fill out National Scholarship Trust Fund application.
3. Call C&S Bank about Jacques Foundation scholarship.
4. Write to NAACP for scholarship application.
5. Complete University of Georgia scholarship application:
   (List here everything you need for the application to be complete and ready to submit.)

- Essay required
- Need two recommendations, one from teacher and one from principal
6. Complete Rhodes College application:
   (To give yourself a sense of accomplishment in the midst of so many tasks you have yet to do, always list the activities you have already finished.)
   - Essay completed
7. Finish Georgia College application.
8. Fill out the University of Alabama application.
9. Fill out the Zeta Phi Beta scholarship application.

February

1. Finish the Centre College application:
   - Essay needed
   - Recommendations needed
2. Furman University deadline:
   - Need essay
   - Need recommendations
3. Oglethorpe University application deadline.

March

1. Complete application for Wesleyan College:
   - Essay required
   - Recommendation required
2. Finish Wendy's scholarship application.
3. Find War Memorial scholarship application.
4. Complete National Negro Business and Professional Women's Club scholarship application.

April

1. Winthrop College application needs the following:
   - Essay
   - Recommendation
2. Finish Herbert Lehman scholarship application.

May

Rest!!!

The most essential contributions to my scholarship success were organization and preparation. *Do not wait to start your scholarship search!* Don't wait until you actually get accepted to the school of your dreams to apply for scholarships. In fact, you don't even have to wait until senior year. It does not matter if you are a middle school or high school student. There are scholarships you can win as early as age six; see chapter 26, "Scholarships for Younger Students—from Kindergarten to 11th Grade."

Prior knowledge is the key to improved preparation and eventual success. If you are not a high school senior, the information you find now about scholarships and awards should be kept up to date until you are eligible to apply. Visit the organization's website every six months, and e-mail them with questions about anything you don't understand or for which you need more information. For example, I have worked with many students who are U.S. citizens but are residents of U.S. territories such as the Virgin Islands or Puerto Rico. Sometimes, when these students peruse the online applications or even try to sign up to receive e-mail reminders, the online system does not show their location. After e-mailing the scholarship organizations, they'll discover it is just a system oversight, and they are indeed eligible because they are U.S. citizens. So start early, stay updated, and check your eligibility if there seems to be a discrepancy or something confusing. And don't forget that many of the largest scholarship programs have deadlines in the fall or early January and February. So be prepared to submit an application at any time for the best possible chance of success!

7

GETTING THE MOST FROM YOUR COUNSELOR

> Nothing great was ever achieved without
> enthusiasm.
>
> —Ralph Waldo Emerson

If you are serious about pursuing a college career, any counselor who truly cares will try to help you. However, many of them are swamped with the day-to-day details of registering students for classes or various other activities, so they don't have time to come to you with scholarship opportunities. You must make a special effort to get to know your counselor. Make an appointment with him or her and discuss your hopes for the future and your need for scholarship money. Identify your academic strengths and weaknesses. When you draft your résumé, make sure your counselor is the first to get a copy, even if you don't need a recommendation yet. Stay in close contact with your counselor by visiting the office often to learn about various colleges and scholarship opportunities that may cross his or her desk. Let the counselor know you are willing to apply for all scholarships for which you are qualified. But don't be annoying—be cognizant about the counselor's time and workload. If the counselor or career center director has a system you should follow for getting scholarship and college information or even getting recommendations, follow the system. If you don't, the counselor may write a recommendation that is less than complimentary for you, which could hurt your scholarship chances.

Your goal in visiting your counselor should be to let the counselor get to know you, your talents, your skills, your situation, and other characteristics about you so that you don't get a form-letter recommendation—that is, one that could be used for any student at your school with the exception of a name change and a few word substitutions. One student I worked with

Did You Know?

In some school systems, counselors are so swamped with other activities that they now have career center directors who can help you with your scholarship search. If your school has one, make sure to visit that office, too!

had a profound speech impediment that unfortunately had never been treated. I suggested he get to know his counselor. He visited her for a few minutes monthly throughout his junior and senior year. As a result of those visits, in every recommendation she wrote for him, the counselor commented on his ability to persevere through high school and in clubs such as Toastmasters despite his disability. If he had not visited the counselor and instead submitted a request for a recommendation via a letter, e-mail, or online, she would never have known to include that information. Unfortunately, counselors, particularly in large schools, rarely have extra time to request additional information about a student.

Scholarship programs often inform the counselors of opportunities and request names of students who would be interested in applying for a particular scholarship. Some programs will consider an applicant on the basis of a recommendation from the counselor only. Therefore, make sure your counselor always has your name on a list of qualified and interested students.

In your senior year, confirm that your counselor has your final transcript or midyear report prepared and ready to go at a moment's notice. Some high schools have a list in the registrar's office for students to place the names of colleges and programs where they need their final transcripts sent. Many colleges and universities will not allow you to register for classes if they have not received your final transcript. Likewise, some scholarship programs may disqualify your application without your transcript, a midyear report, or a copy of your grades. If you are using the Common Application, a common, standardized first-year application form for use at over 400 colleges and universities participating in the Common App system (http://www.commonapp.org), confirm that your counselor and other school officials have received notification (usually via e-mail) about forms they need to complete and submit online. Recommendations may also be requested electronically via the Common Application or another online system used by a college, university, or scholarship program. Follow up to confirm they received the request, which can sometimes get lost in a flood of e-mails. Usually you can check your application status and confirm that all recommendations and required forms have been completed. Put a reminder in your scholarship monthly calendar to check this status.

You should have information about scholarships, grants, and monetary aid in abundance in your household by now, but just to make sure all the bases are covered, ask your counselor for additional information, especially for local scholarships. Some counselors hand out information generated from the U.S. Department of Education (address is given in chapter 2), but they may have information neither you nor I have discovered. The counselors may also have a mini-library that includes financial aid books and resources that you might find useful. If you ask, you may be able to borrow or use their reference books. The counselor might also be able to speak with your school's media specialist or librarian about getting copies of other helpful books. Speak with the counselor about these possibilities.

You can also ask your counselor if he or she would consider setting up a database of scholarships that students at your school, in your community, and in your state are eligible for. Many counselors may already have a paper-based list, which you should make sure you have. They might also put their database on the Internet, especially if your high school has a website. Numerous counselors around the country have done this.

Last, ask your counselor to set up a bulletin board to post scholarship information when it's received. This way all students, including you, can see the information without having to stop at the counselor's office, which would probably make you late for class. I should know. I got detention many times when I was in high school, particularly in my junior and senior year, due to stopping at the counselor's office to check on new scholarship information, ask about recommendations, or get a signature. Since I always had some type of extracurricular after-school activity and my detention for being late was usually short, it didn't really bother me. Of course, if there had been a bulletin board I may not have been late as often. And since some schools now count a certain number of tardies as an absence, being late should be avoided as much as possible.

If you need the paper-based FAFSA (explained in chapter 5), counselors may have copies in their possession. Or you could visit your local library. Obtain one and start gathering the information the form requires as soon as possible, even though it cannot be completed and mailed until after January 1 of the year you plan to enter college. Most colleges require the FAFSA or the CSS—Financial Aid PROFILE for scholarship consideration, even for merit-based scholarships. The FAFSA can also be completed online, which is the easier and faster way. Visit http://www.fafsa.ed.gov for more information about completing the FAFSA. Your counselor can also answer your questions about the CSS—Financial Aid PROFILE or you can visit http://student.collegeboard.org/css-financial-aid-profile or http://www.collegeboard.org and search for keyword "profile."

If you need a recommendation from your counselor, give him or her at least two months' advance notice. If possible, include a copy of your résumé and a stamped addressed envelope (if it needs to be sent as a hard copy). Your résumé will help the counselor to include actual examples of your activities and awards in her recommendation. The pre-addressed envelope makes it more convenient for your counselor to return your recommendation to those programs that require them rather than returning them directly to you. Remember to have a checklist due date for the recommendation's return.

You can use the following letter to request a recommendation from your counselor or another person. Please note that when applying for a scholarship requiring a recommendation, some online application systems automatically send e-mails to each person you submit as a recommender. So be sure to send a letter such as the following *before* applying so your counselor or any other person you want to recommend you has additional information about the scholarship and from your résumé *prior to* receiving an online recommendation request from the scholarship program.

Sample Letter Requesting a Recommendation from Your Counselor

> *Your street address°*
> *Your city, state, and zip code*
>
> October 15, 20XX

Name
Title
Address
City, State, Zip Code

Dear *Name of Your High School Counselor:*

I am interested in applying for the *XYZ Example Scholarship Program.* This award is *sponsored by XYZ Example Foundation. As a high school*

°Items in italics and small type can be changed. If an online recommendation request will be sent by the program, change your letter to read as follows: *I would like to request a recommendation letter from you for my application to this scholarship program. This request will be sent automatically to your e-mail address directly from the organization with instructions for how to complete the recommendation and submit it online.* If the request will be made via e-mail, you can delete the line in the letter referencing a pre-addressed envelope.

junior interested in pursuing my education beyond high school, I am eligible to apply for this scholarship. However, in order to do so, I need your help. This scholarship program requires *three recommendation letters.* I would like to request a recommendation letter from you, as my high school counselor, for my application to this scholarship program.

I have enclosed the following information to assist you in writing a recommendation for me:

- My résumé
- Additional information about me and other activities in which I am involved
- A pre-addressed envelope to send to the program

The recommendation must be completed and sent by *January 15, 20XX*. If you have any questions or need additional information to complete this recommendation, you can reach me at *(XXX) XXX-XXXX* or via e-mail at *xyz@aol.com.*

> Thank you in advance for your help,
> *Your signature*
> *Your name, typed*

Many scholarship applications need a counselor's signature, and may need other information that only your counselor or registrar has access to, such as class size, your class ranking, grade point average, and the exact number of credits you have earned. Since counselors are responsible for many tasks in a high school, give them a little time to gather this information. Make sure you routinely check with them to see if they have the information you need. Once you have fully compiled all of the materials required for an application, put everything in the envelope, affix the proper postage, address the envelope (include your return address), and give it to your counselor. Tell the counselor it needs to be mailed immediately. Make sure your application is mailed in adequate time to make its deadline. In addition to making the deadlines, some scholarships are based on a first-come, first-served basis. Therefore, go to your counselor's office often to ensure that your application will be received well ahead of its deadline. Again, some of your information may be requested from the counselor using an online application system. Let your counselor know what to expect by supplying a list of the scholarships and other programs that may be requesting information for you via e-mail. Check your application status frequently well before any deadlines to confirm that all required information has been submitted. When visiting your counselor's office, remember to be diligent but not pushy. A pleasant demeanor will go a long way toward enlisting your counselor's help and getting a great recommendation. Always say "please" and "thank you."

THE COUNSELOR VISITATION TIMETABLE

Freshman Year

- Meet with your high school counselor to develop a course plan for the next year.
- Ask about scholarship competitions that are generally available to students at your school or in your area. Ask about past winners and their qualifications. See if the counselor can get a copy of the winning essay or essays if one or several were required. Also ask for copies of old applications, if the school has any, or find out when applications are usually received or may be available online. If applications are received in the mail or via e-mail at a certain time, come back at that time to ask for a copy even if you're not eligible to apply that year.
- Begin volunteering for many activities and organizations. Volunteer activities are heavily favored in many large scholarship competitions and even smaller ones. By the way, you can start applying for scholarships now. (See chapter 26.)

Sophomore Year

- Once again, ask your counselor for an extra copy of scholarship applications as they come in throughout the year. Read these applications thoroughly to see if there are particular activities or characteristics they are looking for in applicants—especially when you compare your own résumé to those of past students who have won the scholarships. Make sure to write down the essay questions and try to answer them.
- Once again, do a review of your courses with your counselor to make sure you are on the right track. You should also consider taking the PSAT this year. Get information for this test from your counselor and confirm it is available for you to take. Even though testing this year will not qualify you for the National Merit/Achievement Scholarship Qualifying Test, it will give you a good opportunity to practice for next year when it will count, and it's good practice for the SAT also.

- Begin to review your résumé with your counselor. If you are not currently involved in any activities, speak with your counselor and discuss extracurricular activities that might suit your interests, particularly those within the community.
- Ask the counselor about free financial aid and test-taking workshops, such as The Scholarship Workshop, which you might be able to attend in preparation for your college and scholarship search.

Junior Year

- September—Do a review with your counselor of the classes required for college. Also discuss the AP courses you could take in your strong areas.

My counselor says since I'm a junior that I should wait until senior year to take the SAT and the ACT. Should I wait this long?

If possible you should take the SAT late in your junior year. Doing so will give you an opportunity to assess areas in which you didn't do well and in which you could possibly take improvement courses or use preparation books to help raise your score. This will give you time to retake the test early in your senior year and have scores ready to send to colleges. On the other hand, if you do well the first time you take the test, in your junior year, you can relax all during your senior year knowing that one major task is behind you.

- January—Discuss with your counselor when and what tests you should take, such as the ACT, SAT, and SAT subject tests.
- February—Meet with your counselor to discuss challenging courses to take in your senior year that will help you in applications for scholarships.
- March—Meet with your counselor to discuss the colleges you are interested in applying to. Also ask your counselor's recommendations for books to read to prepare for college and your scholarship search.
- April—Discuss your standardized test scores from the tests you have already taken to identify areas for improvement.

Senior Year

SEPTEMBER

- Begin to discuss with your counselor awards and scholarships that you obtained applications for in your freshman year. If you have already written essays for questions on the application that were used several times in prior years, review them with both your counselor and your English teacher to see how well they think you have answered the questions and shown your qualities.
- Arrange a meeting with your counselor to discuss your activities résumé and make sure it's thorough and well presented.
- Ask the counselor if he or she has any ideas about local organizations that might offer scholarships to students in the community.
- Give your counselor a list of the scholarships you're planning to apply to, their deadlines, whether you need a recommendation or a transcript sent, and any additional items you are planning to include with your applications, such as your résumé.
- Ask your counselor for a schedule of college fairs or of visiting student or college representatives.
- Ask your counselor about the AP tests you should take and the registration materials for them. You should also discuss taking the AP exam with the teachers of these advanced placement courses.

OCTOBER

- Meet with your counselor for an update on recommendations, midyear reports, and transcripts that have been sent for you. Or check your application status online.

8

TAKING TESTS

All common things, each day's events,
That with the hour begin and end,
Our pleasures and our discontents
Are rounds by which we may ascend.

—Henry Wadsworth Longfellow

The Scholastic Assessment Test (SAT) is a necessity for many scholarship programs, especially those for specific colleges and universities. Although some institutions no longer use standardized test scores as one of the primary requirements for admission, many still want your scores from the ACT Assessment or the SAT to determine your eligibility for admission. For private outside scholarships, it depends on the program. The ACT is also a popular exam that is widely accepted by colleges and universities.

The SAT exam lasts 3 hours and 45 minutes and is composed of ten sections that measure mathematical and critical reading abilities. The ten sections consist of six 25-minute sections on mathematics, critical reading, and writing; two additional 20-minute sections on mathematics, critical reading, and writing; a 25-minute essay, and one 10-minute multiple-choice writing section. The reading section assesses your verbal comprehension and includes reading passages and sentence completions. The writing section includes a short essay and multiple-choice questions that focus on improving grammar and usage and identifying errors. The math section contains questions on arithmetic operations, algebra, geometry, statistics, and probability.

SAT scores for each reading, writing, and mathematics section range from 200 to 800. For example, if you scored perfectly on all sections, your score would be 2400. Likewise if you scored 590 on the math section, 800

What's the difference between the ACT and the SAT? Should I take both?

The ACT Assessment is based on information you learned in your high school classes. The SAT tests critical thinking and problem solving so it is more generally based on information you have learned in class. For example:

- The ACT includes a science-reasoning test, trigonometry in the math section, and a test of English grammar whereas the SAT does not.
- The score range on the ACT is from 1 to 36. The SAT score range is from 200 to 800.
- The ACT has four tests (English, reading, math, science). There is an optional writing test. The SAT has three primary sections, math, critical reading, and a required writing section.
- The ACT composite score is an average of the four test scores. The SAT adds your scores from each section
- The ACT has only multiple-choice items. The SAT has an essay section.
- The ACT does not have a penalty for guessing. Wrong answers carry a penalty on the SAT, so guessing randomly to answer all questions can hurt your score.

Yes! You should take both tests. Since the ACT more closely assesses what you have learned and are currently learning in high school, your scores may be higher on this test. On the other hand, if your critical thinking skills are well developed you may do better on the SAT. Take both tests so you can find out for yourself. Based on your scores, you can determine which one you can do better on if you decide to retake one of them.

on the reading section, and 500 on the writing section, your score would be 1890. For the writing section, "subscores" are also given, which are not included in the example above. The multiple-choice writing section score ranges from 20 to 80; and the essay "subscore" ranges from 2 to 12.

The ACT is a national college admission examination that consists of tests in English, reading, math, and science. Many colleges and universities will accept results from the SAT or the ACT. The ACT includes 215 multiple-choice questions and usually takes approximately 3 hours and 30 minutes including breaks. The test scores range from 1 to 36. The ACT provides an assessment of your skills in the four different subject areas. The ACT also provides you with an interest inventory that can help you in planning your future career and educational goals. You can find more information about the ACT at http://www.actstudent.org or http://www .act.org.

When should I take the SAT or the ACT?

If possible, you should take both tests in your junior year or before so you will have enough time to improve your weak areas and retake one or both of the tests again.

When should I start preparing for the test?

Since you have about three to four weeks from the time you register for the test and when you actually take the exam, you should register for a test date at least two months in advance. During the time between registration and the test, prepare for the exam as much as possible. Don't make the mistake of showing up for the test just to see how well you can do, even if it is your first time.

Regular registration for the SAT or the ACT Assessment usually occurs about three to four weeks before the date of the exam. During this time, you should learn as much as you can about the test you plan to take. With Internet access, you can prepare for the SAT, ACT, or the SAT subject tests (discussed later in this chapter) by using the following websites and social media platforms:

PREPARING FOR THE SAT

http://www.collegeboard.com—click on SAT Practice
http://socialmedia.collegeboard.org
Facebook: https://www.facebook.com/thecollegeboard
Twitter: @CollegeBoard
YouTube: http://www.youtube.com/collegeboard

PREPARING FOR THE ACT

http://www.act.org or http://www.actstudent.org
Facebook: https://www.facebook.com/theacttest
Twitter: @ACTStudent

One of the best ways to prepare for the SAT is to visit the SAT practice area of the College Board website and review sample questions, learn about the test and how it is scored, and review answers. You can also download and take a free practice SAT through the College Board's website.

Similar to the SAT, you can prepare for the ACT by thoroughly reviewing the booklet *Preparing for the ACT,* which can be found at many high schools and colleges, or you can download it from the http://www.actstudent.org website. This free booklet includes valuable information about the test as well as a complete practice test with answers.

With both the SAT and ACT, publications and services to help you prepare for the exams are available for purchase. These range from additional versions of the exams to help you practice to test-taking strategies for each type of question.

Many students do not take the time to read test preparation publications or visit the website test preparation sections for the ACT and the SAT. As a result, they often miss out on important facts, especially if it is the first time they are taking these tests. For example, on the SAT points are deducted for wrong answers, so those who randomly guess at answers may be lowering their scores considerably; also, questions at the beginning of the tests are sometimes much easier than those at the end. Preparation booklets and online resources show you how the tests are scored, and the practice tests give you a chance to score your own.

Take the practice tests in the publications, books, or software programs you get under conditions that will be similar to the actual testing situation. Set up a room with a clear desk or small table and declare it off-limits to family members. All noise should be kept to a minimum. Take the test using a sharpened No. 2 pencil; have an extra nearby. If possible, take the test in the morning beginning at 8:30 a.m. Have someone monitor the time. If you run out of time while attempting to complete a section, do not finish it. Go on to the next section, as you will be expected to do on the day of the actual test. After you have finished the practice test, go over your incorrect responses and the correct solutions and their explanations carefully. Finish the questions you did not have time for and then look at the solutions for those. Try to establish a pattern in the questions you habitually miss. If you do find a pattern, there may be a concept or word that you do not fully understand that causes you to select the incorrect answer.

If you can, take the SAT *and* the ACT. Some students do much better on one or the other. Both tests also have preliminary versions, the PSAT and PLAN (pre-test similar to the ACT offered in the tenth grade). If you wish, you can start by taking those to warm up for the actual tests. When I took the preliminary versions years ago, they seemed somewhat harder than the actual SAT or ACT tests. If this is the case, practicing with these will give you a very good background, especially if you take them first in middle school, if available.

THE PSAT: A MEGA-SCHOLARSHIP OPPORTUNITY

The Preliminary SAT (PSAT), usually taken in the eleventh grade, is also a qualifying test for the National Merit/Achievement Scholarship Competition (officially named Preliminary SAT/National Merit Scholarship Qualifying Test—PSAT/NMSQT). The PSAT can be taken prior to the eleventh grade, but it will not qualify you for the competition. Scoring well on this test can reap great rewards. Top scorers will be placed in a large national competition that goes through several different levels. Students who become finalists in this competition are eligible for many scholarship opportunities from corporations and institutions.

Scholarship and Recognition Programs That Open Their Doors for Students Who Take the PSAT

- National Merit Scholarship Program
- National Achievement Scholarship Program
- National Hispanic Recognition Program
- National Scholarship Service and Fund for Negro Students
- Telluride Association

The PSAT is normally given at high schools. To get more information about the test and to help you prepare for it, get a copy of the *PSAT/NMSQT Student Bulletin*. Your high school should have them available in early fall, before the October test. In addition to test-taking tips, sample questions, and a practice test, the bulletin contains extensive information about the PSAT as a qualifying test for two scholarship programs, the National Merit Scholarship Program and the National Achievement Scholarship Program for Outstanding Negro Students. For more information about these programs, contact the National Merit Scholarship Corporation, 1560 Sherman Avenue, Evanston, IL 60201-4897; (847) 866-5100; http://www.nationalmerit.org. In order to take advantage of the opportunities that these scholarships provide, you should begin familiarizing yourself with standardized tests as soon as possible.

THE NATIONAL MERIT SCHOLARSHIP COMPETITION

The National Merit Scholarship Corporation (NMSC) was founded in 1955 as a not-for-profit organization that administers the awarding of National Merit and National Achievement scholarships to academically talented high school students. This program is currently one of the largest scholarship competitions in the United States. For more than fifty years, over two million students have won scholarships through the NMSC valued at more than $1 billion. Initially, funding for the scholarship program was provided by grants from the Ford Foundation. Currently, the awards are supported by independent sponsors and also by funds from the National Merit Scholarship Corporation. Sponsoring organizations include corporations and businesses, foundations, professional associations, and colleges and universities. Corporate and business sponsors also provide special scholarships each year. Armstrong World Industries sponsors a scholarship for the sons and daughters of Armstrong employees that is administered by the National Merit Scholarship Corporation. As a student in Macon, Georgia, a location in which Armstrong has a ceilings plant, I received a National Achievement Scholarship sponsored by Armstrong each year for the four years I attended Florida A&M University in Tallahassee, Florida. Also, by naming Florida A&M as my first-choice school and becoming a finalist for the National Achievement Scholarship Program, I received a university-sponsored scholarship from Florida A&M valued at more than $50,000 over four years.

What's on the PSAT?

- Two 25-minute verbal sections
- Two 25-minute math sections
- One 30-minute writing skills section

The test usually takes two hours and 10 minutes.

If I take the PSAT, what score will definitely win me a scholarship?

Since the top scorers of all those who take the PSAT become semifinalists in the scholarship competition, there is no specific score that will definitely win you a scholarship. It depends on how well others do who take the test. In addition, to become a finalist, you must satisfy other eligibility requirements.

To qualify to enter this huge scholarship competition, you must take the Preliminary SAT/National Merit Scholarship Qualifying Test (PSAT/NMSQT) early in your junior year of high school, usually in October. The top 5 percent of all scorers of the PSAT/NMSQT are eligible for National Merit Scholarships and become semifinalists in the competition. The top scorers are notified of their status in April, following the October test administration of the previous year. The notification invites them to name two colleges or universities to which they would like to be referred by NMSC. In September, the top scorers are then notified through their schools that they have qualified as either a Commended Student or Semifinalist. Commended students, or about 34,000 of the top scorers, receive letters of commendation from NMSC but do not continue in the competition for Merit Scholarship awards. However, some who do not advance in the competition may become candidates for special scholarships sponsored by corporations and businesses. The remaining group of approximately 16,000 students—narrowed down from 50,000 and formed by taking the top scorers from all fifty states—advance to the next stage in the Merit Scholarship competition and become semifinalists.

Sometime in February of each year, the semifinalists who meet academic and all other requirements are notified that they have advanced to the finalist stage of the competition. In March, NMSC notifies approximately 8,300 of the finalists that they have been selected to receive one of the National Merit Scholarship awards. The National Merit Scholarship awards they receive could be any of the following:

- National Merit $2,500 Scholarship
- Corporate-sponsored Merit Scholarship
- College-sponsored Merit Scholarship

Corporate-sponsored scholarships usually go to students who qualify as finalists and whose parents are employees of the corporate sponsor, or the scholarships can go to students in an area where the company has operations. The NMSC evaluates the qualifications of the students and makes the decisions about the winners. If too few students qualify for the number of scholarships the corporation has agreed to sponsor, the NMSC may award the scholarships to other qualified finalists.

Individual colleges and universities also sponsor Merit Scholarships. Finalists who indicate plans to attend a participating university are eligible for the scholarships sponsored by that institution. Universities that

I plan to graduate in my junior year of high school and start college. When should I take the PSAT to qualify for the National Merit and National Achievement Scholarship Competition?

- Take the PSAT/NMSQT in either your *next-to-last year* or the *last year* you will be in high school.
- If you take it in the *next-to-last year* of high school, you will enter the competition for a possible award as your high school career ends.
- If you take the PSAT/NMSQT in your *last year* of high school, you will be competing for awards that will be available as you are completing your college freshman year.

have routinely courted National Merit and/or National Achievement Scholars in the past are Harvard University, Rice University, Texas A&M, Florida A&M University, University of Alabama, University of Southern California, Princeton University, Howard University, Yale University, University of Chicago, University of Florida, and Stanford University. Many more not listed will also treat you very well if you are a finalist for the National Merit or National Achievement Competition. Some universities and colleges may also provide full scholarships if you become a finalist in the competition and name the institution as your first choice selection in the forms sent to you by the National Merit Scholarship Corporation. If you're wondering about a school and its offerings to National Merit or National Achievement finalists, visit its website, and most important, call and ask.

THE NATIONAL ACHIEVEMENT SCHOLARSHIP PROGRAM

Established in 1964, the National Achievement Scholarship Program is an academic competition created to provide recognition for outstanding Black American students. Black students can enter both the National Achievement Program and the National Merit Program by taking the PSAT/NMSQT and meeting other eligibility requirements. The two annual programs, National Merit and National Achievement, are conducted simultaneously but operated and funded separately—a student's standing is determined independently for each program. However, although Black American students can qualify for recognition and be honored as Scholars in the National Merit Program as well as the National Achievement Program, they can receive only one monetary award from NMSC. Students who wish to be considered for the National Achievement Program can do so in a special section of the PSAT/NMSQT answer sheet. If you need more information about how to do this, ask your counselor for assistance, visit http://www.nationalmerit.org to see a sample of where this indication should be made on the answer sheet, or look for wording such as the following: *"If you are a Black American and wish to enter the National Achievement Program as well as the National Merit program, fill in this circle."*

Currently, more than 160,000 students enter the National Achievement Program each year. Nearly 5,000 are honored yearly for their performance on the PSAT/NMSQT. Approximately 3,000 students from this group of honored students are referred to over 1,000 colleges that may also offer scholarships or special admissions consideration. About 1,600 students from the group are designated as semifinalists who have an opportunity to advance in the competition for Achievement Scholarship awards. After submitting applications and meeting other requirements, about 1,300 semifinalists advance to become finalists and are notified of their status in late January following the test administration. From this group of finalists approximately 800 Achievement Scholarships are offered. Winners are notified in mid- to late February. Currently there are two types of Achievement Scholarships:

- National Achievement $2,500 Scholarships
- Corporate-sponsored Achievement Scholarships

Some colleges and universities may offer certain scholarships to students who are finalists in the National Achievement Program. Use sites such as http://www.meritaid.com to explore these institutions or do an advanced Internet search for "scholarships" and "national achievement finalist." You can also search on your favorite university's website or include the name of the university in your advanced search. (See chapter 3 for more information about advanced Internet searches.)

Besides being a great way to prepare for the SAT and qualify for scholarships, the PSAT also gives you a projected SAT score as part of the score report you get back after you take the test. If your projected score isn't high enough for you, then it can give you more motivation to focus on key areas you need to improve in. I suggest that you take the PSAT in the tenth grade and the SAT in the eighth or ninth grade or before to get as much practice as possible and to give you a clear path for improving in areas that badly need it. Since the PSAT could be very helpful in winning scholarships, you should try to do as well as you can on this test before eleventh grade, when it counts as the National Merit Scholarship Qualifying Test. In some cases, you may not be able to take the PSAT prior to tenth grade (the test can only be taken through a high school), and since there are no age restrictions for the SAT, I suggest taking the actual SAT as practice before tenth grade if you choose to do so as preparation for the PSAT in eleventh grade. Taking the SAT early will help you become familiar with the test, which is helpful since the finalist stage of the National Merit and National Achievement Competition rests on your SAT score as well as other supporting factors and documents. Ask your counselor about the Preliminary SAT Scoring Service (PSSS), which some schools and organizations may use to test sophomores and younger students with a previously used version of the PSAT/NMSQT. Although the PSSS is not associated with the National Merit Scholarship Corporation or used by other scholarship programs, the PSSS can give you and your parents comprehensive, personalized feedback on your academic skills and help you prepare for the upcoming PSAT and SAT. There are also various test preparation and strategy guides you can use to help boost your PSAT scores.

Do not feel that if you are past the seventh, eighth, or tenth grade and have not taken these tests that all hope is lost. I personally did not start my scholarship search until the beginning of my senior year. However, I laid the preliminary groundwork for it years earlier, as I had already been involved in various extracurricular activities and had taken the SAT twice. It may help if you take the SAT as many times as you can afford. Also, since the tests are timed, it may eventually improve your score to become more familiar with the formats of the SAT and ACT. I will caution you, though, by saying you should not take the SAT, ACT, or PSAT on a lark just to see what it's like. All of your scores, not just your latest or the best, are reported when you have them sent to colleges, although the College Board currently has Score Choice (for a fee), which allows you to pick your best scores to send. If you feel you aren't ready to give it your best effort, even if you plan to take it several times more, don't take it and have a dismal score reported along with your others. On the other hand, if you want to take the test several times but don't think you can afford it, there are fee waivers for those who cannot afford to pay the full price. Speak with your counselor to get more information. To register for or obtain more information about the SAT, ACT, or other standardized tests, visit the College Board website at http://www.collegeboard.org or the ACT website at http://www.act.org.

For those of you who have taken standardized tests before or have already taken the SAT and done poorly, SAT and ACT scores can vary for a number of reasons. Many students are not good test takers in any situation. Others are plagued by anxiety attacks. Some may not have had enough sleep the night before the test. The testing environment may be poor. Many factors can contribute to a low test score other than lack of knowledge. Scholarship programs and colleges take these factors into account. Most programs concentrate on the well-rounded student who is active in his or her high school and community. If you exhibit excellent qualities in other areas, your test-taking skills or lack thereof will not hold you back. This is not to say that improving test scores is not important. What it does say is that a student who has excellent grades, excellent test scores, and is also involved in a variety of extracurricular activities has an even better chance for taking advantage of scholarship opportunities.

When you receive your test scores, carefully note weak areas. There are various books in the library and the bookstores for improving test scores, but I suggest that you retake a sample test and go over your answers to each question afterward, making sure you understand why you got certain answers correct and why you got certain answers incorrect. For those incorrect answers focus special attention on understanding the type of question and content it relates to so you can effectively study for improvement. Once you've retaken and analyzed an old practice exam, try a new one using the same process of taking the test under exam-day conditions.

Finally, when you do register to take the SAT test, you can decide to pay for the Student Answer Service (SAS) or the Question and Answer Service (QAS). The QAS provides you with a review copy of the verbal and math sections of the actual test you took for the SAT: Reasoning Test. QAS also gives you a record of your answers to each question, the correct answers, scoring instructions, and information on the types of questions and their level of difficulty. The SAS will provide you with a computer-generated report that will tell you if you answered questions correctly, incorrectly, or omitted them. It will also include the question and content type in the verbal and math sections of the test you took. Both of these services can help you to find your weak areas after you have taken the test.

They can help you pinpoint the sections of the test you should focus on improving for the next time around. The QAS will be the most helpful to you since it relates to the actual test you took and your answers. This could give you extra questions to review for practice later if you decide to take the test again.

After you take the SAT, you will also receive a score report for the test. The score report will advise you if you can expect your test scores to change if you take the test again. Even if it doesn't say that you can expect your scores to change noticeably, I would advise you to think about taking it again anyway, especially if you think you can and should do better. As mentioned before, scores on standardized tests can vary for a variety of reasons. The room could have been too cold or too quiet. You may not have entirely understood the instructions. You may have been tired from too much sleep or not enough. You know yourself best and the situation you were in when you took the test. Think about it and make the choice about taking it again.

My personal suggestion for improving critical reading and writing scores is to read as much as possible. Extensive reading helps increase your vocabulary as well as your word usage. Effective reading skills can improve your ability to understand situations, make accurate evaluations, and compare ideas, which are skills needed for the critical reading and writing portions of the SAT and ACT. Another way to improve your vocabulary is to learn the meanings of as many prefixes, suffixes, and roots of the English language as you can. Courses in Latin can be very helpful in this area. If you have a good understanding of the English language and its origins, you will be able to easily grasp and understand the meanings of words you have never seen before. For example, the prefix *mono-* means "single" or "one." Therefore, the following words preceded by *mono-* have definitions that all include the words *single* or *one*. These words and definitions have been extracted from *Webster's New World Dictionary*.

monodrama: a drama acted or written to be performed by *one* person
monody: in ancient Greek literature, an ode sung by a *single* voice
monomerous: having *one* member
monogamy: the practice or state of being married to only *one* person at a time
monomania: an excessive interest in or enthusiasm for *one* thing
monocle: an eyeglass for *one* eye only

Always keep a dictionary and a thesaurus handy to look up unfamiliar words when you're reading. This will help you become accustomed to using and comprehending a variety of words.

My suggestion for improving your math scores is not to shirk the hard courses. Take the most challenging courses you can handle. And if you need it, ask for extra help from your teachers to understand hard concepts. Then practice as much as you can with as many problems as you can. Try to practice on problems formatted in the way you will see them on a standardized test such as the SAT: Reasoning Test.

The SAT, PSAT, and AP exams can be excellent sources of information for you. When registering for the SAT, students who fill in the *Yes* oval on the registration form that asks whether you would like to participate in the Student Search Service will receive free information about colleges and universities. You'll also receive information about scholarship programs sponsored by colleges and universities as well as the government. The information you provide on your registration form is transmitted to other scholarship programs that may be interested in you as one of their scholars; this information includes your name, place of residence, birth date, intended college major, ethnic background, and grade level. If the programs are interested they will send you information. When you receive it, read everything; some may offer wonderful scholarship packages.

The registration forms for the SAT and ACT ask you to list scholarship programs and institutions that you want to receive your scores. If you do not have them available at the time of your registration, then you will have another chance to make your request and any corrections when you reach the test site on the day of the test.

For most scholarships, college or private, you will need to take some type of standardized test. For U.S. citizens it is usually the SAT or the ACT. For some colleges, you may also need to take one of the SAT Subject Tests, which focus on specific subject areas that may be required or recommended by an institution for its admissions requirements. Currently, there are twenty subject tests, including Math Level I; Math Level II; Literature; U.S. History; World History; Biology E/M; Chemistry; Physics; French; French with Listening; German; German with Listening; Spanish; Spanish with Listening; Modern Hebrew; Italian; Latin; Japanese with Listening; Korean with Listening; and Chinese with Listening. Your score on one or more of these tests may be used in combination with other information you provide about yourself, such as your high school record, recommendations, or résumé showing extracurricular activities, by admissions officers to help predict your future performance if you are admitted to the college or university. Starting early and taking these tests as soon as possible, well before your senior year of high school, will boost your confidence and your scores. To help you prepare, visit http://www.collegeboard.org to get preparation tips and additional information.

9

WRITING YOUR SCHOLARSHIP RÉSUMÉ: HOW TO STAND OUT AND WHY GRADES DON'T MEAN EVERYTHING

> A successful man is one who has tried
> not cried; who has worked, not dodged;
> who has shouldered responsibility, not evaded it;
> who has gotten under the burden instead of
> standing off, looking on and giving advice.
>
> —Eliot Hubbard

For someone to invest, he or she must first have a reason to invest. In order for someone to invest in you, it is necessary to promote yourself through words and actions. In chapter 11 we will deal with words. In this chapter we are concerned with actions in the form of your personal résumé.

MYTH 1

You must be an A student to win a scholarship.

FACT:

There are many students who do have A averages and have been unable to obtain scholarship funds. The Coca-Cola Scholars Foundation conducts one of the largest corporate-sponsored scholarship programs in the United States. As a student who participated in the 1991 Coca-Cola Scholars competition, I became aware of many recipients of the $4,000 and $20,000 scholarship awards who were not A students. Essentially, the winners were determined by factors such as community-based extracurricular activities. Although a good academic record is a contributing factor, having an A average would not exclusively qualify a student as a Coca-Cola Scholar. Coca-Cola Scholars are well-rounded, unique, and independent individuals. Note: Coca Cola Scholarships are now $10,000 and $20,000.

MYTH 2

B or C students cannot get scholarships because they are just average.

FACT:

Students who have B or C averages can get scholarships. The Coca-Cola Scholars Foundation is one example where a B average and being well-rounded can get you a scholarship. The David Letterman Telecommunications Scholarship, funded by David Letterman, the television talk show host, is aimed at creative individuals who may not have higher than a C average and so, too, is the Horatio Alger Association Scholarship. There are many scholarships that are not determined solely on the basis of grades. In fact, many sources of financial aid are "grade-blind," meaning that these programs do not recognize grades as a primary determining factor.

MYTH 3

Minorities and impoverished students get scholarships because they are underprivileged. The middle-class student is always left out.

FACT:

The majority of my scholarships were based on merit, which has no regard to ethnic background or need. I am a minority student, but economically I am middle class. Although many scholarships are aimed at minorities, many are based solely on individual merit. There are numerous merit-based scholarship programs. Addresses and information for many of them can be found in Appendix A. Others can be found by using the methods described in chapter 2, "The Scholarship Search: Discovering Hidden Treasures," chapter 3, "Using the Internet and Social Media in Your Scholarship Search," and chapter 4, "The Local Scholarship Search: Finding Scholarships in

Your Backyard." Myths 1, 2, and 3 are just that—myths. Grades do not make a well-rounded individual, and minorities and the poor do not get all the good scholarships.

Be Descriptive for Maximum Impact with Your Résumé

Many activities may be popular in a school, community, region, or even a state. However, these activities may not be popular elsewhere. If you have an activity or activities you believe are unusual, include an explanation similar to the example below.

The Telegraph Teen Board—Group of students from high schools throughout Macon who assist the local newspaper in reporting stories, gathering photographs, and formatting the layout for the weekly news section devoted to high school students in the community.

Member	*2020*
Photographer	*2018*

Good grades play an important role in the scholarship process, yet they should not be used as an excuse not to apply for scholarships. Most scholarship programs look for well-rounded individuals who not only excel academically but are involved in extracurricular activities as well. To them the perfect candidate would be one who has a perfect score on the SAT (2400), the ACT (36), and a 4.0 grade point average or higher, depending on the grading scale for honors classes. When I tell people that my grade point average was 4.67, they usually look at me with an expression of disbelief. A 4.67 was possible for me, as it may be for many of you, because honors classes at our high school were on a five-point scale system. A variety of honors courses, especially advanced-placement courses, may boost your grade point average above the usual perfect 4.0. In addition to perfect test scores and a perfect record in the classroom, colleges look for the ingredient that can label a student as a "total package": extracurricular activities in school and the community. The student who has these qualities will not have a problem being accepted at any college or in winning the money to pay for it. However, even an ideal student needs self-motivation, determination, and persistence, because unless you are an athlete who has received a lot of publicity, most schools will not come to you waving scholarship money. You still need to work hard.

EXTRACURRICULAR ACTIVITIES

Extracurricular activities tell scholarship program administrators that as a student you are willing to devote your time and effort to your community and school. By investing their scholarship dollars in you, they are not only investing in your future, they are investing in the future of the community and the country. Participating in projects for your school and community conveys that you are a self-motivated leader with potential. Involvement in extracurricular activities not only expresses your leadership qualities, it builds them as well. A list of these activities on your résumé is impressive when you include it with your application.

Highlight Your Leadership and Use Action Words

Lead with your role, then state the activity. Alternatively, you can make sure your leadership role is very clear by including it on a separate line under the activity, as you'll see in some of the example résumés.

For instance, you might include in your résumé "Student Officers' Club for Community Programs, Founder." Instead, you should write: "Founder—Student Officers' Club for Community Programs."

A typical job-focused résumé often includes a description of your role in a particular job function. For a scholarship résumé, a description is not necessary UNLESS you need to describe an activity that is uncommon or atypical OR you need to expand your résumé to reduce white space OR your role was influential. If any of these conditions apply, then lead with action words to describe your role.

For example, see the action words in bold face:

- *Founder*—Student Officers' Club for Community Programs
  - ***Organized*** a group of student officers from the community and Northeast High School to form an initiative for ***implementing*** community programs to address childhood obesity
  - **Led** the group in organizing three initial programs that focused on ***targeting*** groups in need, **outreach** to the groups, educational workshops, and **implementation** of formal exercise programs for each target group

Participation in contests and other activities related to your specific interests, such as piano or dance recitals, horse shows, or poetry or oratorical contests, can also show an impressive side to you. Participation in various contests shows that you are not afraid of competition and creates an impression of a well-rounded and involved student. My special interest was writing. The condensed form of my résumé (Résumé A, which follows) shows mostly awards won in writing competitions. It is organized as follows: Departmental Clubs/Activities, with another heading for Honorary Clubs, and yet another heading for Community Clubs/Activities. Then I list awards and honors under a separate heading, beginning with the ninth grade. I prepared several variations of this basic résumé for different programs. One excerpt from a variation, shown in Résumé B, displays the amount of hours spent for each activity; another excerpt lists a club I was involved in and under it the awards I won through that club. These résumés are merely examples to give you guidelines to follow. The way you organize your résumé may be according to your own personal involvement, style, and preference. One applicant for the Ragins/Braswell National Scholarship Competition, a scholarship that I fund, decided to include a chart of his activities as well as a résumé. An example of this type of chart is shown in Résumé C.

School field trips for the purpose of participating in seminars or workshops for educational or community-interest projects can also be included in your résumé as extracurricular activities. You can create a separate heading for special-interest activities. As you review my résumé you may wonder if it is necessary to be involved in so many activities. No, it's not necessary to be involved in as many clubs and activities as I was. It's easy to stretch yourself too thin. I like to be involved in everything, but you don't have to do the same. One or two activities you're really interested in are fine, especially if you have a position of leadership. Please note that when asked on surveys, many scholarship programs stated that the average recipient of their scholarship participated in eight to nine activities. If you are not a member of any club and don't participate in outside activities, I strongly suggest you become involved in some type of extracurricular activity. Participation of any type can help you grow and improve in many areas. One key area is interaction with others in a group setting, beyond the typical classroom environment. This shows your willingness to get involved in your surroundings and make a positive contribution. Also, in reference to winning awards for your activities, even if you have not received honors it looks good to participate. Repeated and improved participation shows that you are not only a good sport, but you can learn from your mistakes.

Clubs and activities that are considered impressive are the Beta Club, Student Council, and the National Honor Society. The National Honor Society also conducts a scholarship program for members of the society. It really doesn't matter what clubs or activities you become involved in,

Getting Involved Can Pay Off in Scholarship Money!

Active participation and leadership in clubs, extracurricular, community, and volunteer activities helps differentiate you from other students. This will definitely help you win scholarship money and also give you a lot to write about in your essays.

Activities can pay off in another way, too. If you are a member of the following clubs and organizations, you may be eligible for a scholarship directly from the organization.

- National Honor Society
- Junior Achievement
- National Beta Club
- Boy Scouts of America (Eagle Scouts)
- Girl Scouts U.S.A.
- Distributive Education Clubs of America (DECA)
- Future Business Leaders of America (FBLA)
- Mu Alpha Theta
- Golden Key International Honour Society (for college students only)

If you continue your participation in some of the organizations above as a college student, you may still be eligible to enter their scholarship competition.

but these are nationally known for leadership, service, and involvement in the community. If you don't have any of these clubs at your high school, contact a national or local representative and start one. Scholarship programs like to see students who initiate and carry out challenging ideas.

Using the format of Résumé A or B, and using the style of C or D is fine. Some scholarship programs request your activities listed in a certain order, and you should comply with their rules. In most cases all forms are acceptable.

SAMPLE RÉSUMÉ A

Marianne Ragins *(Substitute your name and address.)*
P.O. Box 176
Centreville, Virginia 20122

Northeast Comprehensive High School *(Substitute your school name and address.)*
1646 Upper River Road
Macon, Georgia 31201

Departmental Clubs/Activities *(Here list all activities you are involved in at your school.)*

Academic Bowl Team 9th–12th *(List activity and grades in which you participated.)*
  Captain 11th *(List any positions of leadership and the grade as a subheading.)*
  Drama Club 9th–12th

Salmagundi Literary Magazine 10th–12th
    Assistant Editor 10th
    Co-Editor 11th
    Editor-in-Chief 12th

Student Council 9th–12th
    President 12th

Honorary Clubs *(List all clubs you have been inducted into because of outstanding performance.)*

Mu Alpha Theta 10th–12th
National Honor Society 10th–12th

Community Clubs/Activities *(Your clubs or activities within the community.)*

Macon Telegraph and News Teen Board 2025 *(List the calendar year[s] involved.)*
Red Cross Youth Volunteer 2023–2025
Y Club 2021–2024, vice president 2023–2024

Awards/Honors *(List all the awards have won throughout high school. Include certificates of participation.)*
Best Poem in State—Georgia Scholastic Press Association
National English Merit Award
Certificate of Participation—Mathematics Meet 2025

SAMPLE RÉSUMÉ B

Marianne Ragins *(Substitute your name and address.)*
P.O. Box 176
Centreville, Virginia 20122

Northeast Comprehensive High School *(Substitute your school name and address.)*
1646 Upper River Road
Macon, Georgia 31201

School Activities, Awards, and Honors
(Here list all positions of leadership, number of hours spent in each activity, and awards won.)
Academic Bowl Team Captain (11th, 12th; 15 hours/month)
Macon Telegraph and News Teen Board Layout Editor (12th; 28 hours/month)
Salmagundi Literary Magazine Assistant Editor (10th, 20 hours/month)
   First Place—Georgia Scholastic Press Association 2024 *(List awards won as a member of the organization.)*
   First Place—Columbia Scholastic Press Association 2022

SAMPLE RÉSUMÉ CHART C

TABLE 8

	Dates From–To	No. Hours Per Week	Responsibilities/ Special Accomplishments
A. School Activities			
1. Sophomore JV, Varsity Football	2023–11/2024	15	Lettered in junior year of high school
2. Sophomore Varsity Track and Field	2021 and 2022	15	300-, 400-meter hurdles, 4×4 Relay
3. Senior Calendar	9/2023–2024	5	Organized senior activities
B. Community Activities			
1. Portland Youth Golf Association	2021–present	2	Youth Tournament Award
2. Prospective Gents Club	2022–present	3	Club Secretary

(Continued)

C. Volunteer Services			
1. Boys & Girls Club	2021–2022	1	Youth Camp Counselor
2. Dombecher Children's Hospital	2022–2024	1	Mailings for Donor Support
D. Work for Pay			
1. Albina Community Bank	2021–2022	2	Clerical
2. Portland Rose Garden	3/2024–present	16	Merchandise Seller
3. R & J Company	2023–2024	10	Janitor

SAMPLE RÉSUMÉ D

JOHN H. BROWN JR.

354 XYZ Avenue • Macon, GA 31201 • (478) 555-1212 (home) • abc@xyz.net

OBJECTIVE: To obtain a scholarship and gain acceptance to a challenging university or college for the study of accounting, engineering, or electronics.

EDUCATION

Hutchings Career Center   **Macon, Georgia**
Expected Graduation Date—May 2026

EMPLOYMENT AND LEADERSHIP

2026

Current
Advance Auto Parts   **Macon, Georgia**
Cashier

Hutchings Career Center   **Macon, Georgia**
In-Class Tutor—Communications
   Technology Course

Skills USA   **Macon, Georgia**
Mock Interviewing Competition

Summer
Warner Robins Air Force Base   **Warner Robins,**
Government Intern (First Intern   **Georgia**
  Ever Selected for Program)

Spring
Semifinalist—Georgia (CTI)   **Macon, Georgia**
  Career and Technology Institute
Competition for State Office President

2025

Hutchings Career Center   **Macon, Georgia**
Group Leader—Foundation for
  Automotive Service Technicians
  Course—Spring Semester
Group Leader—Electronic Systems
  Course—Fall Semester

Fall Leadership Conference—(CTI)   **Atlanta, Georgia**
  Career and Technology Institute

Hughes Honda Internship   **Warner Robins,**
                                     Georgia
AYES Intern Technician (First Intern
  Ever Selected for Program)

Hutchings Career Center Student   **Macon, Georgia**
Representative—*Georgia CTI Meeting*

2022–2026 (part-time during weekends and after school)

J. H. Brown Lawn Service   **Macon, Georgia**
Owner

2022–2026 (occasional)

J. H. Brown Handyman Service   **Macon, Georgia**
Owner

AWARDS AND HONORS

Semifinalist—Merit Based Scholarship Program (2025)

(Continued)

COMMUNITY SERVICE

- Union Baptist Teen Church—10th, 11th, 12th
  - Teen Church Speaker—Interview Preparation (12th grade)
  - Assistant for Teen Church Self-Defense Class (12th grade)
  - Teen Church Mentor (10th, 11th, 12th)
- Provided recommendations to upper management at Warner Robins Air Force Base for an Extended Youth Internship Program (12th)
- Carrabba's Career Technology Institute Night—9th, 10th, 11th, 12th
- Middle Georgia Buddy Walk for Children with Down Syndrome at Mabel White Baptist Church—11th, 12th
- "Kids Yule Luv" Toy Drive—10th, 11th, 12th
- Mentor—Fort Hill Neighborhood Kids (10th, 11th, 12th)
- Math Tutoring—Fort Hill Neighborhood Elementary School Children—9th, 10th

OTHER EXTRACURRICULAR AND ENRICHMENT ACTIVITIES

School Based

Skills USA—9th, 10th, 11th, 12th
Chess Club—9th, 10th, 11th, 12th
Science Tutoring Program—11th
Reading Tutoring Program—11th

Community-Based

Educational Talent Search—2024, 2025
College Tours (George Institute of Technology, Georgia State University, Savannah State University, University of Georgia, Albany State University)—2025, 2026

SKILLS AND HOBBIES

Over the past several years I have thoroughly explored and maintained interest in the following areas: youth and peer tutoring, Tae Kwon Do, computer software application, animation and development, sports, automotive and home repair, and electronics.

For your résumé, make sure to list at the top those activities that were the most meaningful to you or on which you had the most impact, even if listing is not in chronological order. And no matter what format you decide to use, make sure it is well organized and easy to read. Although you may have many noteworthy activities, they won't be noticed if buried in a jumbled mass of text. For example, here is what Résumé A could look like if it were not well organized with enough white space to avoid tiring the eyes of the reader. This résumé is hard to read. Therefore, if you include a résumé similar to this one as extra information for scholarship committee members to read, they may not do so because there is so much text written closely together.

What Your Résumé SHOULD NOT Look Like

Amy N. Student

School Clubs/Activities: Academic Bowl Team 9th–12th; Captain 11th; Drama Club 9th–12th; *Salmagundi* Literary Magazine 10th–12th; Assistant Editor 10th; Co-Editor 11th; Editor-in-Chief 12th; Student Council 9th–12th; President 12th; Mu Alpha Theta 10th–12th; National Honor Society 10th–12th; *The Telegraph* Teen Board 2022; Red Cross Youth Volunteer 2022–2023; Y Club 2022–2024, vice president 2023–2024; Best Poem in State, Georgia Scholastic Press Association; National English Merit Award; Certificate of Participation—Mathematics Meet 2022; Sophomore JV, Varsity Football 2021–11/2024; Lettered in junior year of high school; Sophomore Varsity Track and Field 2021 and 2022; 300-meter, 400-meter hurdles; 4 × 4 relay; Senior Calendar 9/2022–2024.

Community Activities: Portland Youth Golf Association 2021–present; Youth Tournament Award; Prospective Gents Club 2021–present; Club Secretary; Boys & Girls Club 2021–2022; Youth Camp Counselor; Dombecher Children's Hospital 2022–2024—Mailings for Donor Support.

Work for Pay: Albina Community Bank 2021–2022.

Clerical; Portland Rose Garden 3/23–present—Merchandise Seller; R & J Company 2023–2024—Janitor

I plan to graduate in my junior year of high school and start college. Will this affect my scholarship opportunities?

Possibly, yes. This is because so many scholarship programs look closely at your leadership, extracurricular and community service activities, and your overall involvement. An extra year as a senior can give you more time to contribute and build your résumé. On the other hand, if your participation in activities has been stellar thus far, you may be okay. Your chances really depend on the program and how you stack up against other students.

Graduation as a high school junior may also create a situation where you'll need to ask questions because many programs state that the scholarship is available to high school seniors or may have an age requirement. You may need to clarify your status with your counselor and the program to confirm your eligibility.

10

THE APPLICATION

I wonder if the human touch which people have
is not one of the greatest assets that you can
    have. . . .
You read a book, sit before the performance
of a fine actor or read a poem—and there it is—
something that streams into your consciousness . . .
without this human touch, hope has little
on which to feed or thrive.

—George Matthew Adams

At this point in your scholarship journey everything should come together. Your extensive research has rewarded you with numerous applications. The organizational procedures in chapter 6, "Getting Organized," have shown you how to compartmentalize your applications and supporting documents. You have people such as your counselor and principal on your recommendations list. Your academic and extracurricular interests are clearly outlined. You have also taken or registered for the SAT and the ACT. In addition, your résumé, explained in chapter 9, has been completed and will highlight your commitment to society, your school, and your personal improvement. You are now ready to apply for admission to college and for scholarships.

The most crucial stage of your quest for college scholarships will be completing college applications, fees for which range from $10 to $70. The first item that college and scholarship administrators will see is your application. If it is sloppy, they will get that impression of you before they have a chance to formulate a positive one. They could even decide to scrap your

When Can I Apply for Scholarships?

For many scholarship programs you can't actually apply until you are a high school senior. However, you can apply for some in your junior year or before, such as the Nordstrom Scholarship. See chapter 26, "Scholarships for Younger Students—from Kindergarten to 11th Grade."

The most important thing you should remember is to be prepared to submit applications early in your senior year. Do most of your research as a junior or during the summer before your senior year.

And don't ignore scholarship and award opportunities as a 9th-, 10th-, or 11th-grade student.

entire application, and all your painstaking work on the essay, your résumé, and other supporting material will be wasted. So strive for an application that is not only neat but also free of errors and incomplete information. Having followed the instructions provided in the previous chapters, this step should be easy for you.

TIP 1

All applications should be typed, no exceptions—unless the application requests that you print. If so, use black ink. In scholarship competitions, you should always be thinking of how well you stack up against the next applicant. If all things are equal, there is no question that a typed application makes a much better impression than one that is not. With many applications online and the availability of services such as ScholarSnapp (http://www.scholarsnapp.org), you'll get your typing done for you. Just make sure that any supporting documents you send are typed, too! Online fee-based services such as PDF filler (http://www.pdffiller.com) will allow you to enter your information into PDF applications and print them.

TIP 2

Make photocopies of applications as you receive them, or download and print copies. To avoid mistakes fill out the photocopied applications well ahead of the deadline. Use these applications as your guide to complete online applications. Also, make a computer file of frequently asked questions and their answers. You'll find a list of typical questions asked on applications at the end of this chapter. Always keep a copy of your completed applications—you may need them to prepare for interviews. (If the program or school allows it, using a service such as ScholarSnapp (http://www .scholarsnapp.org), or the Common Application (http://www.commonapp .org) helps with entering repetitive information in multiple applications.

Top 10 Mistakes Made on College and Scholarship Applications

1. Not following directions or including required or requested information
2. Missing the deadline
3. Sending in a sloppy or poorly presented application
4. Forgetting to spell-check and proofread after you spell-check
5. Not taking the time to notify those you are asking for a recommendation of e-mail requests they may be receiving from an organization or college/university
6. Not answering the essay question or another question asked
7. Sending in too much additional information
8. Not understanding a question but providing an answer anyway, without asking questions
9. Not listing your most relevant, impactful, or meaningful experiences before listing those that are much less meaningful
10. Not letting someone else proofread your application before submitting online or sending to the organization or college/university

TIP 3

Set up a file system for all copies of applications so that you can locate them easily as deadlines draw near. A filing system is also helpful to refer to an application for information to use on another one. Organizing electronic file folders for downloaded PDF applications and bookmarking websites for online application systems also helps you keep track.

TIP 4

All sections of the application that you are not directly responsible for should be given to those who are responsible for them as soon as possible. For example, recommendation forms for counselors, teachers, and advisors, or secondary and midyear school reports. This is especially important when submitting online applications, because it's easy to forget the sections others need to complete for you. Alternatively, for online applications that send e-mails to those who are completing recommendations and other required forms for you, send a recommendation request letter and/or e-mail ahead of time so the counselor (etc.) knows what to expect and when.

TIP 5

Arrange to have your scores from the SAT, ACT, and any other required standardized tests sent to the colleges shortly after your applications arrive (if you have not already arranged this during the registration phase for the tests). Make sure to check with the colleges and universities to ensure that they have received them. For many colleges and universities, you can check the status of your application online and see whether required forms and recommendations have been received.

TIP 6

Have 2×3-inch black-and-white photographs prepared with a typed label with your name, address, e-mail address, and telephone number on the back. Include a photo only if asked.

TIP 7

Include your personal résumé. Most applications have space to list your activities and special awards, but it looks more professional to include a résumé. Never leave the spaces for this information blank. Instead, type instructions to "see additional information" and include your résumé. For online applications including a résumé may or may not be possible, depending on the system. Some online applications may still require paper-based submissions of some documents. If so, include your résumé with the additional documents unless specifically requested not to do so.

TIP 8

If submitting through the mail, type essays and other supporting material on good-quality paper. Use paper with a weight of at least 24 lb.

TIP 9

Some programs specifically request that additional pages be kept to a minimum, if they are allowed at all. Respect their wishes and don't include your résumé or samples of your work.

TIP 10

Include with your applications articles that may have appeared in your local newspaper about you or your activities, unless you are asked not to send additional information. See Tip 9.

TIP 11

Include samples of your work that are extraordinary or award-winning. Don't be afraid to send along copies of poetry, artwork, or even recordings (although these may be too bulky) that indicate your special talents, which may include singing or dancing or playing the piano. If you have any special talent or hobby, flaunt it. It makes your application stand out from others. When you include extra information, make sure it really is outstanding or extraordinary. (A copy of an award-winning poem I used to include with my applications for scholarships is shown at the end of this chapter.) Try not to overload your application with extra material. If possible, try to fit all of your material into a 9×12-inch envelope and include no more than two or three pieces. Most important, if a scholarship program or college/university asks that you not include additional information, don't.

TIP 12

Many college admissions application packages contain applications for financial aid. Therefore, whether you are applying for admission or a scholarship, pay close attention to all sections of an application because you have to be admitted to a college before you can win a scholarship sponsored by it.

TIP 13

Applications should be turned in as far in advance as possible. Some scholarships are issued on a first-come, first-served basis. Once the funds are depleted, you cannot apply until the following year. Please note that submitting your application early for scholarship consideration is not the same as "early admission," in which students who get accepted to a specific college or university must make an enrollment commitment if they are accepted. Also, be aware that some programs will accept applications only during a certain time period and may destroy or return applications submitted outside of that time period. Organizations normally state this requirement clearly on an application, so as long as you pay attention, you'll be okay. For online application processes, this is less of an issue because the process will not start until the application period is open.

TIP 14

Complete an application for financial aid. There are two primary financial aid forms, the FAFSA (Free Application for Federal Student Aid) provided by the government, and the CSS—Financial Aid PROFILE (College Scholarship Service–Financial Aid PROFILE). The CSS charges a fee for its service. The government FAFSA is free of charge. Contact the schools you are interested in attending to find out which form they prefer. Even if you are not applying for a need-based scholarship, most college scholarship programs require your student aid report (SAR) from the FAFSA. Again, even though you cannot officially file any of these forms until after January 1 of the year you plan to attend college, obtain one of the forms early and gather all the information you will need to fill out the form completely. Visit http://www.fafsa4caster.ed.gov to estimate your financial need in advance. For more information, refer to chapter 6, "Getting Organized," and chapter 5, "Financial Aid Forms and Help from the Government with College Expenses."

TIP 15

For questions that do not apply to you, write "not applicable" in the answer blank, or the abbreviation "NA" to show that you have not overlooked the question.

TIP 16

If you are not sure about the spelling of a word, look it up in the dictionary.

TIP 17

You may be required to list the names and e-mail addresses of your references. Some schools and scholarship programs ask for this so they can send recommendation forms to these individuals directly, without using you as the medium. Create your recommendation request list ahead of time and think carefully about those you plan to ask. For example: Does the individual know you well? Does the individual understand your strengths and your challenges, or obstacles you've overcome? Will this person go beyond a standard recommendation form letter and tailor your recommendation specifically for you? Is this person accustomed to writing recommendations and/or writing in general?

THE MOST FREQUENTLY ASKED QUESTIONS ON COLLEGE APPLICATIONS

Knowing the questions that frequently appear on college applications will help you prepare for filling out multiple applications in the future. Many of these questions are basic, but answering them may require time and a little research, especially queries relating to other family members. You can also download an electronic application that has many of the most generic and frequently asked questions on college applications from http://www.commonapp.org.

1. In what semester or quarter do you plan to enroll? (This question is asked on all college applications; it basically establishes what class you will be in and the period for which you will need financial assistance.)
2. What is your state of legal residence? If you are a resident of the state in which this institution is located, in what month and year did you become a resident? (This question can help qualify you for in-state tuition, if it is a public institution.)
3. What is your intended program of study and major? If you previously attended this institution, what dates did you attend? If you graduated prior to June of the year you are applying to enter the college or university, give an explanation of how you spent the time in between (refer to chapter 11, "Writing Scholarship Essays That Get Noticed").
4. What is your Social Security number?
5. In which country are you a citizen? If you are a legal resident alien, what is your registration number?
6. Give a description of your academic honors (refer to chapter 9, "Writing Your Scholarship Résumé: How to Stand Out and Why Grades Don't Mean Everything").
7. Give a description of your extracurricular and personal activities (refer to chapter 9, "Writing Your Scholarship Résumé").
8. What activities do you plan to participate in during college?
9. What courses are you currently taking in high school?

10. State the names of both parents, their addresses, occupations, and highest level of education completed. If either one attended college, what is the name of the college(s) they attended?

11. What are your birth date and place of birth?

12. What are the name and address of the high school you are currently attending?

13. What are the name, address, and denomination of the church you are currently attending?

14. What are the name and telephone number of your high school guidance counselor?

15. What is the CEEB/ACT Code of the high school you will graduate from? The CEEB Code is an identification code assigned by the College Board to various scholarship programs, colleges, universities, college majors, high schools, and other entities and programs. The ACT Code is a similar identification code assigned by ACT.

16. Have any family members ever worked for this college or university? If so, list their names, dates of employment, and their relationship to you.

17. List the names of any brothers and sisters, their ages, and the colleges they attended.

18. What languages other than English do you speak?

19. What is your first language?

20. If you have taken the SAT and the ACT, list the dates and your scores. If you have not, have you registered to take them? On what dates?

21. What is the class size and your rank in that class? (Refer to chapter 7, "Getting the Most from Your Counselor.")

22. Do you have any physical limitations that require special assistance and consideration?

23. Do you have, or have you had in the past, any emotional problems that would affect your educational performance?

24. What is the name of your hometown newspaper?

THE MOST FREQUENTLY ASKED QUESTIONS ON PRIVATE/OUTSIDE SCHOLARSHIP APPLICATIONS

Additional essay questions you may be asked are included in chapter 11.

1. What is the size of your graduating class, and what is your rank in it?

2. To which schools have you applied? What are the dates that you applied?

3. What schools have accepted you as a student?

4. List any advanced or special courses, or summer courses, you have taken.

5. List any talents or skills (such as music, arts, sports) that you pursue outside of school.

6. Describe a recent experience that has given you a sense of satisfaction or pride.

7. Describe your leadership role in community and extracurricular activities.

8. What qualities or characteristics do you have that distinguish you as a leader in your community or your school?

9. What are your major social concerns? Describe activities you are involved in that address your concerns.

10. Who has influenced you most in your life? How has this person influenced you?

11. What is your current grade point average?

12. What is your mother's annual income? (*May only be asked for scholarships that are partially or fully based on need.*)

13. What is your father's annual income? (*May only be asked for scholarships that are partially or fully based on need.*)

14. How many dependents are in your family? (*May only be asked for scholarships that are partially or fully based on need.*)

15. How many members of your family are in college? (*May only be asked for scholarships that are partially or fully based on need.*)

16. What is the highest educational level completed by your mother and father?

17. What degree do you intend to pursue in college?

18. Do you work? What is your annual income? (*May only be asked for scholarships that are partially or fully based on need.*)

19. Please list all money available for college expenses. (*May only be asked for scholarships that are partially or fully based on need.*)

    Scholarships $_____

    Grants $_____

    Savings $_____

    Parents $_____

    Other $_____

When you estimate the amounts available for college expenses, do not include scholarships that come from colleges or universities unless you are certain of your college choice. Receipt of some National Merit and

National Achievement Scholarships depends on your college choice and your intended major. Unless you are certain your scholarship will "travel" to whichever school you choose and with any major, do not include it.

If the SAR shows that you are eligible for a Pell Grant, do not include the Pell Grant amount; these grants are funneled through the school, and even though you may be eligible for the maximum amount, you may not receive it. You may also be asked for the date you filed the FAFSA, CSS—Financial Aid PROFILE, and other financial aid forms.

In addition, for need-based aid, you may wish to prepare a statement of financial hardship to explain any extenuating circumstance(s) that would prohibit you or your family from contributing to your educational expenses. This statement should be written in essay format and sent along with your application for financial aid if you are applying for a need-based scholarship from a particular college or university. Do not hesitate to call or arrange a visit to a favored college or university to inform the institution that unfortunately you cannot afford to attend because the financial aid package it has offered cannot meet your needs. Some schools may reconsider, especially if you are an exceptional student.

APPLYING ONLINE

Many scholarship organizations and colleges and universities are providing applications for download on their websites. Some organizations have a completely electronic process whereby you can submit your application online. According to many scholarship providers, applying online is the norm rather than the exception. Many institutions also accept the Common Application, which is available for download at http://www.common app.org. The Common Application contains the standardized information common to most college and university applications. Institutions that are more selective may have secondary applications that are sent after receipt of the Common Application, to gain additional information about the applicants. Some institutions allow you to complete supplemental applications online along with the Common Application.

Although applying online to colleges or downloading applications can make the process easier, I recommend that online applications be used sparingly, as a last resort if you really need to save time. I say this because the ease of communication that e-mail and the Internet have given us has also helped many of us forget to proofread the documents we send electronically for spelling and grammatical errors. I have lost count of the many times

I have received e-mail or something over the Internet that looks as if a first grader with a blindfold on had typed it. As a result, to avoid an application with numerous errors and giving those who read it the impression that you can't spell, type, or read, my recommendations for electronic applications, either for colleges or scholarship organizations, are as follows:

- Use the Common Application, if necessary, for colleges that are the least selective and which you may be considering as a backup school. Since many of the most selective institutions often require more information than what is required in the Common Application and have a school-specific supplement, you may save time by directly requesting the application specific to the institution.

- If you do use the Common Application or download an application from a scholarship program website, always print out the entire application before you fill out anything. After you have printed the application, work on your answers for each section. Make sure to print out an additional hard copy of any sections that your counselor or others need to fill out. For essay questions, short-answer essay questions, and any section requiring more than a one-word answer, type your responses in Microsoft Word, or a similar program, making sure to use spell- and grammar-check. Once you have all your answers written on your computer and have printed them out to check for readability, ask a counselor, parent, or friend to give it a once-over for a final check. After you have done this, copy and paste your answers into the online application or into the form to send electronically. Make sure to proofread once again while it's on your screen and print it out again to proofread a hard copy. Be certain that you have not omitted anything. Finally, even if you can send it to the organization online, try to send your application by mail so you can include your résumé or additional information as discussed in chapter 9, "Writing Your Scholarship Résumé." However, if the organization requests the application online only, follow its directions. Use the above online proofreading process for ScholarSnapp applications as well.

COLLEGE APPLICATIONS: SHOULD YOU APPLY FOR EARLY DECISION OR NOT?

Unless you are absolutely certain of your college choice, the answer is no. This is the same as applying for scholarships that require you to pursue a certain major. If you have any uncertainty at all you should not do it. If you do, changing your mind later may cause you to lose your scholarship for that specific school. Likewise, financial aid packages from the college or university you have decided upon may not be as competitive or as large if the school knows you are definitely planning to enroll for the upcoming year. Look at the financial aid package from "Prestigious University" that follows. The loan amount may have been much larger or the aid amount may have fallen short of actual college costs or Melissa's need if the college financial aid administrator had been certain Melissa would attend. If Melissa had applied as an early decision applicant, she might not have received the Alumni or the Skyler Scholarship. These scholarships might have been used instead to help the school attract other students who are not as certain about coming to their campus.

Sample Financial Aid and Scholarship Award Letter

Prestigious University°
Office of Financial Aid
Aid, Georgia 00001

To: Melissa A. Student   000-00-0001
               P.O. Box 4000
               Rockville, Maryland 29333   February 15, 20XX

On behalf of the Financial Aid Committee, I am pleased to inform you that your request for financial aid has been approved for the 20XX–20XX academic year. Please read carefully the conditions listed below and the appropriate messages on the reverse side of this notice.

Approved:

$5,000.00	XYZ Alumni Scholars Scholarship
$10,000.00	Nancy Y. Skyler General Scholarship
$2,000.00	Federal College Work-Study
$3,500.00	Federal Perkins Loan
$20,500.00	**Total Approved**

Allison Grant
Director of Financial Aid

°The above-named individuals, organizations, and scholarships are fictitious.

Sample of Special Work to Include with Your Application

"Best Poem in State" Georgia Scholastic Press Association 1989

Hourglass

Thoughts . . .
drifting aimlessly
through deep dark regions.
A glimmer of light
rushes in and fades away
to join the others that have
long been forgotten.
Quickly,
another flickers into the powerhouse that is my
mind
only to slink stealthily back, unworthy
of further notice.
Another
bursts forth in a mushroom
of clearness.
I have it!
A sound thought
worthy of notice
worthy of praise
and worthy of me.

—Angel Ragins

(Author's Note: I used my nickname, Angel, for everything as a high school student.)

11

WRITING SCHOLARSHIP ESSAYS
THAT GET NOTICED

Words, when well-chosen and presented, have so
great a force in them, that a description often gives
us more lively ideas than the sights of the things
themselves.

—Joseph Addison

Writing essays is one of the most essential components of your scholarship search, so learning to write a good essay is important to your success. Essay composition is required for most college and private scholarship applications. The images created with words and the values revealed in the essays you submit to scholarship programs are often instrumental in the selection of scholarship winners. In fact, many scholarship competitions are based solely on the quality of your essay.

The main purpose of essays is to give an in-depth view of you as a unique individual. Most essay questions are designed to help evaluators discover the values, ideals, achievements, and traits that make up your personality. Therefore, a well-written essay may give evaluators a glimpse of your inner self through your ability to write a cohesive, well-thought-out writing sample. An essay can also explain any special circumstance that has had an impact on your life. For instance, if you had a period in school in which your academic performance was less than satisfactory, write an essay explaining why and include it with all your applications. Some scholarship committees will ask for an explanation anyway if this circumstance applies to you.

An essay can achieve one of two major objectives for you. In conjunction with your application, extracurricular activities, and academic record, it can make scholarship administrators eager to meet the person behind the words. This will result in advancing you to the next stage of competition, an interview. An essay can also compel scholarship administrators to reward you for your outstanding effort and make you one of their scholarship recipients. You can fulfill these objectives by making the content of your essay interesting, insightful, and informative.

Scholarship programs are looking for essays that show clear thought patterns, creativity, enthusiasm, and potential. Exhibiting these qualities accurately and uniquely is essential to the effectiveness of your essay as a tool to win scholarships. Essays prepared for competition of any kind need to capture their readers' attention and stand out from other essays. The best way to accomplish this is to use honest, straightforward prose and be true to your natural voice. In addition, you should ensure that your essay is well presented in an attractive format that is easy to read and pleasing to the eye.

To accomplish this you should make the overall presentation of your essay and application look as neat and professional as possible. If you have a computer with a page-layout program such as Microsoft Word, use it. Graphic elements will give you an edge over the other applicants. But keep in mind that fancy layout can only complement the content of your essay, not compensate for lack of skill. Be aware that for many scholarship programs, your initial application and any supporting information such as essays will be submitted online. However if attachments are allowed or you are required to send any supporting documents in the mail, make this additional information as attractively formatted as possible.

For writing essays I have found that the basic five-paragraph format is an easy one to use. For example, here is a simple outline for an essay that can be jazzed up with unique variations.

SAMPLE OUTLINE FOR GENERAL ESSAY FORMAT

I. Introduction—one paragraph
  A. Use a quotation, poem, thought, amazing fact, idea, question, or simple statement to draw your reader into your topic.
  B. The main idea does not have to be stated in the first sentence, but it should definitely lead to and be related to your main idea or thesis statement, which should introduce three main points you will develop in the body of your essay.

    C. Avoid using statements such as, "I am going to talk about . . ." or "This essay is about . . ."

II. Body—three paragraphs

    A. Support the main idea with facts, thoughts, ideas, published poetry, quotes, and other intriguing, insightful material that will captivate your audience.

    B. Present clear images.

    C. If necessary, use a thesaurus to ensure that you are not using the same words repeatedly. Using a word over and over will become monotonous for your readers and distract them from your subject.

III. Conclusion—one paragraph

    A. Restate the main idea in an original way.

    B. You can again use a poem or quotation to leave an impression. However, avoid using this tactic in all three parts of the essay. It may appear repetitious and unoriginal.

    C. Refer to the future in terms of your plans pertaining to the subject of your essay. For example, in an essay describing your future career goals, refer to yourself in the career you have outlined. This reference should project you, and the ideas you presented in the essay, into the future. Refer to the last paragraphs of the three sample essays for an illustration.

SPECIAL NOTE: Using quotations or poems shows that you are well read and imaginative. Be selective and look for quotes that are enlightening and profound.

Early in your scholarship search it is best to prepare two basic essays following the aforementioned format, which can easily be tailored to fit most scholarship application essay requirements. Many essays require descriptions of you and your future career goals. Others may ask you to relate your most memorable experience or to describe the most significant person in your life. A list of typical essay topics appears at the end of this chapter.

WRITING ABOUT YOURSELF: A BASIC DESCRIPTIVE ESSAY

When describing yourself in an essay, select three adjectives that characterize you or your values and support them by telling why these adjectives fit you and your attitude about life. These adjectives will make up the body of your essay and should be used as overall guidelines to provide unity and cohesiveness.

As you elaborate on the descriptive adjectives you have chosen, strive to show the following qualities in your essay:

- Sense of responsibility—Demonstrate your sense of responsibility and diligence. You might convey this by your involvement in extra-curricular activities or through academic achievements.
- Participation in extracurricular activities—In the community and your high school, your out-of-school activities should exhibit initia-tive, leadership skills, and enthusiasm. It is a good idea to have your résumé handy as you write your essays. One of the best ways to stand out from other scholarship applicants is through your activities and personal experiences.
- Your potential for growth—Show how you have grown as a person from participation in extracurricular activities and how your growth could be an asset to the college or university you attend or would like to attend and to your community.

These qualities should be evident in every essay you write. Even if the essay is not a descriptive personal essay, it is still important to show your connection to these qualities.

The four original essay examples in this chapter are creatively written and reflect many of my ideals about the importance of education, the value of communication, and the responsibility of my generation to America. They also won scholarships. It should be noted that each one incorporates some of the same parts, since after writing over thirty different essays I found that the principles of some essays could be easily substituted into others. Recy-cling is perfectly acceptable and can save you time and energy.

The following essays have been reprinted and analyzed according to the five-paragraph format and are presented to assist you in writing essays.

ORIGINAL ESSAY EXAMPLE: "FUTURE CAREER GOALS"

I wrote this essay first. The requirements were to write about my future career goals in relation to a journalism scholarship. The essay revolves around my interest in journalism and describes chronologically how that interest blossomed from early childhood into my young adult years. Clear, original images are presented to reflect my love of journalism. In the conclusion I refer to the future in conjunction with my personal plans and ideals. For variety I added one additional paragraph.

I. Introduction

[1]**Throughout my life, I have been involved in many unique activities, many of which have been oriented in the area of communications and journalism.**[2] Therefore, at an early age, I began to develop a desire to pursue a career in one or both of these fields. This desire has progressed from elementary and middle schools into high school. Anchored to a foundation formed over a span of many years, its roots are now unshakable.

    1. This is the introductory paragraph. It introduces the main idea of the essay, the development of my interest in communications and journalism throughout my school career.
    2. The sentence in bold print is phrased as a simple statement to lead the reader into the essay.

II. Body

[3]**The building blocks of this foundation were laid**[4] in sixth grade when I began to participate in a weekly telecast at Walter P. Jones Elementary School. **As the primary newscaster as well as the student who compiled all the stories for the Jones Elementary news broadcast, I was fascinated by my work. It was challenging and exciting.**[5] As a result, while standing in front of a video camcorder, my **passion for journalism and communications**[6] began. Throughout that year I participated in essay and oratorical contests, debates, and plays. My desire had taken firm root.

    3. Supporting paragraph—shows the development and origin of my interest in journalism and communications.
    4. Imagery—creates an image in the mind of the reader.
    5. Presents facts to support the development of my interest. It also gives evidence of my responsibility and enthusiasm for my work. I point out specific activities I have participated in that support the main idea.

6. Word choice variety—I could have said, "my *interest* in journalism and communications began." *Passion* sounded more exciting and is apt to grab the reader's attention.

[7]Furthermore, in middle school I continued to compete in many contests involving these areas of interest. **The winning oration that I had written for the Optimist International Oratorical Contest (District Level) was one I recited along with several others on Channel 6, here in Macon, Georgia.**[8] **The seedlings of journalistic youth that had been planted in elementary school were mushrooming into boisterous young children of communicative creativity.**[9] **This quote by the English essayist Joseph Addison aptly described my feelings then and still does now. "Words, when well chosen and presented, have so great a force in them that a description often gives us more lively ideas than the sights of the things themselves."**[10]

7. Supporting paragraph.
8. Presentation of fact. Once again I used specific activities and honors from my résumé to support the main idea.
9. Imagery.
10. Quote.

[11]As I progressed into my ninth-grade year in school, my interest in journalism and communication intensified. **Northeast High School encompassed a much broader scope than middle school because it contained the *Salmagundi* literary magazine, the *Golden Star* newspaper, and the *Valhalla* yearbook, which helped me gain more experience in journalism as I became actively involved with an actual publication.**[12] **The children of communicative creativity had now become young adults of journalistic potential.**[13]

11. Supporting paragraph. Outlines the progression of my interests into high school.
12. Fact—this statement shows my potential for growth in this area and that I was aware of that growth. Here, I have also used activities from my résumé to help illustrate my point.
13. Imagery.

III. Conclusion

[14]**I would like to pursue a career in journalism and/or communications because both areas, which are closely interrelated, have become an essential part of my life. Over the years this desire has grown like a sturdy young plant preparing to take over the world or me (whichever comes first).**[15] To me, communication is a marvel because it can open doors into worlds otherwise unknown. **Communication can transport you to the tombs of Egypt, the gold of Africa, or the green hills of Ireland.**[16] Through the power of words, spoken or read, man possesses the ability to convey anything.

14. The first two sentences restate the main idea and form the beginning of the conclusion.
15. Imagery.
16. Imagery.

[17]All of my experiences in writing and speaking have helped me to see the importance of communication; for example, in the field of broadcasting where the presentation of information can influence and motivate. As a child, people and their attitudes provoked curiosity within my young mind. As a young adult, people, their attitudes, and their effect on our changing world fascinate me. Journalism and communications embrace both my curiosity as a child and my fascination as a young adult. **A career in either area would not only satisfy my goals but would I hope make me an asset to my community, state, and eventually the world.**[18]

17. Displays my growth in this area and my potential for future growth.
18. This statement exhibits my commitment to improving the society in which I live and it refers to the future.

ORIGINAL ESSAY EXAMPLE: "WHAT CAN MY GENERATION DO FOR AMERICA?"

This essay was written after I wrote "Future Career Goals." As you can see, parts from that earlier essay were adapted for this one. This topic was specifically requested by a scholarship program for all applicants to write about. It is relayed in chronological order. It is a little different because it weaves in my future career goals but does not include specific activities from my résumé. However, the inclusion of a poem I wrote indirectly shows that one of my interests was writing poetry. I supported the main ideas with clear, original images, and concluded with references to the future. The essay supports the five-paragraph theme and includes a poem for variety.

I. Introduction

[1]**The generation of yesteryear was a generation whose eyes were opened by the dawn of technology and the age of profound change.** The generation of today is one grown accustomed to the passions of technology and one which has **quenched**[2] its thirst from the **wealth**[3] of new knowledge to be learned about the future. The generation of tomorrow, my generation, is one in which a new quest for knowledge will be **launched.**[4] Our **young minds are now bursting with potential.**[5] Yet, our **mature minds will reap the harvest of wisdom**[6] that the generations of yesteryear and today have planted in our thoughts as children and are still planting **as adulthood gradually steals away our carefree days.**[7]

1. Introductory paragraph and statement presenting an idea.
2. Word-choice variety.
3. Word-choice variety.
4. Word-choice variety.
5. Imagery.
6. Imagery.
7. Imagery.

[8]When we were born, my peers and I, we were born into a **country nipping at the heels of progress.**[9] All around us, things were changing rapidly, some changes destined for success, some unfortunately not. Unlike the children of generations before us, **our learning shifted from the responsibility of a few teachers to the new wonder that had appeared on the horizon, the almighty silicon chip.**[10] We began to learn many math and reading skills from the green computer-like screen of Speak'n'Spell and Speak'n'Math, from companies such as Texas Instruments and many others which had

picked up the gauntlet that had been flung to them by the new wonder chip. **We witnessed the arrival of home computers and video games. We enjoyed the pleasure of our own home movies with the aid of video camcorders.**[11] We also witnessed the destruction caused by guns made more and more advanced. Our generation observed an entire **gamut**[12] of change and growth as we grew from childhood into the responsibility and awareness of young adults. **Therefore, my generation is one which is filled with the belief that as a country we must always be aware of reality. In essence we should be aware of our weaknesses as well as our strengths.**[13] For example, in technology, we are lagging behind like a runner in second place, so close to the one in front, often pulling ahead, but repeatedly falling behind at different intervals in time. For America these intervals are not mere minutes, they are years. **My generation can breathe new life into the runner and then the pennant of America will once again stand upon a technological plateau envied throughout the world.**[14]

Recycling Essays

If you have already written general essays about your future career goals or to describe yourself, there is a good chance you can use parts and pieces of them in most of the essays you write later. As you can see in the "What Can My Generation Do for America?" essay I used a section of the "Future Career Goals" essay. I also recycled parts of "Future Career Goals" and another essay, "The Importance of Education," to write the essay for the Coca-Cola Scholarship.

For smaller and community-based scholarship programs and some college and university applications, you may be able to choose your own essay topic. If this is the case, you can use previously written essays, such as descriptive essays, over and over.

8. Second introductory paragraph—this paragraph and the first paragraph are used to present facts, images, opinions, and ideas to introduce the main idea.
9. Imagery.
10. Fact.
11. Fact.
12. Word-choice variety.
13. Main idea.
14. Imagery.

II. Body

[15]We must always be aware of the strengths of America. The bulk lies in its foundation, the generation of yesteryear and today; yet all foundations, no matter how sturdy, are dependent upon the rejuvenating additions of future generations. As a member of one of those generations, I would like to state what I hope will be my addition to the foundation of America. I plan to pursue a career in communications and/or journalism. **To me, communication is a marvel because it can transport you to the tombs of Egypt, the gold of Africa, or the green hills of Ireland. Through the power of words, spoken or read, man possesses the ability to convey anything. A career in either journalism or communications would not only satisfy my goals as a productive member of my generation, it would make me an asset to my community, state, and country.**[16]

15. Supporting paragraph.
16. This section comes from another essay, "Future Career Goals."

[17]Therefore, as a broadcast journalist, I can help to relate the ideas of our country by reporting and interpreting the concepts of technologists, lawyers, doctors, scientists, and the rest of our learned generation. The information I present will have the power to influence and motivate the next generation, twenty years from now, and will eventually mold their contributions to America. My generation, like the generations of yesteryear and today, is merely a reflection of the past and the efforts of our ancestors. A poem I wrote illustrates this statement.

Generations,
sprung from the vital tree of life,
its roots outspread, planted all over the world,
its branches extended throughout the seven continents
hovering over the broad expanse of sea, ocean and lake,
its leaves,
some old,
clinging many years
finally fluttering to the ground to join the nests of
long ago

many,

existing on a plane which could only be termed the middle

suspended between the golden age of yesteryear

and rumblings of the future

and finally,

our generation,

the newly green buds of prosperity

noisy with the rustling of youth

gradually acquiring knowledge,

their freshness and vitality

a symbol of new life

and the herald of change.[18]

17. Supporting paragraph

18. Original poem inserted for variety.

III. Conclusion

[19]**Therefore, it is the responsibility of my generation and generations afterward to expand our learning from history, forge new paths, and leave a trail for the generations of tomorrow to follow.** As our generation looks back on their lives, at the changes that have been wrought in our short lifetimes, it seems as if we are living on a foreign soil. **Yet, our country, which appears to be foreign land now, will seem to be the land of aliens in the future.**[20] Our children and subsequently their children will look on another period of rapid change and growth. **Cars which look like jets without wings at this point in time will be hovering if not flying in the air a few years from now.**[21] Also, like Russia that has one now, we will have fully equipped and manned stations in space. As a result of my generation many changes and improvements will be made. **Then, the runner America resembles will not be one flagging for breath, it will be one who has already won the race and has time to run back and help the others lagging behind.**[22]

19. Concluding paragraph begins with restatement of the main idea.
20. Opinion.
21. Opinion.
22. This statement is an opinion, which presents an image and also refers to the future.

ORIGINAL ESSAY EXAMPLE: "THE IMPORTANCE OF EDUCATION"

This essay was also a specific request by a scholarship program. Applicants were given three choices for topics and I picked this one because of its generality. In short, it could apply to anyone. In order to introduce this essay, I began with a quote as a unique variation. It also incorporates parts of the two previous essays; this one is shortened to two paragraphs. The topic was adequately covered in the three hundred words required.

I. Introduction

[1]The true purpose of education is to cherish and unfold the seed of immortality already sown with us; to develop, to their fullest extent, the capacities of every kind with which God who made us has endowed us.

—John Franklin Jameson

[2]This quote successfully illustrates the value and importance of an education for everyone who inhabits this world. Therefore, it lends **credence**[3] to the idea that **education is the oil upon which we as well-run machines of humanity must operate.**[4] As innocent babies at birth, we begin with a new variation of an old product, the human being. As we grow and progress into adulthood, we continue to refine, rejuvenate, and contribute more and more to the product we were born with. For example, a statement by the English poet George Herbert underlines this point: **"In doing we learn."**[5] **As babies, as children, and eventually as adults, everything we do is a learning process, and as we mature we must continue to update and refine the information we have already absorbed as we travel the winding roads of life.**[6]

1. Introductory quote.
2. Introductory paragraph and also a supporting paragraph.
3. Word-choice variety.
4. Imagery.
5. Quote.
6. Main idea.

II. and III. Body and Conclusion Combined

[7]When we were born, we were born into a country nipping at the heels of progress.[8] In fact, since the dawn of time our world has benefited from mankind's ability to adapt and educate. In time, education may eventually enable us to affect the entire universe in many ways. The generations of yesteryear have laid the basic framework. The generation of today must build upon it by continuing to keep our machines as well as our minds, the powerhouse of the machines well-oiled with education. **Without education, and without the basic fundamentals of learning, mankind cannot operate nor can it prosper.**[9] Eventually humanity will fade away. **Therefore it is the responsibility of my generation and generations afterward to expand our learning from history, forge new paths, and leave a trail for the generations of tomorrow to follow.**[10]

7. Concluding paragraph.
8. Statement regenerated from "What Can My Generation Do for America?"
9. Fact.
10. Main idea restated with a reference to the future.

ORIGINAL ESSAY EXAMPLE FROM THE COCA-COLA SCHOLARSHIP COMPETITION

This essay was different from any that I wrote during my scholarship quest. One of the main reasons why it was so different was the question I had to answer. The question was, "You are at your thirtieth high school reunion. Among your classmates is the president of the United States, yet you are the guest of honor. Why?" The instructions for writing were to demonstrate style, depth and breadth of knowledge, and individuality in 750 words or less. I began the essay by projecting the reader into the audience of my thirtieth high school reunion while I sat at the podium waiting for the speaker to finish introducing me as the keynote speaker and guest of honor.

In this essay, I tried to be as a creative as possible to help it stand out from the many individuals I knew were applying for the same scholarship. Although I stuck to the five-paragraph format, I did it in such a manner it was almost unrecognizable. First I used the introductory paragraphs to set the tone of the essay and establish the reader as part of the audience at the class reunion. I used a second introductory paragraph to help show why I was the guest of honor. Second, I split the paragraphs in the body between the words of the speaker who introduced me and my speech to the audience afterward. The last paragraphs sum up the entire essay and my accomplishments and conclude with an element of surprise that also includes a reference to the future. The element of surprise and my reference to the future was that I expected the President of the United States in the year 2021 to be a woman. The entire essay was also a reference to the future in that none of the activities introduced in the essay had actually happened, although they were loosely based on extracurricular activities from my résumé. The essay was meant to show a blueprint for the future and how I hoped to change the world in such a way that my contributions would be more noteworthy than the president's.

ESSAY TOPIC: You are at your thirtieth high school reunion. Among your classmates is the President of the United States, yet you are the guest of honor. Why?

I. Introduction

[1]The audience spread out before me in a **wave of intense faces**.[2] From my vantage point on the dais I looked out over the top of the **wave at the clock, which appeared to be floating on a blob**,[3] which may have been a wall. The speaker seemed to be clearing his throat an innumerable amount of times. **My attention drifted from the floating clock, the wave of faces, to the rising and falling, bell-like tones of the speaker.**[4] My wandering mind finally focused on the speaker as his voice rose in excitement.

1. First introductory paragraph—sets the tone of the essay and establishes that I was at the class reunion, thinking as I heard someone speak.
2. Imagery.
3. Imagery.
4. Imagery.

[5]"She has helped to turn the youth of America into a productive generation of hardworking individuals almost completely untainted by

drugs with her heartbreaking, often gruesome, yet always informative articles, essays, poems, and any other medium she can find. She has infiltrated the media with her constant television appearances and her numerous newspaper articles. She has approached virtually every school in the country and haunted nearly every street corner, passing out flyers, offering support, and giving on-the-spot interviews. She is known by **destructive dregs of society**[6] as the 'angel of **reform and the herald of change.**'[7]

5. Second introductory paragraph—introduces the primary theme of the essay, showing how I influenced the youth of America through writing and journalism. Also gives details about how I did it.
6. Imagery.
7. Imagery.

II. Body

[8]"She has been chased by the **kingpins of the drug world,**[9] abused by children who have lost hope, and persecuted by adults who are no more than children themselves. Yet she has persevered, and she is slowly winning the battle against drugs, against injustice, and against the **soul-destroying effects of poverty.**[10]

8. Supporting paragraph—supports the main theme of the essay and begins to illustrate how my strategy of change through journalism is working.
9. Imagery.
10. Imagery.

[11]"When our youth began to realize that she was not afraid to walk their streets, that she was unmoved by their rages and filth, and that she remained unaltered from her purpose even in extreme circumstances, they began to respond. And, as you can see by the promise that our youth, the future, now show, they have responded in the most positive ways. I am very proud and pleased to introduce Marianne Ragins." I approached the podium, **showers of praise pelting against my back and down upon my head.**[12] I saw thousands of hands clapping repeatedly. I could feel the thunderous applause reverberating throughout my body. I began to speak.

11. Supporting paragraph—transitions the essay focus from the speaker to me.
12. Imagery.

[13]"Over thirty years ago, I was prepared to take on the world, as I **stepped over the threshold of adolescence**[14] into an adult world plagued by problems which seemed insurmountable. I looked at a nation whose young adults, who should have possessed the potential for greatness, instead held the keys to their downfall and the ultimate decline of that nation. The future of the next generation was bleak. And I, as one of those young adults, became consumed by a desire to beat the statistics and make a difference in some way. At that time, I was not entirely sure of the medium I would use, yet journalism seemed to be a good choice. I remember writing an essay in my senior year which contained this quote by Joseph Addison, **'Words, when well-chosen and presented, have so great a force in them that a description often gives us more lively ideas than the sights of the things themselves.'**[15] I also remember a statement I made in which I said, **'Through the power of words, spoken or read, man possesses the ability to convey anything.'"**[16]

13. Supporting paragraph—begins to explain why I took on this quest.
14. Imagery.
15. Quote—reused from "The Importance of Education."
16. Statement reused from "Future Career Goals."

[17]"Later in my life, I realized that a photograph could accomplish almost as much. Together they made an unbeatable combination. From this **inauspicious**[18] beginning, I set out to tackle the world and solve its problems, starting with my home, America. **The rest, as they say, is history.**[19]

17. Supporting paragraph—begins to introduce photojournalism.
18. Word-choice variety.
19. Memorable cliché.

[20]"As I look back at my ambitious dreams, I cannot believe how optimistic I was. It has dawned on me over the years, that had I not been, I would have become disillusioned very quickly, when so many doors

were slammed in my face, especially when these were the doors of the ones I most wanted to help.

20. Last supporting paragraph.

III. Conclusion

[21]"Throughout my childhood, my family was very concerned with helping to make a positive difference in the lives of others less fortunate and they instilled their concern in me. I would like to believe that I have satisfied their expectations and made a difference in someone's life. **When I see a child, a tiny bud pinched from the clutches of unfair circumstance**,[22] fulfill his dreams as an adult and become a well-adjusted member of society, through my efforts, I know that I have satisfied mine."

21. First concluding paragraph—introduces information from my background.
22. Imagery.

[23]I resumed my seat. The President, seated on my right, flashed a brilliant smile, accompanied by a barely perceptible nod. **I knew she was satisfied as well**.[24]

23. Concluding paragraph.
24. Reference to the future and an element of surprise showing that one of my expectations is that by the year 2021, a woman will be president.

For more information on planning and writing essays for college and scholarship competitions, especially if writing is an unpleasant task for you, visit http://www.scholarshipworkshop.com to learn more about *The Scholarship & College Essay Planning Kit.*

ANSWERING SHORT ESSAY QUESTIONS

For some applications you will be required to answer several questions with short essays. Short essays are usually composed of no more than one hundred words and are generally required in conjunction with a full-length essay. They are primarily concise responses to specific questions on a designated area of the application. Usually you will find these types of questions on applications for competitions consisting of several levels. These questions are designed not only to reveal how effectively you can communicate your thoughts, but also how effectively you can communicate them in a concise and clear manner—hence the designated amount of space in which to write your short essay.

The key points to remember about responding to questions requiring short essays are to answer the questions thoroughly and to strive to keep an upbeat yet serious tone. Once you read a question, jot down possible items to include in your answer. Prioritize them and put the items that are most important at the top. Generally you will be required to answer these essay questions in the spaces allotted, so you may not be able to include everything you think of initially; hence the need for giving some items top priority. The most important concept to remember is to make statements that clearly reflect you. They should be cohesive in their entirety and also reflect a clear thought pattern.

The following are typical short-answer essay questions for many scholarship competitions and for some post-secondary institutions. The italicized items identify the areas in which I specified a major interest. The competition for which the essays were written was for students interested in communications arts.

1. What have you accomplished in *communications* and *English* beyond regular classroom work?

  In the area of communicative arts, my accomplishments have been wide and varied, mainly because my interests are broad. As captain and a member of the Academic Bowl Team, I study all subject areas for competition, especially literature. I have maintained an A average in English for all my school years. I am editor-in-chief of the award-winning *Salmagundi* literary magazine, in which I have been published for the past four years. In 1989, I won First Prize for Best Poem in the State at the Georgia Scholastic Press Association (GSPA) competition at the University of Georgia in Athens. Writing essays for contests is a hobby of mine, and I have won third place for an essay on Alexander Hamilton for the Daughters of the American Revolution (DAR) and first place for one on Sidney Lanier. In the Optimist Club Oratorical contests, I have won first place at the zone level for the past three years and I have repeated my speeches on television. As a member of the Fine Arts and Literary Team, I have been in productions for state contests and participated in reading clubs.

2. Make any statement in support of your selection which you think has not been covered elsewhere in your application.

Quick Tips for Writing Scholarship Essays That Get Noticed

Note: The following tips are essential for essays of 200 words or more. You may not be able to follow these tips for short answer essay questions but try to do so as much as possible.

1. Answer the question. When you're writing an essay, it's easy to ramble. When you finish your first draft, go back and reread the question to make sure you've answered it.
2. Do not give a laundry list of activities—but make sure you write about them. In an essay you can really shine and tell those who read it how you feel about a particular activity. Incorporating your activities—how they have helped to make you into the student or person you are, and how those activities may have helped others—is an important feature to include in your essay and make its content come alive for the readers. Always try to answer these questions when writing about an activity:

   - What is the activity and why are you involved?
   - Who does the activity benefit?
   - How does this activity benefit you or others?

3. Proofread! Proofread! Proofread! Typos and spelling or grammatical errors will not make a good first impression. Don't rely on your computer's spell-check. Reread your essays several times, then ask someone else to read your essays for errors as well.
4. If applicable, include your answers to these questions in your essay:
   - Have you faced any challenges?
   - Have you overcome obstacles or hardships?
   - What makes you unique? For example, a girl on a high school football team would be different.
   - Have your achievements had an incredible impact on others or yourself?
   - Have you significantly changed your life in some way? For example, you transformed from an extremely poor student to a great student.
   - How has your commitment and service to others changed your life or that of another person?

Since I was a little girl, English has been a companion that has followed me. As a child it was a delight, as I revolved in a world of fairy tales, romance, and adventure. As a young adult, literature has become an important bridge to good communication skills that I will utilize throughout my life. I am always writing stories and poems and speaking for contests as well as here at school. Currently I am researching John Steinbeck in terms of the fiftieth anniversary of *The Grapes of Wrath* for a feature article in the *Salmagundi* literary magazine.

Following are some common questions that are asked on scholarship applications for private organizations and colleges or universities. Many of them are seen on standard college and university admissions applications as well.

TYPICAL ESSAY TOPICS FOR SCHOLARSHIP APPLICATIONS FROM PRIVATE ORGANIZATIONS

1. Provide a personal statement. A personal statement is basically a description of yourself, your activities, and your goals.
2. Whom do you admire and respect the most? Why?
3. What activity or program is most meaningful to you? What are your reason(s) for getting involved?
4. What is the most interesting and profound book that you have read recently? Why?
5. What is the worst crisis or problem facing Americans today?
6. Describe your most challenging achievement, how you accomplished it, the obstacles you faced, and its impact on your life.
7. Why should you receive this scholarship or award?
8. Tell us about an extracurricular or volunteer activity that has had the most meaning to you and why.
9. What are your future career goals?

TYPICAL ESSAY TOPICS FOR COLLEGE/UNIVERSITY APPLICATIONS

1. Discuss a political, social, or economic issue that is important to you.
2. Comment on a recent scientific or technological advance and the impact it may have on the future.
3. Why did you choose _____ for a future career choice?

4. Describe your ideal teacher.
5. What is the best advice you have received and why?
6. What characteristics do you have that would contribute to this college or university?

CHECKLIST FOR ESSAY PERFECTION

1. Is your writing truthful and accurate?
2. Did you proofread your printed essay at least three times very carefully? (*Do not proofread exclusively on the computer. Print to thoroughly proofread and avoid mistakes.*)
3. Have you asked someone else to read it?
4. Is your essay neatly presented? (Double-spaced, printed on white paper of good quality, etc.)
5. Did you thoroughly respond to the essay question?
6. Do all the supporting paragraphs contribute to the overall theme of your essay?
7. Have you conveyed your enthusiasm in the presentation of your opinions and ideas?
8. Did you incorporate information about your extracurricular and community service activities in your essay?
9. Did you refer to the future in terms of how you will contribute to a particular university or college, your community, or society overall?
10. Did you use transition words? (A list of transition words is available at the end of this chapter. Read the example essays to see how transition words can be used to make your written words more cohesive.)
11. Use a thesaurus and a dictionary for word variety and appropriate word choice.
12. Help your reader to visualize your subject by using descriptive words and phrases.
13. Show your feelings (positive only, please) about your activities.
14. Don't go over the word limit.

USING TRANSITION WORDS

Use any of the following words to help make your essay more cohesive. They can also help you to establish a flow between your thoughts, words, sentences, and paragraphs.

Transition words that can be used to **contrast** two things. *(You might use one of these when you explain your participation in one activity and another dissimilar activity.)*

    still
    although
    on the other hand
    however
    yet
    otherwise
    even though

Transition words that can be used to **compare** two things. *(You might use one of these when you explain your participation in one activity and another similar or dissimilar activity.)*

    likewise
    also
    while
    in the same way
    as
    similarly

Transition words that can be used to **emphasize a point in your essay.** *("You might use one of these to emphasize why an extracurricular activity is so important to you.")*

    again
    truly
    especially
    for this reason
    to repeat
    in fact
    to emphasize

Transition words that can be used to **conclude or summarize.** *(You might use one of these in your last paragraph.)*

    finally
    as a result

to sum up
in conclusion
last
therefore
all in all
because

Transition words that can be used to **add information.** *(You may need these if you are discussing more than one event or activity in your essay.)*

again	moreover	next
another	additionally	finally
for instance	as well	in addition
for example	besides	furthermore
also	along with	
and	other	

Transition words that can be used to **explain further or clarify.** *(You may need these if you want to add more information or details about an event or activity in your essay.)*

that is	in other words	previously
for instance	as stated	

Transition words that can be used to show **time.** *(You might use these for explaining when you participated in certain activities.)*

while	later	now
first	next	yesterday
meanwhile	at	about
soon	third	during
then	tomorrow	until
after	afterward	throughout
second	as soon as	finally
today	before	

12

SCHOLARSHIP INTERVIEWING TIPS

It's better to be prepared for an opportunity and
not have one, than to have an opportunity and not
be prepared.

—Whitney Young

Your research is done and your applications have been submitted—now it's
time to prepare for interviews. For scholarship awards ranging from $50
to $1,000, usually nonrenewable, interviews are generally not required.
However, for many college/university-sponsored as well as large corporate-
sponsored scholarships an interview (sometimes more than one, depending
on how steep the competition) is typically the final step. If you have made
it to the interview stage you've probably managed to impress at least one
person on a scholarship review committee. That's great! Now let's get you
prepared for some of the most typical interview questions.

When are interviews required?

Interviews are normally required for the largest scholarship competitions that
award the most money.

Some colleges and universities may require an interview, especially if you are
being considered for one of their scholarships.

For smaller scholarships, usually for $2,500 or lower, you probably will not have
to interview.

Interviewers are primarily concerned with meeting you to reinforce the image they have formed through your application, résumé, essays, and recommendations. In the interview stage interviewers mainly want to get to know the person behind the words: *you*. They want you to elaborate on items that stand out immediately on your application or résumé. For example, a line stating that you are an avid birdwatcher or that you helped with the presidential campaign for the current officeholder would attract attention. Items such as these are bound to raise questions. Be prepared to talk about yourself and any activities in an enthusiastic and professional manner.

Interviewers want to meet a self-confident, mature, articulate individual who will present a positive image as one of their scholarship recipients. Scholarship recipients are usually considered to be the "cream of the crop" at most universities. Therefore, most scholarship interviewers are looking for well-groomed and well-rounded students who will represent the organization or institution well.

WHAT TO WEAR

In The Scholarship Workshop presentation and boot camp, as well as my motivational speeches and seminars, I advise scholarship interviewees to wear what feels and looks comfortable yet still presents a professional image. Whether your interview is in person or online via webcam, you should look professional. If you're doing a Web-based interview, clean your camera lens, clean the room you will be in, test your audio, and make sure you're in a quiet area with no family members or friends to make noise or distract you.

Gentlemen: Understated tie and jacket, pale, pastel shirt, dark shoes, no earrings or excessive jewelry. Wear matching dress socks. Do not wear white athletic socks or socks in patterns that could be distracting if seen. No flashy, loud colors unless you're a clothes designer. If you dress the part, draw attention to this fact—don't let them think it's not deliberate. Do not wear sneakers. Polished, dark leather shoes are the most appropriate for interviews.

Ladies: Pale or dark muted colors, feminine suit or dress. Avoid flashy colors or designs. Hosiery, if worn, should be flesh-colored with no designs. No excessive jewelry or spike heels. Wear something classic, definitely not flamboyant, unless your future career goal is that of a designer. If you dress the part, make sure to draw attention to this fact so that your interviewers will know it's deliberate.

PREPARATION TIPS

Depending upon the stage of competition (semifinalist or finalist) and the amount of money involved, I have discovered a general pattern. The more money and prestige of a college/university or program, the more interviewers a program enlists. For large scholarship competitions that have several levels there is an average of four to six interviewers per interviewee. You are usually invited into a midsize room and seated at one end of a table with interviewers flanking both sides. If they give you time to relax and get your bearings, use it wisely and remember that they are not out to get you. All the interviewers I encountered were very nice. So be calm.

If you're interviewing via telephone, have a few notes for reference and your résumé in front of you before the call. Review them quickly before the interview but turn them over before you start. You don't want to be tempted to read your answers. You also don't want to get sidetracked by looking at them and missing a question or comment made by the interviewer.

Tip 1

Interviewers usually ask questions about what you have written on your application or in your essays, so always review your copy before you go into an interview. Recommendations from teachers, counselors, and administrators are usually not mentioned, so don't be worried that they will bring up what was said about you. They are primarily concerned with you and your responses.

Tip 2

Be well versed about your activities and various roles you play in the community and in your school.

Tip 3

Talk about your hobbies and special talents in a clear, knowledgeable manner. If asked, you should explain how you became interested in a particular hobby. If you profess to be a writer you should know about the subject and also have in mind a few writers you admire and the reasons why.

Tip 4

Whether or not you like to read or write, you should be able to name a favorite author or book in your conversation with the interviewer and explain why that book or author is your favorite.

Tip 5

Be informed about current events. Form an opinion on prominent issues and have a solid basis for your standpoint. If one of the activities you list in your résumé is formal debating, some interviewers will attempt to debate a particular point with you.

Tip 6

The answers you give should be well thought out. When you are asked a question, take a few seconds to contemplate your response and then give a well-prepared answer. In addition, always try to use positive, decisive words. Take every chance possible to show your leadership skills, potential, and self-motivation in your answers. Approach questions as if you are giving an impromptu speech.

Steps for impromptu speeches include restating the question; stating your position; giving two or three supporting points; and in conclusion, restating the question and your position again. As you end an impromptu speech, clarify your statements and emphasize important ideas. Then reaffirm your answer.

Alternatively you could answer questions by doing the following: (1) Outline the situation, (2) Explain your action, (3) Whom did it benefit— you or someone else? For example, the question or subject could be, "Tell me about yourself." Your answer following these instructions could be: (1) I am a highly motivated individual. (2) For example, I have organized several book drives for the Happy Sunrise Senior Citizens' Home in

Macon for the past three years. (3) As a coordinator for this activity, I have honed my leadership and interpersonal skills, which will really help me as a student at XYZ College and in the future. But most important, I've been able to donate thousands of books through my efforts that have really helped to brighten the days of those at the senior citizens' home.

Tip 7

Usually competitions requiring interviews last more than one day, and program administrators often give you a chance to meet your interviewers at a reception or in some type of informal setting. Don't miss the chance to talk to them, and if—and only if—you admire something the interviewer has done that is public knowledge, don't hesitate to say why you admire his or her actions. Usually interviewers are public officials, published writers, or upper-level managers of corporations, so you may already know a little bit about them. If you have prior knowledge, try to use it to your advantage. Most scholarship programs don't tell you who your interviewers are before you arrive at a competition, but if they do, try to research your interviewers thoroughly. Also research the mission, goals, and history of the scholarship program or organization. Sometimes you may be asked to tell an interviewer what you know about the company or the program and you'll want to have an answer. Visiting an organization's social media platforms such as Facebook or Twitter may help.

Tip 8

Relax. Remember, many of the interviewers themselves have gone through what you are going through, and they understand your feelings. Therefore, don't be so nervous that you can barely talk. If you have a dynamic application (which you should, if you have followed the advice of this book) then the judges who interview you will go out of their way to make you feel comfortable, because they are interested in the person behind the words of that application.

Tip 9

Arrive at the interview site early. This not only demonstrates your enthusiasm and responsibility, it also eliminates the added nervousness that rushing causes. Arriving early will give you time to collect your thoughts and relax. Hence your demeanor will be calm and tranquil as you walk into the interview. If your interview is via telephone or online with a webcam, be seated where you plan to have the interview early. Once again, this can help to minimize any nervousness due to rushing or trying to find a quiet place.

Tip 10

Wait until you are invited to sit down. If you are not asked, stand up for the entire interview.

Tip 11

Practice a firm handshake while looking the person in the eye. This conveys honesty, confidence, and respect.

Tip 12

Send handwritten thank-you notes to your interviewer(s) after the interview. The note should express your gratitude for the time he/she/they spent with you. It should also reaffirm your interest in the institution or program. If a handwritten note is not possible due to time or lack of an address, you can send an e-mail. But keep in mind that handwritten notes will help you stand out since very few people write thank-you notes anymore.

Tip 13

At the interview, look your interviewer(s) in the eye at regular intervals. Frequent eye contact is silent communication with the interviewer(s) that expresses your confidence and knowledge. Shifty eyes display dishonesty. A tendency to look at the ceiling shows unfamiliarity with a topic.

Tip 14

If you have brought along some of your work to show, place it on a table near you. If there is no table, place it by your side on the floor along with your handbag or briefcase, if you have one.

Tip 15

Be pleasant and smile often.

Tip 16

Before the interview, eliminate unnecessary stressful activities. For example, if driving is stressful for you, do not drive to your interview. Also, avoid speaking with someone who habitually upsets you. Instead, talk to someone who always puts a smile on your face and has a positive attitude or listen to one of your favorite upbeat songs in the car.

Tip 17

Since most large scholarship competitions where more money is involved usually require students to travel to a central location for interviews and tours of either the scholarship organization or campus, join the Frequent Flyer programs of major airlines, especially those that service your city the most. Even if you don't ultimately win the scholarship you will earn Frequent Flyer miles, which can add up if accumulated from several scholarship trips. They could earn you a free flight to use for a student excursion or a trip home later.

Tip 18

Do an Internet search to research frequently asked questions for well-known scholarship competitions. Reviewing questions asked in the past can help you get prepared.

Tip 19

Do a practice or mock interview using the *Frequently Asked Questions* at the end of this chapter. Or add some questions you may have found online as per Tip 18.

Tip 20

If you are doing a Web-based or telephone interview where you initiate the call, be exactly on time. If the interviewer is in another time zone, use http://www.time.gov to know the exact time in the time zone where you are calling. Promptness helps to convey your professionalism and interest.

FREQUENTLY ASKED QUESTIONS DURING AN INTERVIEW

1. What would you contribute to the community of _____ College/University?
2. In what activities would you involve yourself?
3. Why would you like to attend _____ College/University?
4. If you could do anything in the world right now, what would you do?
5. Who's your favorite author? Why? If you could have dinner with him or her, what would you ask?
6. Whom do you admire most in the world? Why? This person can be someone you haven't met but would like to meet.
7. What do you see yourself doing in ten or fifteen years?
8. What sets you apart from the other applicants?
9. What will be your contribution to the world?
10. What do you plan to do with your career as a _____?
11. Is there anything you would like to add that we haven't covered?
    Hint: Have a prepared statement for this part, because they almost always ask it. If they don't, say that you would like to add something once they conclude their questions. At this point you should clear up any statements you might have made that sounded misleading and reiterate your leadership abilities, potential, and motivation. Memorize your connection with those qualities for all interviews. If you thought of three adjectives that describe you, as suggested in chapter 11, "Writing Scholarship Essays That Get Noticed," you could use one for your parting words. For example, if your adjectives were "self-motivated," "spirited," and "service-oriented," you could say: "Yes. I am a self-motivated individual who has participated in many activities that exhibit this quality, such as starting a chapter of Mu Alpha Theta at my high school in my freshman year and starting a book drive for the local senior citizens' home. If I win this scholarship I hope to continue using this attribute as a student at XYZ University, in my future career, and in the community where I will eventually reside."

13

THE ART OF GETTING GOOD RECOMMENDATIONS
AND REQUESTING NOMINATIONS

> The doors we open and close each day decide the
> lives we live.
>
> —Flora Whittemore

Many applications require recommendations from at least three reference sources. You should prepare a list of references that include your high school's supervising principal or another key administrator, an English teacher, an employer (if you have one), and your minister, rabbi, or other spiritual leader. I recommend English teachers because they have usually mastered the art of writing recommendations for their students, but any teacher can do this, especially one who knows you well. You should have at least ten others on the list who will write recommendations for you, to achieve variety and avoid tiring the main contributors on your list. When you make your list, include e-mail addresses for each person you plan to ask. For online recommendation systems that some organizations use, an e-mail address will be required.

To make the process of requesting recommendations easier, draft a version of a recommendation letter stressing key points about your character that those you ask can use as a reference. If you've included someone on your recommendations list for an online application that uses an online recommendation system, send a heads-up e-mail along with a recommendation request letter (shown at the end of this chapter) so they know what to expect and when.

My counselor has asked me to write my own recommendation for her to sign. What do you think of this?

At my workshops I have been asked this question by students or parents who are speaking on behalf of their children. They tell me that some counselors, due to lack of time, are requesting that students write their own recommendations for the counselors to approve and then sign. In a survey of scholarship sponsors and administrators, many of whom supplied information for use in this book, 90 percent of them strongly disagreed with this practice. If your counselor asks you to do this, consider giving him/her copies of recommendations that have been written for you by others. This should provide a good view of you from someone else's perspective, which may help your counselor create a recommendation for you. Also make sure you give the counselor a copy of your résumé for a good overall view of you and your activities, which can also help in drafting a good recommendation.

It is important to note that many programs frown upon including recommendations from friends, relatives, or neighbors. Be careful when including recommendations of this type. Speak with your counselor or a teacher first to get his or her opinion before sending one.

For the recommendations you need to complete your applications, mark special dates on your calendar at least three to four weeks before an application deadline. Set checkpoint dates each week afterward, to remind your references of a letter they may need to complete. You can use *The Scholarship Monthly Planner* (see http://www.scholarshipworkshop.com) to help you with reminders. With some online recommendation systems, used by many colleges, universities, and scholarship programs, an e-mail reminder is automatically sent to those you've asked for recommendations. Also, be certain that when you ask someone to write a recommendation for you, give them a copy of your résumé (discussed in chapter 9) to use for reference.

If an application requires that a recommendation be returned directly to the program instead of to you, give the person recommending you a pre-addressed envelope with the correct postage. Once a person has completed your recommendation, make sure to send him or her a handwritten thank-you note. Or at least send an e-mail thank-you, although a handwritten note is more memorable.

You should also make a recommendation chart for future reference. The sample that follows will give you an idea of how to do it. With a chart you

Quick Reminder

For all recommendations you should do the following:

- Give the person a description of the scholarship and/or program.
- Include your résumé and extras.
- Include a SASE with two stamps if needed.
- Ask at least three to four weeks before the deadline.
- Follow up with each person you ask, using your recommendation chart to stay organized.
- Send handwritten thank-you notes (preferred) or e-mails to each person once they have completed your letter.

can easily see who will be best to write a particular type of recommendation. For example, if you need a recommendation that emphasizes your leadership ability, you would approach Mr. B. Gooden, who knows of your skills from the time you spent as captain of the team for which he was an advisor. If you need a recommendation that emphasizes your position as an outstanding member of your high school community, then you would contact Ms. S. Samson. This chart will also keep you informed of who has written recommendations for you in the past and who is currently preparing one. This chart might also come in handy when asking teachers and administrators to submit nominations for you to scholarship programs that don't place limits on the number of nominations submitted from a high school, college, or state.

Although putting people on your recommendation list may seem like an easy task, you should give it careful thought. Not only should you think about how the person knows you, you should also think about whether he or she has have the ability to write well—or even enjoys writing. Even though other qualifications about a student may not be wonderful, an outstanding recommendation could help to sway some scholarship committees. Likewise, a poor recommendation could actually hurt some students who have outstanding supporting documents in every other area. For example, as a scholarship committee member, I once saw a recommendation that was badly photocopied and addressed to the wrong scholarship program. It received quite a few negative comments from the scholarship selection committee. When the individual rating points were tallied in the recommendation area, the student did not receive a very high number. On another

Sample Recommendation Chart

TABLE 9

Name of person, e-mail address, and telephone number	Has this person done a recommendation for me before?	Is this person doing a recommendation for me now? When is it due?	How does this person know of me?
Mrs. A. Brown Example@scholarship workshop.com (703) 555-1212	No	No	Neighbor. Retired English teacher. I have volunteered as an assistant with her Girl Scout troop for six years.
Mr. B. Gooden Gooden@scholarship workshop.com (703) 555-1212	Yes	Yes	Advisor of Science Bowl team. I have been the captain of the team for two years.
Ms. S. Samson Samson@scholarship workshop.com (703) 555-1212	Yes	Yes. Due on 2/28/2028.	Principal of my high school.
Mrs. F. Champion Champion@scholarship workshop.com (703) 555-1212	Yes	No	Red Cross youth coordinator. I have been a volunteer for four years.

scholarship committee, I saw a recommendation that wasn't even considered because the entire letter consisted of one line that basically stated that the person highly recommended the student—and that was it! Also consider that if your résumé is filled with information about one significant activity, some committees might question why you don't have a recommendation from someone associated with the activity.

SAMPLE LETTER REQUESTING A RECOMMENDATION

Your street address°
Your city, state, and zip code

October 15, 20XX

Name
Title
Address
City, State, Zip Code

Dear *Name of Person You Are Requesting a Recommendation From:*

I am interested in applying for the *XYZ Example Scholarship Program.* This award is *sponsored by XYZ Example Foundation. As a high school junior interested in pursuing my education beyond high school, I am eligible to apply for this scholarship.* However, in order to do so, I need your help. This scholarship program requires *three recommendation letters.* Since you are the *advisor for the XYZ program* that I have been involved in for the *past two years,* I would like to request a recommendation letter from you for my application to this scholarship program.

I have enclosed the following information to assist you in writing a recommendation for me:

- My résumé
- Additional information about me and other activities in which I am involved
- A stamped envelope pre-addressed to send to the program

The recommendation must be completed and sent by *November 30, 20XX.* If you have any questions or need additional information to complete this recommendation, you can reach me at *(XXX) XXX-XXXX* or via e-mail at *xyz@aol.com.*

Thank you in advance for your help,
Your signature
Your name, typed

If an online recommendation request will be sent by the program, change your letter to read as follows: "Since you are the advisor for the XYZ program that I have been involved in for the past two years, I would like to request

---

°Items in italics and small type should be changed.

a recommendation letter from you for my application to this scholarship program. This request will be sent automatically to your e-mail address directly from the organization with instructions for how to complete *the recommendation* and submit *it online*." If the request will be made via e-mail, delete the line in the example referencing an enclosed pre-addressed envelope.

ASKING FOR A NOMINATION

Asking for a nomination is similar to requesting a recommendation. Unlike recommendations, however, scholarship programs that require nominations usually limit the number of nominations from schools, states, or regions. As a result, if you're not already being considered as a student who should be nominated for a specific program or scholarship competition, you'll have to make your interest known and convince one person— your principal, president of your college or university, the financial aid office, your counselor, or a nominating committee—not only of your desire to be considered but also of your qualifications. You'll have to give compelling reasons why you should be nominated over others being considered. For example, if you were asking for a nomination, you should first get all the information you can about the program, especially the eligibility requirements and characteristics of past winners. Then if you're eligible and you believe your background and skills fit the specific criteria the program is looking for, you should request a nomination from the appropriate person or office at your school. You can do so by submitting a letter similar to the sample letter that follows. If you are nominated, make sure to say thank-you.

SAMPLE LETTER REQUESTING A NOMINATION

Your street address°
Your city, state, and zip code

October 2, 20XX

Name
Title
Address
City, State, Zip Code

Dear *Name of Person You Are Requesting a Nomination From:*

As a student who has been actively involved for the past *four* years in various *leadership, community*, and *professional development* activities, I am interested in being nominated for the *XYZ Example Program*. As you may already be aware, this is an award *open to high school students who have a consistent record of academic excellence, been active in school programs, and been recognized as leaders by peers and instructors*. I believe I am eligible for this award based on my experience in numerous extracurricular activities such as *Student Council, DECA, FBLA, and as the creator for the Students Helping Students program, our after-school tutoring program run by students in Honors and AP courses.*

I have enclosed the following information to assist you in determining whether my nomination for this program is appropriate:

- My résumé
- Additional information about me and other activities in which I am involved

Nominations are required by *November 15, 20XX*. If you have any questions or need additional information, you can reach me at *(XXX) XXX-XXXX* or via e-mail at *xyz@aol.com*. I really appreciate your consideration.

Thank you,
Your signature
Your name, typed

°Items in italics and small type should be changed.

14

SCHOLARSHIPS AND AWARDS FOR COMMUNITY SERVICE, VOLUNTEERING, AND WORK

Much effort, much prosperity.

—Euripides

If you've been pretty active in helping out in your community during high school, then you not only have an edge in many of the general scholarship programs; you have opened another avenue of scholarship opportunity for yourself. Why? Because some scholarship programs are based almost entirely on your assistance to others—so you could win a scholarship primarily because of your community service and volunteer work. And for some programs that aren't based on community service you can get extra points in your favor because your community service can help distinguish you from others competing for the same scholarship.

Also, some scholarships and sources of college financial aid are awarded based on your willingness to work, sometimes in areas where there is a shortage of talent and human resources. Some examples are nursing- or teacher-oriented loan forgiveness programs or scholarships. For example, with a loan forgiveness program, any loans you used to complete your degree may be forgiven (meaning you don't have to pay them back) or partially forgiven if you agree to work for a period of time, usually in a specific area. To find out what's available in your state, go to chapter 5, "Financial Aid Forms and Help from the Government with College Expenses," to get the contact information for the financial aid agency in your state.

Other programs that offer scholarships or monetary awards for your service include the National Guard or even a community service–oriented program such as AmeriCorps. If you're willing to give up some time either before, after, or during your pursuit of an educational degree, one of these programs just might work for you.

Here a few scholarships that are based almost entirely on community service or that require a service commitment once you complete your degree program and/or an internship requirement during your college career.

A Few Important Items to Remember

- Deadlines change frequently. It is best to visit the website for a listed scholarship program or award for the most current deadline. Or you can review *The Scholarship Monthly Planner* on our website at http://www .scholarshipworkshop.com, which has deadlines updated frequently. Also join us on Facebook (http://www.facebook.com/scholarshipworkshop) and follow us on Twitter (@ScholarshipWork) for frequent alerts on new scholarships and upcoming deadlines. Join our mailing list to get the latest updates about scholarships and other helpful information. Text "SCHOLARSHIP INFO" to 22828 or visit our website to join.
- Do not send blanket e-mails requesting an application from an organization. Many organizations have a large number of people interested in their programs and may not respond.
- Do not rely solely on the following scholarship list. It is best to use the strategies described in chapter 2, "The Scholarship Search: Discovering Hidden Treasures," chapter 3, "Using the Internet and Social Media in Your Scholarship Search," and chapter 4, "The Local Scholarship Search: Finding Scholarships in Your Backyard," to uncover the most opportunities available to you.
- Some programs change their application requirements and eligibility guidelines. Please review their websites carefully for any changes.
- If you've reviewed their website thoroughly and still have questions, use the e-mail address and/or telephone number, if provided.
- Programs can and do stop awarding scholarships or suspend their scholarship programs. Don't get discouraged. You can still find available scholarships. But please know that there are no guarantees about the availability of a given scholarship, or that you will win it.

SCHOLARSHIPS FOR VOLUNTEERING, COMMUNITY SERVICE, AND WORK
AMERICORPS EDUCATION AWARD

AmeriCorps
1201 New York Avenue NW
Washington, DC 20525
(202) 606-5000

Website: http://www.americorps.gov

Additional Information: Students who participate in the AmeriCorps program are eligible to receive an education award of up to $5,550 based on the number of years or hours they spend in service. The award can be used to do one or a combination of the following:

- Repay qualified existing or future student loans
- Pay all or part of the current education expenses to attend a qualified institution of higher education, including some vocational programs
- Pay expenses while participating in an approved school-to-work program

Some colleges and universities will match the amount of your AmeriCorps Education Award.

BOREN UNDERGRADUATE SCHOLARSHIPS

Boren Scholarships and Fellowships
Institute of International Education, 7th Floor
1400 K Street, NW
Washington, DC 20005-2403
(800) 618-NSEP
E-mail: boren@iie.org
Website: http://www.borenawards.org
Social Media: Follow Boren Awards on Twitter and Facebook
Additional Information: Boren Scholarships are available for U.S. undergraduate students to study abroad in areas of the world that are important to U.S. interests. This scholarship will provide up to $20,000 and applies to underrepresented areas such as Africa, Asia, Central and Eastern Europe, Eurasia, Latin America, and the Middle East. The Boren Scholarships specifically exclude Western Europe, Canada, Australia, and New Zealand. For a complete list of countries included, visit the website. Boren Scholarships also have a preference for students who are interested in studying less commonly taught languages, including but not limited to Arabic, Chinese, Korean, Portuguese, Russian, and Swahili. The program prefers students who plan to work in the federal government. The National Security Education Program (NSEP) funds the Boren Scholarships. Those interested in the scholarship should clearly identify how their study abroad, as well as their future academic and career goals, will contribute to U.S. national security as broadly defined. This is a service-based scholarship program. You will incur

an NSEP service requirement to work in the federal government for at least one year or for the length of time you received the scholarship, whichever is longer. See the website for additional program requirements and deadlines.

BOREN GRADUATE FELLOWSHIPS

Boren Scholarships and Fellowships
Institute of International Education, 7th Floor
1400 K Street NW
Washington, DC 20005-2403
(800) 618-NSEP
E-mail: boren@iie.org
Website: http://www.borenawards.org
Social Media: Follow Boren Awards on Twitter and Facebook.
Additional Information: Boren Graduate Fellowships are available for U.S. graduate students to study abroad in areas of the world critical to U.S. interests. The fellowship will provide up to $30,000 and is intended to help graduate students add an international language component to their graduate studies. Boren Fellowships support study and research in Africa, Asia, Central and Eastern Europe, Eurasia, Latin America, and the Middle East and exclude Western Europe, Canada, Australia, and New Zealand. For a complete list of countries that are included, visit the website. Boren Fellowships have a preference for students who want to pursue study in less commonly taught languages, including but not limited to Arabic, Chinese, Korean, Portuguese, Russian, and Swahili. This is a service-based fellowship program. You will incur an NSEP service requirement to work in the federal government for at least one year or for the length of time you received the scholarship, whichever is longer. See the website for additional program requirements and deadlines.

CARING AWARDS

The Caring Institute
228 7th Street SE
Washington, DC 20003
(202) 547-4273
E-mail: info@caring.org
Website: http://www.caring-institute.org
Additional Information: If you haven't yet graduated from high school

or reached your eighteenth birthday, you can be nominated for a $2,000 Caring Award from the Caring Institute if you've been deeply involved in activities that show your depth of caring for your community, state, region, or the world. Winners of this award are considered role models with an extraordinary sense of public service. Past winners have received this award for activities such as founding organizations designed to serve others and/or making a meaningful impact in their high school, community, state, or beyond.

CENTRAL INTELLIGENCE AGENCY—UNDERGRADUATE SCHOLARSHIP PROGRAM

Central Intelligence Agency
Office of Public Affairs
Washington, DC 20505
(703) 482-0623
Website: http://www.cia.gov (click on *Student Opportunities* or search for "Scholarship")
Additional Information: This program provides scholarships of up to $18,000 per school year for tuition, fees, books, and supplies as well as paid summer employment with the CIA. It is available to high school seniors planning to enroll in a four- or five-year college program and also to college sophomores. If awarded the scholarship, you must maintain full-time college status and a minimum cumulative 3.0 GPA. After your college graduation you must agree to continue employment with the Agency, which will require relocation to Washington, D.C., for a period of 1.5 times the length of your college sponsorship. For example, if you received the scholarship for four years, then you must work for the agency for a period of six years. The Agency will pay the cost of transportation between your school and the D.C. area and provide a housing allowance during your summer employment. To apply, you must be a U.S. citizen; 18 years of age by April of your senior year (for high school seniors); have scores of at least 1500 on the SAT or 21 on the ACT (for high school seniors); have a 3.0 (on a 4.0 scale) GPA or higher; demonstrate financial need (household income ceiling of $70,000 for a family of four, and $80,000 for a family of five or more); and meet the same employment standards as permanent employees. The deadline is October 15 of each year.

THE CHRISTOPHER REEVE AWARD

Heart of America Foundation
401 F Street NW, Suite 325
Washington, DC 20001
E-mail: scholarships@heartofamerica.org
Website: http://www.heartofamerica.org
Additional Information: The Heart of America Foundation recognizes outstanding students who are high school seniors or younger with the Christopher Reeve Award. The award is a $1,000 scholarship from Merriam-Webster, Inc. to be used for your higher education. To be eligible for this award, you must have demonstrated tremendous compassion and caring in service to your community. You must also be nominated. The Heart of America Foundation is a national nonprofit headquartered in Washington, D.C., whose goal is to combine volunteerism and literacy. The organization's focus is to provide children in need nationwide with the tools to read, succeed, and make a difference. See website for additional details.

COMCAST LEADERS AND ACHIEVERS SCHOLARSHIP

Website: http://corporate.comcast.com/our-values/community-investment/youth-education-leadership or see http://corporate.comcast.com (search for "Leaders and Achievers" or "scholarship")
Additional Information: This scholarship rewards high school seniors for their leadership, community involvement, and academic achievement. To enter this competition, you must live in a community that is served by Comcast and be nominated by your high school principal or guidance counselor. Winners are recognized with one-time scholarship grants of $1,000 from the Comcast Foundation to pursue higher education, which can include vocational or technical school. See website or consult your counselor for additional details. (See chapter 13 for additional information about requesting nominations.)

JESSE BROWN MEMORIAL YOUTH SCHOLARSHIP PROGRAM

Disabled American Veterans
Voluntary Services Department
P.O. Box 14301
Cincinnati, OH 45250-0301

Advice on Self-Nominations

If possible, always request that someone else nominate you for an award or scholarship. It adds more strength to your nomination if an organization can see the admiration someone else has for you and your dedication to community service or other achievements. It lends validation to your efforts as well. Always consider your competition: if your self-nomination is compared to another student who has been nominated by someone else and all things are equal, the other student may win the award over you.

Don't be afraid to ask for help. Many may be willing to nominate you. Give those you ask your résumé and tell the person about the award as well as the mission and goals of the scholarship program. See chapter 13 for additional help on requesting nominations.

Alternatively, if you have tried to get a recommendation from someone but have not been successful in time to make the program's deadline, go ahead and self-nominate. If the program offers you that opportunity, take advantage of it if you must.

An Interesting Note

One of the students who attended The Scholarship Workshop presentation (http://www.scholarshipworkshop.com) in Arlington, Virginia, won the Kohl's Scholarship when she was eleven years old. Imagine having $10,000 won before you even start your high school scholarship search!

Website: http://www.dav.org (click on *Voluntary Services\Jesse Brown Scholarship*) or link to http://www.dav.org/volunteers/Scholarship.aspx
Additional Information: The Jesse Brown Memorial Youth Scholarship Program was established to recognize youth volunteers age 21 or younger who have volunteered for a minimum of 100 hours at a VA medical center during the previous calendar year. You must be nominated for this program and write a 750-word essay titled "What Volunteering Has Meant to Me." You can also nominate yourself. See the website for additional eligibility criteria, current deadlines, and the nomination form. Scholarship amounts can be up to $20,000.

KOHL'S CARES SCHOLARSHIP PROGRAM

(319) 341-2932 (indicate you need information for the Kohl's Cares Scholarship Program)
E-mail: kohls@act.org
Website: http://www.kohlskids.com or http://www.kohlscorporation.com/ CommunityRelations/scholarship/index.asp
Additional Information: If you are a student between the ages of 6 and 18 who has made a difference in your community, you can be nominated to win a $10,000 scholarship from Kohl's Corporation. They have been awarding these scholarships since 2001 to recognize young students who have made amazing contributions in their communities. The deadline is usually mid-March of every year. Since the program's inception, Kohl's has awarded more than $3.5 million in scholarships and prizes. If you're interested in this program, see the website for details. If you're wondering how to get nominated, see chapter 13, "The Art of Getting Good Recommendations and Requesting Nominations."

THE PRUDENTIAL SPIRIT OF COMMUNITY AWARDS

Website: http://spirit.prudential.com
Additional Information: Sponsored by Prudential in partnership with the National Association of Secondary School Principals (NASSP), this program recognizes students in grades 5 through 12 who have demonstrated exemplary community service. Local honorees are selected at participating schools and organizations in November, and from these winners, two state honorees are chosen from each state and the District of Columbia. State honorees receive an award of $1,000, an engraved silver medallion, and an all-expense-paid trip to Washington, D.C. National honorees receive an additional award of $5,000, an engraved gold medallion, a crystal trophy for their school or organization, and a $5,000 grant from the Prudential Foundation to donate to a nonprofit charitable organization of their choice. Although this program is not officially a scholarship, the funds you win, if you're an avid volunteer, could add nicely to the money in your college fund.

SODEXO FOUNDATION

Stephen J. Brady STOP Hunger Scholarships
9801 Washingtonian Blvd.

Gaithersburg, MD 20878

(615) 320-3149 (indicate your call is about the Sodexo Foundation Stephen J. Brady STOP Hunger Scholarships)

E-mail: http://STOPHunger@applyists.com

Website: http://www.sodexofoundation.org (click on *Scholarships*)

Additional Information: Stephen J. Brady STOP Hunger Scholarships are open to students in kindergarten through graduate school who are enrolled in an accredited educational institution in the United States. Students must have performed unpaid volunteer service to stop hunger within the last 12 months. Additional consideration is given to students working to fight childhood hunger. A community service recommendation form, a type of form used to independently verify your community service, is required for this application so ask recommenders, who must not be family members, for their recommendations early. For more on requesting recommendations, see chapter 13.

UNITED STATES PEACE CORPS

Paul D. Coverdell Peace Corps Headquarters
1111 20th Street NW
Washington, DC 20526
(855) 855-1961

Website: http://www.peacecorps.org

Additional Information: Two to four years of service in the U.S. Peace Corps can eliminate a significant part of your college loan debt. Fifteen percent of Perkins Loans, including interest, can be canceled for each of your first and second years of service and a 20 percent loan cancellation is available for your third and fourth years of service. Please note that while in the Peace Corps, you are not paid a salary. Instead, you receive a stipend to cover basic necessities such as food, housing expenses, and local transportation. Although the amount of the stipend varies from country to country, you will receive enough money to live at the same level as the people you serve. Your personal expenses, including any souvenirs or vacation travel, are your responsibility. The Peace Corps will also pay for your transportation to and from your country of service and provide you with complete medical and dental care. When you complete your service you will receive a "readjustment allowance" of $7,425, which can be used to pay college expenses or help in transitioning back home.

While you are a volunteer, you can defer repayment of your Stafford,

Perkins, Federal Consolidation, and Direct loans, as well as some commercial loans. However, the Peace Corps does not grant deferments, cancellations, or grace periods for government or private loans. These must be obtained directly from your lender. Peace Corps recruiters will explain the rules that apply to each type of loan. Answers to questions concerning outstanding student loans are also on the website.

U.S. OFFICE OF PERSONNEL MANAGEMENT (OPM) SCHOLARSHIP FOR SERVICE

Scholarship for Service Program Office
200 Granby Street, Suite 500
Norfolk, VA 23510-1886
E-mail: sfs@opm.gov
Website: http://www.sfs.opm.gov/
Additional Information: If you are willing to pursue your course of studies with an emphasis in information assurance (coursework focusing on the protection of sensitive data), attend one of the participating institutions, and are willing to work for the federal government once you graduate, then this may be just the program for you. The OPM Scholarship for Service program, funded through grants awarded by the National Science Foundation, offers college funding in exchange for a student's commitment to work for a federal agency designated by OPM after graduation. The program is designed to increase the number of federal information assurance professionals in order to better protect the government's critical information infrastructure. The program provides scholarships that fund the typical costs that students pay for books, tuition, and room and board while attending an approved institution of higher learning; for example, stipends of up to $20,000 per year for undergraduates, $25,000 for master's degree students, and $30,000 per year for doctoral candidates. Each institution manages the actual amounts of funding for participating students. Approved institutions include Carnegie Mellon University, Florida State University, Georgia Tech, University of Idaho, Iowa State University, Hampton University, Mississippi State University, Naval Postgraduate School, University of North Carolina—Charlotte, Norwich University, Polytechnic University of New York, Purdue University, Syracuse University, the University of Tulsa, and many others. In addition to the full-ride scholarships, students in the program also receive stipends of up to $8,000 for undergraduates and $12,000 for graduate students. While still in school, students who are

funded for more than a year will also serve a paid internship at a federal agency. The agency may offer students other paid employment while they are on scholarship if it does not interfere with their studies. In exchange for the scholarship (including the stipend), students agree to work for a federal, state, local, or tribal government organization for a period equivalent to the length of the scholarship or one year, whichever is longer.

NATIONAL INSTITUTES OF HEALTH (NIH) UNDERGRADUATE SCHOLARSHIP PROGRAM

Undergraduate Scholarship Program
Office of Intramural Training and Education
National Institutes of Health—DHHS
2 Center Drive, Building 2, Room 2E24
Bethesda, MD 20892-0230
(301) 594-3318
E-mail: ugsp@nih.gov
Website: https://www.training.nih.gov/programs/ugsp
Additional Information: This program awards scholarships on a competitive basis of up to $20,000 per academic year for tuition, educational expenses, and reasonable living expenses to students from disadvantaged backgrounds who are committed to careers in biomedical, behavioral, and social science health-related research. Scholarships are awarded for one year and you can reapply for up to four additional years. To be eligible for this program, you must be a U.S. citizen or qualified non-citizen; be enrolled or accepted for enrollment as a full-time student for the upcoming academic year at an accredited undergraduate institution; and have a grade point average of 3.3 on a 4.0 scale (or be within the top 5 percent of your class). You must also come from a low-income family. Consult the website or contact the program for specific income guidelines based on the size of your family.

For each full or partial scholarship year after you receive this award, you will incur two types of service obligation: a Summer Laboratory Experience in which you will serve 10 weeks as a paid summer research employee in an NIH research laboratory, and one year of full-time employment in an NIH research laboratory for each year you received the scholarship.

NATIONAL HEALTH SERVICE CORPS (NHSC)

U.S. Department of Health and Human Services
Bureau of Clinician Recruitment and Service
5600 Fishers Lane
Rockville, MD 20857
(800) 221-9393
E-mail: GetHelp@hrsa.gov
Website: http://nhsc.hrsa.gov
Additional Information: This program offers two ways you can use your medical- or health-related training to help the nation's underserved and at the same time benefit from the scholarship program to pay the costs of your medical training or the loan repayment program to pay off your qualifying education loans.

- *NHSC Scholarship Program*—This is a competitive scholarship program designed for students committed to providing primary health care in communities of greatest need. As a recipient of this scholarship you must serve where you are most needed upon completion of your training. To be eligible for the program, you must be a U.S. citizen enrolled or accepted for enrollment in a fully accredited U.S. medical or dental school, or a nurse practitioner or nurse-midwife, or physician's assistant program. Check the website for complete eligibility requirements. After your training, you must serve a period of one year for each year of support you received, with a two-year minimum commitment. The program provides the following benefits for up to four years of education: payment of tuition and fees; twelve monthly stipend payments per year; and payment of other reasonable educational expenses, such as books, supplies, and equipment.

NHSC LOAN REPAYMENT PROGRAMS

The National Health Service Corps (NHSC) loan repayment program (LRP) offers primary health care providers loan repayment assistance in return for working or teaching in a rural, urban, or frontier community that has limited access to care. These areas, throughout the United States, are termed health professional shortage areas (HPSAs). Based upon the HPSA score and whether you are working or teaching in that area you can get up to $60,000. There is a minimum two- or four-year service commitment depending upon whether you are full-time or half-time. There are three different types of loan repayment programs:

- *NHSC Loan Repayment Program*—Available for licensed primary care medical, dental, and mental and behavioral health providers who are employed or seeking employment at approved sites.
- *NHSC Students to Service Loan Repayment Program*—Available for allopathic and osteopathic medical students in their fourth year at an accredited medical school.
- *State Loan Repayment Program*—Available for primary care providers who are deemed eligible in participating states. Providers should apply to the individual state program. See your state's financial aid agency or higher education commission. Refer to chapter 5, "Financial Aid Forms and Help from the Government with College Expenses," for information on your state financial aid agency.

15

UNUSUAL SCHOLARSHIP OPPORTUNITIES

*Your living is determined not so much by what life
brings to you as by the attitude you bring to life.*

—John Homer Miller

There are many different types of scholarships offered for a variety of reasons, as you've seen throughout this book. Some are even more different than others. Although many of these scholarships are quite specific in nature and could go unused because few or none qualify, it illustrates that scholarships can be established and awarded for all types of reasons, not just grades and test scores. Who knows? If you fall into one of the categories the scholarship or award is designed to target, this opportunity just may have been waiting for you! If you want to find out if an organization has a Facebook page, Twitter handle, or YouTube channel, use the strategies in chapter 3, "Using the Internet and Social Media in Your Scholarship Search." Also refer to chapter 14 to review "A Few Important Items to Remember."

SCHOLARSHIPS BY ASSOCIATION

Dr. Angela E. Grant Memorial Scholarship Fund
P.O. Box 84481
Pearland, TX 77584
Website: http://www.drangelagrantscholarship.org
Additional Information: In memory of Dr. Angela E. Grant, this scholarship seeks to recognize future scholars who have been affected by cancer and who are dedicated to community service and celebrating the spirit

of life. High school seniors or current college students who are cancer survivors or who have an immediate family member who has been diagnosed with cancer are eligible to apply.

Kathern F. Gruber Scholarship Program
Blinded Veterans Association
477 H Street NW
Washington, DC 20001-2694
(202) 371-8880
Website: http://www.bva.org
Additional Information: This scholarship is available to dependent children and spouses of veterans of the U.S. Armed Forces who are blind (either service or non-service connected). You do not need to be a member of the Blinded Veterans Association.

Millie Brother Scholarship
ATTN: CODA Scholarship Committee
Dr. Jennie E. Pyers, Associate Professor of Psychology
Wellesley College
106 Central Street
Wellesley, MA 02481
Website: http://www.coda-international.org (please visit website to confirm current address for applications)
Additional Information: Open to high school seniors who are hearing children of deaf parents. Award is based on essay, reference letters, and transcript. Winning essays are published in the CODA newsletter and are available online. Award amounts up to $3,000.

LEFT-HANDED STUDENTS PLEASE STAND UP!

Frederick and Mary F. Beckley Scholarship
Juniata College
Office of Student Financial Planning
1700 Moore Street
Huntington, PA 16652
(877) JUNIATA
Website: http://www.juniata.edu
Additional Information: Inspired by the love story of two left-handed

students at Juniata College, Frederick and Mary Beckley, this scholarship of $1,000 to $1,500 a year is available to sophomores, juniors, or seniors attending Juniata, a small liberal arts college located in Huntington, Pennsylvania.

WILLING TO STAND OUT AT YOUR PROM?

"Stuck at Prom" Contest
ShurTech Brands
32150 Just Imagine Drive
Avon, OH 44011
Website: http://duckbrand.com/promotions/stuck-at-prom
Facebook: http://www.facebook.com/ducktape
Additional Information: Contest is open to U.S. citizens who are high school students at least fourteen years of age who attend a high school prom in the spring wearing complete attire or accessories made from Duck-brand duct tape. You can enter through the Facebook page or by visiting the contest website. Entrants must enter as a couple (two individuals) and submit a color photograph in their prom attire along with other documentation. The winning couple will be selected based on a variety of criteria, including originality, workmanship, quantity of Duck tape used, use of colors, and creative use of accessories. Award amounts range from $500 to $5,000. Contest begins in early to mid-March and ends in early July.

DOES THE FUTURE GRAB YOUR INTEREST?

L. Ron Hubbard's Writers of the Future Contest
P.O. Box 1630
Los Angeles, CA 90078
(323) 466-3310
Website: http://www.writersofthefuture.com or http://www.writersofthefuture.com/contest
Additional Information: The L. Ron Hubbard Writers of the Future Contest is an ongoing competition designed to discover new and amateur writers of science fiction. You can submit all types of science fiction, fantasy, and horror with fantastic elements. The contest does not require an entry fee and you retain all rights to your story. All entries must be submitted in

English, previously unpublished in professional media, and be original works of prose, up to 17,000 words in length. Open to U.S. citizens and non-citizens. Award amounts range from $500 to $5,000.

L. Ron Hubbard's Illustrators of the Future Contest
P.O. Box 3190
Los Angeles, CA 90078
(323) 466-3310
Website: http://www.writersofthefuture.com or http://www.writersofthe future.com/contest
Additional Information: The contest is open to entrants from all nations, though written communication must be in English. You can submit all themes of science fiction and fantasy illustrations. No entry fee is required and you retain all rights to your entries. Award amounts range from $500 to $5,000.

BEING SHORT OR CALLED A LITTLE PERSON CAN HELP WITH SCHOLARSHIPS

Little People of America Scholarship
250 El Camino Real, Suite 201
Tustin, CA 92780
(888) LPA-2001 (English and Spanish) or (714) 368-3689
E-mail: info@lpaonline.org
Website: http://www.lpaonline.org
Additional Information: The Little People of America (LPA) is an association of people who are 4'10" or less in height, family members, or those who have demonstrated an interest in issues relating to dwarfism. Scholarships are awarded, to the following, in order of preference: members of LPA who have a medically diagnosed form of dwarfism; immediate family members of dwarfs who are also paid members of LPA; people with dwarfism who are not members of LPA; disabled students in general; non-disabled students who can demonstrate a need for financial educational assistance.

INTERESTED IN SHOOTING MARBLES TO WIN A SCHOLARSHIP?

National Marbles Tournament Competition
10908 Bornedale Drive
Hyattsville, MD 20783

Website: http://nationalmarblestournament.org

Additional Information: The annual National Marbles Tournament, held in June of each year, provides up to $5,000 in scholarships, prizes, and various awards to mibsters (marble shooters) ages 7 to 14. The tournament began in 1922 and is operated by a national committee composed of individuals throughout the country with a common interest in the game of marbles. Mibsters play more than 1,200 games over the four-day tournament. The competition starts at the local level.

BEING TALL COULD HELP YOU WIN A SCHOLARSHIP

Tall Clubs International Scholarship Program
3417 Iberia Street
Las Vegas, NV 89146

Website: http://www.tall.org (click on *Scholarships*) or visit http://tall.org/tci-acts/scholarships-2/

Additional Information: Tall Clubs International (TCI) offers a scholarship for tall students, funded by the TCI foundation. Individual chapters of TCI may also offer local awards. In order to be considered for a TCI scholarship you must contact a TCI Member Club (visit the website for a list of locations—pick the one closest to you for contact). If they do not have an active Student Scholarship campaign, they can appoint you as their candidate. To qualify for the scholarship, you must be at least 5'10" if you're a woman or 6'2" if you're a man.

CREATE A FASHION DESIGN FOR THE PLUS-SIZE

NAAFA (National Association to Advance Fat Acceptance)
P.O. Box 4662
Foster City, CA 94404-0662
(916) 558-6880

Website: http://www.naafa.org

Additional Information: The National Association to Advance Fat Acceptance offers a $1,000 scholarship to encourage student fashion designers to specialize in the design of fashions for the plus-size body. They also offer a $1,000 scholarship to encourage further study for undergraduates and graduates across a variety of disciplines that incorporate Health At Every Size (HAES) tenets and principles. Visit the website for more details.

MADE ANY GARMENTS WITH WOOL LATELY?

National Make It with Wool Competition
Marie Lehfeldt, National Director
Box 175
Lavina, MT 59046
Website: http://www.sheepusa.org or http://www.makeitwithwool.com
/home.html
Additional Information: Awards of up to $2,000 are available in this competition designed to promote the beauty and versatility of wool fabrics and yarns; to encourage personal creativity in sewing, knitting, and crocheting with wool fabrics and yarns; to recognize creative skills; and to help you develop life skills such as responsibility and good sportsmanship. As a contestant you must select, construct, and model your own garments. If you made the garment for someone else, the intended wearer must model the garments. Entries are judged on appropriateness to contestant's lifestyle, coordination of fabric/yarn with garment style and design, presentation, quality, and creativity. Contest is open to age groups ranging from preteens, 12 and under, to adults, 25 and older. For more information send a stamped, self-addressed envelope to the contest address above.

ARE YOU MAJORING IN LANGUAGE STUDY WITH A MINOR IN KLINGON?

Klingon Language Institute Kor Memorial Scholarship
P.O. Box 794
Blue Bell, PA 19422 USA
Website: http://www.kli.org/scholarship/
Additional Information: The purpose of the Kor Memorial Scholarship is to recognize and encourage scholarship in fields of language study. Familiarity with Klingon or other constructed languages is not required but creative and innovative applicants are preferred. This scholarship is a $500 award made available to an undergraduate or graduate student each year. The recipient is announced yearly at the annual conference of the KLI, the *qep'a'*. Students must be nominated by their academic department chairs/heads and/or deans. Each may submit only one undergraduate and one graduate nomination for consideration per award year. To be nominated you must be a full-time student at the time of the award and in a program leading to a degree in a field of language study.

DO YOU ABSTAIN FROM SMOKING, ATTEND BUCKNELL, AND AVOID STRENUOUS ATHLETIC ACTIVITY?

Gertrude J. Deppen Scholarship Fund
Bucknell University
Lewisburg, PA 17837
Website: http://www.bucknell.edu (click on *Endowed Scholarships*)
Additional Information: The Gertrude J. Deppen Scholarship Fund
was established for students attending Bucknell University by Joseph H.
Deppen, Class of 1900, in memory of his sister Gertrude, Class of 1902.
The fund is meant to provide scholarships to those who have resided in
Mount Carmel for ten years, who are graduates of Mount Carmel Public
High School, who are not habitual users of tobacco, liquor, and narcot-
ics, and do not participate in strenuous athletic contests. Award amount
varies.

WHAT'S IN A NAME? SCHOLARSHIPS BASED SOLELY ON YOUR LAST NAME

Zolp Scholarships
Financial Aid Office
Sullivan Center
6339 N. Sheridan Road
Chicago, IL 60626
(773) 508-7704
Website: http://www.luc.edu (click on *Other Scholarships*)
Additional Information: If you're Catholic and your last name is Zolp
you could be eligible for a scholarship award toward tuition at Loyola University. The last name of Zolp must appear on your birth certificate and
confirmation certificate. Award amount varies.

SERIOUS ABOUT GRAPES AND WINE?

American Society for Enology and Viticulture
ASEV Scholarship Committee
P.O. Box 1855

Davis, CA 95617-1855

(530) 753-3142

E-mail: society@asev.org

Website: http://www.asev.org (click on *Scholarship Program*) or http://asev.org/scholarship-program/

Additional Information: ASEV awards scholarships to North American (Canada, Mexico, or the United States) undergraduate juniors and seniors or graduate students pursuing a degree in enology, viticulture, or in a curriculum emphasizing a science basic to the wine and grape industry. The awards are not in predetermined amounts and may vary from year to year. Previous applicants and recipients are eligible to reapply each year in open competition with new applicants.

DO SPORES, MOLD, AND FUNGI INTEREST YOU?

Mycological Society of America

Website: http://www.msafungi.org (see *Awards*)

Additional Information: Applicants must be student members of the MSA, candidates for a Ph.D., and must reside during their fellowship tenure in any Canadian or U.S. university. Previous recipients of these fellowships are not eligible to apply. Applicants for these awards are evaluated on the basis of their scholastic merit, research ability, and promise shown as a mycologist. The fellowships are supplementary grants and may be used in any way to further your graduate studies. Award amounts up to $2,000.

CAN YOU CALL A DUCK?

Chick and Sophie Major Memorial Duck Calling Contest

Website: http://stuttgartarkansas.com (click on *Duck Festival\Scholarship Contest*)

Additional Information: The contest is open to any high school senior in the United States who can call ducks. The scholarships can be used to further your education in any field. As a contestant you will have 90 seconds to use four calls—hail, feed, comeback, and mating, and you must follow the rules ordained by the World's Championship Duck Calling Contest. There is no entry fee for this contest. Award amounts range from $500 to $2,000.

GOLF CADDIES LISTEN UP!

Evans Scholars Foundation
1 Briar Road
Golf, IL 60029
(847) 724-4600
Website: http://www.wgaesf.org (click on *Scholarships*)
Additional Information: The Evans Scholars Foundation provides full tuition and housing grants to golf caddies. Most Evans Scholars attend one of the fourteen universities where the Evans Scholars Foundation owns and operates a chapter house. Applicants for these scholarships must be nominated by their golf clubs, and have a documented caddie record with a minimum of two years of outstanding service. You must also have an excellent high school academic record, have a B average in college prepa-ratory classes, and submit your ACT scores. Applicants must also demon-strate significant financial need.

Ouimet Scholarship
(774) 430-9090
Website: http://www.ouimet.org
Additional Information: The Ouimet Scholarship is a renewable, need-based, competitive undergraduate scholarship. To be eligible, you must have completed two years of service to golf as a caddy or helper in the pro shop, or course operations superintendent at a golf club in Massachusetts. This does not include off-course driving range, miniature golf, or country club dining room, kitchen, office, pool, or tennis employees. You can apply as a high school senior or as a college undergraduate. See website to request an application. The deadline is usually in early December. Ouimet awards range from $1,500 to $15,000 per year.

SCHOLARSHIPS AND REDUCED TUITION FOR PARENTS
OF TWINS AND OTHER MULTIPLES

Illinois Organization of Mothers of Twins Clubs, Inc.
Website: http://www.iomotc.org
Additional Information: The Illinois Organization of Mothers of Twins Clubs awards four scholarships each year to mothers and fathers of multiples

in Illinois who are continuing their education. To be eligible for these scholarships, parents of multiples must be enrolled in a junior or four-year college or university, be residents of Illinois, and be involved in community service or be a member of a mothers of twins club. Award amount varies.

Although not technically a scholarship for multiples, many colleges and universities will offer reduced tuition if more than one student from a family attends during the same time period. Contact the financial aid office of the colleges and universities your children are interested in attending for specific information about opportunities that may be available to you.

HAVE YOU BEEN AFFECTED BY THE DEATH OF PARENT?

LIFE Lessons Scholarship Program
LIFE Foundation
Website: http://www.lifehappens.org/life-lessons/
Additional Information: The LIFE Foundation sponsors the LIFE Lessons Scholarship Program for college students and college-bound high school seniors. Those interested in the program can submit essays or videos about how the death of a parent or guardian impacted their lives. You could win up to $15,000 in scholarship money. Note: If your parent died as a result of cancer, see the Dr. Angela E. Grant Memorial Scholarship Fund earlier in this chapter.

DO YOU LIKE YOUR VEGGIES?

Vegetarian Resource Group
P.O. Box 1463
Baltimore, MD 21203
(410) 366-8343
E-mail: vrg@vrg.org
Website: http://www.vrg.org
Additional Information: Each year the Vegetarian Resource Group awards $10,000 (2 awards of $5,000 each) in college scholarship money to graduating U.S. high school seniors who have promoted vegetarianism in their high schools and/or their communities. Vegetarians do not eat meat, fish, or fowl. Early submission is encouraged. Entries will be judged on

having shown compassion, courage, and a strong commitment to promoting a peaceful world through a vegetarian diet/lifestyle.

DO YOU HAVE AN INTRIGUING INVENTION?

Collegiate Inventors Competition
(800) 968-4332, option 5
E-mail: collegiate@invent.org
Website: http://www.invent.org
Additional Information: This competition recognizes, encourages, and rewards students to share their inventive ideas with the world. To compete, you must be enrolled (or have been enrolled) full-time in any U.S. or Canadian college or university at least part of the 12-month period prior to the date the entry is submitted. For teams, which can have up to four students, at least one member must meet the full-time eligibility criteria. The other team members must have been enrolled on a part-time basis (at a minimum) sometime during the 12-month period prior to the date the entry is submitted. Your entry must be your original idea and product. See website for complete entry requirements. Awards vary up to $15,000.

LUCKY? AND GOOD AT TAKING OPEN-BOOK TESTS?

American Fire Sprinkler Association Scholarship
Second Chance Scholarship Contest
Website: http://www.afsascholarship.org
Additional Information: Current college or trade school students can win $1,000 in the AFSA Second Chance Scholarship Contest. To enter, you must read the "Fire Sprinkler Essay" about automatic fire sprinklers. Then complete the registration page with all requested information. Finally, you need to take a ten-question multiple-choice test, which is open book. For each question you answer correctly, you will get one entry into a drawing for one of three $1,000 scholarships. For each question answered incorrectly, you will be given one more chance at the end of the exam to answer those questions correctly. A total of ten (10) entries into the drawing is possible if you answer all ten questions correctly.

16

SCHOLARSHIPS FOR THE UNNOTICED ATHLETE

It is impossible to win the race unless you venture to run, impossible to win a victory unless you dare to battle.

—Richard M. De Vos

If you've got athletic talent but haven't been noticed by a college recruiter for a team, you may still have an opportunity to get an athletic scholarship, even if you're not the star player for your high school football or basketball team. If you are, then you probably don't need to be reading this section because there's a good chance you have more than your fair share of scholarship money being waved at you. Just as most people don't think much about local or regional scholarship opportunities that could be in their backyard, many parents and students don't think about the scholarship opportunities that could be available for sports like lacrosse, bowling, volleyball, or gymnastics.

If you're pretty good but maybe not the best athlete *and* have considerable experience playing a particular sport, you also have a chance to win scholarship money to showcase your talent on a college team. But, in order to tap in to these dollars, you will definitely need to promote yourself heavily.

Don't forget to keep your options open by continuing to search for scholarships that don't depend on your athletic skills. Even if your grades aren't the most perfect, scholarships from private companies and associations as well as colleges and universities can be won based on your overall qualifications (community and extracurricular activities, work experience, essay, etc.). The key to being successful at having your college expenses covered by scholarships is to keep your options open. This means that if you have athletic qualifications, use them to pursue athletic scholarships but still go after every other scholarship for which you meet the eligibility requirements.

Don't Forget: Athletic Associations and Organizations Could Offer You a Scholarship

Make sure to check all types of organizations for scholarship and award opportunities as discussed in chapter 2, "The Scholarship Search: Discovering Hidden Treasures." If you're an athlete you should also check athletic-focused organizations. For example, the Northern Virginia Athletic Directors, Administrators and Coaches Association will award $2,000 scholarships to senior scholar-athletes with financial needs. Candidates are judged on high school athletic participation, academic performance, positive involvement in the school and community, writing skills, and a recommendation.

To launch an athletic scholarship search, you should do as follows:

1. Learn the Athletic Recruiting Process

Athletic coaches at colleges and universities may get information about you from your high school coach, alumni, news articles, or through recruiting services and scouting reports. Or, they may have certain cities they habitually keep an eye on by studying local news from certain areas, or communicating with coaches at target high schools, or visiting sports camps or competitions held during the summer.

Once coaches at colleges and universities have an idea of recruitable talent, they may send questionnaires to you asking about your background and athletic talents. Based on your responses to this or follow-up telephone calls or e-mails, they may actually visit your school or next sporting event to see you in action, evaluate your talents, and see if you might be a match for the sports program at their college or university. You might also receive a personal visit from a coach before or after a sporting event in which you participate. This is generally the process for larger sports programs and highly recruited students. You may also want to consult websites such as http://www.collegesportsscholarships.com and the NCAA Eligibility Center (http://www.eligibilitycenter.org).

2. Research and Gather Information

Meet with the coach of your high school team. Discuss your eligibility and options for obtaining a sports scholarship at various colleges and universities. Ask about scholarships that are offered in your sports area. For example, if you bowl, your coach might give you information on scholarships offered through the United States Bowling Congress (http://www .bowl.com) or he or she may give you information on colleges and universities that have teams for this sport. If your coach doesn't have this information available, ask if he or she can help you out with finding some. You might also visit http://www.ncaachampionships.com to see a list of schools and the areas where they have winning teams. If the college or university is listed as a championship winner in one or more years for bowling, then that school would be a good candidate for you to approach about scholarship opportunities. Also consult books such as *The Student Athlete's Guide to Getting Recruited: How to Win Scholarships, Attract Colleges and Excel as an Athlete* by Stewart Brown and *Peterson's Four-Year Colleges* (http:// www.petersons.com), which have comprehensive information about athletic programs.

If you're getting started early, perhaps in the 7th, 8th, or 9th grades, you may want to participate on more than one athletic team. For example, if you notice that lacrosse is played and championships have been won at most of the schools you would be interested in attending and you're also interested in pursuing your volleyball talents on a team, you may want to play on both the volleyball and the lacrosse team as a high school student in order to maximize your chances for scholarships once you graduate from high school. A caution, however: this approach could result in your not being able to hone your skills as much as if you only played one sport. It could also detract from your ability to handle your regular classwork in addition to extracurricular and/or community activities. Discuss with your parents which sport you can or should continue playing. Sports require a lot of time, energy, and money from both you and your parents, so figure out the sports area you should focus on as soon as possible.

Once you have a list of schools that participate heavily in your best sport, visit each college or university's website to get the correct spelling and name of the coach for your sport. You can also call the athletic department for each school. If you do call, be prepared for the chance that they may put you through to the coach. Have your résumé handy and your three adjectives in mind (refer to chapter 11, "Writing Scholarship Essays That Get Noticed," and chapter 12, "Scholarship Interviewing Tips"), especially as they relate to your sports experience just in case you need to answer questions on the spot.

3. Prepare Your Athletic Scholarship Marketing Package

Athletic Scholarship Marketing Package

- Résumé and cover letter
- Business card
- High school coaches' recommendation
- Website (if you're starting the process early)
- News clippings
- Video (YouTube and CD-based)

- Create a résumé that strongly outlines your athletic accomplishments. You can use the résumé you have written for your general scholarship search as outlined in chapter 9, "Writing Your Scholarship Résumé," but you should move your athletic section to the top. In the section detailing your athletic accomplishments, make sure to include any letters earned, records you've broken, sports statistics for your team while you've been on it, honors you've received, and titles of articles in which your name has been mentioned in connection with the sport. If you've attended any sports camps or clinics, you should also outline these in your résumé.

For example, the section might look like the following:

Personal Statistics (*include personal statistics that are important to your sport such as weight for wrestling or height for basketball*)
    Weight: 157 lbs.

Athletic Achievements and History (*include special accomplishments*)
Wrestling: 7th–12th grades
    Captain, 11th–12th grades
    "Local wrestling team does it again!"—*The Telegraph* article, January 10, 2026
    Southern Regional Wrestling Sports Camp—Atlanta, Georgia, Summer 2027, 2028
    State Champion—2026, 2027
    State Finalist—2028

- Write a letter detailing your sports-related accomplishments and your academic interests. This should be included with the résumé you send to the coaches at the schools on your list. The summary of your athletic information should include height, weight, times, other statistics, and any athletic awards. Also include a summary of your academic information as well; for example, your grade point average or class rank. Your letter should resemble a cover letter that your parents or someone who's entering the workforce might write for a job.

- Include a business card with your letter. There are many ways to create inexpensive, professional-looking business cards. Visit your local Office Depot, OfficeMax, or Staples to find one that fits your budget. The following example shows information you may want to include on your business card:

Fiction Athlete

Northeast High School—Macon, Georgia
Expected Graduation—May 2028, Current GPA: 3.0
Expected Field of Study—Business Economics
Sports Experience—Wrestling, Soccer

Personal Statistics—Height (5'10"); Weight (157 lbs.)

Athletic Highlights—Wrestling State Champion—2026, 2027
Wrestling State Finalist—2028

P.O. Box 176 • Centreville, VA 20122 • (703) 579-4245
Website: http://www.marianneraginsports.com • E-mail: mnr@aol.com*

- Create a Web or Facebook page to send coaches for more updated information about you. You may want to include a picture on your website, your personal statistics, your résumé, articles and clippings, academic interests, and so on. This would come in handy if you need to send a last-minute e-mail to a coach who has just come up on your radar screen and you don't have time to send a full set of your marketing materials. A website can also be helpful if you start promoting yourself when you're a sophomore or junior. Keep your site updated with current information about yourself and your accomplishments. Once you have done this, you can send coaches periodic e-mails or call to let them know there is new information about your achievements they may want to see. Also, with digital cameras, your parents probably have pictures of you in action that you can post on your website to make it more interesting.
- Ask your high school coach to write a general letter of recommendation for you to include with your marketing package.

---

* This is a fictional website and e-mail address.

- Last, include one or two news clippings about you and/or your high school team.

4. GET THE BALL ROLLING

Once you have completed your list of schools and coaches you want to target and you have your athletic scholarship marketing materials complete, it's time to start stuffing envelopes. Alternatively, you could send a PDF of the information in your marketing package and a link to your website and YouTube video via e-mail. If you're a senior, you should do this as soon as possible so you'll have time to visit colleges and meet coaches personally. If the coaches show interest, you may decide to attend a summer sports camp and invite them to see you in action. If you're not a senior, you can still send your materials early, especially if you send a business card and have a website. As you progress on the road to becoming a senior they can refer to your business card and keep an eye on you through your website. You can also periodically call coaches and send update letters or e-mails to let them know you're still interested in their school and hope to obtain an athletic scholarship.

5. FOLLOW UP

About two to three weeks later, follow up your letters and e-mails with calls (particularly for the schools in which you are most interested) to inquire if they have received your materials and have any questions for you.

17

SCHOLARSHIPS FOR MINORITIES: WHAT'S THE DIFFERENCE IN A MINORITY SCHOLARSHIP HUNT?

> Everybody, my friend, everybody lives for
> something better to come. That's why we want to
> be considerate of every man—who knows what's in
> him, why he was born and what he can do?
>
> —Maxim Gorky

The hunt for scholarships by members of minority groups involves all of the steps discussed throughout this book. As a minority member, you will still have to research scholarships to find those that you are eligible to win. You will still need to get organized and submit complete applications with the usual required essays. Essentially everything that a non-minority applicant must do, you must do also. The primary difference between the scholarship hunt for minorities and one for a non-minority is that the pool of scholarship money you can win is much larger. Not only can you apply for general scholarships, you can also apply for scholarships only open to minorities. Many organizations, colleges, and universities attempt to level the educational playing field by offering special scholarships to members of minority groups only. One of the reasons for this is that minorities are typically underrepresented at the post-secondary educational level. For instance, let's look at three different scholarships. If you are Native American, you can apply for a mainstream scholarship like the Coca-Cola Scholarship. You can also apply for a scholarship available only to Native Americans such as the one offered by the Presbyterian Church U.S.A. You would also be eligible for a general minority scholarship such as the Jackie Robinson scholarship. As a result, being a Native American qualifies you for all three scholarships, an African American would be qualified for two of the scholarships, and a non-minority would be qualified for the Coca-Cola Scholarship alone.

Moreover, as a member of a minority group, you have a lot of bargaining power at schools where minorities are traditionally underrepresented. Therefore you should be able to get funds specially designated to increase the minority population and diversity of a college or university. Being a member of a minority group is a fact you should make clear to financial aid offices, if unknown, especially if you are appealing for more scholarship aid.

If you are in a minority group you should make the most of the scholarship opportunities currently available to you. It is very important to remember that although the pool of funds for the minority is larger, it is still necessary to use all of the strategies discussed throughout this book to win them. Review chapters 2, 3, and 4 thoroughly to learn how to uncover as many scholarship opportunities as you can.

On some college campuses you may be considered a minority only as it relates to the student population at that particular campus. For example, this might be the case for a Caucasian student at a "historically black college or university" (HBCU). In some instances, you may be able to get a scholarship specifically at that institution because you add diversity to the campus.

Following is an abbreviated list of scholarship and fellowship opportunities for various minority groups. Although many of the scholarships shown here can be used for any field of study, some opportunities are specific to some of the most popular fields of study such as law, medicine, and business. Please check Appendix A for additional minority opportunities, and if you are pursuing law, medical school, or an advanced business degree (MBA), visit chapter 19, "Going Beyond the Undergraduate Degree— Paying for Graduate School."

GENERAL MINORITY SCHOLARSHIP AND FELLOWSHIP OPPORTUNITIES

See "A Few Important Items to Remember" on page 181 for additional tips.

AMERICAN ASSOCIATION OF UNIVERSITY WOMEN (AAUW) EDUCATIONAL FOUNDATION

Selected Professions Fellowships
c/o ACT, Inc.

P.O. Box 4030
Iowa City, IA 52243-4030
(319) 337-1716, ext. 60
E-mail: aauw@act.org
Website: http://www.aauw.org
Additional Information: See chapter 19.

CONGRESSIONAL BLACK CAUCUS FOUNDATION SCHOLARSHIPS

1720 Massachusetts Avenue NW
Washington, DC 20036
(202) 263-2800
E-mail: info@cbcfinc.org
Social Media: The Congressional Black Caucus Foundation is on Facebook, Twitter, LinkedIn, and YouTube
Website: http://www.cbcfinc.org (click on *Scholarships*)
Additional Information: The Congressional Black Caucus (CBC) Foundation administers the CBC Louis Stokes Health Scholars Program; CBC Spouses Education Scholarship Fund; the CBC Spouses Education Scholarship; the CBC Spouses Visual Arts Scholarship; CBC Spouses Heineken USA Performing Arts Scholarship; and the CBC General Mills Health Scholarship. You must reside or attend school in a congressional district represented by a Congressional Black Caucus member to be eligible for these scholarships. Each scholarship has different eligibility requirements and award amounts vary but can be as much as $8,000.

CONSORTIUM FOR GRADUATE STUDY IN MANAGEMENT

Consortium Fellowships
229 Chesterfield Business Parkway
Chesterfield, MO 63005
(636) 681-5553
E-mail: recruiting@cgsm.org
Website: http://www.cgsm.org
Additional Information: The Consortium for Graduate Study in Management is an alliance of business schools and corporate entities. The Consortium provides merit-based full fellowships and offers professional development opportunities to U.S. citizens who are African American, His-

panic American, or Native American (American Indian or Alaskan Native) to assist them in pursuing managerial careers in business, government, or nonprofit organizations. To be eligible to apply and for admittance to one of the Consortium schools, you must hold a bachelor's degree in any academic discipline from an accredited institution recognized by Consortium member schools. You can apply for a Consortium Fellowship at up to six of the Consortium business schools. See the website for a current list of schools. Admission decisions are made by the school(s) of your choice. If you are admitted to a Consortium member school, you become eligible to compete for the Consortium Fellowship at that school.

GATES MILLENNIUM SCHOLARS

P.O. Box 10500
Fairfax, VA 22031-8044
(877) 690-GMSP
E-mail: contactus@gmsp.org
Website: http://www.gmsp.org
Additional Information: The Gates Millennium Scholars (GMS) program was established in 1999 through a grant from the Bill and Melinda Gates Foundation. The goal of the program is to provide outstanding African American, American Indian/Alaska Natives, Asian Pacific Islander Americans, and Hispanic American students with significant financial need with an opportunity to complete an undergraduate college education, in all discipline areas. The program also provides graduate school funding for students pursuing studies in mathematics, science, engineering, education, or library science. To be eligible, you must be nominated by your principal, teachers, guidance counselor, tribal higher education representative, or another professional educator. Students nominated for the program should have strong leadership potential and a demonstrated commitment to community service. Students are required to provide a completed Nominee Personal Information Form. The deadline is usually in January of each year. See the website for current deadline and additional eligibility requirements.

GEM PH.D. SCIENCE FELLOWSHIP

National GEM Consortium
1430 Duke Street

Alexandria, VA 22314

(703) 562-3646

E-mail: info@gemfellowship.org

Website: http://www.gemfellowship.org

Additional Information: The National Consortium for Graduate Degrees for Minorities Engineering and Science, Inc. (GEM) Fellowship programs provide opportunities for underrepresented minority students to obtain M.S. degrees in engineering and Ph.D. degrees in engineering and the natural and physical sciences through a program of paid summer internships and graduate financial assistance. GEM provides three Fellowship Programs:

- **M.S. Engineering**—The objective of this program is to increase the pool of minority engineering graduates by providing funds to assist in continued education. The fellowship provides a practical engineering summer work experience through an employer sponsor as well as a portable academic year fellowship of tuition, fees, and a stipend that may be used at any participating GEM member university where the GEM Fellow is admitted.
- **Ph.D. Engineering**—The program provides doctoral fellowships to underrepresented minority students who have either completed or are currently enrolled in a Master's in Engineering program. The fellowships can be used at any participating GEM member university where the GEM Fellow is admitted. During the first academic year of doctoral study, the GEM Consortium pays the stipend and a cost-of-instruction grant to the institution where the Fellow is enrolled. After the first year, the fellowship cost is paid by the participating GEM university. Fellows are also provided a practical summer work experience for at least one summer.
- **Ph.D. Science**—This program offers fellowships to pursue doctoral degrees in the natural science disciplines: chemistry, physics, earth sciences, mathematics, biological sciences, and computer science. You can apply in your junior or senior year in college, as a Master's of Engineering graduate student or as a working professional. These are portable fellowships and can be used at any participating GEM member university where the GEM Fellow is admitted.

JACKIE ROBINSON FOUNDATION

Scholarship Program
75 Varick Street, 2nd Floor
New York, NY 10013-1917
(212) 290-8600
E-mail: requests@jackierobinson.org
Website: http://www.jackierobinson.org
Additional Information: Open to high school seniors who are members
of a minority group and have been accepted into a four-year college or university. Applicants must also be U.S. citizens. The scholarship provides up
to $7,500 per year and the deadline is normally in early February.

KPMG FOUNDATION DOCTORAL SCHOLARSHIP PROGRAM

KPMG Foundation
3 Chestnut Ridge Road
Montvale, NJ 07645
Website: http://www.kpmgfoundation.org
Additional Information: To apply for this scholarship, you must be African American, Hispanic American, or Native American; a U.S. citizen or
a permanent resident of the United States (possess a green card); and
enrolled, on campus, in a full-time, AACSB-accredited accounting business doctoral program by September of the year you apply for the scholarship. This is a $10,000 yearly scholarship, renewable for up to five years or
a total of $50,000. The funds provided by the KPMG Foundation are not
meant to replace funds that might normally be made available by the doctorate granting institution. Therefore, the KPMG Foundation recom-
mends that the institution you attend provide the following: a $5,000
annual stipend unrelated to assistantships; teaching and research assistantships; and a waiver of tuition and fees.

NATIONAL MEDICAL FELLOWSHIPS

347 Fifth Avenue, Suite 510
New York, NY 10016
(212) 483-8880
E-mail: info@nmfonline.org

Website: http://www.nmfonline.org/

Additional Information: National Medical Fellowships (NMF) are need-based scholarships and awards available primarily to first- and second-year medical students. The mission of this program is to provide scholarships for underrepresented minorities in medicine. Current scholarships and awards include the Aetna Foundation/NMF Healthcare Leadership Program; NMF Emergency Scholarship Fund; Hugh J. Andersen Memorial Scholarship; Lawrence Brown Memorial Scholarship; Lincoln Fund Need-Based Scholarship; Mary Ball Carrera Scholarship; National Medical Association (NMA) Special Awards Program; and United Health Foundation Scholarships. Visit the website for program updates, specific eligibility requirements for each scholarship, and respective deadlines.

FORD FOUNDATION PREDOCTORAL FELLOWSHIPS

Fellowship Office, Keck 576
National Research Council
550 Fifth Street NW
Washington, DC 20001
(202) 334-2872
E-mail: infofell@nas.edu
Website: http://national-academies.org/fellowships

Additional Information: The Ford Fellowship program awards approximately 60 predoctoral fellowships to provide three years of support for individuals engaged in graduate study leading to a Ph.D. or Sc.D. degree. The fellowships are awarded in a national competition administered by the National Research Council (NRC) on behalf of the Ford Foundation. The awards are made to individuals who demonstrate superior academic achievement, are committed to a career in teaching and research at the college or university level, show promise of future achievement as scholars and teachers, and are well prepared to use diversity as a resource for enriching the education of all students. Although the program is open to all U.S. citizens who have not previously earned a doctoral degree, special consideration may be given to members of six minority groups whose underrepresentation in some fields has been severe and long-standing. These minority groups are: Alaska Natives (Aleut, Eskimo, or other indigenous people of Alaska); Black/African Americans; Mexican Americans/Chicanas/Chicanos; Native American Indians; Native Pacific Islanders

(Hawaiian/Polynesian/Micronesian); and Puerto Ricans. This fellowship provides an annual stipend of $16,000 and three expense-paid trips to attend conferences of Ford Fellows.

THE PH.D. PROJECT

Website: http://www.phdproject.org

Additional Information: The Ph.D. Project is not a doctoral or scholarship program but an information clearinghouse for underrepresented minorities who are interested in pursuing a Ph.D. to become a business school professor. The mission of the organization, founded by the KPMG Foundation, is to attract African Americans, Hispanic Americans, and Native Americans to business doctoral programs and provide support during the doctoral programs. The organization defines itself as the definitive source for everything you need to know to reach the goal of obtaining a business doctoral degree. Each year the organization sponsors a Ph.D. Project conference that brings together minority students interested in obtaining a doctoral degree from all over the world. Although there is a registration fee (refundable if you enter a Ph.D. program), your travel expenses are paid. Interested individuals must apply and be selected to attend. Although the Ph.D. Project does not offer any funding to doctoral students, the KPMG Foundation offers scholarships to African Americans, Hispanic Americans, and Native Americans pursuing an accounting doctoral degree. And many business doctoral programs will waive the student's tuition and fees and provide a stipend and/or research/teaching assistantships.

NOTE: I was selected to attend the Ph.D. Project conference in 1997. For those interested in pursuing a doctoral degree, the information and contacts obtained through attending this conference are invaluable. Participants are able to interact with and ask questions of current doctoral students, and faculty and admission staff from business doctoral programs.

ROBERT TOIGO FOUNDATION

180 Grand Avenue, Suite 450
Oakland, CA 94612
(510) 763-5771
Website: http://www.toigofoundation.org
Additional Information: See chapter 19.

THURGOOD MARSHALL SCHOLARSHIP FUND

901 F Street NW, Suite 300
Washington, DC 20004
(202) 507-4851; fax: (202) 652-2934
E-mail: info@tmcfund.org
Website: http://www.thurgoodmarshallfund.net
Additional Information: See Appendix A.

XEROX TECHNICAL MINORITY SCHOLARSHIP

Website: http://www.xerox.com/jobs/minority-scholarships/enus.html or
http://www.xerox.com (click on *Scholarships*)
Additional Information: The Xerox Technical Minority Scholarship
provides between $1,000 and $10,000 to qualified minorities with a 3.0 or
higher GPA who are enrolled in a technical degree program at the bachelor level or above. Applicants must be U.S. citizens or visa-holding permanent residents of African American, Asian, Pacific Island, Native
American, Native Alaskan, or Hispanic descent. You must be currently
enrolled as a full-time undergraduate or graduate student in any of the following technical fields: Chemistry, Information Management, Computing
and Software Systems, Material Science, Printing Management Science,
Laser Optics, Physics, and Engineering (Chemical, Computer, Electrical,
Imaging, Manufacturing, Mechanical, Optical, or Software). The application deadline is normally in September of each year.

AFRICAN AMERICAN MINORITY
SCHOLARSHIP AND FELLOWSHIP OPPORTUNITIES

**100 BLACK MEN OF AMERICA'S FUTURE LEADER
SCHOLARSHIP PROGRAM**

100 Black Men of America, Inc.
ATTN: National Scholarship Administrator
141 Auburn Avenue
Atlanta, GA 30303
Website: http://www.100blackmen.org (click on *Scholarship*)
Additional Information: This program is open to current undergradu-
ate students or high school students with a minimum 2.5 GPA who have

completed 50 hours of active community service within the past twelve months (with certified documentation) and been involved in activities as a student leader. See the website for additional information and current deadlines. Deadlines are normally in late February.

AFRO-ACADEMIC, CULTURAL, TECHNOLOGICAL AND SCIENTIFIC OLYMPICS (ACT-SO)

4805 Mt. Hope Drive
Baltimore, MD 21215
(410) 580-5650
E-mail: actso@naacpnet.org
Website: http://www.naacp.org
Additional Information: ACT-SO is an enrichment program for African American high school students designed to recruit, stimulate, improve, and encourage high academic and cultural achievement while providing students with the opportunity to earn cash scholarships. At the national level, gold, silver, and bronze medals are awarded along with cash scholarships of $2,000, $1,500, and $750 in each of 25 categories of competition in the sciences, humanities, and performing and visual arts. You must be an amateur in the competition category you enter. Students must compete in a local ACT-SO program to qualify for the National ACT-SO competition. Local winners are awarded certificates and many other prizes. Contact your local NAACP branch office for more information. If your local branch does not operate an ACT-SO program, contact the national office using the information above. To be eligible, you must be an African American high school student, enrolled in grades 9–12, and a citizen of the United States.

DR. ARNITA YOUNG BOSWELL SCHOLARSHIP

National Hook-Up of Black Women, Inc.
Scholarship Committee
1809 East 71st Street, Suite 205
Chicago, IL 60649
Website: http://www.nhbwinc.com (click on *Scholarships*)
Additional Information: This scholarship is awarded to African American freshmen, sophomore, junior, or senior students enrolled in an accredited college or university. Awards are a minimum of $1,000. A 2.75 GPA and

essay between 300 to 500 words are required. The deadline is usually in March.

THE HERBERT LEHMAN EDUCATION FUND

99 Hudson Street, Suite 1600
New York, NY 10013
Website: www.naacpldf.org/herbert-lehman-education-fund-scholarship or www.naacpldf.org (click on *Our Work\Scholarships*)
Additional Information: To apply for a Herbert Lehman Scholarship, you must be a senior in high school, a high school graduate, or a freshman currently enrolled at a college or university. In your application, you must present strong academic records, test scores, and personal essays, and have a track record of community and school involvement that reveals exceptional leadership potential with an ability to work well in diverse settings. Strong recommendations from teachers, community representatives, or employers are also required. The scholarship award is $2,000 and can be renewed for up to four years if you remain in good academic standing and program funds remain available. The application deadline is usually in March. Students who are not U.S. citizens are eligible to apply for this scholarship. Although the scholarship was originally intended for African American students, it is currently open to all students who meet eligibility requirements. Visit the website for an application and specific deadline date.

MCKNIGHT DOCTORAL FELLOWSHIP PROGRAM

201 East Kennedy Boulevard, Suite 1525
Tampa, FL 33602
(813) 272-2772
E-mail: mdf@fefonline.org
Website: http://fefonline.org/mdf.html or http://www.fefonline.org
Additional Information: The McKnight Doctoral Fellowship program addresses the underrepresentation of African American faculty at colleges and universities in the state of Florida by increasing the pool of qualified African Americans with Ph.D. degrees. The program provides up to 50 fellowships for study at one of nine participating Florida universities: Florida A&M University; Florida Atlantic University; Flor-

ida Institute of Technology; Florida International University; Florida State University; University of Central Florida; University of Florida; University of Miami; and the University of South Florida. Each fellowship provides annual tuition of up to $5,000 for three academic years plus an annual stipend of $12,000 (an additional two years of support at this level is provided by the participating institution). Hispanic students are also eligible to apply. The deadline is normally in January of each year. Check the website for additional eligibility requirements and application process.

NATIONAL ACHIEVEMENT SCHOLARSHIP PROGRAM FOR OUTSTANDING NEGRO STUDENTS

1560 Sherman Avenue, Suite 200
Evanston, IL 60201-4897
(847) 866-5100
Website: http://www.nationalmerit.org
Additional Information: African American applicants qualify for this competition by taking the PSAT in their junior year of high school with plans to enroll in a bachelor's degree program. The program offers $2,500 National Achievement Scholarships; corporate-sponsored scholarships (amounts vary); and in some cases college-sponsored scholarships (amounts may vary). Refer to the section "The National Achievement Scholarship Program" in chapter 8.

NATIONAL ASSOCIATION FOR THE ADVANCEMENT OF COLORED PEOPLE

4805 Mt. Hope Drive
Baltimore, MD 21215
(410) 580-5650
Website: http://www.naacp.org
Additional Information: The NAACP offers several scholarship programs annually. Visit the NAACP website address above for more information about each scholarship and the eligibility requirements. To apply for one of the scholarships, visit http://www.uncf.org (click on *For Students\ Scholarships*).

NATIONAL BLACK MBA ASSOCIATION, INC. SCHOLARSHIP PROGRAMS

180 N. Michigan Avenue, Suite 1400
Chicago, IL 60601
(312) 236-BMBA (2622); fax: (312) 236-4131
Website: http://www.nbmbaa.org (see *Programs\Scholarship Programs*)
Additional Information: The National Black MBA Association (NBM-BAA) provides scholarship awards to undergraduate and graduate students each year for the pursuit of careers in business, academia, and related professions. Applicants must demonstrate academic excellence, strong communication skills, community involvement, and leadership ability. Scholarship awards range from $1,000 to $15,000 and are contingent upon funding levels each year. Local NBMBAA chapters conduct scholarship programs and award funding to students in their area. Consult the website or write for specific eligibility requirements and deadlines.

NATIONAL URBAN LEAGUE, INC.

Website: http://www.nul.org
Additional Information: Contact your local Urban League to determine if scholarships are available in your area, or visit the website to find your local Urban League, or conduct an advanced Internet search for your state using the terms "Scholarship" and "Urban League."

RON BROWN SCHOLAR PROGRAM

1160 Pepsi Place, Suite 206
Charlottesville, VA 22901
(434) 964-1588
E-mail: info@ronbrown.org
Website: http://www.ronbrown.org
Additional Information: This organization awards scholarships to academically talented and highly motivated African American high school seniors who intend to pursue full-time undergraduate degrees. Award is based on financial need, leadership, academics, and community activities. Typically, students applying for this program have an A average, are in the top 10 percent of their high school class, and may participate in up to ten extracurricular activities. Interviews and essays are required. Essay questions from previous years have been as follows: (1) List your extra-

curricular, community, and other activities in order of importance. Choose the most important and tell why it is significant; (2) Submit an essay you plan to send as part of your college applications; (3) What issue or concern will most significantly affect African Americans in the twenty-first century?

There are generally two deadlines for this $40,000 scholarship ($10,000 payable for four years). The first is November 1, which gives you an opportunity to have the Ron Brown Scholarship program forward your information to other scholarship providers. The second is January 9, which is the final deadline. Visit the website to learn about current scholars and the application process.

UNITED NEGRO COLLEGE FUND

Attention: Scholarships
1805 7th Street NW
Washington, DC 20001
(800) 331-2244
Website: http://www.uncf.org (see *For Students\Scholarships*)
Additional Information: Visit the UNCF website where hundreds of scholarships and paid internships from corporate sponsors are listed.

DR. WYNETTA A. FRAZIER "SISTER TO SISTER" SCHOLARSHIP

National Hook-Up of Black Women, Inc.
Scholarship Committee
1809 East 71st Street, Suite 205
Chicago, IL 60649
Website: http://www.nhbwinc.com (see *Scholarships*)
Additional Information: See chapter 20.

HISPANIC/LATINO MINORITY SCHOLARSHIP AND FELLOWSHIP OPPORTUNITIES

HISPANIC SCHOLARSHIP FUND

1411 W. 190th Street, Suite 325
Gardena, CA 90248

(877) HSF-INFO (877-473-4636)
E-mail: scholar1@hsf.net
Social Media: Follow Hispanic Scholarship Fund on Facebook and Twitter.
Website: http://www.hsf.net (click on *Find a Scholarship* or *Scholarships*)
Additional Information: The Hispanic Scholarship Fund was founded in 1975 to help Hispanic American college students complete their education. The Fund provides scholarships to community college, four-year college, and graduate students of Hispanic heritage. Scholarship award amounts range from $1,000 to $15,000 with the average award amount being $2,500 for students at four-year institutions and $1,250 for students at two-year institutions. See the website for specific scholarships available along with eligibility requirements and deadlines.

LULAC NATIONAL EDUCATION SERVICE CENTERS INC.

National Headquarters
1133 19th Street NW, Suite 1000
Washington, DC 20036
E-mail: scholarships@lnesc.org
Social Media: Follow LNESC on Facebook and Twitter
Website: http://www.lulac.org (click on *Programs—Education—Scholarships*) or http://www.lnesc.org (click on *Scholarships*)
Additional Information: The LULAC National Scholarship Fund (LNSF) provides scholarships to Hispanic students attending colleges and universities. Under the LNSF program, local LULAC councils, along with local and national businesses, award scholarships to students in their communities. LNSF is administered by the LULAC National Educational Service Centers, Inc., a nonprofit educational organization. Hispanic students should contact the LULAC national office to find a local educational service center to get more information about specific scholarship programs. Visit the website for additional information about specific scholarships available, eligibility requirements, and deadlines.

MEXICAN AMERICAN LEGAL DEFENSE AND EDUCATION FUND

634 S. Spring Street, 11th Floor
Los Angeles, CA 90014

Website: http://www.maldef.org (click on *Education\Scholarship Resources*)
Additional Information: MALDEF provides a scholarship resources guide for high school students, a law school scholarship program, and a DREAM Act Student Activist Scholarship for current college students. The MALDEF Law School Scholarship Program awards scholarships of up to $5,000 each year to deserving individuals in their first, second, or third year of law school. Students must be enrolled in law school full-time to qualify. The scholarships are awarded to students based upon their demonstrated involvement in and commitment to serve the Latino community through the legal profession, academic and professional achievement, and financial need. MALDEF also offers scholarships of up to $5,000 each to deserving DREAM Act student activists. All current college and graduate students are eligible to apply as well as students seeking to enroll in college or university for the first time (or to re-enroll following a leave of absence).

MCKNIGHT DOCTORAL FELLOWSHIP PROGRAM

201 East Kennedy Boulevard, Suite 1525
Tampa, FL 33602
(813) 272-2772
E-mail: mdf@fefonline.org
Website: http://fefonline.org/mdf.html or http://www.fefonline.org
Additional Information: See the African American section of this chapter.

NSHMBA SCHOLARSHIP PROGRAM

National Society of Hispanic MBAs
450 East John Carpenter Freeway, Suite 200
Irving, TX 75062
(877) 467-4622 or (214) 596-9338
Website: http://www.nshmba.org (click on *Scholarship Program*)
Additional Information: The National Society of Hispanic MBAs (NSHMBA) provides scholarships to outstanding Latinos pursuing master's degrees in management or business. The scholarships are awarded on a competitive basis to full-time and part-time graduate students. To apply you must be of Hispanic heritage, be a U.S. citizen or a legal permanent resident, be enrolled or planning to enroll in a graduate management/

business major at an accredited college/university, and be enrolled in the upcoming fall term. You must also have a NSHMBA membership. However, applicants who are not currently members can become an associate member for free. Awards range from $2,500 to $10,000.

CONGRESSIONAL HISPANIC CAUCUS INSTITUTE (CHCI)

911 2nd Street NE
Washington, DC 20002
(202) 543-1771
Website: www.chci.org (click on *Scholarships*)
Social Media: Follow CHCI on Facebook and Twitter
Additional Information: CHCI provides scholarship opportunities to Latino students in the United States who have a history of performing public service–oriented activities in their communities and who demonstrate a desire to continue their civic engagement in the future. There is no GPA requirement or need to major in a specific field of study. Students with excellent leadership potential are encouraged to apply. Scholarship amounts range from $1,000 to pursue an associate degree, to $2,500 to pursue an undergraduate degree, to $5,000 to pursue graduate-level study.

NATIVE AMERICAN/INDIAN SCHOLARSHIP AND FELLOWSHIP OPPORTUNITIES

AMERICAN INDIAN COLLEGE FUND

National Headquarters
8333 Greenwood Blvd.
Denver, CO 80221
(800) 776-3863 or (303) 426-8900
E-mail: scholarships@collegefund.org
Social Media: Follow College Fund on Facebook, Twitter, LinkedIn, YouTube, and Google+
Website: http://www.collegefund.org (see *Students\Scholarships*)
Additional Information: Established in 1989, the American Indian College Fund provides scholarships to American Indian/Alaska Native students to attend tribal colleges but also provides scholarships for Ameri-

can Indian/Alaska Native undergraduate and graduate students to attend any other accredited public and nonprofit private college in the United States. Visit the website for specific information about available scholarships and deadlines.

AMERICAN INDIAN GRADUATE CENTER

3701 San Mateo NE, #200
Albuquerque, NM 87110
(505) 881-4584 or (800) 628-1920
E-mail: fellowships@aigcs.org
Social Media: Follow AIGC on Facebook and YouTube
Website: http://www.aigcs.org (click on *Scholarships*)
Additional Information: To be eligible for an AIGC fellowship, you must be an enrolled member of a federally recognized U.S. American Indian tribe or Alaska Native group, or possess one-fourth degree (federally recognized) Indian blood through the submission of a Tribal Eligibility Certificate (TEC). You must also be pursuing a master's or doctorate as a full-time graduate student at an accredited U.S. graduate school; or pursuing an undergraduate degree as a full-time student at an accredited U.S. undergraduate school, or be a high school sophomore or junior planning to attend an accredited undergraduate school in the United States. In addition, you must have financial need. See the website for specific scholarships available, deadlines, and additional eligibility requirements.

AMERICAN INDIAN SCIENCE AND ENGINEERING SOCIETY SCHOLARSHIP PROGRAMS

P.O. Box 9828
Albuquerque, NM 87119-9828
(505) 765-1052
E-mail: info@aises.org
Website: http://www.aises.org (click on *What We Do\Programs\Scholarships*)
Additional Information: The mission of the American Indian Science and Engineering Society (AISES) is to substantially increase the representation of American Indians and Alaskan Natives in engineering, science, and other related technology disciplines. The Society administers several

scholarship programs. Please see the website for current scholarships available, specific eligibility requirements, and deadlines, which often occur in the spring.

INTERNATIONAL ORDER OF THE KING'S DAUGHTERS AND SONS

Director, North American Indian Department
P.O. Box 1040
Chautauqua, NY 14722-1040
Website: http://iokds.org (click on *Scholarship Programs*)
Additional Information: This organization offers scholarships with no restrictions placed upon tribal affiliations or Indian blood quantity. However, applicants must provide a tribal registration number and fulfill other requirements. For more information about the North American Indian Scholarship Program and to request an application, send a stamped, self-addressed envelope to the address above. Scholarships are available for technical, vocational, or undergraduate college or university. Usually you must request applications by March 1. Visit the website for additional eligibility requirements and current deadlines.

NATIONAL SOCIETY DAUGHTERS OF THE AMERICAN REVOLUTION SCHOLARSHIPS FOR AMERICAN INDIANS

Website: http://www.dar.org (see *National Society\Scholarships*)
Additional Information: The DAR American Indian Scholarship is a nonrenewable $1,000 award and is available to help Native American students of any age, any tribe, in any state who are striving to get an education. This scholarship can be used for vocational training or college/ university at the undergraduate or graduate level. Graduate students are eligible, but undergraduates are given preference. Proof of American Indian blood is required and you must have a GPA of 3.25 or higher. All awards are judged based on financial need and academic achievement. For more information, send a stamped, self-addressed envelope to the address above. This organization also awards the Frances Crawford Marvin American Indian Scholarship yearly to one student, who must be enrolled full-time at a college or university. Applicants for this scholarship must be Native American, and proof of American Indian blood is required. Award is based on demonstrated financial need and academic achievement, and applicants must have a 3.25 GPA or higher. A recipient can

reapply for this scholarship. The amount of the scholarship may vary each year based on total return of the endowment. The Anne Trevarthen Memorial Scholarship is also available to high school seniors specifically to attend the College of William and Mary. See the website for additional details and eligibility requirements for all scholarships as well as current deadlines.

18

SCHOLARSHIPS FOR CURRENT COLLEGE STUDENTS AND TRANSFER STUDENTS

Don't waste life in doubts and fears;
spend yourself on the work before you,
well assured that the right performance
of this hour's duties will be the best preparation
for the hours or ages that follow it.

—Ralph Waldo Emerson

You may at this point be pondering the question: Are there scholarships for me if I'm already in college? The answer to your question is yes, there are definitely scholarships for students already in college. In some cases students who are enrolled in a college or university have a better chance at winning certain scholarships, especially those that are college/university sponsored, mainly because of close proximity to the source of those scholarships. In addition, undergraduates and graduate students have numerous chances to get involved in organizations and associations affiliated with their majors that also sponsor scholarships. The National Society of Professional Engineers and the National Association of Black Accountants are two such organizations.

A primary focus of this book has been to help you realize that no institution or organization gives money without reason. Being aware of those reasons, along with meeting general requirements such as making deadlines, preparing for a dynamic interview, creating an outstanding personal narrative through an essay, composing a flawless and impressive résumé, and thoroughly completing an application give you the best chance of scholarship success. These objectives can be achieved whether you are a high school senior, an undergraduate, or a graduate student. The primary keys to success in finding scholarships are preparation and determination. Therefore, the ideas I have presented in the previous chapters can apply at any stage of the educational process.

SEARCHING FOR SCHOLARSHIPS AS A CURRENT COLLEGE STUDENT— THE DIFFERENCE BETWEEN YOU AND OTHER STUDENTS

- *As a high school senior*—Scholarships may be more abundant, particularly small amounts in the community.
- *As a college student currently enrolled*—Undergraduate scholarships may not be as abundant, but you have the campus/community as a resource and can still search for funds based on your interests, major, or career goals.
- *As a transfer student* (from a two-year/community college)— Undergraduate scholarships may not be as abundant, but you have the campus/community as a resource and you can still search for funds based on your interests, major, or career goals. You also have the opportunity for transfer scholarships. Visit Phi Theta Kappa's list of institutions offering transfer scholarships at http://www.ptk.org (search for "scholarships"). College Fish (http://www.collegefish.org) is also a great resource for students transferring from two-year colleges to four-year institutions and the site includes information about college money for transfer students.
- *As a nontraditional student*—Scholarships for adult students may not be as abundant, but you too have the campus/community as a resource, just as currently enrolled students do. Nontraditional students should also revise their thinking. Search for scholarships targeting adult students as well as those for college students or college undergraduates.
- *For all students*—Look for scholarships based on who you are, where you are, what you are, and your interests. For example, many organizations, particularly those designed to serve a specific population (like women), could be an opportunity for you! So, if you are female, search for scholarships targeting women. Are you interested in culinary arts? If so, then search for scholarships targeting culinary arts. Are you a cancer survivor? If so, then search for scholarships intended for survivors of cancer.

As outlined above, you'll see that there are many scholarships available, intended for all types of people. You just need to spend the time and expend the effort to find them.

DON'T MAKE ASSUMPTIONS WITH YOUR SEARCH

Look at eligibility requirements carefully. A scholarship program may mention student classification but not age. For example, a scholarship directory or database entry may look like this one.

> Council of Citizens with Low Vision International
> Attn: Fred Scheigert Scholarship
> 324 S. Diamond Bar Blvd., #128
> Diamond Bar, CA 91765
> http://www.cclvi.org/scholarship.htm
> Amount: $3,000
> To qualify to receive a scholarship award, you must be:
> - a full-time college/trade/vocational student for the upcoming academic year
> - registered for at least 12 undergraduate units (9 graduate units)
> - have a minimum cumulative 3.2 GPA

As you can see, the eligibility requirements do not mention age. The example above only mentions qualifications as they relate to your status in college.

Entries in scholarship and award directories might also include a category showing target applicants. For example, the entry might include a section such as this one:

> TARGET APPLICANT:
> - College student
> - Graduate student
> - Adult student

Once again, the entry above does not mention age, only classification. As a result, if you are a currently enrolled college student or a community college student transferring to a four-year institution, reviewing directories that include entries with target applicants such as the one above could uncover several scholarship sources for you.

As a student already enrolled in college, review the checklist below for additional sources of financial aid at the undergraduate level.

ASSOCIATIONS AND ORGANIZATIONS OF PROFESSIONALS IN YOUR AREA OF STUDY CAN BE SCHOLARSHIP GOLD MINES!

To find associations and organizations in your area of study to see if any of them offer scholarships, look at the *Encyclopedia of Associations* published by Gale Research, which can usually be found at your local library. You can also visit the Internet Public Library (http://www.ipl. org) and go to the Special Collections area to search for "Associations on the Net."

This section is organized by category. Thus if you're looking for associations that are affiliated with engineering, you can go directly to that section. When I did this, I found the National Society of Professional Engineers (NSPE) website as well as many others. I went to the NSPE website and used their site's search engine to search for scholarships. Using this method I found the $10,000 Paul H. Robbins, P.E., Honorary Scholarship for undergraduate students.

You can also use Web searches such as Yahoo! to search for organizations in your field. I conducted an advanced Internet search (explained in chapter 3) for accounting societies and associations and found quite a few that offer scholarships. In the area of accounting, there were at least six organizations that offered scholarships. They included the National Society of Public Accountants, the American Institute of Certified Public Accountants, the American Accounting Association (AAA), the International Association of Hospitality Accountants (IAHA), the Institute of Management Accountants, and the American Society of Women Accountants. All of these organizations offered some type of accounting scholarship to students already enrolled in college.

Be aware that membership can definitely have its privileges. Some associations may require you to be a member of their organization to be eligible for a scholarship. If so, the membership fee is usually reduced for currently enrolled students.

CHECKLIST FOR OTHER SOURCES OF FINANCIAL AID

1. Magazines directed toward career and success-oriented people, such as *Money, Black Enterprise,* and *Fortune.*
2. Try to get a paid internship. Many corporations sponsor internship programs for undergraduates and graduates. Some will also sponsor

scholarships for interns who have performed well academically. Even if they do not fund all or part of the education of an intern, the job experience will enhance your résumé for future employment and scholarship consideration.

3. Contact the athletic office if you participate in any type of sport. Athletic scholarships can be offered for many different athletic activities such as swimming, lacrosse, and tennis. To get a sports scholarship, you don't always have to play football, basketball, or baseball. Refer to chapter 16, "Scholarships for the Unnoticed Athlete."

4. Contact the financial aid office at your college or university. Read your college or university catalog for a list of fellowships, endowments, and scholarships to get an idea of money you might qualify for. You should also visit the financial aid section of your school's website. It's good to have an idea of the school's available student aid funds so you can ask specific questions about money to help you finish your education.

5. If you participate and have a serious interest in activities such as music, dance, theater, or art, contact those departments to see if scholarships are available in those areas.

6. Review directories that list grants in specific areas to see if there might be aid opportunities that could apply to you. For example, check out the online directory *Foundation Grants to Individuals* or *The Foundation Directory* at http://www.foundationcenter.org. You may also be able to obtain this directory in your local library.

7. See if you are eligible for an out-of-state tuition waiver if you attend a public college or university out of your home state but in a neighboring state.

8. Try to get a company to sponsor you in exchange for your endorsement of its products or services.

Other Strategies for Paying the College Bill

- Volunteer to be a resident advisor if the position is unfilled.
- Consider ROTC scholarships—usually incurs a military commitment. See chapter 27.
- Join national community service organizations such as AmeriCorps.
- The National Guard can also help pay your tuition bill. See chapter 27.

For more information about community and work-related aid, read chapter 14, "Scholarships and Awards for Community Service, Volunteering and Work."

9. Consider cooperative education. With this option you may alternate attending school with extended periods of work for a company or agency that needs students in your area of study. This period could last from several months to a year. The company or agency you work for generally pays your tuition bill, or provides a salary designed to cover your tuition, in exchange for your services. In this arrangement your school may also give you academic credit based on the work experience you are accumulating in your field while working with the company or agency.

10. Contact honor societies in your area of study.

11. Check out companies in need of future employees in your area of study or a related area.

12. Check with organizations that benefit certain groups to which you belong (for example, legally blind, women, minority, etc.).

13. Contact alumni associations, particularly in the city you're from, for scholarships. Contact the national alumni association office for your college or university as well.

14. Contact your state financial aid agency. See chapter 5, "Financial Aid Forms and Help from the Government with College Expenses."

15. If you attend a United Negro College Fund (UNCF) college or university, see http://www.uncf.org for information about numerous scholarships that may be available to you.

16. If you haven't already, read chapter 2, "The Scholarship Search: Discovering Hidden Treasures," for more ways to find sources of educational aid.

17. Contact professionals who are already working in the field you are planning to enter. Ask if they know of associations or organizations that could help you complete your education. For example, if you're studying in the field of veterinary medicine, contact a veterinarian. Alternatively, if it's anthropology, contact an anthropologist. Doing so may or may not help you find a scholarship opportunity, but it could get you a paid internship and/or valuable work experience that can help you win scholarships, grants, or open doors to other opportunities. You should do this in addition to trying to find national associations and organizations that may be listed in a book or online, because professionals in your area may know of smaller, community and regionally based organizations that offer support to students. On social media sites such as Facebook or Twitter, search for associations that are affiliated with your field. For example, you can input "marketing" into the search bar and see if any promising organizations

come up. Reading a few Tweets or glancing at the Facebook page will give you an idea of whether it may be helpful to you in your search.

THE LOCAL SEARCH FOR CURRENT COLLEGE STUDENTS

The local search is the one most often ignored by the typical student. I covered this subject as it pertains to all students in an earlier chapter, but I will reiterate the steps for students already in college. Many students in search of scholarships use a few scholarship directories and an Internet search service such as Fastweb.com, which are great first steps, but they need to go further. In some cases an Internet search service is the only resource used. Unfortunately, if *your* scholarship quest only includes directories and the Internet or even the Internet alone, you could be overlooking some valuable scholarship opportunities.

The best way to do a complete scholarship search is to search locally in your community, state, and region in addition to directories and the Internet. Most of the scholarships you find in directories and on the Internet are national, which means that if you apply you are among many others who hope to win the scholarship. This makes winning the scholarship harder because it is more competitive. For many local scholarships the number of applications is smaller, and thus less competitive. This is because local scholarships are generally smaller in monetary value and a lot of students feel they aren't worth the time and effort. Fortunately, smaller, easier-to-win scholarships do add up and should not be ignored. In my scholarship total of more than $400,000, awards as small as $50 were included.

For a local scholarship search, you should contact or review the following sources:

- The career center at your institution.
- The department office for your major or your minor course of study.
- Your college or university website for special Web pages listing scholarships that can be used at your school but are not specific to your institution. For example, Georgetown University has maintained a page listing outside scholarships for many years.
- Your college or university's website to become aware of scholarships, grants, and fellowships specific to your university. Although you may not qualify currently, you may in the future if you can meet the requirements.

- Community foundations—visit http://www.novacf.org for an example of a community foundation and the types of scholarships a community foundation might offer. See chapter 3, "Using the Internet and Social Media in Your Scholarship Search," for more information about conducting an advanced Internet search for community foundations.
- Local clubs and organizations—examples of these would be the Soroptimist Club, the Optimist Club, Exchange Clubs of America, Daughters of the American Revolution, YMCA/YWCA, the Kiwanis Club, the Rotary Club, the Lions Club, or the Knights of Columbus. Also look for sororities and fraternities. For more examples of clubs and organizations based in local communities throughout the United States, refer to chapter 2. Alpha Kappa Alpha Educational Advancement Foundation (http://www.akaeaf.org) is an example of a foundation affiliated with a sorority that offers scholarships to current college students.
- Your company, which may offer tuition reimbursement. Contact the human resources department for more information.
- Companies you've interned with in the past or recently to request financial assistance to complete your education—some companies may automatically offer interns a scholarship once the program is completed.
- Companies and banks located in your community—some may have scholarships available to local residents. Call the company's personnel or human resources department to inquire if they offer scholarships to students in the community. Your local newspaper or chamber of commerce may be able to assist you in identifying local companies.
- Your parents' employers—some employers offer scholarships to children of their employees.
- Your parents' union, to find out if they offer scholarships to the children of their members. Union Plus is an example of a union that maintains a scholarship program.
- Any organization to which you or your parents belong, local or national, to determine whether they have a scholarship program for their members. Your church or faith-based organization might be an example.
- Your professors and/or advisors—some educators form groups to offer scholarships to students in special areas.
- Your credit union, if you have one—some credit unions have scholarship opportunities for their members.

FUNDING SOURCES FOR CURRENT COLLEGE STUDENTS

Explore each of the following for sources of aid to assist you with your continued education. Some are mentioned in earlier sections, but here's a quick summary:

- *Federal aid*—Visit the Federal Student Aid section on the Department of Education's website (http://www.ed.gov) to determine if you are eligible for any federal aid or grant programs.
- *State aid*—Find the organization in your state designated to administer funds for residents. For example, in Virginia, this organization is the State Council of Higher Education for Virginia (SCHEV). See chapter 5 for your state financial aid agency.
- *Membership organizations*—If you are a member of any organization on campus or in your community, determine if scholarships or general college funding are available to members. Your church or faith-based organization might be one. Another is the NAACP, a community-based civic organization, which has scholarships available to its members and others. You should also ask your parents about their membership in organizations, since some may have scholarships available to members' children.
- *Scholastic honor societies*—Honor societies such as Golden Key International Honour Society (www.goldenkey.org) or Phi Theta Kappa (www.ptk.org) and many others have scholarships available to their members. Hundreds of scholastic societies cover interest areas from music to chemistry and beyond. Read my book *College Survival and Success Skills 101* to find out more about scholastic honor societies. This book focuses on success strategies for current college students.
- *Associations*—There are thousands of associations in the United States, and many have scholarships available to students who want to continue their studies and pursue a career in specific fields or interest areas.

STUDENT RÉSUMÉ EXAMPLES

Once you have uncovered the scholarship and free aid opportunities that are available to you, know that students who are enrolled in colleges and universities are expected to be more professional than high school

One-page résumé example (when printed on 8 1/2×11-inch sheet of paper)

Marianne N. Ragins

University Address	**Permanent Address**
FAMU Box 00000	P.O. Box 176
Tallahassee, Florida 32307	Centreville, Virginia 20122
Telephone: (904) 555-1234	Telephone: (703) 579-4245

Objective: Effective utilization of my extensive literary, analytical, and organizational skills for a major business entity.

Education: Presently matriculating as a junior at Florida Agricultural and Mechanical University's School of Business and Industry.

Major:	Business Administration
Expected Graduation:	April 1995
Grade Point Average:	3.88/4.0

Relevant Course Work: Honors English I and II; Principles of Economics I and II; Legal Environment of Business; Principles of Marketing; Intermediate Accounting I and II; Managerial Accounting; Quantitative Methods for Business Decisions I; Financial Accounting

Achievements: Winner of more than $400,000 in scholarship awards; cover story, *Macon Telegraph,* May 2 and 4, 1991; national headlines, Associated Press, May 3, 1991; cover story, *Parade* magazine; featured in *Essence, Newsweek, Money, Jet, Reader's Digest, People, Black Enterprise,* and *YSB* magazines; appeared on *Good Morning America* (ABC), *The Home Show* (ABC), *Teen Summit* (BET); January 11 declared *Marianne "Angel" Ragins Day* in Wilmington, Delaware; Dean's List—Fall Quarter 91/Spring Quarter 92/Fall Quarter 92/Spring Quarter 93; Coca-Cola Scholar; Armstrong Scholar; Wendy's Scholar; National Dean's List 1991–1993; Outstanding Service Award 1991; Letter of Commendation from Thomas B. Murphy, Speaker of the House, Georgia General Assembly 1991; Letter of Commendation from Clarence Thomas, Supreme Court Justice 1991.

Organizations: Presidential Scholars Association; Phi Eta Sigma National Honor Society; University Honors Council; volunteer coordinator for Special Olympics 1991; volunteer speaker for local area middle and high schools; Red Cross volunteer; Coordinator, *Benjamin D. Hendricks Undergraduate Honors Conference* 1993 and 1994; panel speaker, *The 21st Century—Education Beyond the Classroom* 1993; Mock Trial Team, Florida Collegiate Honors Conference 1992; Southern Regional Collegiate Honors Conference 1991; international speaker at the Crystal Palace, Nassau, the Bahamas 1993; Director of Organization and Planning, *Hometown News*; coordinating manager, *Close-up.*

Publications: Author and publisher (first and second editions) of *Winning Scholarships for College: The Inside Story;* national publisher for third and future editions, Henry Holt and Company, Inc., New York.

Work Experience:
06/93 to 08/93
EDS Belgium N.V.—*Overseas Internship Assignment in Brussels, Belgium*
• Assistant for the Sales, Finance, and Government divisions of EDS
• Extensive involvement with the preparation of financial documents and sales presentations.

06/92 to 08/92
Electronic Data Systems (EDS)—*Internship Assignment in Raleigh, North Carolina*
• Proposal Manager:
  • Entailed managing and editing material from proposal and technical writers, coordinating staff meetings and project deadlines, as well as overseeing all aspects of production concerning the submission of EDS' proposal for the Tallahassee Integrated Public Safety System.
• Proposal Team Staff Member:
  • Desktop publishing, word processing, and production for various proposals.

Computer Proficiency: WordPerfect, Lotus 1-2-3, Ventura Publisher, Microsoft Word, MacDraw, Microsoft Excel, Microsoft PowerPoint, ABC Flowcharter, Photostyler, Freelance Graphics, Lotus Notes

References Available Upon Request

Multiple-page résumé

Marianne N. Ragins

University Address
FAMU Box 00000
Tallahassee, FL 32307
Telephone: (904) 555-1234

Permanent Address
P.O. Box 176
Centreville, Virginia 20122
Telephone: (703) 579-4245

Professional Objective: Effective utilization of my extensive literary, analytical, and organizational skills for a major business entity.

Education: Presently matriculating as a junior at Florida Agricultural and Mechanical University's School of Business and Industry.

Major:	Business Administration
Expected Graduation:	April 1995
Grade Point Average:	3.88/4.0

Work Experience: 06/93 to 08/93
EDS Belgium N.V.—*Overseas Internship Assignment in Brussels, Belgium*
Description of Work Assignment:
• Assistant for the Sales, Finance, and Government Divisions of EDS
• Extensive involvement with the preparation of financial documents and sales presentations.

06/92 to 08/92
Electronic Data Systems (EDS)—*Internship Assignment in Raleigh, North Carolina*
Description of Work Assignment:
• Proposal Manager:
  • Entailed managing and editing material from proposal and technical writers, coordinating staff meetings and project deadlines, as well as overseeing all aspects of production concerning the submission of EDS' proposal for the Tallahassee Integrated Public Safety System.
• Desktop publishing, word processing, and production for the following proposals:
  • North East Ohio Information Network (NEOMIN)
  • The City of Savannah
  • The City of Broken Arrow
  • Indianapolis Sewer System
  • City of Indianapolis Collections System

Honors/Organizations

COLLEGE

Dean's Lists—Fall Quarter 91/Spring Quarter 92/Fall Quarter 92/Spring Quarter 93
Phi Eta Sigma National Honor Society
Member of the University Honors Council
Presidential Scholars Association
Volunteer Coordinator for Special Olympics
Red Cross Volunteer
January 11 declared *Marianne "Angel" Ragins Day* in Wilmington, Delaware
Author of *Winning Scholarships for College: The Inside Story*
LGB Scholars Association

Professional Speaking Engagements
Department of Family and Children's Services—Fort Gaines, Georgia
James Farmer Scholars Program—Mary Washington College, Fredericksburg, Virginia
Positive Teens—Wilmington, Delaware
Delta Sigma Theta—Atlanta, Georgia
Keenan Program—Bethune-Cookman College, Daytona Beach, Florida
Crystal Palace—Nassau, The Bahamas

Certificates of Appreciation—Speaker
Griffin Middle School—Tallahassee, Florida
Havana Middle School—Tallahassee, Florida
Bethel AME Church—Tallahassee, Florida
Bethel Baptist Church—Tallahassee, Florida
Northeast High School—Macon, Georgia
Southwest High School—Macon, Georgia
Church of God in Christ—Macon, Georgia
Stubbs Chapel Baptist Church—Macon, Georgia
Union Baptist Church—Macon, Georgia
Regional Honors Convention—Roanoke, Virginia
McEvoy Middle School—Macon, Georgia
GED Graduation—Macon, Georgia
Riverside Optimist Club—Macon, Georgia
Regional Honors Convention—St. Augustine, Florida

Newspapers and Articles
May 2, 1991—front-page news story, *Macon Telegraph and News*
May 3, 1991—front-page story picked up by the Associated Press
May 4, 1991—front-page news story, *Macon Telegraph and News*
Appeared in articles for *Essence, Newsweek, Money, Jet, Reader's Digest, People, Black Enterprise, YSB*
September 17, 1991—cover story of *Parade* magazine

Television shows:
May 6, 1991—appeared on *Good Morning America*, ABC morning news show
June 14,1991—appeared on the *Home* show, ABC home improvement show
Karla Heath Show
Channel One News
America's Best College Buys
August 22, 1991—taping of *You Bet Your Life*, pilot game show starring Bill Cosby

Radio Shows:
"Your Personal Finance with Charles Ross"
"WABC News"
"WBZT News"
"Bob Laws Night Talk Show"

HIGH SCHOOL ACTIVITIES AND HONORS

- Academic Bowl Team
- Debate Team
- Drama Club
- Literary Team
- Math Club
- Math Team
- *Salmagundi* Literary Magazine
  - Assistant Editor—Sophomore Year
  - Co-Editor—Junior Year
  - Editor-in-Chief—Senior Year
- Science Bowl Team
  - Captain—Junior and Senior Year
- Science Club
- Spanish Club
- Spirit Club
- Student Council
  - President—Senior Year
- Quill and Scroll National Honor Society

- Mu Alpha Theta
- National Honor Society
- *Macon Telegraph and News* Teen Board
- Project Link
- Red Cross Youth Volunteer
- Y Club
  - Vice-President—1989–90
- Gold Medallion—First Place Optimist Oratorical Contest 1987
- Silver Medallion—Second Place Optimist Oratorical Contest 1987
- Second Place—(Oratory) Winter Forensics Forum 1988
- Bronze Medallion—Third Place Math Olympics 1988
- Certificate of Academic Achievement in Science 1988
- Certificate of Outstanding Achievement 1988 and 1989
- National Science Merit Award
- Scholarship—Summer Journalism Workshop at the University of Georgia 1989
- "Best Poem in State" Georgia Scholastic Press Association 1989
- Plaque—"Best Bill" Georgia 44th Youth Assembly, awarded by the *Atlanta Journal and Constitution* 1989
- Black Youth and Business Entrepreneurship Program, Georgia College
- Trophy—Science Bowl Regional Competition 1989 and 1990
- Trophy—Biology
- Georgia Council Teachers of English Writing Award 1989
- Coordinator—Science Fair 1989
- Georgia Council Teachers of English Student Achievement Award 1989 and 1990
- Northeast Student of the Month—November 1989
- Alternate for the Georgia Governor's Honors Program 1990
- Who's Who in American High School Students 1990
- National Leadership Service Award 1990
- National English Merit Award 1990
- Plaque—Project Link, Student Leadership Program 1990
- First Place Medallion—Optimist International Essay Contest 1990
- Trophy—Chemistry 1990
- Trophy—Outstanding Service Award 1990
- Northeast Observer for Model U.N. 1990
- Delegate for Summit Conference on Bibb County Education 1990
- Black Georgia Scholar Award
- Duval County Academic Invitational Tournament 1989, 1990 and 1991
- Certificate of Commendation—Regional Winner, Red Clay and Skyscrapers Georgia Alliance for Public Education 1990
- Georgia Certificate of Merit awarded by the State of Georgia 1990
- Letter of Nomination—Congressional Youth Leadership Conference 1990
- Champion Journalist 1990
- National Council of Teachers of English Writing Award 1990
- Published in "Minescape" GCTE magazine
- Letter of Commendation from Thomas B. Murphy, Speaker of the House, Georgia General Assembly 1991
- Letter of Commendation from Clarence Thomas, Supreme Court Justice 1991

students in their speech, manner of dress, and especially in presenting a résumé to an organization for a part-time job, internship, or a scholarship. To help you present your list of achievements and qualifications, the above résumés are examples of those I used as a college student. When you are applying for a job or an internship, include a one-page résumé. If you are applying for a scholarship to a scholarship committee, include the multiple-page résumé unless there are specific requirements you need to follow. Also, if you are a junior or senior in college, you may not want not to include high school activities unless they are particularly noteworthy or you wish to show a long-standing interest in a particular area. For example, if you are applying for a journalism scholarship you would want to show that your interest and focus in this area has been concentrated for a number of years.

SCHOLARSHIP OPPORTUNITIES FOR CURRENT COLLEGE STUDENTS

See "A Few Important Items to Remember" on p. 181 for additional tips.

100 BLACK MEN OF AMERICA'S FUTURE LEADER SCHOLARSHIP PROGRAM

100 Black Men of America, Inc.
ATTN: National Scholarship Administrator
141 Auburn Avenue
Atlanta, GA 30303
Website: http://www.100blackmen.org (click on *Scholarship*)
Additional Information: Open to current undergraduate students or high school students with a minimum 2.5 GPA who have completed 50 hours of active community service within the past twelve months, with certified documentation, and have been involved in activities as a student leader. See the website for additional information and current deadlines. Deadlines are normally in late February. Award amounts range from $1,000 to $3,000.

ADVANCING ASPIRATIONS GLOBAL SCHOLARSHIPS

ATTN: Womenetics
99 West Paces Ferry Road NW, Suite 200
Atlanta, GA 30305
E-mail: scholarships@womenetics.com
Website: http://www.womenetics.com (click on *Scholarships*)
Additional Information: Available to undergraduate students in an

accredited college or university who are U.S. citizens or legal residents of the United States. To apply, you must write an essay of 2,500 words or less discussing certain questions. Scholarships range from $1,500 to $5,000. See the website for additional details and current deadlines.

ALPHA KAPPA ALPHA EDUCATIONAL ADVANCEMENT FOUNDATION

5656 South Stony Island
Chicago, IL 60637
(800) 653-6528
Website: http://www.akaeaf.org/
Additional Information: This organization offers merit and financial need scholarships. To be eligible for the merit scholarships, you must have completed a minimum of one year in a degree-granting institution and be continuing a program of education in such an institution; demonstrate exceptional academic achievement, as evidenced by a GPA of 3.0 or higher; and show evidence of leadership by participation in community or campus activities. For the financial need scholarships you must have a minimum GPA of 2.5, have completed a minimum of one year in a degree-granting institution, and be continuing your studies in such an institution. For financial need scholarships you can also be a student in a non-institutional program that may or may not grant degrees, provided you include a course-of-study outline. These awards are usually given to individuals who have endured great hardship to accomplish their educational goals and aspirations. Visit the website to download applications. This organization does not accept requests for applications via e-mail, fax, or in writing.

AMERICAN FIRE SPRINKLER ASSOCIATION SCHOLARSHIP SECOND CHANCE SCHOLARSHIP CONTEST

Website: http://www.afsascholarship.org
Additional Information: Current college or trade school students can win $1,000 in the AFSA Second Chance Scholarship Contest. To enter, you must read the website's "Fire Sprinkler Essay" about automatic fire sprinklers. Then you'll be eligible to complete the registration page with all requested information. Finally, you'll need to take a ten-question multiple-choice test which is open book. For each question you answer correctly, you will get one entry in a drawing for one of three $1,000 scholarships. For each question answered incorrectly, you will be given

one more chance at the end of the exam to answer the question correctly. A total of ten (10) entries in the drawing is possible if you answer all ten questions correctly.

THE AYN RAND INSTITUTE

Essay contest on Ayn Rand's novel *Atlas Shrugged*
E-mail: info@aynrandnovels.com
Website: www.aynrand.org/contests
Social Media: Follow Ayn Rand Novels on Twitter and Facebook.
Additional Information: High school seniors, current college students, and graduate students can win up to $10,000 by writing an essay based on Ayn Rand's novel *Atlas Shrugged*. See the website for contest details and current deadline.

BUICK ACHIEVERS SCHOLARSHIP PROGRAM

(800) 537-4180
E-mail: buickachievers@scholarshipamerica.org
Website: http://www.buickachievers.com
Social Media: This program is currently managed by Scholarship America, which you can follow on Facebook and Twitter for updates about this and other open scholarships.
Additional Information: If you are active in the community and have a will to succeed, the Buick Achievers Scholarship Program could be an opportunity for you. This program is available to current college undergraduates as well as high school seniors who are interested in careers related to the automotive industry and are majoring in or planning to major in the broad range of fields that contribute to the automotive industry. Possible majors range from engineering and business administration to graphic design, mathematics, finance, and accounting. Currently this program has more than 1,000 scholarships available in amounts up to $25,000 per year. Winners are chosen based on academic achievement, financial need, participation and leadership in community and school activities, work experience, and demonstrated interest in pursuing a career in the automotive or related industries. Other factors considered are whether you are a first-generation college student, a woman, a minority, a military veteran, or a dependent of military personnel. See the website for complete details and deadlines.

Another scholarship program intended to encourage students to pursue a career in the automotive field is the Automotive Hall of Fame Scholarship. See http://www.automotivehalloffame.org/education/scholarships or http://www.automotivehalloffame.org (search for "Scholarships") for additional information.

THE COLLEGIATE INVENTORS COMPETITION

Invent Now Collegiate Inventors Competition
3701 Highland Park NW
North Canton, OH 44720-4535
E-mail: collegiate@invent.org
Social Media: Follow Collegiate Inventors on Twitter and Facebook.
Website: http://www.invent.org/collegiate/
Additional Information: The Collegiate Inventors Competition (CIC) is an international awards program designed to encourage college students active in science, engineering, mathematics, technology, and creative invention while stimulating their problem-solving abilities. To participate in this competition, you must be enrolled, or have been enrolled, full-time in any college or university at least part of the twelve-month period prior to the date your entry is submitted. If you are submitting a team entry (you can have a maximum of four students) at least one member of the team must meet the full-time eligibility criteria. The other team members, at a minimum, must have been enrolled part-time sometime during the twelve-month period prior to the date the entry is submitted. Currently, you or your team can submit an unlimited number of entries to the competition; however, only one prize per student or team will be awarded. Graduate students entering this competition can win up to $15,000 and undergraduates can win up to $12,500. Inventions submitted are judged on the originality of the new idea, process, or technology. The idea must be complete, workable, and well articulated. Entries are also judged on their potential value to society—socially, environmentally, and economically—and on the range or scope of use. See the website for complete details and entry requirements.

COLLEGE JUMPSTART SCHOLARSHIP

College JumpStart Scholarship Fund
4546 B10 El Camino Real, No. 325
Los Altos, CA 94022

E-mail: admin@jumpstart-scholarship.net
Website: http://www.jumpstart-scholarship.net
Additional Information: See Appendix A.

CREATE-A-GREETING-CARD SCHOLARSHIP CONTEST

Website: http://www.gallerycollection.com/greetingcardscontests.htm or
http://www.gallerycollection.com/greeting-cards-scholarship.htm
Additional Information: This $10,000 scholarship contest is open to all
high school and college students and members of the armed forces who can
create a winning Christmas card, holiday card, birthday card, or all-occasion
greeting card. Legal residents of the fifty United States, the District of
Columbia, American Samoa, Guam, the Commonwealth of the Northern
Mariana Islands, the U.S. Virgin Islands, and Puerto Rico are eligible to
enter. International students who have a student visa to attend school in the
United States are considered legal residents and are also eligible to enter.

DR. ARNITA YOUNG BOSWELL SCHOLARSHIP

National Hook-Up of Black Women, Inc.
Scholarship Committee
1809 East 71st Street, Suite 205
Chicago, IL 60649
Website: http://www.nhbwinc.com (see *Scholarships*)
Additional Information: See chapter 17.

ELIE WIESEL PRIZE IN ETHICS ESSAY CONTEST

Elie Wiesel Foundation for Humanity
555 Madison Avenue, 20th Floor
New York, NY 10022
(212) 490-7788
Website: http://www.eliewieselfoundation.org or www.ethicsprize.org
Additional Information: Contest is open to registered undergraduate
full-time juniors or seniors at accredited four-year colleges or universities
in the United States during the fall semester. You do not have to be a U.S.
citizen for this contest. Students must write essays on topics related to ethics
or topics suggested by the foundation. Prizes range from $500 to $5,000.
Essays should be between 3,000 to 4,000 words.

FRAME MY FUTURE SCHOLARSHIP CONTEST

E-mail: churchhillclassics@diplomaframe.com; enter "Frame My Future Scholarship Contest" in the Subject line
Website: http://www.diplomaframe.com (search for "Frame My Future")
Additional Information: This contest is open to community college, undergraduate, or graduate school students attending a U.S. college or university full-time in the current academic year. To enter you must also be a U.S. citizen. To qualify, you must create an essay that shares what you want to achieve in your personal and professional life after college. You should incorporate the theme: This is how I "Frame My Future." You must submit your entry online in a .JPG file, and it must be fully viewable and/or readable online as one image. The entry form must include a short description of your entry piece (maximum of 500 characters). Student winners win $1,000 and one grand prize winner will win an additional $1,000 matching donation to their school. Finalists are judged based on their entry and description. Winners are ultimately chosen by online vote. For additional information and current deadline, visit the website.

GO DADDY .ME SCHOLARSHIP

E-mail: scholarship@godaddy.com.
Website: http://www.godaddy.com/scholarship/mescholarship.aspx or http://www.godaddy.com (search for "Scholarship")
Additional Information: High school seniors and current college students with a 3.0 GPA who can describe in 500 words or less how technology has contributed to their success in school or beyond are eligible to enter this contest. To become a Go Daddy Scholar and win $10,000 for college you must be at least 16 years of age or older and a legal resident of the fifty United States including the District of Columbia (but excluding Puerto Rico). See website for additional eligibility requirements and current deadline dates. The .ME Scholarship is named for the .ME Registry, operator of the .ME domain extension.

"LEADING THE FUTURE II" SCHOLARSHIP

The Scholarship Workshop
P.O. Box 176
Centreville, VA 20122

(703) 579-4245
E-mail: scholars@scholarshipworkshop.com
Website: http://www.scholarshipworkshop.com
Social Media: Follow Scholarship Workshop on Facebook and Twitter @ ScholarshipWork.
Additional Information: The "Leading the Future" Scholarship is designed to elevate students' consciousness about their future and their role in helping others once they receive a college degree and become established in a community. It is open to high school seniors or current college undergraduates who are U.S. residents. Visit the website to download an application.

THE LEOPOLD SCHEPP FOUNDATION

551 Fifth Avenue, Suite 3000
New York, NY 10176-3201
(212) 692-0191
Website: http://www.scheppfoundation.org
Additional Information: See Appendix A.

LIFE LESSONS SCHOLARSHIP PROGRAM

LIFE Foundation
Website: http://www.lifehappens.org/life-lessons/
Additional Information: See chapter 15.

NATIONAL ASSOCIATION FOR CAMPUS ACTIVITIES EDUCATIONAL FOUNDATION

NACA
13 Harbison Way
Columbia, SC 29212
(803) 732-6222
E-mail: info@naca.org
Website: http://www.naca.org/
Additional Information: This organization offers various scholarships for undergraduate and graduate students involved in on-campus activities or holding positions of leadership on a college campus. Please see the website for additional details on each scholarship available.

Scholarship Drawings Could Win You Big Bucks If You're Lucky

The GotChosen $40,000 Scholarship Giveaway!
http://www.gotchosen.com

The GotChosen scholarship is open to all students who are 18 years or older. This includes current students, previous students with outstanding loans, and even future college students in the United States, Brazil, Canada, Chile, Colombia, or Mexico. The Got Chosen Giveaway is free and 100 percent transferable if you win.

Many scholarship drawings are available. If you're willing to share information about yourself, encourage others to visit specific websites, or to read about certain issues that potentially have numerous marketing efforts directed your way, consider entering one or more drawings, particularly if the stakes are high. Just make sure you don't share personal identifying information such as Social Security numbers or bank account numbers. And if you're wondering about a giveaway, see "Places to Check Out Offers That Sound Too Good to Be True," in chapter 2.

PROJECT YELLOW LIGHT SCHOLARSHIP/HUNTER GARNER SCHOLARSHIP

Julie Garner
One Shockoe Plaza
Richmond, VA 23219.4132
(804) 698-8203
Website: http://projectyellowlight.com
Additional Information: High school and college students who want to encourage fellow students to develop safe driving habits can enter the Project Yellow Light scholarship competition. Your entry, which will consist of a video designed to motivate, persuade, and encourage your peers not to drive distracted, can win you up to $5,000 for your education. The winning video will be turned into an Ad Council PSA that will be distributed nationally to 1,600 TV stations, and the top two winners will also earn the opportunity to attend a one-day survival skills class at the Skip Barber Racing School. To apply, access the entry form and submit your video through the website.

THE RAGINS/BRASWELL NATIONAL SCHOLARSHIP

The Scholarship Workshop
P.O. Box 176
Centreville, VA 20122

(703) 579-4245

E-mail: scholars@scholarshipworkshop.com

Website: http://www.scholarshipworkshop.com

Social Media: Follow Scholarship Workshop on Facebook and Twitter @ScholarshipWork.

Additional Information: This scholarship is available to high school seniors, undergraduates, and graduate students who attend The Scholarship Workshop presentation or an online class given by Marianne Ragins, winner of more than $400,000 in scholarships. Award is based on use of techniques taught in the workshop; application; essay; and extracurricular activities. Interested students should visit the website for more details and class information. The deadline is usually in April.

RONALD REAGAN COLLEGE LEADERS SCHOLARSHIP PROGRAM

The Phillips Foundation

1 Massachusetts Avenue NW, Suite 620

Washington, DC 20001

(202) 250-3887

Website: http://www.thephillipsfoundation.org (click on *Ronald Reagan College Leaders Scholarship Program*)

Additional Information: To apply for this merit-based scholarship, you must be a U.S. citizen who is a least a college sophomore but not yet a college senior and enrolled full-time in good standing at any accredited, four-year degree-granting institution in the United States or its territories. If you win, you will receive the scholarship for your junior year and may apply for renewal before your senior year. If you attend a two-year school, you can apply as a junior for a one-time scholarship for the senior year when you transfer to a four-year institution. You need to submit an essay of 500 to 750 words describing your background, career objective, and scope of participation in leadership activities promoting freedom, American values, and constitutional principles. Award amount ranges from $1,000 to $7,500.

SCHOLARSHIP AMERICA'S DREAM AWARD

Website: http://www.scholarshipamerica.org

Additional Information: This award is intended to target students who have gotten beyond their college freshman year and need additional funding to complete their college education. The awards range from $5,000 to

$15,000 each year, beginning in the second year, and grow by $1,000 each year until graduation (up to a 5-year degree program). The Dream Award includes scholarships for general disciplines and also those that are STEM-related (science, technology, engineering, and math). To be eligible, you must have a 3.0 GPA or higher and have successfully completed your first year of a post-secondary degree or certificate program.

19

GOING BEYOND THE UNDERGRADUATE
DEGREE—PAYING FOR GRADUATE SCHOOL

> It is knowledge that influences and equalizes the
> social conditions of man; that gives to all, however
> different their political position, passions which are
> in common, and enjoyments which are universal.
>
> —Benjamin Disraeli

Although the amount of scholarship money available for graduate school may not be as plentiful as it is for undergraduates or high school seniors, there is still money available to students who wish to pursue their studies beyond an undergraduate degree. The federal government and many universities offer numerous funding sources for promising students. It may take more effort to find and win scholarship or fellowship money, but the effort should still be made because there is money to be won. Many of the strategies suggested in chapter 2, "The Scholarship Search: Discovering Hidden Treasures," chapter 3, "Using The Internet and Social Media in Your Scholarship Search," and chapter 14, "Scholarships and Awards for Community Service, Volunteering, and Work," should be used to explore other scholarship opportunities. You should also do the following to find sources of aid available to you:

- Start researching funds for graduate school early. Ideally, you should do this at least one academic year before you are ready to begin your graduate studies.
- Fine-tune your résumé. Students who are well rounded and involved in community service, leadership, academic, and career-oriented

activities, are more competitive when it comes to getting money for undergraduate and graduate school. Optimally, you should have been involved in these types of activities well before you begin thinking about graduate school. But if not, start increasing your involvement level at least one year before you need to start applying for funding.

- Much graduate aid is specific to a field of study, research area, or area of practice. So your search should be more focused on awards in your specialized area and less on general scholarships. You should definitely put a lot of thought into the area you want to pursue so you can target your search for funding. Those sources of funding could include any of the following:
  - Look for scholarship opportunities. Scholarships are available based on many criteria, such as club or religious affiliations, ethnic origins, heritage, career aspirations, your city, your state, your willingness to write an essay on a certain topic, personal characteristics, and many other factors. Exploring the chapters mentioned in the first paragraph above will help you uncover these opportunities.
  - Search for fellowships in your area of study. Fellowships are explained in chapter 2, and are very similar to scholarships in that they can be need-based, merit-based, or a combination of the two. Many can also be quite lucrative, often covering some portion of tuition as well as living expenses. Both Cornell University (http://www.gradschool.cornell.edu/fellowships) and UCLA (http://www.gdnet.ucla.edu/grpinst.htm) offer excellent databases to assist students with finding fellowships.
  - Research grants may be available in your area of study as well.
  - For all of the above—scholarships, fellowships, and grants—conduct an advanced Internet search for these terms along with your area of study to help you find funding sources specific to you. (See chapter 3 for more information on an advanced Internet search.)
- Review the schools you want to attend for graduate study. Review your field of study. Look at the school's employment rate for recent graduates in your area of study. Also review the *Occupational Outlook Handbook* (http://www.bls.gov/ooh). Although you can certainly obtain funds for graduate study, there is the possibility that you will incur loans for some of your study or other expenses. If this is the

case, prepare yourself by understanding the job outlook and salary level once you complete your graduate degree.

- Take any required standardized tests. Most graduate programs require that you take a standardized test, such as the Graduate Records Examination (GRE) or Law School Admissions Test (LSAT). Most schools review these types of standardized test scores as part of their admissions process and some use it to determine how much aid to offer you. Depending upon your scores and the areas you need to work on, you may want to take some preparation courses.

- Speak with professors about various fellowship and research opportunities that might fund your studies. Contact the faculty head of your field's department to inquire about scholarship opportunities. If you are not currently enrolled at a university, then visit the institution at which you would like to pursue your graduate work and ask these questions.

- Refer to scholarly journals and publications in your field for fellowship opportunities.

- Contact your area of study's department to find out if it has scholarships available to students who wish to pursue graduate work.

- Find out if there is an arrangement for students from your school to attend another corresponding institution and offer scholarships to them—sometimes called "graduate feeder programs."

- Contact national and professional associations and organizations in your area of graduate study. For example, marketing students might contact the American Marketing Association, or architectural students might contact the American Institute of Architects, and so on. To find associations in your area of study, look at the *Encyclopedia of Associations* published by Gale Research, which can usually be found at your local library. You can also visit the Internet Public Library (http://www.ipl.org) and go to the section for "Associations on the Net," which is organized by category. Thus if you're looking for associations that are affiliated with law, you can go directly to that section. When I did this, I saw the American Political Science Association website. I used their website search engine to search for scholarships. I found the Pi Sigma Alpha/Howard Penniman Graduate Scholarships. Some associations may require that you be a member of their organization to be eligible for their scholarship. Many others do not. For those that do require you to be a member, the membership fee is usually reduced for current students.

- Contact local companies to ask if they will offer funds for your studies in return for your agreement to alternate work experience with educational study. This could include a cooperative education or internship agreement with the company until you complete your education. If the companies you contact employ many students with graduate degrees in your area of study, then they could be very interested in supporting your continued education.
- Within the academic year you're ready to begin your studies you should complete the FAFSA. This will help determine any federal or state aid you could receive, which could include federal loans. Visit http://www.fafsa.ed.gov for more information.
- Consider a Ph.D. in your area of study. Why? Study at the doctoral level often gives you the opportunity for assistantships and tuition waivers from many universities. The section below has more information about assistantships.
- Look at possible tax credits. Refer to IRS Publication 970 for more information, consult your tax professional, visit http://www.studentaid.ed.gov, or see chapter 5.
- Check out honor societies associated with your field.

Some of the most common funding sources for graduate students are those that provide payment for services performed. Sources of this type usually fall into three general areas: assistantships, internships, and cooperative education.

GRADUATE ASSISTANTSHIPS

Assistantship students receive a stipend, which is either paid in a lump sum each semester or paid over a period of weeks or months. Usually, schools also provide a partial or full tuition fee grant or a partial or full tuition fee reduction. In the assistantship the student usually does work related to his or her field of study but it does not necessarily coincide with academic work.

- Graduate Teaching Assistantships—Teaching Assistants (TAs) are graduate students who get an assistantship to teach undergraduate students.
- Graduate Research Assistantships—Assistantships in this area are given to graduate students who assist the faculty of a particular institution with research projects.

- Graduate Administrative Assistantships—These assistantships can be obtained to perform administrative or support services for an institution.

INTERNSHIPS

Internships can be obtained by graduate students at companies or other institutions and can provide a way for you as a graduate student to receive payment for work performed and also receive invaluable work experience. Academic credit can sometimes be obtained for internships. Internships and the money earned from them can help significantly with the costs of your education.

COOPERATIVE EDUCATION

Cooperative education combines academic study with work experience. These assignments are usually paid and generally last longer than internships.

Tuition Reimbursement

For graduate students who are already employed, you should contact your company's human resources or professional development department to inquire about a tuition reimbursement program. In these programs, employees pay the tuition for courses you take either individually or as part of a degree program. Once a satisfactory grade has been earned, the company will then reimburse you for all or part of the tuition you paid. Also, review chapter 14, "Scholarships and Awards for Community Service, Volunteering, and Work," for more information about programs that may fund your studies in return for a service commitment once you complete your degree. Even if your company does not have a tuition reimbursement program, you may still be able to get tuition help if you can make your graduate study add value to the current work you do. For example, your master's degree in communication could help you revamp the corporate website, e-mail marketing campaign, or social media strategy. In addition, consider employment at a university because some offer free or reduced tuition to their employees. Please note that some graduate programs limit the amount of hours students work or require full-time status. For example, this is definitely the case with some doctoral programs.

PERSONAL STATEMENTS FOR GRADUATE SCHOOL

If you are applying for graduate school admission and scholarships, you will usually be required to submit a personal statement. This statement should outline your reasons for continuing your education beyond an undergraduate degree, and touch on the experience you have acquired over the years either through working or some other pursuit—did you work for a couple of years before deciding to attend graduate school? Many schools will require at least two years of work experience—or activities during your undergraduate years (if you decided to go to graduate school immediately upon receiving your undergraduate degree). The personal statement can also take the form of a response to a specific question, or it can be a basic descriptive essay about you. Refer to chapter 11 for more details on constructing responses in an essay format. The personal statement is similar to an essay. Its main objective is to convey a mature, professional view of you. It should reflect your intellect, academic goals, and the self-growth gained during your undergraduate experience or as an employee.

I wrote the following personal statement for acceptance into George Washington University.

STATEMENT OF PURPOSE

SUBMITTED TO GEORGE WASHINGTON UNIVERSITY—
WASHINGTON, D.C.

For the past six years I have juggled the roles of student, author, public speaker, consultant, volunteer, marketing representative, and entrepreneur. As the author of three nonfiction books, owner of a consulting and motivational speaking business, and as an Armstrong marketing representative responsible for consulting with architects, interior designers, and contractors on such projects as the State Department and the Pentagon, the decision to attend George Washington University where flexibility is normal rather than an exception was an easy one. My interest in obtaining a Master's of Business Administration at George Washington University also stems from a firm belief in continuous education; a desire to enhance and expand upon the practical knowledge I have gained through my position with Armstrong and other endeavors; as well as an interest in prior preparation for obtaining a doctoral degree.

My belief in continuous education and my public speaking career originated in early childhood. When I was four, my sister began teaching me the rudiments of language arts and mathematics. My lessons advanced quickly, soon allowing me to read chapters of the Bible to numerous amazed audiences. My most vivid childhood memory, however, is not of my teacher's shocked face as I flew through sentences of Dick and Jane's life on the first day of school, but of the big, red F I received for a coloring activity clearly showing my ignorance of all colors in the spectrum. I, who at the age of five could read passages from the Bible that even adults stumbled over, have been humbled by that experience since. At the time, my childish pride and superiority complex had egged me into tantrums that put a premature end to the lessons my sister had tried without success to continue. As a result, the lessons had stopped, first grade began, and my first F became engraved forever into my memory as a reminder that education should never end.

Furthermore, the skills I have obtained in my marketing and sales position with Armstrong will broaden by study at George Washington University as well as interaction with other individuals of similar interest. While gaining further knowledge of marketing as a graduate student at George Washington University to complement my work experience, I can also contribute the insight I have of marketing and sales as it relates to consulting, publishing, and manufacturing, with hope resulting in a mutual transfer of information.

Moreover, earning my master's in Business Administration will also serve as preparation for my long-range goal of acquiring a doctoral degree. It is my hope that the educational background I gain along with continuous work experience at Armstrong will be an excellent foundation for doctoral study and my eventual contribution in front of the classroom.

Acceptance to your program will satisfy (for now) my desire for continuous education, augment the experience I have gained as a marketing representative and entrepreneur, and also serve as a building block for future doctoral study. Additionally, George Washington University, with its flexibility, will not only provide an excellent learning environment with a global flair but will also allow me to continue juggling my various roles successfully.

SCHOLARSHIP AND FUNDING OPPORTUNITIES

The following opportunities are mostly general within each field, although some may be for specific areas within the field or may target specific groups such as women. However, if you are a minority, you should review chapter 17, "Scholarships for Minorities—What's the Difference in a Minority Scholarship Hunt?" for additional funding options to pay for your graduate and professional school education. Once again, make sure to review chapters 2, 3, and 14, as mentioned at the beginning of the chapter.

See "A Few Important Items to Remember" on p. 181 for additional tips.

General Funding

THE AYN RAND INSTITUTE

Essay Contest on Ayn Rand's Novel *Atlas Shrugged*
E-mail: info@aynrandnovels.com
Website: http://www.aynrand.org/contests
Additional Information: See chapter 18.

When Searching for Money for Medical School and Health-Related Fields . . .

When searching for funds to attend medical school or complete your education in the medical field, contact hospitals in your local area. This can be an important source of funding for you because some of the hospitals in your area may have scholarship programs to help you continue your medical school studies.

For example, the Laporte Hospital Foundation in Laporte, Indiana, offers scholarships for students pursuing health care careers. So too does the Virginia Hospital Center in Arlington, Virginia, for those interested in nursing careers.

You can also contact community foundations such as the Berks County Community Foundation in Pennsylvania, which offers the Community General Hospital Foundation June A. Roedel Healthcare Scholarship.

FORD FOUNDATION PREDOCTORAL FELLOWSHIPS

Ford Foundation Fellowships Office, Keck 576
National Research Council
550 Fifth Street NW
Washington, DC 20001
(202) 334-2872
E-mail: infofell@nas.edu
Website: http://national-academies.org/fellowships
Additional Information: See chapter 17.

FRAME MY FUTURE SCHOLARSHIP CONTEST

E-mail: churchhillclassics@diplomaframe.com: Include "Frame My Future Scholarship Contest" in the Subject line.
Website: http://www.diplomaframe.com (search for "Frame My Future")
Additional Information: See chapter 18.

GATES MILLENNIUM SCHOLARSHIP PROGRAM

P.O. Box 10500
Fairfax, VA 22031-8044
(877) 690-GMSP
E-mail: contactus@gmsp.org
Website: http://www.gmsp.org
Additional Information: See chapter 17.

THE LEOPOLD SCHEPP FOUNDATION

551 Fifth Avenue
Suite 3000
New York, NY 10176-3201
(212) 692-0191
Website: http://www.scheppfoundation.org
Additional Information: See Appendix A.

HARRY S. TRUMAN SCHOLARSHIPS

712 Jackson Place NW
Washington, DC 20006
(202) 395-4831
E-mail: office@truman.gov
Website: www.truman.gov
Additional Information: This highly competitive scholarship program is open to college juniors planning to continue their education with graduate study. Applicants must be U.S. citizens who want to be a "change agent" and pursue a career in public service. If you're considering this program, you'll need to have an extensive record of community and volunteer service as well as campus involvement. In addition, you need to be nominated by your college or university. The deadline is usually in early February. The scholarship is usually $30,000 toward your graduate education.

RAGINS/BRASWELL NATIONAL SCHOLARSHIP

The Scholarship Workshop
P.O. Box 176
Centreville, VA 20122
(703) 579-4245
E-mail: scholars@scholarshipworkshop.com
Website: http://www.scholarshipworkshop.com
Additional Information: See chapter 18.

MONEY FOR MEDICAL SCHOOL AND HEALTH RELATED FIELDS

ALLMAN MEDICAL SCHOLARSHIPS

Miss America Organization
ATTN: Scholarship Department
222 New Road, Suite 700
Linwood, NJ 08221
(609) 653-8700
E-mail: info@missamerica.org
Website: http://www.missamerica.org/scholarships/
Additional Information: The Allman Medical scholarship is available to
women who have competed within the Miss America system on the state,
local, or national level from 1998 to the present, regardless of whether a
title was won. One or more scholarships per year may be awarded depending upon the qualifications of applicants.

NATIONAL HEALTH SERVICE CORPS

U.S. Department of Health and Human Services
Bureau of Clinician Recruitment and Service
5600 Fishers Lane
Rockville, MD 20857
(800) 221-9393
E-mail: GetHelp@hrsa.gov
Website: http://nhsc.hrsa.gov
Additional Information: See chapter 14.

INTERNATIONAL ORDER OF THE KING'S DAUGHTERS AND SONS HEALTH CAREERS SCHOLARSHIPS

Director, Health Careers Department
P.O. Box 1040
Chautauqua, NY 14722-1040
Website: http://iokds.org (click on *Scholarship Programs*)
Additional Information: The scholarship offered by this organization is $1,000 and can be won by students who are U.S. or Canadian citizens and enrolled full-time in a school located in the U.S. or Canada. Students must be preparing for careers in medicine, dentistry, pharmacy, physical or occupational therapy, and medical technologies. Your application must be for at least the third year of college unless you are an R.N. student, in which case you must have completed the first year of schooling. Premed students are not eligible to apply. If you are seeking an M.D. or D.D.S., your application must be for at least the second year of medical or dental school. There is no age limit for this scholarship. For an application, students should send a stamped, self-addressed envelope to the address above no later than April 1.

NATIONAL SOCIETY DAUGHTERS OF THE AMERICAN REVOLUTION MEDICAL SCHOLARSHIPS

Alice W. Rooke Scholarship and Irene and Daisy MacGregor Memorial Scholarship
Website: http://www.dar.org
Additional Information: To apply for either of these awards, visit the website to download the application and get the current information for submission. The award amount is $5,000 annually for up to four years—maximum of $20,000.

- Alice W. Rooke Scholarship and Dr. Francis Anthony Beneventi Medical Scholarship—Awarded to students who have been accepted into or are pursuing an approved course of study to become a medical doctor. Award must be used at an approved, accredited medical school and cannot be used for premedical study, osteopathic medicine, veterinary studies, or study to become a physician assistant.
- Irene and Daisy MacGregor Memorial Scholarship—Awarded to students of high scholastic standing and character who have been accepted into or are pursuing an approved course of study to become

a medical doctor. Award must be used at an approved, accredited medical school and cannot be used for premedical study, osteopathic medicine, veterinary studies, or study to become a physician assistant. This scholarship can also be used for study in the field of psychiatric nursing (graduate level) at an accredited medical school. Preference is given to qualified women.

NATIONAL SOCIETY DAUGHTERS OF THE AMERICAN REVOLUTION NURSING SCHOOL SCHOLARSHIPS

Website: http://www.dar.org
Additional Information: This organization offers the following $1,000 scholarships for nursing school. To apply for these awards, visit the website to download the application and get the current information for submission.

- Caroline E. Holt Nursing Scholarship—Awarded to students who plan to attend or are attending an accredited school of nursing and have financial need.
- Mildred Nutting Nursing Scholarship—Awarded to students who have been accepted or are currently enrolled in an accredited school of nursing. Applicants from the greater Lowell, Massachusetts, area are given preference for this award.
- The Occupational/Physical Therapy Scholarship—Awarded to students with financial need who have been accepted to or are attending an accredited school of occupational therapy (including art, music, or physical therapy).

PFIZER POSTDOCTORAL FELLOWSHIP PROGRAMS

Website: http://pfizercareers.com/university-relations/postdoc
Additional Information: Postdoctoral training programs allow individuals to pursue extended research opportunities in the areas of disease biology, drug delivery and mechanisms of action, as well as the engineering of novel therapeutic proteins, vaccines, and nucleic acids. The fellowship provides support for up to four years. Consult the website for additional information.

TYLENOL SCHOLARSHIP

Website: http://www.tylenol.com/scholarship
Social Media: Facebook: https://www.facebook.com/TylenolScholarship
Additional Information: This scholarship is open to current college students and graduate students pursuing degrees related to the health care industry. The deadline is usually in May of each year. Award amounts range from $5,000 to $10,000.

MONEY FOR LAW SCHOOL

AMERICAN BAR ASSOCIATION LEGAL OPPORTUNITY SCHOLARSHIP FUND

321 North Clark Street
Chicago, IL 60654
E-mail: legalosf@americanbar.org
Website: http://www.ambar.org/DiversityScholarship
Additional Information: This scholarship is available to those attending an American Bar Association (ABA) accredited law school. Award amount is $5,000 annually. Freshmen with satisfactory academic performance in law school can renew the award for up to two additional years for a total potential award opportunity of $15,000.

FEDERAL CIRCUIT BAR ASSOCIATION SCHOLARSHIPS

1620 I Street NW, Suite 801
Washington, DC 20006
(202) 466-3923
Website: http://www.fedcirbar.org (click on *Scholarships*)
Additional Information: This association provides scholarship awards between $5,000 and $10,000 to students pursuing a juris doctor (J.D.) degree in any law school accredited by the American Bar Association. You must also have financial need, and show a demonstrable interest in one of the many topics that lie within the procedure, substance, or scope of the jurisdiction of the U.S. Court of Appeals for the Federal Circuit (international trade, government contracts, patents, trademarks, certain money claims against the U.S. government, federal personnel, and veterans' benefits). Students with interests solely in areas such as family, public interest,

bankruptcy, or criminal law and those pursuing advanced degrees (e.g., LL.M.) are not eligible to apply. See the website for additional eligibility requirements and deadlines.

JUDGE JOHN R. BROWN AWARD FOR EXCELLENCE IN LEGAL WRITING

Judge John R. Brown Scholarship Foundation
1177 West Loop South, 10th Floor
Houston, TX 77027
Website: http://www.brownsims.com (click on *About Brown Sims\Affilia-tions*)
Additional Information: The Judge John R. Brown Scholarship Foundation recognizes excellence in legal writing in American law schools with a $10,000 award. Any law student currently enrolled in an accredited law school in the United States seeking a J.D. or LL.B. degree is eligible to submit a paper. As an example, a previously submitted paper that won an award was titled "Control Share Acts, Closed-End Funds, and the Battle for Corporate Control," written by Daniel S. Alterbaum of Yale Law School.

NAPABA LAW FOUNDATION SCHOLARSHIPS

1612 K Street NW, Suite 1400
Washington, DC 20006
(202) 775-9555
E-mail: nlfstaff@napaba.org
Website: http://www.napaba.org (see *Scholarships*)
Additional Information: The National Asian Pacific American Bar Association (NAPABA) administers various scholarships ranging from $2,500 to $7,500 to law students. Most scholarships awarded are to applicants with a commitment to serve the needs of the Asian Pacific American community.

MONEY FOR BUSINESS SCHOOL

To obtain scholarship money for an MBA or graduate business degree, the university you plan to attend should be your primary source. For example, the Darden Graduate School of Business Administration at the University of Virginia does an excellent job of letting prospective and current students know about the financial aid available for its business school education. If you're interested in the Darden school or would like to see an example of this, visit http://www.darden.virginia.edu (click on *Costs and Financial Aid\Scholarships*). Many universities may have special pamphlets or Web pages that list scholarships and financial opportunities available to you for studies at their institution.

Also check out the following sources for ways to pay for your business school education. These are meant to give you a general idea of money that may be available to you. To find other sources for funding your education, look into associations and organizations based on your specific professional area, as mentioned in the beginning of this chapter. For example, if you're interested in the field of accounting, the American Accounting Association (AAA) administers the Accounting Doctoral Scholars Program as well as the Educational Foundation for Women in Accounting and awards numerous scholarships at the undergraduate, graduate, and postgraduate levels. Also review Appendix A for additional funding.

AMERICAN ASSOCIATION OF UNIVERSITY WOMEN EDUCATIONAL FOUNDATION SELECTED PROFESSIONS FELLOWSHIPS

ACT, Inc.
P.O. Box 4030
Iowa City, IA 52243-4030
(319) 337-1716, ext. 60
E-mail: aauw@act.org
Website: http://www.aauw.org
Additional Information: The AAUW awards Selected Professions Fellowships to women to pursue a full-time course of study at accredited institutions in one of the designated degree programs in which women's participation has been traditionally low. The designated degree programs are Architecture (M.Arch., M.S.Arch.), Computer/Information Sciences (M.S.), Engineering (M.E., M.S., Ph.D.), and Mathematics/Statistics (M.S.). Fellowships in the following degree programs are restricted to women of color, who have been underrepresented in these fields: Business Administration (M.B.A., E.M.B.A.), Law (J.D.), and Medicine (M.D., D.O.). All applicants must be U.S. citizens or permanent residents.

CONSORTIUM FOR GRADUATE STUDY IN MANAGEMENT

http://www.cgsm.org
Additional Information: See chapter 17.

KPMG FOUNDATION DOCTORAL SCHOLARSHIP PROGRAM

KPMG Foundation
3 Chestnut Ridge Road
Montvale, NJ 07645
Website: http://www.kpmgfoundation.org
Additional Information: See chapter 17.

ROBERT TOIGO FOUNDATION

180 Grand Avenue, Suite 450
Oakland, CA 94612
(510) 763-5771
Website: http://www.toigofoundation.org
Additional Information: To become a Toigo Fellow, you must be a minority defined by the U.S. Department of Labor (i.e., African American, Asian American/Pacific Islander, Hispanic/Latino, Native American/Alaska Native, and/or South Asian American) and a U.S. citizen or legal resident pursuing a career in finance after graduation. You must also be applying to or accepted into one of the following: an accredited U.S.-based two-year MBA program, a JD/MBA, master's in Real Estate, or a master's in Finance. There is an application fee for this program but it is reduced if you apply early.

THE PH.D. PROJECT

http://www.phdproject.com
Additional Information: See chapter 17.

MONEY FOR GRADUATE STUDY IN ENGINEERING,
MATHEMATICS, OR SCIENCE

FANNIE AND JOHN HERTZ FOUNDATION

2300 First Street, Suite 250

Livermore, CA 94550

(925) 373-1642

Website: http://www.hertzfndn.org

Additional Information: The Hertz Foundation supports graduate students working toward a Ph.D. in the physical sciences ranging from electrical engineering to molecular biomedicine. Students studying applied physics, applied chemistry, applied mathematics, applied modern biology, and all areas of engineering are eligible to apply for the fellowship. You must also be a citizen or permanent resident of the United States, and be willing to commit to make your skills available to the United States during a time of national emergency. The fellowship is based on merit only, not need, and consists of a cost-of-education allowance, accepted by all of the tenable schools in lieu of all fees and tuition, and a personal-support stipend, which is currently between $31,000 and $36,000 depending upon fellowship option chosen. Refer to the website for additional eligibility requirements and deadlines.

GEM PH.D. SCIENCE FELLOWSHIP

National GEM Consortium

1430 Duke Street

Alexandria, VA 22314

(703) 562-3646; fax: (202) 207-3518

E-mail: info@gemfellowship.org

Website: http://www.gemfellowship.org

Additional Information: See chapter 17.

NATIONAL DEFENSE SCIENCE AND ENGINEERING GRADUATE FELLOWSHIPS

American Society for Engineering Education

1818 N Street NW, #600

Washington, DC 20036

(202) 649-3831

E-mail: ndseg@asee.org

Website: http://www.asee.org/ndseg/

Additional Information: The National Defense Science and Engineering Graduate (NDSEG) Fellowships are awarded to applicants pursuing a doctoral degree in, or closely related to, one of the following specialties: aeronautical and astronautical engineering, biosciences (includes toxicology), chemical engineering, chemistry, civil engineering, cognitive, neural, and behavioral sciences, computer science, electrical engineering, geosciences (includes terrain, water, and air), materials science and engineering, mathematics, mechanical engineering, naval architecture and ocean engineering (includes undersea systems such as autonomous vehicles and other networked platforms), oceanography (includes ocean acoustics, remote sensing, and marine meteorology), or physics (includes optics). NDSEG fellowships are intended for students at or near the beginning of their graduate studies in science or engineering. Those who accept the fellowship, which can be used at any university, will not incur a military or service obligation to the DoD or related agency. NDSEG Fellowships last for three years and pay for full tuition and all mandatory fees, a monthly stipend, and up to $1,000 a year in medical insurance.

OAK RIDGE ASSOCIATED UNIVERSITIES FUNDING OPPORTUNITIES

Website: http://www.orau.org (click on *Science Education and Peer Review\ Science Education*)
Additional Information: Through the online catalog and website, learn about academic fellowships and scholarships, research experiences, sabbaticals, and internships funded by a wide range of government agencies. These science education programs are administered by ORAU, many of them through the U.S. Department of Energy's Oak Ridge Institute for Science and Education (ORISE).

XEROX TECHNICAL MINORITY SCHOLARSHIP

Website: http://www.xerox.com/jobs/minority-scholarships/enus.html or http://www.xerox.com (see *Scholarships*)
Additional Information: See chapter 17.

20

SCHOLARSHIPS FOR NONTRADITIONAL STUDENTS—DISTANCE LEARNERS AND ADULTS RETURNING TO COLLEGE

> All things are possible to him who believes.
> They are less difficult to him who hopes.
> They are more easy to him who loves,
> and still more easy to him who perseveres
> in the practice of the three virtues.
>
> —Brother Lawrence

Many of the scholarships discussed in this book are also available to undergraduates and graduates regardless of age or whether their schooling hit a bump in the past and is now back on track. As a result, nontraditional students or individuals returning to college after a brief or prolonged period may also be eligible for these. There are even special scholarships for such students, especially women.

Aid may also be available for online education. In fact, some students may choose online education as a way to help finance their education since distance learning reduces the amount of money spent on food, lodging, and transportation.

Whether you're interested in returning to an actual college campus or becoming educated via your computer in an accredited online program, you should review all the strategies in this book for securing the aid to pay for your continued education. Make sure to read chapter 5, "Financial Aid Forms and Help from the Government with College Expenses," to learn

272 / Winning Scholarships for College

about tax benefits for education as well as other financial aid from the government.

SEARCHING FOR SCHOLARSHIPS AS A NONTRADITIONAL STUDENT— THE DIFFERENCE BETWEEN YOU AND OTHER STUDENTS

- *As a nontraditional student*—Scholarships for adult students may not be as abundant, but you still have the campus/community as a resource, just as on-campus students do. Nontraditional students should also revise their thinking to search for scholarships targeting adults as well as undergraduates. You may also benefit from credits or awards given for life experience (explained later in this chapter).
- *For all students*—Look for scholarships based on who you are, where you are, what you are, and your interests.
- *As a high school senior*—Scholarships may be more abundant, particularly small amounts in the community.
- *As a college student currently enrolled*—Undergraduate scholarships may not be as abundant, but you can use the campus and community as a resource and can still search for funds based on your interests, major, or career goals.
- *As a transfer student* (from a two-year/community college)—Undergraduate scholarships may not be as abundant, but you'll have the campus/community as a resource and can still search for funds based on your interests, major, or career goals. You also have the opportunity for transfer scholarships. Visit Phi Theta Kappa's list of institutions offering transfer scholarships at http://www.ptk.org (search for "Scholarships"). College Fish (http://www.collegefish.org) is also a good resource for students transferring from two-year colleges to four-year institutions, and the site includes information about college money for transfer students.

As outlined above, many scholarships are available, intended for all types of people. You just need to expend the time and effort to find them.

Don't Make Assumptions with Your Search

Look at eligibility requirements carefully. A scholarship program may mention student classification but not age.

For example, a scholarship directory or database may look like this one.

Council of Citizens with Low Vision International
Attn: Fred Scheigert Scholarship
324 S. Diamond Bar Blvd., #128
Diamond Bar, CA 91765
http://www.cclvi.org/scholarship.htm
Amount: $3,000
To qualify to receive a scholarship award, you must be:
- a full-time college/trade/vocational student for the upcoming academic year
- registered for at least 12 undergraduate units (9 graduate units)
- have a minimum cumulative 3.2 GPA

As illustrated in the above example, the eligibility requirements do not mention age. The example mentions qualifications only as they relate to your status in college. Please note that this can apply to you even if you have not yet started at your college since many deadlines will occur before the start of your first or next semester or quarter. As long as you will be starting your program in the immediate future (for example, the next regular session at your college or university), the scholarship check or award will be disbursed directly to the school during their next award period, so you can usually still apply. Check with the organization or program to confirm.

Books listing multitudes of scholarship and award opportunities might also include a category for "target applicants." For example, an entry might include a section such as this:

TARGET APPLICANT:
- College student
- Graduate student
- Adult student

Once again, the entry above does not mention age, only classification. As a result, if you are a nontraditional student, reviewing directories that include entries such as this one could uncover scholarship sources for you.

As a nontraditional or adult student, use the following checklist for additional sources of financial aid.

1. Review magazines directed toward career and success-oriented people, such as *Money*, *Black Enterprise*, and *Fortune*.

2. Try to get a paid internship. Many corporations sponsor internship programs for undergraduate and graduate students. Some will also sponsor scholarships for interns who have performed well academically. Even if the program does not fund all or part of the education of an intern, your job experience will enhance your résumé for future employment and scholarship consideration.

3. Contact the athletic office if you participate in any type of sport. Athletic scholarships can be offered for many different athletic activities such as swimming, lacrosse, and tennis. To get a sports scholarship, you don't always have to play football, basketball, or baseball. Refer to chapter 16, "Scholarships for the Unnoticed Athlete."

4. Contact the financial aid office at your college or university. Make sure to read your college or university catalog for a list of fellowships, endowments, and scholarships to get an idea of money you might qualify for. You should also visit the financial aid section of your school website. Get a good idea of the school's available student aid funds so you can ask specific questions about money to help you finish your education.

5. If you participate and have a serious interest in activities such as music, dance, theater, or art, contact those departments and ask if there are scholarships available in these areas.

6. Review directories that list grants in specific areas to see if there might be aid opportunities that could apply to you. For example, check out the online directory *Foundation Grants to Individuals* or *The Foundation Directory* by visiting http://www.foundation center.org.

7. See if you may be eligible for an out-of-state tuition waiver if you attend a public college or university out of your home state.

8. Try getting a company to sponsor you in exchange for your endorsement of their products or services.

9. Consider cooperative education. With this option you may alternate attending school with extended periods of work for a company or agency that needs students in your area of study. This period could go from several months to a year. The company or agency you work for generally pays your tuition bill or provides a salary designed to cover your tuition, in exchange for your services. In this arrangement your school may also give you academic credit based on the work experience you are accumulating in your field while working with the company or agency.

Other Strategies for Paying the College Bill

- Volunteer to be a resident advisor if the position is unfilled.
- Consider ROTC Scholarships—usually incurs a military commitment. See chapter 27.
- Join national community service organizations such as AmeriCorps.
- The National Guard can also help in paying your tuition bill. See chapter 27.

For more information about community and work-related aid, read chapter 14, "Scholarships and Awards for Community Service, Volunteering, and Work."

10. Contact honor societies in your area of study; for example, for Engineering, Anthropology, and other fields.
11. Check out companies in need of future employees in your area of study or a related area.
12. Check with organizations that benefit certain groups to which you inherently belong (e.g., legally blind, women, minority, etc.).
13. Contact alumni associations, particularly in the city where you're from, for scholarships. Contact the national alumni association office for your college or university as well.
14. If you attend or are planning to attend a United Negro College Fund (UNCF) college or university, visit http://www.uncf.org for information about numerous scholarships.
15. Contact community-based foundations and groups. See chapter 3, "using the Internet and Social Media in Your Scholarship Search," for more information about conducting an advanced Internet search for community foundations.
16. If you haven't already, read chapter 2, "The Scholarship Search: Discovering Hidden Treasures," for more ways to find sources of educational aid.
17. Contact professionals who are already working in the field you plan to enter. Ask about associations or organizations that could help you complete your education. For example, if you're studying in the field of veterinary medicine, contact a veterinarian. Doing so may or may not help you find a scholarship opportunity, but it could get you a paid internship and/or valuable work experience, which can help you win scholarships, grants, or open doors to other opportunities. You should do this in addition to your own efforts to find

national professional associations and organizations, because professionals in your area may know of smaller community and regionally based organizations that may offer support to students. On social media sites such as Facebook or Twitter, search for associations that may be affiliated with your field. For example, you can input "marketing" into the search bar and see if any promising organizations are found. Reading a few Tweets or glancing at the Facebook page will give you an idea of whether it may be helpful to you in your search.

ASSOCIATIONS AND ORGANIZATIONS OF PROFESSIONALS IN YOUR AREA OF STUDY

To find associations and organizations in your area of study and see if any of them offer scholarships, look at the *Encyclopedia of Associations* published by Gale Research, which can usually be found at your local library. You can also visit the Internet Public Library (http://www.ipl.org) and go to the Special Collections area to search for "Associations on the Net."

This section is organized by category, so if you're looking for associations that are affiliated with engineering, you can go directly to that section. When I did this, I found the National Society of Professional Engineers (NSPE) website as well as many others. I went to the NSPE website and used their site search engine to search for scholarships. Using this method I found the $10,000 Paul H. Robbins, P.E., Honorary Scholarship for undergraduate students.

You can also use Web search engines such as Yahoo! to find organizations in your field. I conducted an advanced Internet search (see chapter 3) for accounting societies and associations and found quite a few that offer scholarships. For accounting, there were at least six organizations that offered scholarships. They included the National Society of Public Accountants, the American Institute of Certified Public Accountants, the American Accounting Association (AAA), the International Association of Hospitality Accountants (IAHA), the Institute of Management Accountants, and the American Society of Women Accountants. All of these organizations offered some type of accounting scholarship to students already enrolled in college.

Be aware that membership can definitely have its privileges. Some associations may require you to be a member to be eligible for a scholarship.

Many others do not. For those that do require you to be a member, the membership fee is usually reduced for currently enrolled students.

THE LOCAL SEARCH FOR NONTRADITIONAL STUDENTS

The local search is one most often ignored by the typical student. I covered this topic for all students in an earlier chapter of this book, but I want to reiterate the steps for nontraditional students because they often use only a few scholarship directories and an Internet search service such as Fastweb.com, but they need to go further. Unfortunately, if your scholarship quest includes only directories and the Internet, or even just the Internet, you could be overlooking some valuable scholarship opportunities.

The best and most complete scholarship search includes your community, state, and region. Most of the scholarships you find in directories and on the Internet are national, which means that if you apply, you are among many others who hope to win the scholarship. In addition, an Internet search for scholarships for nontraditional students can be frustrating because currently so few resources address scholarships for you specifically.

For a local scholarship search, consider the following sources:

- The career center at your institution
- The department office for your current or future major or minor course of study
- Your current or intended university's website for pages listing scholarships that can be used at your school but are not specific to your institution. For example, Georgetown University has maintained a page listing outside scholarships for many years.
- Your college or university's website for scholarships, grants, and fellowships specific to your university. Also do this for universities you're contemplating but have not yet applied to. Although you may not qualify currently, you may in the future if you can meet the requirements. You need to take charge of your scholarship quest by keeping track of your current and future scholarship eligibility at your institution.
- Community foundations. Visit http://www.novacf.org for an example of a community foundation and the scholarships offered.
- Local clubs and organizations. Examples of these would be the Soroptimist Club, the Optimist Club, Exchange Clubs of America,

Daughters of the American Revolution, YMCA/YWCA, the Kiwanis Club, the Rotary Club, the Lions Club, or the Knights of Columbus. Also look for sororities and fraternities. For more examples of clubs and organizations based in local communities throughout the United States, read chapter 2. Alpha Kappa Alpha Educational Advancement Foundation (http://www.akaeaf.org) is an example of a foundation affiliated with a sorority that offers scholarships.

- Your place of employment. Your company may offer tuition reimbursement. As someone returning to college or an older student who is currently employed, check to see if your company has an Employee Reimbursement Program or an Educational Assistance Program. If so, you can be reimbursed for the cost of tuition and fees once courses you take have been completed and you have received a satisfactory grade. Some employers may require that employees work a specific period of time after receiving their degree as a form of repayment.
- Where you interned, in the past or recently. You may be able to request financial assistance from the company to complete your education. Some companies may automatically offer interns a scholarship once the program is completed.
- Companies and banks in your community. Some may have scholarships available to local residents. For some individuals in the medical field such as nurses, some hospitals offer educational assistance if you are willing to work in their hospital for some period of time. Your local newspaper or the chamber of commerce may be able to assist you with identifying local companies.
- Your union. If you belong to a work-related union, ask if scholarships are available to you as a member.
- Any organization to which you belong, local or national. Determine whether they have a scholarship program for their members. Your church or faith-based organization might be an example.
- Professors and/or advisors at your current campus or the one you're planning to attend. Some educators form groups to offer scholarships to students in special areas.
- Credit unions. Some have scholarship opportunities for their members.
- Check to see if your intended college or university offers the Osher Reentry Scholarship program, which is supported by the Osher

Foundation. It provides grants directly to reentry students who are defined by Osher as individuals who have experienced an interruption in their education of five or more years and want to resume their education at the undergraduate level. The scholarship is intended to benefit students who have considerable years of employability ahead of them—ideally, aged 25 to 50. See the website for a list of participating institutions at http://osherfoundation.org.

FUNDING SOURCES FOR NONTRADITIONAL STUDENTS

Explore each of the following sources of aid that could assist you with your continued education. Some are mentioned in earlier sections, but here's a quick summary:

- *Federal aid*—Visit the Federal Student Aid section on the Department of Education's website (http://www.ed.gov) to determine if you are eligible for any federal aid or grant programs.
- *State aid*—Find the organization in your state designated to administer funds for students who are residents. For example, in Virginia, this organization is the State Council of Higher Education for Virginia (SCHEV). See chapter 5 to find your state's financial aid agency.
- *Membership organizations*—If you are a member of an on-campus organization or one in your community, determine if scholarships or general college funding is available to members. Your church or faith-based organization is an example, another is the NAACP, a community-based civic organization that has scholarships available to its members and others.
- *Scholastic Honor Societies*—Honor societies such as Golden Key International Honor Society (http://www.goldenkey.org) or Phi Theta Kappa (http://www.ptk.org) and many others have scholarships available to their members. Hundreds of scholastic societies cover interest areas from music to chemistry and beyond. Read my book, *College Survival and Success Skills 101* to find out more about scholastic honor societies and whether any of them give awards in the field you're currently in or planning to pursue. *College Survival and Success Skills 101* focuses on success strategies that include additional college funding for current college students.

Are you a woman returning to school after suspending your education for a number of years?

If you are, there are many women's organizations that may have funding for you to complete or further your education. For example, visit the following organizations and others you find by exploring your community's phone book for more information or conducting an advanced Internet search. They may be able to help you in your continued studies:

- Business and Professional Women's Foundation
- American Association of University Women
- Jeannette Rankin Foundation
- Association for Women in Science

Also visit http://www.advancingwomen.com for more information on associations and organizations focused on helping women in all areas of their lives, including furthering their education.

- *Associations*—An excellent resource for students of all ages are the thousands of associations in the United States. Many of them have scholarships available to students who want to continue their studies and pursue a career in their interest area.

ONLINE EDUCATION

Online education programs are becoming the medium of choice for many students who want to return to college but cannot accommodate traveling to take courses at an institution. With distance learning, students can get the degree they want, whether it's needed to upgrade their skills at present jobs or to qualify them for new ones, without ever leaving their homes or offices. This method of obtaining a degree also helps to decrease overall costs since you'll be studying from your home or office and avoiding expenses such as transportation and meals.

However, always be aware of the fake degrees offered by disreputable distance-learning or online education programs. When considering a program, you should call the human resources department of local companies in the area where the program is physically located to find out if they hire or have ever hired anyone with a degree from the program you are considering. Check the Better Business Bureau for complaints about the program and conduct an Internet search for the organization and check for any poor reviews, scam alerts, or complaints. Consult the career center for the educational organization and ask about graduation rates and job placement statistics. Confirm whether the educational organization has an accredited degree or certificate program. If it does, you may be able to get financial aid from the federal government. Visit http://www.studentaid.ed.gov for more information. For most scholarships and awards, you need to be attending an accredited college or university. To determine if the school you're interested in is accredited, visit one or both of these websites: Council for Higher Education Accreditation (http://www.chea.org) and the U.S. Department of Education Office of Post-Secondary Education (http://www.ope.ed.gov/accreditation). Please note that inclusion in the CHEA or OPE database does not automatically qualify the organization as legitimate. You should still do your due diligence.

CREDIT FOR LIFE EXPERIENCE

Keep in mind that some colleges sponsor reduced or non-tuition programs for older students returning to college. Some universities offer Life Experience Credit Awards or some other type of experience-based award for mature students whose life experience may be credited toward the requirements of a degree program. Contact your colleges and universities of interest for more information.

Attending college online or later than usual is common for many individuals who join the military or National Guard after graduating from high school. If you are a veteran or are currently in the military, refer to chapter 27 for the "Scholarships and College Funding for the Military and Their Family," for information about your funding options based on military service.

SCHOLARSHIP OPPORTUNITIES FOR NONTRADITIONAL STUDENTS, DISTANCE LEARNERS, AND ADULT STUDENTS RETURNING TO COLLEGE

DISTANCE LEARNERS AND ALTERNATIVE EDUCATION

Below are sources that can be useful for distance learners or those in online degree programs and adult students returning to college, or if you

Scholarship Giveaways for Nontraditional Students

If you don't want to write an essay but you're willing to share your name and e-mail address for potential marketing offers, you can enter many scholarship giveaways that may result in you winning big dollars.

- Scholarships4Moms $10,000 Monthly Scholarship Giveaway—http://www.scholarships4moms.net
- Scholarships4WorkingAdults $10,000 Monthly Scholarship Giveaway—http://www.Scholarships4WorkingAdults.com
- A similar program requires only a three-sentence essay, Return2College Scholarships—http://www.return2college.com/scholarship.cfm

Giveaways are especially prone to disappearing as quickly as they appear. The programs may or not be available by the time you visit one of the sites above. Be certain not to share personal information such as Social Security numbers to enter these types of giveaways.

just graduated from high school and you're considering putting off going to college, see "A Few Important Items to Remember" on p. 181 for additional tips.

ADULT STUDENTS IN SCHOLASTIC TRANSITION

Executive Women International Scholarship Program
3860 South 2300 East
Salt Lake City, UT 84109
(801) 355-2800
E-mail: ewi@ewiconnect.com
Website: http://www.ewiconnect.com (see *ASIST*)
Additional Information: This ASIST award is open to adult students at transitional points in their lives. They may be single parents, individuals just entering the workforce, or displaced workers. Scholarships are awarded through chapters. See the website for participating chapters and deadlines.

AMERICAN ASSOCIATION OF UNIVERSITY WOMEN (AAUW)
EDUCATIONAL FOUNDATION

Career Development Grants
ACT, Inc.

P.O. Box 4030
Iowa City, IA 52243-4030
(319) 337-1716, ext. 60
E-mail: aauw@act.org
Website: http://www.aauw.org
Additional Information: AAUW awards Career Development Grants to women who already have a bachelor's degree and are preparing to advance their careers, change careers, or reenter the workforce. Preference is given to AAUW members, women of color, and women pursuing their first advanced degree or credentials in nontraditional fields. Applications are usually available between August 1 and December 15, the deadline for applications. This program has an application filing fee. Award amounts range from $2,000 to $12,000.

ASSOCIATION FOR NONTRADITIONAL STUDENTS IN HIGHER EDUCATION SCHOLARSHIPS

Website: http://www.myantshe.org (see *Scholarships*)
Additional Information: If you are a nontraditional student, you are eligible to join ANTSHE, which is an organization dedicated to the support and encouragement of adult students who are pursuing their degrees in higher education. You must be a member to apply for one of their scholarships. The association administers the Marius "Gabe" Degabriel Scholarship for undergraduates and the Kazimour Scholarship for graduates. Award amounts vary.

BUSINESS AND PROFESSIONAL WOMEN/USA FOUNDATION

Career Advancement Scholarship Program
Website: http://www.bpwusa.org
Additional Information: The Career Advancement Scholarship Program is designed to award financial assistance to women who wish to advance in their careers, or will soon enter or reenter the workforce. To be eligible for this award you must be female, 25 years of age or older, and a U.S. citizen. You must also demonstrate a critical need for financial assistance, have clearly defined career plans, and be officially accepted into a program or course of study at an accredited institution in the United States, Puerto Rico, or the U.S. Virgin Islands. If awarded the scholarship, you must graduate within twelve to twenty-four months from the date of

grant. The scholarships are awarded through the Foundation's Legacy Partners for STEM (Science, Technology, Engineering, and Math)-related fields. Visit the website to find a legacy partner in your area for the availability of this scholarship opportunity and others.

COLLEGE JUMPSTART SCHOLARSHIP

c/o College JumpStart Scholarship Fund
4546 B10 El Camino Real, 325
Los Altos, CA 94022
E-mail: admin@jumpstart-scholarship.net
Website: www.jumpstart-scholarship.net
Additional Information: See Appendix A.

COLLEGE IS POWER SCHOLARSHIP

E-mail: service@collegeispower.com
Website: http://www.collegeispower.com/scholarship.cfm
Additional Information: This scholarship is available to students 17 years of age or older who plan to start a program of higher education within the next twelve months or who are currently enrolled in a program of higher education. You must be a full- or part-time student, attend a campus-based or online program and be a citizen or permanent resident of the United States. Award amount is $1,500. Deadline is usually in May.

DR. WYNETTA A. FRAZIER "SISTER TO SISTER" SCHOLARSHIP

National Hook-Up of Black Women, Inc.
Scholarship Committee
1809 East 71st Street, Suite 205
Chicago, IL 60649
Website: http://www.nhbwinc.com (see *Scholarships*)
Additional Information: The scholarship is open to mature African American women (at least 30 years of age and older) who are returning to college without the support of a spouse. Possible applicants may have dropped out of college to seek employment or care for their children. Scholarship is for $500. Deadline is usually in March.

JEANNETTE RANKIN FOUNDATION

Women's Education Fund
Jeannette Rankin Foundation
1 Huntington Road, Suite 701
Athens, GA 30606
E-mail: info@rankinfoundation.org
Website: http://www.rankinfoundation.org
Additional Information: The Jeannette Rankin Foundation awards grants on an annual basis to low-income women, 35 years of age and older, who are in an undergraduate or vocational training program. Those applying for funds must have a vision of how their education will benefit themselves, their families, and their communities. Applications may be downloaded from the website beginning in November. Deadline is usually March 1.

LINDA LAEL MILLER SCHOLARSHIP FOR WOMEN

Website: http://www.lindalaelmiller.com (see *Linda's Scholarship*) or http://www.lindalaelmiller.com/lindas-scholarship/
Additional Information: These $1,000 scholarships are awarded annually to nontraditional women students 25 years or older who may have had a difficult time finding scholarships for which they qualify. Generally, the scholarship funds may be used not only for tuition and books, but also for child care, transportation, and other expenses not covered by traditional scholarships. See website for additional details and an application. A 500-words-or-less essay is required covering the following points:

- Why you are applying for a Linda Lael Miller Scholarship for Women
- How achieving your educational goals will enhance your and your family's future
- The specific purpose for which you would use the funds
- The dollar amount you are seeking in a Linda Lael Miller Scholarship

"LEADING THE FUTURE II" SCHOLARSHIP

The Scholarship Workshop
P.O. Box 176
Centreville, VA 20122
(703) 579-4245

E-mail: scholars@scholarshipworkshop.com
Website: http://www.scholarshipworkshop.com
Additional Information: The "Leading the Future" Scholarship is designed to elevate students' consciousness about their future and their role in helping others once they receive a college degree and become established in a community. It is open to high school seniors or current college undergraduates who are U.S. residents. Visit the website to download an application.

THE LEOPOLD SCHEPP FOUNDATION

551 Fifth Avenue, Suite 3000
New York, NY 10176-3201
(212) 692 0191
Website: http://www.scheppfoundation.org
Additional Information: See Appendix A.

MEXICAN AMERICAN LEGAL DEFENSE & EDUCATION FUND (MALDEF)

634 S. Spring Street, 11th Fl.
Los Angeles, CA 90014
Website: http://www.maldef.org (click on *Education\Scholarship Resources*)
Additional Information: See chapter 17.

THE RAGINS/BRASWELL NATIONAL SCHOLARSHIP

The Scholarship Workshop
P.O. Box 176
Centreville, VA 20122
(703) 579-4245
E-mail: scholars@scholarshipworkshop.com
Website: http://www.scholarshipworkshop.com
Additional Information: See Appendix A.

SODEXO FOUNDATION

Stephen J. Brady STOP Hunger Scholarships
9801 Washingtonian Boulevard
Gaithersburg, MD 20878

(615) 320-3149 (indicate your call is about the Sodexo Foundation STOP Hunger Scholarships)
E-mail: STOPHunger@applyists.com
Website: http://www.sodexofoundation.org (see *Scholarships*)
Additional Information: see chapter 14.

SOROPTIMIST INTERNATIONAL OF THE AMERICAS—WOMEN'S OPPORTUNITY AWARDS

1709 Spruce Street
Philadelphia, PA 19103-6103
(215) 893-9000
E-mail: siahq@soroptimist.org
Website: http://www.soroptimist.org
Additional Information: The Women's Opportunity Awards program was established by Soroptimist International of the Americas in 1972 and is designed to give women heads of household who are the primary source of financial support for their families the opportunity to achieve their career goals. To be eligible, you must be a woman head of household who is attending, or has been accepted to, a vocational/skills training program, or an undergraduate degree program. You must demonstrate financial need, be a resident of a Soroptimist International of the Americas member country or territories, and must not have already earned an undergraduate degree. The award can be used for any expenses related to your education, including tuition, books, housing, child care, and transportation. The program begins at the community level. Local winners from the community then become eligible to receive regional awards ranging from $3,000 to $5,000. The first-place winners from each region then become eligible to receive one of three $10,000 finalist awards. The deadline is normally December 1.

WOMEN'S INDEPENDENCE SCHOLARSHIP PROGRAM, INC.

4900 Randall Parkway, Suite H
Wilmington, NC 28403
(910) 397-7742
Website: http://www.wispinc.org
Additional Information: The Women's Independence Scholarship Program (WISP) was created in 1999 to help formerly battered women overcome the barriers to education necessary to become employable and

financially stable. Women who are U.S. citizens or legal U.S. residents who have survived partner abuse and have been separated from their abuser for a minimum of one year are eligible to apply. You must have applied to or have been officially accepted into an accredited course of study at a U.S. institution. You must also demonstrate a critical need for financial assistance, exhibit a strong desire, along with the ability, to complete a training and/or academic program, and have a definite plan to use the training to upgrade skills for career advancement, to train for a new career field, or to enter or reenter the job market. Please see the website for additional eligibility requirements and deadlines.

21

SCHOLARSHIPS FOR INTERNATIONAL STUDENTS AND STUDY ABROAD FUNDING FOR U.S. STUDENTS

> Things don't turn up in this world until somebody turns them up.
>
> —James Garfield

For international students who want to study in the United States, your primary vehicle for receiving scholarships are the colleges and universities themselves. Research the colleges and universities you are interested in attending by visiting their websites, then sending letters or e-mails to inquire about scholarships for international students. Institutions that have large international studies programs may also award a substantial amount of scholarship money to international students, and there may also be numerous graduate scholarships and fellowships available to them. For example, you might be able to secure funding for your education in the United States from one or more of the following sources:

- Private organizations, foundations, and international agencies based in the United States and abroad
- U.S. federal government agencies as well as foreign governments, through assistantships, fellowships, and some special awards
- Colleges and universities, through scholarships, fellowships, grants, and assistantships for graduate students, including those from other countries
- Direct exchange programs, for a full or partial waiver of tuition and fees through your home-country university and a U.S.-based university

For American students who want to study at colleges and universities abroad, various sources of funds are available to you as well. Some of the funds are specifically for short terms of study abroad. Others are for longer educational periods abroad.

The following includes addresses for obtaining further information about scholarships and financial aid for foreign students and Americans who want to study abroad.

See page 181, "A Few Important Items to Remember," for additional tips.

SCHOLARSHIP PROGRAMS AND INFORMATION FOR INTERNATIONAL STUDENTS AND THOSE WHO WANT TO STUDY ABROAD

Database and Research Sites for International Scholarship Opportunities

EDUCATIONUSA

http://www.educationusa.info
Website sponsored by the U.S. Department of State to help international students pursue U.S. higher education opportunities.

EDUPASS

http://www.edupass.org
Primarily an information site for international students who want to finance college.

INSTITUTE OF INTERNATIONAL EDUCATION (IIE) FUNDING FOR U.S. STUDY

http://www.fundingusstudy.org
Scholarship database for international students.

INTERNATIONAL EDUCATION FINANCIAL AID

http://www.IEFA.org
Primarily a scholarship search database for international students.

SCHOLARSHIPS CANADA

http://www.scholarshipscanada.com
Primarily a scholarship search database for Canadian students.

STUDENTAWARDS.COM

http://www.studentawards.com
Primarily a scholarship search database for international students.

INSTITUTE FOR THE INTERNATIONAL EDUCATION OF STUDENTS (IES)

33 West Monroe Street, Suite 2300
Chicago, IL 60603-5405
(800) 995-2300 or (312) 944-1750
E-mail: info@IESabroad.org
Website: http://www.iesabroad.org
Additional Information: This site provides scholarship information and includes information about scholarships for international students funded by IES.

Scholarship Programs for International Students

AMERICAN ASSOCIATION OF UNIVERSITY WOMEN (AAUW)
EDUCATIONAL FOUNDATION INTERNATIONAL FELLOWSHIPS

AAUW Fellowships and Grants
ACT, Inc.
P.O. Box 4030
Iowa City, IA 52243-4030
(319) 337-1716 (indicate you are inquiring about the AAUW International Fellowships)
E-mail: aauw@act.org
Website: http://www.aauw.org
Additional Information: AAUW International Fellowships are awarded for full-time study or research in the United States to women who are not U.S. citizens or permanent residents. The fellowship can be used for graduate and postgraduate studies at accredited U.S. institutions. To be eligible, you must have completed an academic degree equivalent to a bachelor's degree from a U.S. college or university by the time you apply for this fellowship. In addition, you must have applied to your proposed institution of study by the time you submit your application. Your application should show excellent academic achievement and a demonstrated commitment to women and girls. If you are selected, you are expected to return to your

home country to become a leader in business, government, academia, community activism, the arts, or the sciences after completion of your studies.

THE COLLEGIATE INVENTORS COMPETITION

(800) 968-4332, option 5
E-mail: collegiate@invent.org
Website: http://www.invent.org
Awards: Up to $15,000
Additional Information: see chapter 15.

CREATE-A-GREETING CARD SCHOLARSHIP CONTEST

Website: http://www.gallerycollection.com/greetingcardscontests.htm or http://www.gallerycollection.com/greeting-cards-scholarship.htm
Additional Information: See chapter 18.

ELIE WIESEL PRIZE IN ETHICS ESSAY CONTEST

Elie Wiesel Foundation for Humanity
555 Madison Avenue, 20th Fl.
New York, NY 10022
(212) 490-7788
Website: http://www.eliewieselfoundation.org or http://www.ethicsprize.org
Additional Information: See chapter 18.

FOSTER CARE TO SUCCESS (FC2S) SCHOLARSHIP PROGRAMS

(formerly Orphan Foundation of America)
21351 Gentry Drive, Suite 130
Sterling, VA 20166
(571) 203-0270; fax: (571) 203-0273
E-mail: info@fc2success.org
Website: www.fc2success.org
Additional Information: See Appendix A.

INTERNATIONAL ORDER OF THE KING'S DAUGHTERS AND SONS HEALTH CAREERS SCHOLARSHIPS

Director, Health Careers Department
P.O. Box 1040
Chautauqua, NY 14722-1040
Website: http://iokds.org (see *Scholarship Programs*)
Additional Information: See chapter 19.

L. RON HUBBARD'S ILLUSTRATORS OF THE FUTURE CONTEST

P.O. Box 3190
Los Angeles, CA 90078
(323) 466-3310
Website: http://www.writersofthefuture.com or http://www.writersofthe future.com/contest
Additional Information: See chapter 15.

L. RON HUBBARD'S WRITERS OF THE FUTURE CONTEST

P.O. Box 1630
Los Angeles, CA 90078
(323) 466-3310
Website: http://www.writersofthefuture.com or http://www.writersofthe future.com/contest
Additional Information: See chapter 15.

PAUL AND DAISY SOROS FELLOWSHIPS FOR NEW AMERICANS

400 W. 59th Street
New York, NY 10019
(212) 547-6926
E-mail: pdsoros_fellows@sorosny.org
Website: http://www.pdsoros.org
Additional Information: The purpose of this program is to provide opportunities for new Americans to achieve leadership in their chosen fields. If you value the U.S. Constitution and the Bill of Rights, this could be a great opportunity to pursue additional study in your chosen field. A new American could be any of the following: a resident alien holding a

green card, someone naturalized as a U.S. citizen, or the child of two parents who are both naturalized citizens. You must also be a college senior or a college graduate with a bachelor's degree or, if in graduate school, not yet have completed your second year in it. As of the application deadline, you must not have reached 31 years of age.

The Paul and Daisy Soros Fellowships for New Americans can support up to two years of graduate study—in any field and in any advanced degree-granting program—in the United States. Each fellowship awarded consists of up to $25,000 in maintenance grants and up to $20,000 in tuition support for each year of graduate study, for a maximum of $90,000. The deadline for submission of completed applications is usually in early November. Consult the website for current deadlines and specific application requirements.

SHIRE CANADA ADHD SCHOLARSHIP PROGRAM

2250 Alfred-Nobel Blvd., Suite 500
Saint-Laurent, Quebec, H4S 2C9, Canada
(514) 787-2300 or (800) 268-2772
Website: http://www.shireadhdscholarship.com/CA-EN/
Additional Information: This scholarship is intended for Canadian students who are of the age of majority in their province of residence and have been diagnosed with ADHD. You must be a legal resident of Alberta, Ontario, or Quebec and have been accepted or currently enrolled in a post-secondary program at a Canadian accredited two- to four-year college, university, trade school, technical school, or vocational school located in Alberta, Ontario, or Quebec. You must also be under the care of a licensed health care professional for ADHD.

SOROPTIMIST INTERNATIONAL OF THE AMERICAS—WOMEN'S OPPORTUNITY AWARDS

1709 Spruce Street
Philadelphia, PA 19103-6103
(215) 893-9000
E-mail: http://siahq@soroptimist.org
Website: www.soroptimist.org
Additional Information: See chapter 20.

For U.S. Students Studying Abroad

BOREN UNDERGRADUATE SCHOLARSHIPS

Boren Scholarships and Fellowships
Institute of International Education, 7th Floor
1400 K Street NW
Washington, DC 20005-2403
(800) 618-NSEP
E-mail: boren@iie.org
Website: http://www.borenawards.org
Additional Information: See chapter 14.

BOREN GRADUATE FELLOWSHIPS

Boren Scholarships and Fellowships
Institute of International Education, 7th Floor
1400 K Street NW
Washington, DC 20005-2403
(800) 618-NSEP
E-mail: boren@iie.org
Website: http://www.borenawards.org
Additional Information: See chapter 14.

COUNCIL ON INTERNATIONAL EDUCATIONAL EXCHANGE SCHOLARSHIP PROGRAMS

300 Fore Street
Portland, ME 04101
(800) 40-STUDY
E-mail: studyinfo@ciee.org
Website: http://www.ciee.org
Social Media: Follow CIEE on Twitter and Facebook.
Additional Information: Annually, CIEE awards millions of dollars in scholarships to students who want to study abroad. Please visit the website or use the contact information above to obtain specific eligibility requirements for each of these scholarships.
  • CIEE GAIN Scholarship
  • CIEE LIFT Scholarship
  • Ping Foundation Scholarships, which include:

- CIEE International Study Program Scholarships
- Jennifer Ritzmann Scholarship for Studies in Tropical Biology
- John E. Bowman Travel Grants
- Kathleen McDermott Scholarship
- Michael Stohl Scholarship
- Peter Wollitzer Scholarship, for study in Asia
- Robert B. Bailey Scholarship

FOUNDATION FOR GLOBAL SCHOLARS SCHOLARSHIPS

12050 N. Pecos Street, Suite 320
Westminster, CO 80234
Website: http://www.foundationforglobalscholars.org/scholarships-over view/
Additional Information: To apply, you must be a U.S. or Canadian citizen currently enrolled in a North American college or university that accepts transfer credit from an academic program abroad. Credit will be applied to your degree being earned. Scholarships are open to college freshmen, sophomores, juniors, or seniors or students in medical school, law school, graduate school, or a two-year community college. Scholarships range between $500 and $2,500. See the website for additional details and deadlines.

KYMANOX'S JAMES J. DAVIS MEMORIAL SCHOLARSHIP FOR STUDENTS STUDYING ABROAD

Website: http://www.kymanox.com/scholarship
Additional Information: This $1,000 scholarship is designed to encourage students to broaden their horizons by experiencing something new abroad. To apply, you must be a U.S. citizen or U.S. permanent resident, and a college undergraduate enrolled in a full academic year or fall, spring, or summer semester/quarter study at an accredited university abroad. Less than eight weeks' study is not eligible for this program. Preference will be given to students with financial need, students studying in a non-English-speaking country, and those who are majoring in Engineering, Math, or Science.

MARSHALL SCHOLARSHIPS

E-mail: apps@marshallscholarship.org
Website: http://www.marshallscholarship.org
Social Media: Follow Marshall Scholar@marshallscholar on Twitter.

Additional Information: Marshall Scholarships provide funding for young Americans of high ability to study for a degree in the United Kingdom. Up to forty scholars are selected each year to study at the graduate level at a UK institution in any field of study. The scholarship is open only to U.S. citizens who hold a first degree from an accredited four-year college or university in the United States with a minimum GPA of 3.7. The scholarship covers university fees, cost of living expenses, annual book grant, thesis grant, research and daily travel grants, fares to and from the United States and, in some cases, a contribution toward the support of a dependent spouse. Amounts vary.

SARA'S WISH FOUNDATION SCHOLARSHIP PROGRAM

23 Ash Lane
Amherst, MA 01002
(413) 256-0914
E-mail: info@saraswish.org
Website: http://saraswish.org
Social Media: Follow Sara's Wish on Facebook.
Additional Information: The Sara's Wish Foundation was established in memory of Sara Christie Schewe. In 1996 Sara was killed in a fatal bus crash in India while participating in a Semester at Sea program. The scholarship was established to perpetuate Sara's ideals and create opportunities for other students who share Sara's zest for life, love of adventure, and zeal to excel. To be eligible for this scholarship, you must have a commitment to public service, a strong record of scholarship, a history of leadership experience, a sincere interest in the work of Sara's Wish Foundation, and a willingness to join its ongoing efforts to improve safety awareness. The scholarship provides financial assistance for young women who want to pursue international travel experiences in the areas of education, health care, or public service. Please note that only U.S. citizens can apply for this program. For more information and an application, visit the website.

For International Study—United States or Other Countries

THE WORLD BANK JOINT JAPAN/WORLD BANK GRADUATE SCHOLARSHIP PROGRAM

1818 H Street NW, MSN J4-402
Washington, DC 20433 USA

(202) 473-6849
E-mail: jjwbgsp@worldbank.org
Website: http://www.worldbank.org/wbi/scholarships/
Additional Information: This program awards scholarships to individuals from World Bank member countries for graduate study at universities renowned for their development research and teaching. Scholarships cannot be used for study in the scholar's own country. Visit the website or contact the address above for more information.

22

SCHOLARSHIPS FOR DISABLED STUDENTS

Sooner or later, those who win are those who think
they can.

—Richard Bach

Scholarship opportunities are available to students with all types of disabilities or physical handicaps. As emphasized throughout this book, students should use *all* of the strategies discussed in this book for finding sources of aid and securing the funds to pursue their education further. However, to get information specific to students with disabilities, you should contact the financial aid office and the office of Disability Support Services at the college or university you attend or are planning to attend.

Make sure to conduct an advanced Internet search for your specific type of disability as well. To conduct an advanced search, go to a search engine such as Yahoo! On the main tool bar at the top of the page, look on the right-hand side for a dropdown box. In the dropdown list that appears, choose "Advanced Search." You should see options on the page that appear similar to the image below.

Show results with all of these words	scholarship	any part of the page ▼
the exact phrase	hemophilia	any part of the page ▼
any of these words		any part of the page ▼
none of these words		any part of the page ▼

This example search was made specifically to find scholarships for individuals with hemophilia. The National Hemophilia Foundation at http://www.hemophilia.org was one of the top results listing scholarship and funding resources for those with hemophilia. Use an advanced search such as this one, based on Boolean search logic, to find scholarships for your specific type of disability.

Don't forget that all other scholarships are still open to you as well. In fact, obstacles you may have overcome to pursue your education while dealing with your disability may even help you in writing compelling essays for scholarship consideration. The following sources may be helpful in your search to find aid specific to students with disabilities:

See "A Few Important Items to Remember" on page 181 for additional tips.

GENERAL SCHOLARSHIP OPPORTUNITIES FOR THE DISABLED

CENTRAL INTELLIGENCE AGENCY UNDERGRADUATE SCHOLARSHIP PROGRAM

Office of Public Affairs
Washington, DC 20505
(703) 482-0623
Website: http://www.cia.gov (see *Student Opportunities* or search for "Scholarship")
Additional Information: The Undergraduate Scholarship Program has a special goal of attracting minorities and students with disabilities. It provides scholarships of up to $18,000 per school year for tuition, fees, books, and supplies, as well as paid summer employment for those who qualify. It is available to high school seniors planning to enroll in a four- or five-year college program and to college sophomores as well. If awarded the scholarship, you must maintain a full-time college status and a minimum cumulative 3.0 GPA. You must also agree to employment with the Agency, which will require relocation to Washington, D.C., after your college graduation for a period of 1.5 times the length of your college sponsorship. For example, if you received the scholarship for four years, then you must work for the agency for a period of six years. You will also have summer employment with the agency. The Agency will pay the cost of transportation between your school and the D.C. area and also provide a housing allowance during the summer. To apply, you must be a U.S. citizen, 18 years of age by April of your senior year (for high school seniors), have scores of at least 1500 on the SAT or 21 on the ACT (for high school seniors), have a 3.0 (on a 4.0 scale) GPA or higher, demonstrate financial

need (household income ceiling of $70,000 for a family of four, and $80,000 for a family of five or more), and meet the same employment standards as permanent employees. The deadline is October 15 of each year.

DISABLEDPERSON, INC., SCHOLARSHIP COMPETITION

disABLEDperson, Inc.
P.O. Box 230636
Encinitas, CA 92023-0636
(760) 420-1269
E-mail: info@disabledperson.com
Website: http://www.disabledperson.com
Additional Information: To enter this competition, you must sign up on disABLEDperson.com as a community member. You must also write an essay of no more than 750 words on the current topic and complete a registration form. Please note that correct spelling and grammar are imperative and you should submit only carefully edited versions of the essay you write since it is the primary basis for the scholarship award. In addition, you must be enrolled in a U.S.-based two- or four-year accredited college or university and be a full-time student (minimum of 12 credits for undergraduate, 9 credits for graduate). You must also be a U.S. citizen. If you win this $1,000 scholarship, you must prove disability through your Disability Student Services department. The program defines disability according to the ADA description: a physical or mental impairment that substantially limits one or more major life activities.

LITTLE PEOPLE OF AMERICA, INC., SCHOLARSHIPS

Little People of America Inc.
250 El Camino Real, Suite 201
Tustin, CA 92780
(888) LPA-2001 (English and Spanish), direct: (714) 368-3689
E-mail: info@lpaonline.org
Website: http://www.lpaonline.org
Additional Information: Little People of America (LPA) is made up of those who are 4'10" or less in height, family members, or someone who has demonstrated a well-founded interest in issues relating to dwarfism. Scholarships are awarded in order of preference to any one of the following: members of LPA who have a medically diagnosed form of dwarfism, immediate family members of dwarfs who are also paid members of LPA,

people with dwarfism who are not members of LPA, disabled students in general, and non-disabled students who can demonstrate a need for financial educational assistance.

For Individuals Who Are Blind or Legally Blind

AMERICAN COUNCIL OF THE BLIND SCHOLARSHIPS

American Council of the Blind
2200 Wilson Boulevard, Suite 650
Arlington, VA 22201-3354
(202) 467-5081; fax: (202) 467-5085
E-mail: info@acb.org
Website: http://www.acb.org (see *Scholarships*)
Additional Information: This organization provides scholarships ranging from $1,000 to $2,500 to vocational students or entering college freshmen, undergraduate and graduate college students who are legally blind, maintain a 3.3 GPA, and are involved in their school/local community. Deadline is normally in early March. See the website for additional details.

CHRISTIAN RECORD SERVICES, INC., SCHOLARSHIPS

Christian Record Services, Inc.
4444 South 52nd Street
Lincoln, NE 68516-1302
(402) 488-0981; fax: (402) 488-7582
E-mail: info@christianrecord.org
Website: http://www.christianrecord.org
Additional Information: To apply for these scholarships you must be legally blind and planning to attend or currently attending college at the undergraduate level to secure training that will enable independence and self-support. The deadline is generally April 1 of each year. Applications are accepted between November 1 of the present year and April 1 of the following year for assistance in the next fall term.

NFB SCHOLARSHIP PROGRAM

National Federation of the Blind Scholarship Committee
200 East Wells Street at Jernigan Place

Baltimore, MD 21230
(410) 659-9314, ext. 2415
E-mail: scholarships@nfb.org
Website: http://www.nfb.org
Additional Information: Applicants must be legally blind in both eyes
and studying or planning to study full-time at the post-secondary level. An
additional scholarship is also available to a full-time employee who is also
attending school part-time. Scholarships are awarded based on academic
excellence, community service, and financial need. Please visit the website
or e-mail for additional details and eligibility requirements. The deadline
is normally March 31 each year and awards range from $3,000 to $12,000.
Scholarship winners must also participate in the NFB convention.

For Individuals Who Are Hearing Impaired

ALEXANDER GRAHAM BELL ASSOCIATION FOR THE DEAF COLLEGE SCHOLARSHIPS

Alexander Graham Bell Association
3417 Volta Place NW
Washington, DC 20007
(202) 337-5220
E-mail: financialaid@agbell.org
Website: http://www.agbell.org
Additional Information: This is a merit-based competitive scholarship
program offering several scholarships for full-time students who have a pre-
lingual bilateral hearing loss in the moderately severe to profound range,
use listening and spoken language, and are pursuing a bachelor's, master's, or
doctorate (not law or public policy) degree at an accredited mainstream college or university. Available scholarships vary annually in amounts ranging
from $1,000 to $10,000. Please visit the website for application and current
deadline. This scholarship is open to international students.

HARD OF HEARING OR DEAF SCHOLARSHIP PROGRAM

Sertoma Headquarters
1912 E. Meyer Boulevard
Kansas City, MO 64132
(816) 333-8300

E-mail: infosertoma@sertomahq.org
Website: http://www.sertoma.org (see *Scholarship*)
Additional Information: This program offers a $1,000 scholarship to cover tuition, books, and supplies. To be eligible, you must have a minimum 40dB bilateral hearing loss, as evidenced on audiogram by an SRT of 40dB or greater in both ears, and be a U.S. citizen. You must have a 3.2 GPA and be pursuing a bachelor's degree on a full-time basis at a college or university in the United States. This program is open to high school seniors and current college students. See the website for additional details and current deadline.

MINNIE PEARL SCHOLARSHIP PROGRAM

Bridges
ATTN: Minnie Pearl Scholarship Program
415 Fourth Avenue South, Suite A
Nashville, TN 37201
(615) 248-8828 (voice/TTY) or (615) 290-5147
E-mail: info@hearingbridges.org
Website: http://www.hearingbridges.org
Additional Information: The Minnie Pearl Scholarship is a four-year undergraduate scholarship of up to $4,000 ($1,000 per year). Applicants must be high school seniors with a 3.0 GPA. Students must have a signifi-cant bilateral hearing loss and must be of mainstreamed hearing-impaired status. All applicants must have been accepted at an accredited four-year college or university and be U.S. citizens.

For Individuals with Learning Disabilities or Attention-Deficit/ Hyperactivity Disorder

ALLEGRA FORD THOMAS SCHOLARSHIP

National Center for Learning Disabilities
Anne Ford Scholarship
381 Park Avenue South, Suite 1401
New York, NY 10016-8806
(888) 575-7373
E-mail: AFScholarship@ncld.org
Website: http://www.ncld.org
Additional Information: The Allegra Ford Thomas Scholarship is a $2,500 one-time need-based scholarship awarded to a graduating high

school senior with a documented learning disability (LD) and who will be enrolled in a two-year community college, a vocational or technical training program, or a specialized program for students with LD. The ideal Allegra Ford Thomas Scholar is a student who is active in his or her school or community, clearly demonstrates the importance of self-advocacy, has demonstrated perseverance, and is committed to achieving personal goals despite the challenges of LD. Please note: Attention-Deficit/Hyperactivity Disorder (ADHD) alone is not considered to be a learning disability. To be eligible for this program, you must also have a specific learning disability. The deadline is normally December 31 of each year.

ANNE FORD SCHOLARSHIP

National Center for Learning Disabilities
Anne Ford Scholarship
381 Park Avenue South, Suite 1401
New York, NY 10016-8806
(888) 575-7373
E-mail: AFScholarship@ncld.org
Website: http://www.ncld.org
Additional Information: The Anne Ford Scholarship is a $10,000 need-based scholarship ($2,500 a year over four years) open to graduating high school seniors with a 3.0 GPA who have a documented learning disability and who plan to enroll in a full-time bachelor's degree program. The ideal Anne Ford Scholar is a student who is active in his or her school or community, clearly demonstrates the importance of self-advocacy, has strong leadership skills, has demonstrated academic achievements consistent with college and career goals, and plans to contribute to society in ways that increase opportunities for individuals with LD. Please note: Attention-Deficit/Hyperactivity Disorder (ADHD) alone is not considered to be a learning disability. To be eligible for this program, you must also have a specific learning disability. The deadline is normally December 31 of each year.

SHIRE ADHD SCHOLARSHIP PROGRAM

(855) 474-4732
Website: http://www.shireadhdscholarship.com
Additional Information: To be eligible for a national scholarship, you must be a U.S. citizen and a legal resident of the fifty states or the District

of Columbia. You must also have been accepted to or currently enrolled in an undergraduate program at an accredited two- or four-year college, university, trade school, technical school, vocational school, or other "eligible educational institution." When you submit an application for this scholarship, you must have been diagnosed with ADHD and currently under the care of a licensed health care provider for it, although no specific future or ongoing plan of management or treatment for your ADHD is required to be eligible to receive a scholarship. The scholarship includes a $2,000 monetary award and a prepaid year of ADHD coaching from the Edge Foundation to help you in the transition to higher education. The selection of scholarship winners is based on community service, volunteer and extracurricular activities, and a personal essay describing how ADHD has affected your life.

For additional information about scholarship and financial aid specific to the disabled and their families, read *Financial Aid for Persons with Disabilities and Their Families* by Gail Ann Schlachter and R. David Weber. Visit http://www.rspfunding.com for more information about this publication.

23

I AM HOMESCHOOLED—CAN I STILL
WIN SCHOLARSHIPS?

I find the greatest thing in this world not so much
where we stand, as in what direction we are
    moving.
To reach this port of heaven, we must sail
    sometimes
with the wind, and sometimes against it but we
    sail,
and not drift, nor live at anchor.

            —Oliver Wendell Holmes

Yes, you can. However, in order to win you will need independent outside evaluation of your activities, skills, and hobbies. What does that mean? Well, for starters, being president of your homeschool's student council will not do much for you. That is definitely an example of a "big fish in a small pond," even if there are numerous brothers and sisters and neighbors included in your homeschool. But being president of your church or synagogue's youth group or a leader in your area's Boy Scout troop or the winner of 4-H competitions or even a winner in national, state, or regional competitions for athletic skills, special hobbies, or musical talents can all help validate how wonderful you are. Pay special attention to chapter 9, "Writing Your Scholarship Résumé—How to Stand Out in a Crowd and Why Grades Don't Mean Everything."

In addition to meeting the requirements for homeschooling in your state or region (including whether courses need certain accreditations), homeschooled students should consider taking community college courses. Many of the most competitive students, even those with traditional schooling, are adding community college courses to their résumé, which can help them stand out from the crowd.

Of course, as a homeschooled student you should also take standardized tests such as the ACT and SAT. In addition, take AP exams for areas in which you excel. If you do well, it could help you in two ways: possible exemption from a future college course *and* additional validation of the A's and high GPA you may have on your homeschool transcript. Some states even sponsor online AP courses if you are interested in taking one to get prepared for an AP exam. Visit http://www.collegeboard.org for additional information.

If you want to be considered for the National Merit Achievement/National Merit Scholarship competitions, you should also take the PSAT. Contact a principal or counselor at a local public or independent high school to make arrangements to take the PSAT/NMSQT at their school. Be sure to make contact well in advance of the mid-October test dates for your junior (third year) of high school. You should make contact preferably during the previous June. Visit http://www.nationalmerit.org for additional information. Also see chapter 8, "Taking Tests," for additional information.

Most important, homeschooled students should follow all of the steps in this book to find and win scholarships that a traditional student might follow since you may be eligible for most if not all of them. And don't forget, community service and extracurricular activities along with leadership roles are essential to winning many scholarships.

24

I DO NOT HAVE AN A AVERAGE—CAN I GET SCHOLARSHIPS FOR COLLEGE?

Our lives are not determined by what happens to
us but by how we react to what happens, not by
what life brings to us, but by the attitude we bring
to life.

—Anonymous

Absolutely! You can certainly win scholarships for college. Having an A average can certainly help in your quest to win scholarships *but* a vast majority of
scholarships awarded by programs are not tied to colleges and universities.
These are often called "outside scholarships." These types of programs may
not require a certain GPA or the requirement for GPA may be a 3.0 or lower.
This includes those that are merit-based. So if you can achieve a B average,
you can qualify for most scholarships. Even if you don't have a 3.0 GPA, you
still have opportunities—essay contests, artistic contests, video contests, and
even contests based on blogging and texting—that do not require information about your grades. In addition, if you've been involved in your community, many programs are more impressed by your service to others and the
volunteer aspects listed in your résumé. See chapter 14, "Scholarships and
Awards for Community Service, Volunteering, and Work."

It is important to remember that most outside scholarship programs are
looking for well-rounded students. They want students who not only perform well in the classroom but excel beyond academics. What does this
mean? If you've been involved in leadership activities, community activities,
special hobbies, athletic activities, tutoring, mentoring, or even show an

awareness of important global and social issues and how you might positively influence the world, you can impress a scholarship program. If you can showcase your activities and your potential, you have a great chance to win scholarships. So don't let your less-than-stellar grades discourage you. And don't let test scores discourage you, either, because there are many outside scholarship programs that *do not* request specific test scores.

For scholarships that are tied to specific colleges and universities, your ability to be accepted must meet those requirements. As a result, if the college or university shows that a certain GPA or test score is required for admission or if you don't come close to the average GPA and test scores of admitted students, then it will be difficult for you to win a scholarship with that particular school even if you meet all other requirements. For example, there are some scholarships sponsored by alumni based on certain characteristics, for which you qualify. Unfortunately, those characteristics won't matter if you can't get accepted to the college or university.

However, don't think I'm telling you that grades and test scores do not matter in winning scholarships. You do need to make every attempt to get your grades and test scores as high as possible. However, even if you don't achieve an A or even a B, there are still scholarships that might be right for you. Keep looking!

Quick Tips to Finding College Money for Middle Class Students

- Review chapter 2 to research scholarships in all areas specific to your personal characteristics, situation, and location.
- Look for local scholarship and award opportunities by reading chapter 4.
- Review chapter 3 for tips on finding specific scholarships via the Internet. For example, you can perform an advanced Internet search (explained in chapter 3) for "merit scholarships" or "non-need scholarships."
- Thoroughly peruse Appendix A for general scholarships as well as other chapters in this book for specific scholarships that apply to you. For example, if you are disabled, a minority, or perhaps qualify for an unusual scholarship, there are chapters specifically focusing on scholarship in these areas.
- Most importantly if you're an avid volunteer, consider awards and scholarships based on your charitable work such as those outlined in chapter 14.
- Also if you're an incredible writer, public speaker, a videographer, or skilled in some other area, look out for scholarships and awards for these characteristics as well. I include a lot of them in this book. But do your own research to find others that apply to you and what you do.
- If you're a social media fan, don't forget there are even college money opportunities based on texting, blogging, and many other endeavors. Keep your eyes open! And good luck!

25

ARE THERE SCHOLARSHIPS FOR
MIDDLE-CLASS STUDENTS?

We shape our dwellings, and afterwards our
dwellings shape us.

—Sir Winston Churchill

As the author of this book, a successful scholarship winner, and a workshop leader, I frequently get asked if there are scholarships for middle-class students. My answer is, yes, of course. Although there are many need-based scholarship programs, there are also numerous merit-based scholarship programs, awards, and contests. Are you wondering how to find them? First, when reading through any of the lists of scholarships in this book, scholarship directories, or program websites, the additional eligibility guidelines will usually state whether a program is need-based. Even if the guidelines do not state so, if the application requests certain information such as annual income, a statement of financial need, or shows specific income levels for a certain family size, then it is need-based. It is important to note that even though some programs may state that financial need is required, the definition of need can vary. So be very clear what determines financial need by thoroughly reviewing the program's site and the application. Ask additional questions if necessary. You should also be aware that some smaller community-based programs faced with few or no applicants and a strong desire to award an annual scholarship, may still award a deserving student without financial need but who shows strong potential in terms of leadership and community service. In addition, some need-based programs may ask for a statement from you indicating why you should still be considered for a scholarship when you do not meet stated income limits. If given this opportunity, take it. Explain that care for extended family members, for example, or even residing in a high cost-of-living area can really stretch an income.

Overall, the successful, organized student should apply for all scholarships for which he/she is eligible. Look for merit scholarships, awards, contests, and competitions that generally do not require a financial need statement. Be aware that when you read the fine print, some do. If it does not require too much additional time and it's a regional or community-based award, apply anyway. You may be the exception. Otherwise there are still plenty of merit-based opportunities for you as a middle-class student. You just need to do the research to find them. Review chapters 2, 3, and 4 to steer you in the right direction for finding scholarships specifically for you and your situation.

26

SCHOLARSHIPS FOR YOUNGER STUDENTS
—FROM KINDERGARTEN TO 11TH GRADE

Act quickly, think slowly.

—Proverb

Can you imagine winning a scholarship or award before you even become a senior? This could mean extra freedom for you when you reach your senior year—you could devote all of your time to being a senior and focus on your dream college or university. Of course, scholarships and awards change every year, but currently you can win one as early as age six, particularly if you have already started volunteering and helping out in the community.

If you win a scholarship before you actually start your college studies, the money is usually held for you by the sponsoring organization. Once you notify the organization about your college or university choice, funds are usually disbursed directly to the school. Or, you can win some awards that are not technically considered scholarships and the funds may be sent directly to you immediately. This information is normally included in the sponsor's program materials or website. If funds are remitted directly to you, save it! Don't spend it!

To give you a jumpstart on money you can win before 12th grade, here's a list of opportunities you can start pursuing even before you leave kindergarten or attend middle school.

See "A Few Important Items to Remember" on p. 181 for additional tips.

AYN RAND'S NOVELETTE ANTHEM ESSAY CONTEST

E-mail: info@aynrandnovels.com
Website: http://www.aynrand.org/contests

Additional Information: Open to 8th, 9th, and 10th grade students who submit an essay of 600 to 1,200 words. Awards range from $30 to $2,000. Deadline is usually in March.

AMERICAN LEGION NATIONAL HIGH SCHOOL ORATORICAL CONTEST

(317) 630-1200
E-mail: oratorical@legion.org
Website: http://www.legion.org (click on *Programs\Family and Youth\ Scholarships\National High School Oratorical Contest*)
Additional Information: Open to students in grades 9 through 12 who are less than 20 years of age (as of the national contest deadline) and are U.S. citizens or lawful permanent residents of the United States. You must be currently enrolled in a high school or middle school (public, parochial, military, private, or state-accredited homeschool) in which the curriculum is considered to be of high school level. You must be able to prepare and deliver speeches in public to win these awards. In addition to the scholarships awarded by the national headquarters, several hundred scholarships may be awarded by intermediate organizations to participants at the post, district, county, or department levels of competition. Visit the website for more details and current deadlines. Award amounts range from $1,500 to $18,000.

AYN RAND'S NOVEL THE FOUNTAINHEAD ESSAY CONTEST

E-mail: info@aynrandnovels.com
Website: http://www.aynrand.org/contests
Additional Information: Open to 11th- and 12th-grade high school students who submit an essay of 800 to 1,600 words. Awards range from $50 to $10,000. The deadline is usually in April.

BEST BUY SCHOLARSHIP PROGRAM

Website: http://pr.bby.com (click on *Community Relations\Scholarship Programs*) or https://bestbuy.scholarshipamerica.org

The Best Buy Scholarship Program awards scholarships to 9th- through 12th-grade students in the United States and Puerto Rico. To be eligible you must plan to enter a full-time undergraduate course of study after graduating from high school. Good students with strong participation in community service or who have work experience are urged to apply for these $1,000 scholarships. Best Buy has awarded over $20 million in scholarships to more than 16,000 students since 1999. This program is administered for Best Buy by Scholarship Management Services, which is a division of Scholarship America. Visit the Scholarship America website at http://www .scholarshipamerica.org for more information about this scholarship program and other open scholarships.

CARING AWARDS

The Caring Institute
228 7th Street SE
Washington, DC 20003
(202) 547-4273
E-mail address: info@caring.org
Website: http://www.caring-institute.org
Additional Information: See chapter 14.

THE CHRISTOPHER REEVE AWARD

Heart of America Foundation
401 F Street NW, Suite 325
Washington, DC 20001
E-mail: scholarships@heartofamerica.org
Website: http://www.heartofamerica.org
Additional Information: See chapter 14.

COLLEGE JUMPSTART SCHOLARSHIP

College JumpStart Scholarship Fund
4546 B10 El Camino Real, 325
Los Altos, CA 94022
E-mail: admin@jumpstart-scholarship.net
Website: http://www.jumpstart-scholarship.net
Additional Information: This scholarship is open to high school grades 10 through 12 college students, and nontraditional students who are U.S. citizens or legal residents. You must be attending or planning to attend an

accredited two-year, four-year, or vocational/trade school in the United States and be committed to using education to better your life and that of your family and/or community. Deadlines are normally in April and October.

CREATE-A-GREETING-CARD SCHOLARSHIP CONTEST

Website: http://www.gallerycollection.com/greetingcardscontests.htm or http://www.gallerycollection.com/greeting-cards-scholarship.htm
Additional Information: See more on this scholarship in chapter 18, "Scholarships for Current College Students and Transfer Students."

DAVIDSON FELLOWS SCHOLARSHIP

Davidson Institute for Talent Development
9665 Gateway Drive, Suite B
Reno, NV 89521
(775) 852-3483, ext. 435
E-mail: DavidsonFellows@davidsongifted.org
Website: http://www.davidsongifted.org/fellows or http://www.davidson fellows.org
Social Media: Follow DavidsonGifted on Twitter, Facebook, and YouTube.
Additional Information: The Davidson Fellows Scholarship awards range from $10,000 to $50,000 for students age 18 and under who have completed a significant piece of work. The program looks for students whose projects are at or close to the college-graduate level with a depth of knowledge in their particular area of study. The application categories are Science, Technology, Engineering, Mathematics, Literature, Music, Philosophy, and "Outside the Box." To apply you must be a U.S. citizen, a permanently resident, residing in the United States, or living overseas due to active U.S. military duty. There is no minimum age for eligibility. The deadline for preliminary submissions is in January. See the website for specific details and guidelines for entering this competition.

DOODLE 4 GOOGLE

E-mail: doodle4google-usteam@google.com
Website: http://www.google.com/doodle4google
Additional Information: Doodle 4 Google is an annual program that encourages K–12 students in the United States to use their artistic tal-

ents to think big and redesign the Google homepage logo for millions to see. Previous themes have been "My Best Day Ever" and "What I Want to Do Someday." Winning student artists will see their artwork appear on the Google homepage and receive a $30,000 college scholarship and a $50,000 technology grant for their school, along with other prizes. Visit the website for complete eligibility guidelines, templates, and submission information.

THE DUPONT CHALLENGE

DuPont Office of Education
P.O. Box 80357
Wilmington, DE 19880-0030
E-mail: thechallenge@usa.dupont.com
Website: http://thechallenge.dupont.com
Additional Information: Open to high school students in grades 7–12 (who must be at least age 13) attending public or private high schools in the United States and its territories. Awards are given based on an original science essay of 700 to 1,000 words written by applicants and signed by their science teacher. Award selection is based on the scientific accuracy of the essay and the student's writing ability. Visit the website to obtain an entry form which must accompany your essay and to get additional information and contest rules. The deadline is normally in January or early February. Prizes range from $1,000 to $5,000 in savings bonds.

THE GLORIA BARRON PRIZE FOR YOUNG HEROES

The Barron Prize
545 Pearl Street
Boulder, CO 80302
Website: http://www.barronprize.org
Additional Information: Each year, the Gloria Barron Prize for Young Heroes honors outstanding youth leaders ages 8 to 18 who have made a significant positive difference to people and our planet. Top winners in this program receive a $2,500 cash award to support their service work or higher education. You must be nominated for this prize. The deadline is usually in April. Visit the website for additional information about nominations, application requirements, and other details.

JESSE BROWN MEMORIAL YOUTH SCHOLARSHIP PROGRAM

DAV (Disabled American Veterans) National Headquarters
Voluntary Services Department
P.O. Box 14301
Cincinnati, OH 45250-0301
Website: http://www.dav.org (click on *Voluntary Services\Jesse Brown
Scholarship*) or http://www.dav.org/volunteers/Scholarship.aspx
Additional Information: See chapter 14.

KOHL'S CARES SCHOLARSHIP PROGRAM

(319) 341-2932 (indicate you need information for the Kohl's Cares Schol-
arship Program)
E-mail: kohls@act.org
Website: http://www.kohlskids.com or http://www.kohlscorporation.com
/CommunityRelations/scholarship/index.asp
Additional Information: See chapter 14.

NORDSTROM SCHOLARSHIP

(206) 373-4550 or (319) 341-2248
E-mail: nordscholar@nordstrom.com or NordstromScholarship@act.org
Website: http://www.nordstrom.com/scholarship
Additional Information: Since 1994, Nordstrom has been awarding
$10,000 scholarships (award is paid in annual amounts of $2,500 over four
years) to hardworking high school juniors to pursue their education. Scholarships are awarded on the basis of academic achievement, awards/hon-
ors, leadership, school activities, community/volunteer activities, as well
as financial and employment history. The awards are granted without
regard to race, creed, color, religion, gender, or national origin for students
in the following eligible states: Alaska, Arizona, California, Colorado,
Connecticut, Delaware, District of Columbia, Florida, Georgia, Hawaii,
Idaho, Illinois, Indiana, Kansas, Maryland, Massachusetts, Michigan, Minnesota, Missouri, Nevada, New Jersey, New York, North Carolina, Ohio,
Oregon, Pennsylvania, Rhode Island, Tennessee, Texas, Utah, Virginia, and
Washington.

NATIONAL YOUNG ARTS FOUNDATION

Programs Department
2100 Biscayne Boulevard
Miami, FL 33137
(800) 970-ARTS or (305) 377-1140; fax: (305) 377-1149
E-mail: info@youngarts.org
Website: http://www.ARTSawards.org or http://www.nfaa.org
Additional Information: This talent search competition is open to high
school students between the ages of 15 and 18 (or in grades 10 through 12)
with talent in the arts such as dance, writing, music, theater, visual arts,
and jazz. Awards can be used in any field of study. To apply, you must be a
citizen or permanent resident of the United States or its official territories
(e.g., Puerto Rico). The deadline for final submission is in October. There
is an application fee for this program. See the website for details.

OPTIMIST INTERNATIONAL ORATORICAL CONTEST

Programs Manager
4494 Lindell Boulevard
St. Louis, MO 63108
(800) 500-8130 or (314) 371-6000
E-mail: programs@optimist.org
Website: http://www.optimist.org (click on *Members/Scholarship Con-
tests)*
Additional Information: This scholarship is based on your ability to prepare and present a timed four- to five-minute speech on a specific topic.
Contestants, who must be no more than 19 at the time of contest entry, must
speak about the official oratorical contest subject, which changes each year.
For example, one year's contest subject was, "Why My Voice Is Important."
Contest is open to citizens of the United States, Canada, and the Caribbean. You must enter the contest through your local Optimist Club; use
the e-mail address above to get contact information for your local Optimist Club. Students must compete in several levels. Visit the website for
more details. Award amounts range up to $2,500.
NOTE: I competed in the Optimist International Oratorical Contest for
several years at various levels beginning in the 6th grade, usually winning
at each level but not the final level. Although I did not win the $1,500
award available at that time, I did gain invaluable experience in public

speaking and in writing speeches, which also helped me to write essays. These are very important skills to have, especially if you want to win scholarships. The ability to speak well in public will help you in both interviews and in preparing essays.

OPTIMIST INTERNATIONAL ESSAY CONTEST

Programs Manager
4494 Lindell Boulevard
St. Louis, MO 63108
(800) 500-8130 or (314) 371-6000; fax: (314) 371-6006
E-mail: programs@optimist.org
Website: http://www.optimist.org (click on *Home\Members\Scholarship Contests*)
Award Amount: $650 to $5,000
Additional Information: This is a multilevel essay-writing contest. Students at the district and international level win scholarships. Contestants must be no more than 19 at the time of contest entry. Contest is open to citizens of the United States, Canada, and the Caribbean. You must enter the contest through your local Optimist Club. Use the e-mail address above to get contact information for your local Optimist Club. Visit the website for more details. The award amount is $2,500.

PROFILE IN COURAGE ESSAY CONTEST

Columbia Point
Boston, MA 02125
(617) 514-1600
E-mail: profiles@nara.gov
Website: http://www.jfkcontest.org
Additional Information: In recognition of one of President Kennedy's most important legacies, this contest is designed to promote the involvement of young people in the civic life of their country. High school students in grades 9 through 12 can participate in this essay contest by writing a compelling 1,000 word (maximum) essay and citing at least five sources on the meaning of political courage. Registration forms must be submitted with the essay and are available on the website. The first-place winner and the nominating teacher will be invited to receive awards at the Kennedy Library in Boston. Awards range from $500 to $10,000. The contest deadline is usually in early January.

PRUDENTIAL SPIRIT OF COMMUNITY AWARDS

Website: http://spirit.prudential.com
Additional Information: See chapter 14.

SCHOLASTIC ART AND WRITING AWARDS

557 Broadway
New York, NY 10012
E-mail: info@artandwriting.org
Website: http://www.scholastic.com/artandwriting or http://www.artand
writing.org
Additional Information: This award is designed to recognize outstanding talent among students in the visual arts and creative writing. Students
submit individual works of art as well as writing portfolios for this competition. Awards range from $500 to $10,000. You can begin submitting for
one of these awards in the fall, usually September; check the website.

SIEMENS COMPETITION IN MATH, SCIENCE AND TECHNOLOGY

Siemens Foundation
170 Wood Avenue South
Iselin, NJ 08830
(877) 822-5233
E-mail: foundation.us@siemens.com
Additional Information: This program is available to high school seniors
who want to enter individual research projects and to all high school students (from grades 9 to 12) who wish to enter projects as part of a two- to
three-member team. The Siemens Competition is designed to recognize
remarkable talent early and foster individual growth in high school students who are willing to challenge themselves through science research.
Students can achieve national recognition for science research projects
that they complete in high school and earn up to $100,000 in scholarships
for their work. The competition deadline is normally in September.

SODEXO FOUNDATION

Stephen J. Brady STOP Hunger Scholarships
9801 Washingtonian Boulevard
Gaithersburg, MD 20878

(615)-320-3149 (indicate your call is about the Sodexo Foundation STOP Hunger Scholarships)
E-mail: STOPHunger@applyists.com
Website: http://www.sodexofoundation.org (see *Scholarships*)
Additional Information: See chapter 14.

SONS OF THE AMERICAN REVOLUTION JOSEPH S. RUMBAUGH HISTORICAL ORATION CONTEST

Chairman, Joseph S. Rumbaugh Historical Oration Contest
NSSAR Headquarters
1000 South Fourth Street
Louisville, KY 40203-3208
Website: http://www.sar.org/Youth/Oration_Contest or http://www.sar.org (see *Education*)
Additional Information: Oratory competition for high school freshmen, sophomores, juniors, and seniors who submit an original five- to six-minute oration on a personality, event, or document of the American Revolutionary War and how it relates to the United States today. Oration must be delivered from memory, without props or charts. For more information and complete rules, visit the website. Awards range from $200 to $3,000.

U.S. SENATE YOUTH PROGRAM

William Randolph Hearst Foundation
90 New Montgomery Street, Suite 1212
San Francisco, CA 94105-4504
(800)841-7048 or (415) 908-4540; fax: (415) 243-0760
E-mail: ussyp@hearstfdn.org
Website: http://www.ussenateyouth.org
Additional Information: Open to high school juniors or seniors holding a student office. Students must be currently elected to one of the following offices: student body president, vice president, secretary, or treasurer; class president, vice president, secretary, or treasurer; student council representative; or student representative to district, regional, or state-level civic organization. For an application contact your high school principal or state education administrator. Visit the website to find more information about your state's education administrator and the program details. The organization's advice to interested students is to apply in your junior year

so that you will have two years of eligibility, rather than one year if you apply as a senior. Award is a $5,000 college scholarship and an all-expense-paid trip to Washington to experience national government in action. The deadline is usually in early fall. Visit the website at the beginning of your junior or senior year for additional details and current deadlines.

VETERANS OF FOREIGN WARS OF THE UNITED STATES

Voice of Democracy Annual Audio Essay Contest
(816) 968-1117
E-mail: kharmer@vfw.org
Website: http://www.vfw.org (click on *Community Programs*)
Additional Information: This scholarship contest is open to grade 9 through 12 students who write and record a three- to five-minute essay addressing the assigned theme, which changes each year. Previous assigned themes have been "I'm Optimistic About Our Nation's Future," "Freedom's Obligation," "Reaching Out to America's Future," and "What Price Freedom?" To participate in this contest, visit the website for more information, speak with your high school counselor, or contact your local VFW post. Scholarship awards range from $1,000 to $30,000. The deadline is usually November 1 of each year. Submissions should go to your local VFW post. E-mail or visit the website to find your local post.

CAN GRADUATING FROM HIGH SCHOOL EARLY AFFECT YOUR SCHOLARSHIP CHANCES?

One of the questions I have been getting in recent years is whether students should graduate in the 11th grade if they have earned enough credits to do so. My answer: It depends. If you are still hoping to enter and win some of the most competitive scholarship competitions, then losing an additional year of community service, extracurricular activities, and leadership experience could hurt your chances. However, if you've packed an impressive amount of activities into an already outstanding résumé, you could be okay. Really, you never know, because there is no guarantee with scholarship competitions. You can never know the résumés of students you are competing against. And you don't know other factors that could be under consideration when determining winners. Furthermore, if your parents are saving to help you with college, your early graduation reduces the number of years they have available to continue saving. It may force them to start spending for your education before they're fully ready. Or your need for college funds early could interfere with money they need for an older brother or sister already in college. Of course, if they can pay for your freshman year before facing yearly tuition increases that many institutions have, your early graduation may not be so bad. They might even consider it a freshman-year bargain.

27

SCHOLARSHIPS AND COLLEGE FUNDING FOR THE MILITARY AND THEIR FAMILY

> If you would lift me up you must be on higher ground.
>
> —Ralph Waldo Emerson

If you are considering the military as an option for funding for your college education, the following information should be quite helpful in guiding you through the process. Before choosing this route, you should consider your timeline for completing college and whether joining the military is something you really want to do. For example, with an ROTC scholarship you may be able to participate in a school's ROTC program while taking college courses to complete your degree. With ROTC, you would join the military as an officer after you complete your college education. In addition, you can usually take the first year of college courses without incurring an obligation to join the military once you graduate. After the first year, however, if you choose to stay in the program you will have a service obligation. Alternatively, you may decide to join the military before you go to college and use funds through the GI Bill to fund your education once you complete your term in the military. Or maybe you want to attend one of the military academies. Here is a rundown of your college funding options with military service.

IF YOU WANT TO FINISH YOUR DEGREE BEFORE COMPLETING YOUR MILITARY SERVICE COMMITMENT

Reserve Officers' Training Corps (ROTC) Program

With the Reserve Officers' Training Corps (ROTC) program you can get money for college while you're in school. During your college career, you must take one military science course along with your other college courses each semester or quarter. After you graduate you will enter the service as a commissioned officer. With a full ROTC scholarship, most of your tuition, fees, and textbook charges for four years of college will be covered. Here is contact information to get more information about ROTC programs:

ARMY ROTC

(800) USA-ROTC
http://www.armyrotc.com

NAVY ROTC

(800) USA-NAVY
http://www.nrotc.navy.mil

AIR FORCE ROTC

(866) 423-7682
http://www.afrotc.com/

MARINES ROTC

(800)-MARINES
http://www.marines.com

COAST GUARD COLLEGE STUDENT PRE-COMMISSIONING INITIATIVE (CSPI)

http:// www.gocoastguard.com

U.S. Service Academies

If you want to complete your education first, you may be interested in attending a service academy, the four-year institutions of higher education operated by the Army, Air Force, Marine Corps, Navy, and the Coast Guard. If you are accepted into a service academy, you will receive a full scholarship with a small monthly stipend. After you graduate, you will be commissioned as an officer in the Army, Air Force, or Marine Corps, or as an ensign in the Navy or Coast Guard. Getting into a service academy is quite competitive, so be prepared.

For more information:

- U.S. Military Academy in West Point, New York: (800) 822-8762 or see www.usma.edu.
- U.S. Naval Academy in Annapolis, Maryland: (800) 638-9156 or see www.usna.edu.
- U.S. Air Force Academy in Colorado Springs, Colorado: (800) 443-9266 or see www.usfa.af.mil.
- U.S. Coast Guard Academy in New London, Connecticut: (800) 883-8724 or see www.cga.edu.
- U.S. Merchant Marine Academy in Kings Point, New York: (866) 546-4778 or see www.usma.edu.

IF YOU WANT TO WORK ON YOUR DEGREE WHILE YOU'RE IN MILITARY SERVICE

Servicemembers Opportunity Colleges (SOC)

SOC is a consortium of nearly 2,000 colleges and universities that can help you get a college education while you're in the military. With SOC you can complete your coursework on a campus, at military installations and armories, online using a computer, or by correspondence, which allows you the flexibility to obtain your associate, bachelor, and or even a graduate degree while in the military. SOC also operates the Concurrent Admissions Program (ConAP) for those who enlist in the Army or Army Reserves. Essentially, you enlist in the Army and apply for college at the same time. To get more information, contact:

Servicemembers Opportunity Colleges.
1307 New York Avenue NW, 5th Floor
Washington, DC 20005-4701
(202) 667-0079 or (800) 368-5622, fax: (202) 667-0622
E-mail: socmail@aascu.org
Website: http://www.soc.aascu.org

Community College of the Air Force

If you're interested in the Air Force branch of military service, you can take advantage of the Community College of the Air Force (CCAF), which is a two-year college open only to enlisted men and women. The college offers numerous programs leading to an associate's degree in various scientific and technical fields. With its Tuition Assistance Program, the Air Force will pay up to 100 percent of the cost of your tuition and fees for courses. Visit http://www.au.af.mil/au/ccaf and http://www.military.com (click on *Education\Money for School*) for more information.

IF YOU WANT TO COMPLETE YOUR MILITARY SERVICE THEN WORK ON YOUR COLLEGE DEGREE

The following benefits are offered through the Department of Veterans Affairs. Some benefits can be used for college expenses while you're still in military service. Others benefits may not be available until you complete your term of service.

In most cases, benefits may be used for degree or certificate programs, flight training, apprenticeship/on-the-job training, and correspondence courses, as well as remedial, deficiency, and refresher courses (requires special approval). With most of the programs you will receive a monthly benefit check based upon your type of training and training time. For more specific information about these education benefits, visit http://www.va.gov (see *GI Bill*) or http://www.gibill.va.gov or call (888) 442-4551 or (888) GI-BILL.

- **Montgomery GI Bill, Active Duty (MGIB)**—Through the Montgomery GI Bill program you may be eligible for up to thirty-six months of education benefits. Benefits are payable for ten years following your release from active duty.
- **Montgomery GI Bill, Selected Reserve (MGIB-SR)**—Members of the Selected Reserve, which includes the Army Reserve, Navy Reserve, Air Force Reserve, Marine Corps Reserve, Coast Guard Reserve, Army National Guard, and the Air National Guard, may be eligible for education benefits under this program. See the GI Bill website for additional information and eligibility requirements.
- **Reimbursement for Licensing and Certification Tests**—For licensing and certification tests, you may be eligible to receive reim-

bursement for the cost of the tests only. Tests taken must have been specifically approved for the GI Bill.

- **Tuition Assistance "Top-Up"**—The Tuition Assistance Top-Up benefit helps pay the difference between the total cost of a college course and the amount of tuition assistance paid by the military for a course.
- **Veterans Educational Assistance Program (VEAP)**—If you entered active duty between January 1, 1977, and June 30, 1985, *and* you elected to make contributions from your military pay, matched on a $2 for $1 basis by the government, VEAP benefits should be available for your education.
- **Survivors' and Dependents' Educational Assistance Program (DEA)**—This program provides education and training opportunities to eligible dependents of veterans who are permanently and totally disabled due to a service-related condition, or who died while on active duty or as a result of a service-related condition. Those who qualify for the program may be eligible for up to forty-five months of education benefits.
- **Work-Study Program**—If you are currently attending school three-quarter time or more and you are receiving VA education benefits, you may qualify for this program. Through this program you may work at the school veterans' office, VA regional office, VA medical facilities, or at approved state employment offices. As a work-study student, you may be paid at the state or the federal minimum wage, whichever is greater.

To get more information about the programs discussed in this chapter as well as any other information about the military and options for funding a college education with military service, see http://www.gibill.va.gov or http://www.military.com. As an individual in the military or affiliated with the military by family associations, you have many additional funding opportunities open to you. Look at chapter 2 for ways to research specific scholarships. Remember, use all the strategies in this book for finding scholarships because they may be available to you as well.

PRIVATE SCHOLARSHIP OPPORTUNITIES FOR THE MILITARY AND THEIR FAMILIES

TILLMAN MILITARY SCHOLARS PROGRAM

http://www.pattillmanfoundation.org (see *Tillman Military Scholars*)
The Pat Tillman Foundation's Tillman Military Scholars program provides

scholarships to active and veteran service members and their spouses that cover not only direct study-related expenses such as tuition and fees, but also other needs, including housing and child care.

SCHOLARSHIPS FOR MILITARY CHILDREN PROGRAM FROM THE FISHER HOUSE FOUNDATION

http://www.militaryscholar.org

Open to dependent unmarried children under age 23 of active-duty personnel, reserve/guard, and retired military members, or survivors of service members who died while on active duty or who died while receiving retired pay from the military. Applicants and their sponsors must be currently enrolled in the Defense Enrollment Eligibility Reporting System (DEERS) database and have a current dependent military ID card. The DEERS database will be the primary method of verifying eligibility. The Fisher House Foundation also offers scholarships to military spouses.

THE POST 9-11 GI BILL AND MARINE GUNNERY SGT. JOHN DAVID FRY SCHOLARSHIP

http://freedomalliance.org

This scholarship is open to the children of service members who died in the line of duty after September 10, 2001. Eligible children attending school may receive assistance with public, in-state undergraduate tuition and fees, plus a monthly living stipend and textbook allowance for up to thirty-six months of benefits.

AMVETS NATIONAL SERVICE FOUNDATION SCHOLARSHIPS

http://www.amvets.orgs (click on *Programs\Educational Opportunities*)

Scholarships from AMVETS are available to veterans and active military, their children, and their grandchildren. Awards are available to families of deceased veterans as well. The awards are based on academic excellence and financial need and are open to high school seniors, high school JROTC, and veterans in pursuit of higher education.

28

MAKING CHOICES: YOU'VE WON AN AWARD . . . NOW WHAT DO YOU DO?

> One of the rarest things that man does is to do the best he can.
>
> —Josh Billings

Congratulations! You have received a scholarship award letter or e-mail. Usually you need to formally accept or reject the offer by May 1 of the year you plan to begin your post-secondary education. This date is often called the national scholarship deadline. Outside scholarships may have different deadline dates for acceptance.

The following are items you may want to consider before choosing a scholarship offer, regardless of how much money they are offering. These considerations are divided into two categories: scholarships from a particular college or university and scholarships from private organizations. At the end of the chapter I have included several award letters for scholarships from private organizations and colleges and universities.

CATEGORY A: SCHOLARSHIPS AND FINANCIAL AID FROM COLLEGES OR UNIVERSITIES

- Is it a full or partial scholarship? If partial, what does it cover? Does the scholarship cover your costs beyond your first year?
- Are there any other incentives to "sweeten the pot" other than the scholarship itself? For example, some "sweeteners" could be living stipends, a personal computer or tablet for your academic use, internships

with companies in your particular area of study, summer study-abroad programs, a private dormitory room, and the like.

- Can this institution help you get a scholarship, fellowship, grant, or other financial aid to afford graduate school if you need it?
- What will the degree you receive from this particular college or university prepare you for?
- Will the educational benefits from this institution fulfill your post-secondary educational goals?
- How are other graduates faring after they leave the institution?
- Are there many students transferring out of the institution, particularly scholarship students?
- What type of overall reputation does the institution have?
- Will you receive the attention you need to thrive at this institution? Is it a large university with an impersonal environment in an urban area, or is the college small, with an intimate atmosphere in a little town?
- What types of special arrangements are made for scholarship students? For example, some arrangements are honors programs, special advisors, student support groups, special dormitories, fraternities, and sororities.
- What is the average class size?
- Is on-campus housing available for four years or more of your college career, or are upperclassmen expected to move off-campus to allow room for incoming freshmen? If upperclassmen are expected to move into off-campus housing, will the scholarship pay for this arrangement?
- Do you want to attend this college or university regardless of the scholarship or financial aid it offers?
- How many core courses are required?
- What are the hours for the library and computer rooms?
- Are the library and computer facilities adequate for the entire student body?
- What is the job placement rate of graduates from this college or university, especially in your intended major?
- How many years does it take the average student to graduate? How many years does it take the average student to graduate in your intended major? Measure these years against the time your scholarship will cover.
- What situations could result in termination or permanent suspension of the scholarship?
- What grade point average do you need to maintain to keep the scholarship?

- What is not covered by this scholarship offer? For example, summer school courses, books, room and board, courses beyond those allotted to be considered a full-time student, courses that must be repeated, books that must be purchased off-campus and not at the campus bookstore, and similar factors.
- Will you be allowed to use a private outside scholarship to replace a loan in your financial aid package?
- Even with the aid of a full scholarship, can you afford to attend the college of your choice? What additional assistance will you need? For example, examine the cost of living in the city where the college is located. Try to uncover hidden costs. If you think your award package from a specific college or university isn't enough, make an appeal in writing, via telephone or e-mail, and if necessary in person, especially if it's a school you really want to attend.
- Are off-campus classroom sites a regular occurrence for courses in your intended major? If so, it will add to your basic transportation costs.
- Are the costs of lab materials covered in your scholarship? In some cases they are not. Since most schools require at least two basic science courses such as physics or chemistry with corresponding labs, this can be a hidden cost.

Here are some things you should do to help answer some of your questions about a particular institution:

- Talk to other students at the school, especially scholarship students. Talk to alumni. Many schools will have students and also parents call you at your home or e-mail you. Take the time to jot down general questions about your interests and keep it by the phone and on your computer for these times. You may also be able to e-mail or join them in a chat room sponsored by the university or college. You may even be able to review Facebook pages of students or specific groups at the college or university.
- Visit the campus. Speak to students, especially those in the library. These students tend to be more serious about their work and usually won't have the bias of failing grades to color their views or comments. Talk to the professors. Spend the night in the freshman dormitory. Eat in the cafeteria.
- Look at course offerings for required classes and those for your intended major. Look at the sections available each semester or quarter. At any given time, an institution may be facing budget cuts that

could affect the number of courses and the sections for each course they offer. This may cause a problem when the unavailability of a course could mean an extra semester, quarter, or year in school without financial backing from your scholarship.

- Visit the admissions office. Inquire about the dropout rate and the reasons for students leaving.
- Talk to personnel in the career center, if the school has one. If the school doesn't have one, you may want to think twice about attending. If the institution doesn't have the resources to help you find a job or explore options after college, then what's the use of attending?

Review your entire financial aid package by looking at the following areas to compare colleges and universities where you've been accepted. In general, you should give priority to offers that have the most aid in the forms of scholarships, grants, work-study. or federally backed loans. For example, any type of aid from number 1 in the list below is very good, 2 is still good, 3 is great but you'll have a service commitment, which could interfere with future plans, 4 would not be as good, 5 is certainly less attractive, and 6 should be your least preferred option. In some case, you may not have the option of being selective with your choices but if you do, this provides you with a guideline.

1. Scholarships and grants are the best type of aid because there is no need to pay them back. Make sure you understand the terms of the scholarship. Is it for the first year and beyond or one year only? Is it renewable? If you change your major, does the scholarship stop?
2. Work-study can certainly help and can be more flexible than a job off-campus. However it could take time away from your studies.
3. Scholarships with a service commitment—if you accept the scholarship, you must be willing to commit some part of your time either in college or after college to a private organization, company, agency, or within a certain area.
4. Federal student loans—this is money that must be repaid with interest, although a subsidized direct loan from the federal government does not start accruing interest until after you leave school.
5. State loans—this is money that must be repaid with interest; it is not subsidized. The interest rate may be higher than a federal loan and some of the other terms may not be as advantageous. Definitely com-

pare the differences between any loan offers, which should include interest rates, terms, and repayment policies.

6. Private loans—this is money that must be repaid with interest; it is not subsidized. The interest rate may be higher than a federal loan and some of the other terms are usually not as good as a federal loan. Definitely compare the differences between any loan offers, including interest rates, terms, and repayment policies.

CATEGORY B: SCHOLARSHIPS FROM PRIVATE ORGANIZATIONS

- Is it a full or partial scholarship? If partial, what does it cover?
- What situations could result in temporary or permanent suspension of the scholarship?
- What grade point average do you need to maintain to keep the scholarship?
- Will the scholarship "travel"? For example, do you have to attend a specific institution to receive the scholarship? Also, will you have to major in a particular discipline to keep the scholarship?
- What type of support system does the scholarship program have for its scholars?
- How will the funds be transferred to the institution you want to attend? Some scholarship checks do not arrive before the student has to meet the financial obligations at the school he or she plans to attend.
- Once you accept the scholarship, see if the scholarship program has a Facebook, Twitter, or other social media presence. If so, get connected to stay in the know with your scholarship program. Programs often send out information regarding updates, internships, or additional scholarship programs for which you might be eligible to apply. In addition, if there is an e-mail newsletter, make sure to sign up for this as well.

The letters that follow are examples of what you might receive in the mail or, as is often the case, an e-mail. In addition, there may be an online acceptance form that you need to complete as well. So make sure that any e-mail address you supply when applying for a scholarship is one you check regularly and often. Your next e-mail could be a notice of a great scholarship you've won.

CONGRATULATIONS AND AWARD LETTERS

April 24, 1991

Marianne N. Ragins
P.O. Box 6845
Macon, GA 31208

Dear Marianne:

CONGRATULATIONS! We are pleased to inform you that you have been selected to receive a Wendy's Scholarship. You will receive more information and details about your scholarship in a few days from the Scholarship Program Administrator.

A Scholarship Brunch will be held in honor of the recipients on Saturday, May 18, 1990 at 11:00 a.m. Parents or special friends are encouraged to attend. It will be held at the Northwest Atlanta Hilton in Marietta, GA.

Dorothy Wells or Gwen Lewis will contact you during the next week to confirm your attendance for the brunch.

Again, Congratulations.

Sincerely,

Dorothy Wells

WENDY'S INTERNATIONAL, INC.

WENDY'S INTERNATIONAL, INC./375 FRANKLIN ROAD-SUITE 400/MARIETTA, GA 30067/404-425-9778

COCA-COLA SCHOLARS FOUNDATION, INC.

ONE BUCKHEAD PLAZA · SUITE 1000
3060 PEACHTREE ROAD NW
ATLANTA · GEORGIA 30305
404·237·1300

March 25, 1991

Mebane M. Pritchett
president

Ms. Marianne N. Ragins
P.O. Box 6845
Macon, GA 31208

Dear Ms. Ragins:

Congratulations! You have been selected as one of the 151 Finalists in the 1991 Coca-Cola Scholars Program. Reaching this level distinguishes you from among the approximately 60,000 applicants who originally applied to our Program, and you are to be commended for this outstanding accomplishment.

We are pleased to invite you to attend our National Competition, at Foundation expense, to compete for the two tiers of Awards to be granted. Based on the materials previously submitted, as well as personal interviews to be conducted at the Competition, 51 Finalists will be chosen as National Scholars and will receive renewable Awards of $5,000 per year for four years of undergraduate study, a total Award of $20,000. The remaining 100 Finalists will be designated Regional Scholars and will receive four year renewable Awards of $1,000 per year. As a result, all Finalists who attend the National Competition are assured of receiving an Award that will be applicable to the accredited U.S. college or university of their choice.

The National Competition will be held on April 18–20, 1991 at the headquarters of The Coca-Cola Company in Atlanta, Georgia. All Finalists will be flown to Atlanta, with travel

Marianne N. Ragins
March 25, 1991
Page 2

arrangements made by the Foundation, and will stay at the Penta Hotel. Airfare, meals, in-town transportation, and accommodations will be provided by the Foundation at no cost to the Finalists.

To accept our invitation, we ask that you and your parents or guardian sign the enclosed Release and Indemnity Agreement and return it immediately in the postage-paid envelope provided. This form must be received before we can release your airline ticket, so be sure to return it promptly. Your flight arrangements will be based on the travel registration form you returned earlier and your interview schedule.

Finalists will attend a Seminar following dinner Thursday evening. It will be moderated by the Chairman of our National Selection Committee, and four Committee members will discuss aspects of their professions, including education, politics, journalism, and leadership development. Students will then be encouraged to ask questions and interact with the Committee.

In addition to the scheduled interviews, Finalists will be honored at the Coca-Cola Scholars Banquet to be held on Friday evening at the Hotel Nikko Atlanta. Recommended attire for both the interview and the Banquet is coat and tie for men and correspondingly appropriate attire for women.

No preparation is required for the National Competition interviews. However, we do encourage all Finalists to review previously submitted application materials, because questions asked during the personal interviews will be based in part on the information provided therein.

Each Finalist will be interviewed individually during a 20 minute period by a group of four National Selection Committee members. On Saturday afternoon following the interviews, the Selection Committee will determine the recipients of the two levels of Awards. Finalists will be notified of their status by mail the following week.

Marianne N. Ragins
March 25, 1991
Page 3

The following materials are enclosed:

1. Release and Indemnity Agreement—Please return it immediately to allow the release of your airline ticket.

2. Tentative Schedule of Scholar Events for the National Competition.

3. Foundation 1990 Annual Report.

4. List of National Selection Committee Members.

We look forward to your prompt return of the enclosed Agreement, so that we can complete arrangements for your trip to Atlanta. If you have any questions about the Competition, please call the Foundation office at (404) 237-1300.

Once again, congratulations on your achievement in being selected as a Finalist in the Coca-Cola Scholars Program. All of us at the Foundation look forward to meeting you at the National Competition and to making your visit to Atlanta enjoyable and worthwhile.

Sincerely,

MMP/ogh
Enclosures

cc: Northeast High School

RHODES COLLEGE

FOUNDED 1848

February 22, 1991

Ms. Marianne Nicole Ragins
P.O. Box 6845
Macon, GA 31208

Dear Angel:

It is my pleasure to inform you that you have been named a finalist in the competition for the Bellingrath Scholarship. The scholarship covers the full cost of tuition, room and board for four years at Rhodes College. As we received over 700 nominations for our six available scholarships, your selection as one of 36 finalists is a distinct honor indeed.

You are invited to meet with the Selection Committee for the final interview on Monday, March 18, on the campus of Rhodes. At that time you will compete with five other students for the honor of being named a Bellingrath Scholar.

Please note on the enclosed schedule that the program officially begins on Monday at 11:30 a.m. with a reception for all finalists and members of the Selection Committee and ends following the afternoon interviews. However, since the fullness of the schedule on March 18 allows very little time to interact with Rhodes students and gain a feel for the city of Memphis, we encourage you to travel to Rhodes prior to Monday. Our student volunteers, many of whom are former Bellingrath finalists, have prepared a variety of activities for Saturday evening and Sunday that we believe you will enjoy and better acquaint you with the College and city.

I ask that you please complete and return the enclosed reservation form or contact my office by telephone (1-901-726-3700 in-state or 1-800-238-6788 out-of state) prior to Wednesday, March 6 to confirm your attendance.

Angel, I believe it appropriate to say that whatever the outcome of the competition, you will be offered one of our merit-based scholarships, the least of which amounts to one-half of our tuition costs per year. I sincerely hope that our efforts in the weeks ahead will enable you to join us in the fall.

April 22, 1991

Ms. Marianne N. Ragins
P.O. Box 6845
Macon, GA 31208

Dear Marianne:

I enjoyed the opportunity to speak with you recently, and at this time would like to again add my congratulations to those recently extended by Armstrong's President, William W. Adams, on your selection to receive one of our Company scholarships. I am confident that you will never regret the extra effort and perhaps sacrifices you have made to get an excellent education. Your next step, college, will be ever so much more meaningful, and I hope you enjoy it.

In the next several weeks, you will be contacted by Allen Tabor, who will arrange a time and place to make the formal presentation of your scholarship. In the meantime, if you have any questions, please feel free to give me a call at (717) 396-2541.

Again, congratulations on a job well done.

Sincerely,

Bing G. Spitler
Manager, College Relations
Organization Development

MLW

Presbyterian College

CLINTON, SOUTH CAROLINA 29325 • (803) 833-2820

.March 5, 1991

Miss Marianne N. Ragins
P.O. Box 6845
Macon, GA 31208

Dear Angel:

You have been selected to receive a Belk Scholarship valued
at $14,000 for the four years of study at Presbyterian College.
Because this award (amounting to $3,500 annually) is made
on the basis of academic merit, I congratulate you on your
superior intellectual ability as well as on the diligence you
have shown throughout your high school career.

I want to thank you again for applying for consideration as
an Academic Scholar at Presbyterian College. The Scholarship Committee was most impressed with your credentials
and with your potential for outstanding future achievement.
The Committee had the difficult task of choosing sixteen
finalists from a field of 150 highly-qualified semifinalists,
and your selection for a Belk amounts to a real mark of dis-
tinction. In addition to this fine Belk Scholarship, you also
may qualify for other grants based on your need for financial
assistance.

I ask that you let me know by May 1, 1991 (National
Candidates' Reply Date) whether you can accept our offer of
this scholarship. If you need additional financial aid, please
complete the necessary applications. If you have questions
concerning this process, please contact Mrs. Judi Gillespie.
You may call her toll-free at 1-800-476-7272.

I hope it will be my pleasure to welcome you personally to PC next fall and to come to know you as an honor student on our campus. You can look forward to four exciting years at Presbyterian College.

Kindest personal regards.

Sincerely,

Kenneth B. Orr
President

KBO/sga

Enclosures (Please sign and return one agreement and retain the other one for your file.)

29

FOR PARENTS ONLY: HELPING YOUR SON OR DAUGHTER WITH THE COLLEGE AND SCHOLARSHIP PROCESS

> Few things in the world are more powerful than a positive push. A smile. A word of optimism and hope. A "you can do it" when things are tough.
>
> —Richard M. De Vos

As parents, you should start talking to your kids about scholarships as early as ninth grade. Although many kids will tell you they want to go to college, most of them don't even think about how it will be paid for until their senior year or until they have a frank discussion with you, the parent. Wondering why? Believe it or not, your kids probably think you earn enough each year or have saved more than enough money to pay for their college education and their siblings', too. As a result, your children may not think twice about what they can do to help pay the tuition bill. Even if they know how much you've saved they probably have no concept of the amount it could cost each year to send them to college.

I know this based on the hundreds of seminars I have given over the years. In these seminars it has most often been the parents who are the most concerned with how to pay and finding scholarships. In many instances, the parents attend while their kids are at home or involved in some other activity. I once did a seminar where all of the attendees were mostly freshmen in high school. None of their parents attended. And, as you can imagine, the session had to be even more interactive than usual because the students informed me that they had been forced into coming by the session coordinators and their parents, and saw no need to be there. When I asked if they thought they would need money to help pay for their college education, all but three of the them said no, even though 100 percent of them stated they wanted to attend college. I asked them why they didn't think they would have to contribute. The answers were "my parents make enough money" or "my parents have money in an account to pay for it." For students who said money was in an account, I asked how much they thought was in the account. They told me amounts ranging from $2,000 to $5,000. I asked how much money they thought one of their favorite colleges would cost each year. Most of them said a few thousand dollars.

Helping Your Son or Daughter Find Scholarships in Every Nook and Cranny

Parents! Think of every organization or association you or your child may be affiliated with as potential sources of scholarships. For example:

- Do you belong to a credit union?
- Do you belong to a union?
- Do you belong to a fraternity or sorority?
- Do you have any religious affiliations?
- Do you belong to an alumni association for your college or university?

All of the above could be sources of scholarships for your son or daughter. Even associations you may not think offer scholarships could be opportunities for your kids. For example, your electric utility company or an association such as the Military Benefit Association (a nonprofit organization of military personnel and civilian employees of the U.S. government that offers $2,500 scholarships to the children of their members) could be a funding opportunity.

In some cases, if you become an active member of an organization that does not have a scholarship program, you can suggest one. Organizations are often eager to provide educational benefits to their members and to the surrounding communities in which they operate. If they take your suggestion seriously and introduce a scholarship program for their members or children of their members, they may do so in time to benefit your son or daughter. If not, the program will still benefit others in your organization and could also help younger children you might have in later years.

The lesson for parents in this story is that your children may have no idea how much money is needed for their college education. It's up to you to tell them and to get them involved in activities that will help make their scholarship quest successful. It's also up to you to motivate them into wanting to help themselves when it comes to paying for their college education.

To get started in preparing them, look at the scholarship checklist in chapter 32. Familiarize yourself with the various steps to prepare for the scholarship search process. Along the way, be prepared to give gentle reminders or to have discussions with your son or daughter about upcoming milestones and the help or advice your child might want from you. Before embarking on the scholarship search, you should have goal-setting, thought-provoking discussions with your children to establish the following:

- There is a need for them to go to college and why. This should be mostly their input.
- Make sure college is something they want to do.
- Be honest with your soon-to-be college students about your financial situation. Even if it's a good one, make sure they understand that the financing of their college education is as much their responsibility as yours. Both you and your son or daughter should establish and agree that there is a need for them to win scholarships or free money for college before the scholarship search is begun. Make it clear that although their education is very important to you, financing it entirely will be a huge burden, particularly if you are a middle-class family, or have high expenses that are not recognized by the financial aid forms as a basis for need. You should also let your son or daughter know that given the high costs of attending college, all of you will probably have large outstanding loans if they are unable to win scholarships. You should also discuss with them salary projections for their intended career path. You can get these from the *Occupational Outlook Handbook*, which can be found at your local library or online at http://www.bls.gov/ooh. Salary.com is also an excellent resource for information. After you obtain salary projections, you and your children should do a sample financial budget depicting the inflows and outflows of cash both of you will have once they graduate and obtain a job. If you look at the college costs in chapter 1 of this book and compute an approximation of your loan amounts using a financial aid calculator from a website such as http://www.finaid.org, it will be easy to see how much income will be going to loan payments. If your kids haven't seen a need before to secure as much scholarship money as possible, they will after this exercise.

- Prepare an investment plan if you have the resources and the time. Refer to chapter 31, "For Parents Only: Saving for College."
- Encourage your son or daughter to participate in activities, particularly community service. Many scholarship programs place heavy emphasis on an applicant's service in the community. You might visit http://www.nhs.us/scaa/scaa_search.cfm to find some nationally recognized student activities to get your son or daughter involved in.
- Talk to the guidance counselor at the high school your son or daughter attends.
- Encourage and take your son or daughter to visit colleges and talk to financial aid directors.
- Discuss with your son or daughter various majors and introduce him or her to people who have already graduated in that field and who currently work in it. Changing majors in college can cost more money, especially if your student has gotten beyond the core courses. This could add an extra year and thousands of dollars to the total college bill.
- Help with their research for scholarships, but please don't do it for them, unless they are so swamped with extracurricular activities, volunteer work, and a job that they don't have time, and you as the parent holding down a full-time job actually do.
- Make sure you have a computer and Internet access in your home or that your child has access to one nearby or at school. The Internet can help to maximize the time you spend searching for scholarships and make your search more comprehensive. Help your son or daughter integrate social media responsibly into this process. Scholarship programs and government organizations have Facebook pages, Twitter handles, YouTube videos, and more to educate parents and students.
- Prepare for the financial aid forms (FAFSA and/or CSS—Financial Aid PROFILE) you and your soon-to-be college student will have to complete. Manage your finances to maximize your chances of financial aid legally and ethically (refer to chapter 5). Visit http://www.fafsa.ed.gov or www.fafsa4caster.ed.gov to estimate your financial need before actually completing the FAFSA. In addition, you can get information about the FAFSA on YouTube at http://www.youtube.com/user/federalStudentAid. You can also get information about this process using Twitter, @FAFSA.
- Be on the lookout for scholarship scams that may catch your son or daughter unaware. Since many scams require money in some way,

shape, or form, you as the primary providers for your child will probably be asked for the money to pay for them. When asked by your kids for money to pay for any ruse resembling those discussed in the "Scholarship Scams" section of chapter 2, you should get involved.

- Encourage your child to be self-motivated, determined, and highly persistent from an early age, well before they get into high school, if possible. These traits are very important in the pursuit of scholarships and in many areas of life.
- You should also encourage responsibility and independence in your children. To win scholarships and to succeed in college, these traits are also very important.
- Review chapter 35, "Major Reasons Why Some Students Win Scholarships and Others Don't." Ensure that your son or daughter is using the best practices of a scholarship winner and avoiding the pitfalls of those who don't win scholarships.

Most important for parents is to let your student do the work involved in winning scholarships and getting accepted to a college themselves. You should show interest, provide advice, and give support. To stay up to date on their activities and progress with the scholarship and financial aid process, ask to see their monthly scholarship plan, which should be similar to the one shown in chapter 6, "Getting Organized." It is important that you do not hover or panic even though you are concerned about their welfare and want them to do well. However, if you know your son or daughter's weakness is organization and timeliness, then you may need to take a more active role in the process. It's up to you to decide.

For students reading this chapter, to help keep your parents informed make sure you keep your monthly scholarship plan like the one shown in chapter 6 in full view and updated. Put it on the refrigerator door or in another highly visible place to soothe your parents' nerves and to serve as your own constant reminder of tasks you need to do in the scholarship process.

30

FOR PARENTS ONLY: MOTIVATING YOUR KIDS TO WIN SCHOLARSHIPS

> Our greatest weakness lies in giving up. The most certain way to succeed is to always try just one more time.
>
> —Thomas Edison

For many parents, trying to get their kids to research and apply for scholarships can be very difficult. Here are a few tips you can try to help your teenager get more involved in the scholarship search.

- Share your financial situation early. Don't wait until the senior year if you can help it. Estimate the costs of the colleges your son or daughter is interested in attending. Determine your expected family contribution using a financial aid calculator, such as the one on http://www .finaid.org. Suggest to your son or daughter to take a look at some of the videos on the Federal Student Aid YouTube channel at http:// www.youtube.com/user/federalStudentAid. If you're comfortable with it, show them your bank account. Discuss your debts and other responsibilities especially if brothers and sisters will also be attending college. Sometimes kids may not understand how much it takes to keep everything running in your household. Sometimes they grossly overestimate just how well you might be doing. And most students and parents just don't understand how many loans they may end up with to afford a college education. A thorough understanding might help motivate them and help you in the process.

- Give an incentive, especially if it looks to your kids as if paying for college will be very easy for you even though you know looks can be deceiving. For example, you could promise to buy them a new car of their choice if they graduate with a scholarship. Make sure to specify a maximum limit for the car you agree to buy and the type of scholarship they have to win to get it (full-ride, tuition only, etc.). Considering that the cost of a college education could be three times as much as the car you buy, it might work to your financial advantage.

- Be clear on what you will and will not pay for. If your son is not willing to help in securing his own future by trying to win a scholarship, then let him know there are certain schools you will not and cannot afford. Suggest community college as an option. However, don't rule out private or more expensive institutions on the basis of cost alone. Remember, even though the cost of attendance will be higher, your financial need will be greater, and you may qualify for more aid.

- Get your kids talking to other students who have graduated with loans that have to be repaid or who have had to work throughout college in order to stay enrolled. Get other college students who have won scholarships to talk to them. Hearing about their experiences might push them into action.

- If your kids are interested in certain areas such as medicine, law, architecture, engineering, and so on, introduce them to people in these fields. This could help to raise their interest in pursuing certain fields and may aid in their self-motivation. These professionals can also help them and you to get a clear picture of the money it will take to achieve your child's dream.

- Start discussing the scholarship process early. The earlier your daughter prepares by participating in extracurricular and community-based activities, assuming leadership roles, and starting her research, the easier and more stress-free senior year will be for her to enjoy. A well-prepared senior doesn't worry as much about scholarship or college applications because she's already done most of the work by the end of her junior year. Early preparation also provides an opportunity to apply for all of the biggest scholarships, which normally have deadlines early in a student's senior year. This keeps them from scrambling at the last minute to complete applications. Read chapter 32, "It's Never Too Early to Prepare for the Scholarship Search" for more information.

For more information about motivating your kids to win scholarships, consider attending one of my motivational speech presentations. Visit http://www.scholarshipworkshop.com to get more information about attending.

HOW MANY SCHOLARSHIPS SHOULD MY SON OR DAUGHTER PURSUE? CAN THERE BE TOO MANY?

I've had many parents ask this question over the years. Often parents are concerned their son or daughter may work too hard with the scholarship process while still trying to keep up with extracurricular activities. Unfortunately, there are absolutely no guarantees with scholarships. Neither you as parents, nor I as the author of this book, can rarely, if ever, be certain your child will be selected as a winner even if you believe he or she has done everything right. There are many factors that go into the final selections for scholarships and contests. And you can't plan for them all. So my advice to those who ask is to apply for as many scholarships as possible. You just need to work on the process to make it easier to apply. For example, your teenager should follow the strategies I outline for recycling essays. He or she should follow the strategies in chapter 6 for getting organized. Streamline the Internet search by reviewing chapter 3. Get any additional information needed for applications ready and into computer folders. Get prepared for frequently asked questions in interviews. After once going through the initial organization process and steps, applying for multiple scholarships should be much easier. Not only that, don't let your son or daughter think that applying for scholarships is extra work on top of applying for college admission. Why? Because much of the work one needs to do for college admissions can be replicated very easily for scholarship applications. Likewise, much of the work for scholarship applications may also be applicable to the college admissions process. This includes essays, interview preparation, applications, and more. There is a correlation between both processes because colleges and universities (including the top tier) prefer the same types of students that competitive scholarship programs prefer, and vice versa.

31

FOR PARENTS ONLY: SAVING FOR COLLEGE

The secret of success is constancy to purpose.

—Benjamin Disraeli

Many ways exist to save or invest for a college education. In fact, there are so many strategies for saving, based on your income, risk tolerance, and time frame, that I will cover only a few. You should consult a financial planner or a tax professional for more specific and comprehensive information on an investment strategy for you and your family.

The Rule of 72

One simple strategy for investing is to use the Rule of 72. This rule can help you decide on the types of investments you may want to pursue to save for your child's college education. With the Rule of 72, you divide the number 72 by the interest rate for your savings or investment account. The result is the number of years it will take for your investment to double. For example, if you have a savings account that pays 4 percent interest, you would divide 72 by 4. The result is 18. Therefore, if you put $500 into a savings account, it would take 18 years for your money to double into $1,000. Also, using the Rule of 72, if you put your money into a certificate of deposit (CD) paying 6 percent interest, your $500 investment would take only 12 years to increase to $1,000. Depending upon when you read this book, however, 4 percent to 6 percent interest on an investment may or may not be realistic.

If you put your money into stocks your return might earn on average 10 percent (this average changes frequently) and your $500 would increase to

$1,000 in only six years. There are many websites such as http://www
.bankrate.com (my favorite) to help you see current rates for savings, CDs,
money market accounts, 529 savings plan options, and more. In addition,
apps such as Mint (for Mint.com) for your iPhone, iPad, Android, or Android
tablet can help you plan for a specific time frame to meet a college savings
goal. For example, although I will be coaching both of my children to win
as many scholarships, contests, and other free financial aid as possible, I
still have a goal set up in Mint.com to pay for their college education.

U.S. Series EE Savings Bonds and Other Options from Treasury Direct

If you have only a small amount of money to invest, a savings bond of
this type can be purchased for as little as $25. These bonds, issued by the
government, earn a fixed rate of interest. Although you have little risk of
losing your money with this vehicle, you'll also have a lower rate of return
when compared with other investment options. One good thing about a
U.S. savings bond is that if you cash it in to pay for tuition and fees related
to college, you may not be taxed on the interest you earn from the bond.
You may also want to explore I Bonds, Treasury bonds, Treasury notes,
and other government investment vehicles, some of which have potentially
higher rates of return than EE Bonds. If you want more information, call
(800) 722-2678 or go to the website at http://www.savingsbonds.gov or
http://www.treasurydirect.gov.

Prepaid Tuition Plans (Section 529)

You might also consider prepaid tuition plans, which are available in
many states. A prepaid tuition plan is a savings plan for college that is
guaranteed to rise in value at the same rate as college tuition. For instance,
if a family purchases shares of a plan worth half a year's tuition at a state
college, the shares will always be worth half a year's tuition, even ten years
later when tuition rates may have doubled—although plans may run into
trouble if their investments in the stock market perform poorly. Prepaid
tuition plans can also be thought of as allowing participants to buy tuition
credits for their son or daughter that can be used in the future as a waiver
or payment of their college tuition and fees in a specific state. Although
the funds in the plan can be used for an out-of-state college or private
institution, the money paid out from the plan may be based on in-state
tuition rates for that state. Your tuition credit or waiver for a public college

or university may buy you two years in the state the plan was set up, but only one year in another state or one semester at a private institution. Contact your financial advisor, state financial aid agency, or department of education for more information.

Important Note for Parents

Money accumulated in your child's name or an account contributed to by your son or daughter is usually considered a student asset when your financial need at colleges and universities is calculated. If you can, use the money in these accounts for other college preparation expenses or transfer the money to an account in your name before your son or daughter's junior year in high school. Student assets are generally weighed more heavily in determining a family's Expected Family Contribution (EFC) than assets in the parents' name. Speak with your financial advisor about any investment accounts you have for strategies they recommend. Note: 529 Plans that are in a parent's name are considered assets of the parent and do not affect student financial aid eligibility as much as an account owned by your son or daughter.

Section 529 College Savings Plans

Another alternative for accumulating college savings is a 529 College Savings Plan. One of its most important features is that the money you put into the plan grows tax-free for future educational costs. Withdrawals from the plan to pay your son or daughter's qualified college costs are also tax-free, assuming the funds are used for qualified higher education expenses. The 529 Savings Plan usually offers several investment options, including equity mutual funds ranging from aggressive—which may be good for you when your kids are young—to conservative, for when your kids are nearing college age. Since both states and educational institutions offer 529 plans, there are many you can choose from, including those from another state. Most plans are open to out-of-state investors and will allow payouts for the costs of attending any accredited college or university in the country. However, the program in your home state may offer tax advantages such as a state tax deduction or a credit on contributions. Consult your financial advisor for specific advice on funding this type of account as well as the amount you should contribute. You can also visit http://www .savingforcollege.com for additional information.

The biggest difference between the 529 Prepaid Tuition Plan and the 529 Savings Plan is that the Prepaid Tuition Plans allows you to lock in the cost to attend certain in-state colleges and universities. However, with the Section 529 Savings Plan, you run the risk of potential investment loss due to a downturn in the market, which means you may not earn enough to pay the full tuition for your son or daughter's future education.

Coverdell Education Savings Account (ESA)

With this type of savings account, you can contribute a maximum of $2,000 each year and your withdrawals are tax-free when used for qualified higher-education expenses as well as elementary and secondary school expenses. The account can be allocated in any way you choose. Eligibility for this type of account phases out contributions based on income level. See http://www.irs.gov for phase-out levels.

Custodial Account UGMA/UTMA

Custodial accounts can be set up for your children under applicable state law. You or the custodian you designate controls the account until your children reach the age of trust determination, which depends upon your state and type of account. The account will be taxed at your children's rate. You can contribute unlimited amounts and the account can be allocated however you choose. Withdrawals can then be used for anything. Note that this type of account is currently considered a student asset which could affect financial aid eligibility.

CERTIFIED COLLEGE PLANNING SPECIALISTS

If you're interested in using any of the savings options discussed above, consult your tax or financial advisor. Or, to help you evaluate the right savings option for you and help plan for your son or daughter's college education expenses, you may want to consult a Certified College Planning Specialist (CCPS) in addition to your financial advisor. Although your financial advisor may be able to steer you in the right direction for your college savings choices, a Certified College Planning Specialist focuses on these types of investments and may be able to help you more. Those who have the CCPS designation actively assist families in preparing for the financial cost of sending children to college and can help you with strategies for paying for college, saving for college, and advanced college funding planning. You can also see sites such as http://www.finaid.org or http://www.collegesavings.org to learn how various types of accounts could impact your teenager's financial aid package. Also consult *Paying for College Without Going Broke*, published annually by Princeton Review, which is a college financial aid guide with line-by-line instructions for completing the FAFSA and CSS—PROFILE aid forms. It also provides tips for maximizing financial aid eligibility.

GETTING FREE MONEY IN COLLEGE SAVINGS ACCOUNTS FOR THINGS YOU ALREADY BUY

In recent years, several new companies have begun offering some type of automatic rebate on everyday purchases. The rebates you earn accumulate in savings accounts intended to help you pay for your kids' education. Beginning with companies such as Upromise.com to Sage Scholars to Babymint.com, the trend is growing steadily. So far, setting up the accounts is free for those who decide to take advantage. Once the account is established you purchase items as you normally would—for example, buying groceries or gas. And if you shop online, the savings are even better. The beauty of these programs is that when you make a purchase, you automatically get a rebate in your account to use for your children's education expenses. In some cases, you can use the account in any way you choose and your relatives and friends can even join the program and help save for your kids. The following are examples of some of these companies with a short description of their program and how they can help you save for college.

Upromise.com

With Upromise.com you can set up a free online account by registering your credit or debit cards and other loyalty cards such as the CVS Extra-Care Card. When you make online purchases at companies such as Walmart, Sears, Target, Bed Bath & Beyond, Toys "R" Us, and thousands more, you get money back for college as an automatic rebate in your account. Or when you buy groceries at stores such as Giant that have loyalty cards tied to your name you also get money back. Rebates are also available for gas purchases. You can also get a percentage of your total bill back (including tax and tip) at more than 8,000 restaurants. The money you accumulate in the account stays there until you decide to use it, or it can be transferred to a 529 Plan. Most important, anyone can help you save for your children's education by linking to the account you set up. This means that purchases by grandparents, extended family, and even friends can go toward your son or daughter's account to help you accumulate more money faster. I set up an account for my nephew. I also helped him get a scholarship so he didn't need the funds in the account, so I sent Upromise.com a letter indicating I wanted to receive a check for the funds I had accumulated for him. I received the check and invested the funds for my own children who both have steadily growing Upromise.com accounts. You can even save money for yourself or for a child you plan to have in the future. For more information about Upromise.com and some of the many ways opening an account with them can help you save for college, go to http://www.upromise.com. Also look at ways to maximize your savings as well. For example, Upromise.com currently has an add-on for your Internet browser that alerts you any time you visit a merchant online where you might be able to earn funds. They also have many other ways to help you save, including sweepstakes, credit cards, and even periodic scholarship offers directly from upromise.com.

BabyMint

When you join BabyMint you can receive up to a 26 percent rebate on everyday purchases made through BabyMint's network of more than 500 retailers, such as Best Buy, Container Store, Walmart, and Gap. As you make purchases, BabyMint tracks, collects, and deposits your earnings into a tax-free 529 Plan or a Coverdell account. Or you can choose to have your rebates sent to you via check or directed into another BabyMint member's account. Earnings can also be applied to student loans. Grandparents, extended family, and friends can also participate by having their rebates go into your child's account.

In addition to rebates from participating retailers and product manufacturers, BabyMint members can also apply for and use the BabyMint College Savings Credit Card to receive an additional 1 percent rebate on all their purchases, regardless of where they shop. When the BabyMint card is used at their participating in-store merchants, you can get up to an additional 8 percent on all of your purchases.

You can also enroll in BabyMint's Tuition Rewards program where every dollar in shopping rebates you earn is matched by a dollar off tuition at nearly 180 colleges and universities across the United States. For more information, visit http://www.babymint.com, or call (888) 427-1099.

GradSave

Do you, your friends or your relatives like using registries to buy gifts? Do you prefer gift cards because you have no idea what to buy or because you don't like wasting money and want to make sure that whatever you buy will have a likelihood of being used? If you answered yes to either of these questions, then consider GradSave, an innovative program that combines gift-giving with a great way to save for your son or daughter's college education.

To start using this program, register for a free GradSave account and create a profile that includes a picture and a description of your son or daughter. As soon as you do, gift cards from friends and family can be immediately redeemed in the account. You can also spread the word about the account via e-mail, Facebook, and Twitter or when you send invitations to events like baby showers and other celebrations. Encourage friends and family to give your child the gift of a future education instead of a toy, clothes, or other item you really don't need. To start investing your earnings, you can link your GradSave account to your 529 Savings Plan and transfer the funds at any time. Please note, however, that although Grad-Save doesn't charge those who give you a gift card any fees, they do charge a fee when the gift is deposited in your account. So you will not get the full amount of the gift card.

32

IT'S NEVER TOO EARLY TO PREPARE FOR
THE SCHOLARSHIP SEARCH

Just over the hill is a beautiful valley, but you must
climb the hill to see it.

—Anonymous

It may seem a little early to begin searching for scholarships in the seventh
or eighth grade, but an early start will allow you to take advantage of many
opportunities that will ensure college or university dollars for your future.
For example, you can begin your research and gradually build up a database of scholarships that you will be eligible to apply for in your senior year.
In addition, you have a chance to clearly outline your goals and plans for
the future in terms of extracurricular activities and your academic record.
Early preparation is an important factor in a successful scholarship search.
If you are prepared for the process before senior year, you will know
exactly what to do and to which programs you should apply. Early preparation creates two advantages: (1) you know what to expect; and (2) you are
relaxed and calm about it. Prior knowledge and preparation are essential
factors for success in any endeavor. To begin your journey in the seventh
grade is to create a clear and easy path for success.

When you prepare early you will have adequate time to explore numerous scholarship programs, perfect your essay writing and interviewing
skills, participate and excel in various extracurricular activities, and also
improve your SAT scores and your academic record. Note that the largest
scholarship programs, giving scholarships ranging from $4,000 to $30,000
and up, have very early deadlines. Many fall in October and December of

When should you start your scholarship search?

Start your search as soon as possible. Although the majority of scholarships can only be applied for as a senior in high school, it can really pay off if you know what's available and what to expect beforehand by doing your research early. This is mainly because the largest scholarship programs have deadlines early in your senior year. Don't wait until the summer before college starts.

Can you start too early?

Starting your research before you get into high school may be too early for some. If you do, you'll have a great database to start with as a senior. You can also prepare yourself early by starting to participate in activities that interest you and that you'll continue to pursue in high school. You can also take the PSAT early, if available, to start preparing for eleventh grade when it will really count for scholarship consideration. Or you might even decide to take the SAT or ACT early. Also remember that some scholarships can be won as early as age six. See chapter 26.

Can you start too late?

Yes. If you're hoping to win a full ride scholarship, late spring and early summer of your senior year is too late. Scholarships are still available at this time and may also be easier to win, so they shouldn't be ignored, but the amounts you can win are usually smaller. All hope is not lost—you can still win scholarships if you're already enrolled in college.

the applicant's senior year. Early preparation will increase your chances tremendously. It will also ease not only your mind but also your parents' minds to have the scholarship journey well under way. So start as soon as possible.

While it is certainly true that the early bird often gets the worm, eleventh and twelfth graders should not count themselves out. Many battles have been fought, races have been won, and journeys successfully completed with self-motivation, determination, and persistence. Early preparation will definitely make any undertaking easier, but if you begin late it does not take you out of the running. A prime example of success in spite of a late beginning is my own scholarship journey. Many elements contributed to my scholarship success, such as a strong academic record and participation in extracurricular activities throughout high school, but I did not actually begin my scholarship journey until the second day of my senior year in high school. So, you can be successful in spite of a late start, especially if you have a high level of self-motivation, determination, and persistence.

COUNTDOWN: THE SCHOLARSHIP CHECKLIST

Seventh and Eighth Grades

- Begin to think about college. Prepare yourself by listing all the reasons you should go to college and how you or your parents will pay for it.
- If you and your parents haven't formulated an investment plan, you should start doing short-term investment planning. Even if you and your parents can save and invest only $25 a month, this can add up to enough to pay your first semester tuition if you attend a public college or university. It could buy all your books for the first and second year, or it could buy you a new computer or tablet. All of these are things you will need, and money saved to pay for them can help lessen the burden of college expenses. Even if you win enough scholarship money to cover your tuition, fees, and room and board, with additional amounts given to you each year for personal spending, extra money can come in handy, even if only for frequent trips home for a taste of Mom's homemade spaghetti.
- If possible, take the PSAT or SAT to get an idea of your areas of strength and weakness.
- If you have not started to become involved in activities outside of school, you should start now to develop interests you can build on when you get to high school. I began participating in the Optimist Oratorical Contests, essay contests, and debates in the sixth grade. These activities helped me build a foundation for activities I participated in later such as the *Salmagundi* literary magazine, the Literary Team, the Drama Club, and the *Macon Telegraph and News* Teen Board. You will see these activities listed on my résumé in chapter 9, "Writing Your Scholarship Résumé: How to Stand Out and Why Grades Don't Mean Everything."
- Ask your parents to explore joining a program such as Upromise .com now. This is a free program that allows individuals to register credit and frequent shopper cards to earn rebates into a college savings account. Also read the section in chapter 31 titled "Getting Free Money in College Saving Accounts for Things You Already Buy."

Ninth Grade

- When you enter high school you begin with a clean slate. Maintain that clean slate throughout your high school career. Scholarship administrators do not take kindly to suspension or expulsion from any school.
- You should definitely begin to get involved, if you aren't already, in school and community activities such as the Beta Club, Science and Math clubs, or Academic Bowl teams. Activities that you begin participating in now will become part of the résumé you'll eventually submit to colleges, universities, and scholarship programs. You can also become involved in volunteer activities such as the Red Cross or other youth community groups. Some clubs and activities such as DECA and Boy/Girl Scouts of America have special scholarship competitions for their members.
- If you are not involved in some activity within your church or spiritual community, you should consider it. Activities such as church or synagogue youth groups and choirs are considered extracurricular activities and should be included on your résumé. Not only that, as an outstanding and outgoing member of the church or synagogue, the congregation may help to fund your college education.
- Acquire a recommended reading list from an English teacher or from the public library in your area. Reading books from this list will not only help to improve your verbal SAT scores, but will also give you something to talk about during scholarship interviews.

Should I Participate in the International Baccalaureate (IB) Program? Can I Still Apply for Scholarships?

Yes, you can certainly participate in the IB program. However, keep in mind that one of the best ways to distinguish yourself in a scholarship competition is through your extracurricular activities, leadership, volunteer activities, and community service. Sometimes the rigorous requirements of an IB program can limit your participation in these types of activities. If you can handle both the IB program as well as these activities, excellent. If not, the IB program may still be for you, as it relates to your future college and university. But definitely think carefully about what you want to do. Your extracurricular activities, leadership, volunteer activities, and community service also affect the admission decision at some of the most selective colleges and universities. Do a little more research. Discuss with your parents. Then decide! For more information about the IB program, visit http://www.ibo.org.

- Begin to participate in activities and contests such as essay contests, poetry contests, art exhibitions, drama productions, or oratorical contests. Participation shows that you are motivated, even if you do not win. It also enhances your communication skills, which will be useful during interviews and for writing essays. The more you participate and become involved, the more well rounded you will be as a person. Your participation will enhance your chances of getting a scholarship, and will also help you to become a well-prepared and informed member of society.
- Start keeping a list of all activities and contests in which you have participated.
- Review with your counselor the courses you will need to take in the next four years of high school. Make sure you prepare a schedule of courses and units you need to have in order to qualify for some scholarships, prepare for college, and avoid remedial courses. Many colleges and universities require you to have taken certain courses in preparation. These courses usually include four units of English, three units of science (with at least two lab courses), three or more units of math (algebra, trigonometry, and pre-calculus), three units of social studies (American history, world history, economics, and government), and two units of one foreign language. Try to structure your schedule so that you can take these courses in addition to courses in fine arts, a third course in one foreign language, physical education, computer technology, and another laboratory course in science. Review the most rigorous courses at the high school you will be graduating from. If you are looking toward the most competitive scholarships, your class schedule needs to be among the most demanding ones a student at your school can have.
- Review chapter 26, "Scholarships for Younger Students—From Kindergarten to 11th Grade," for scholarships and awards you qualify for now.

Tenth Grade

- Begin to familiarize yourself with standardized tests. Take the PSAT again even if you have taken it before. When taking these tests make sure to darken the *Yes* oval so you can be included in the Student Search Service. Your participation in the Student Search Service will get you on the mailing lists of many colleges and will provide scholarship and academic information. After you receive your scores from these tests, carefully note your weak areas. Talk to your counselor and your teachers about ways to improve your scores in these areas.

- Begin to run for offices in various clubs—which you should already be involved in from your ninth-grade year. Analyze your course schedule and the units you have already taken to see if you can take some advanced placement courses. Discuss this with your counselor. If you take the test given immediately after these courses and earn a high enough score you can be exempted from some college or university courses later, which is a savings in itself. The scores range from 1 to 5, with 5 being the highest score possible. A 3, 4, or 5 is usually acceptable for exemption from a course, subject to specific college and university requirements. Go to http://www.collegeboard.org for more information about AP exams.

- Start researching for scholarships now. Keep a paper file or an electronic file on your computer with information about all programs. Try to get copies of PDF applications and other information by visiting scholarship program websites and registering with free scholarship search services such as http://www.fastweb.com. Look at the essay questions and other requirements. Write essays for the programs and ask your counselor and English teacher to look at them and help you make them better. Although you may not have the same essay question and the scholarship may not be offered when you actually get ready to apply, practice in writing essays for these competitions is very important.

- Review chapter 26, "Scholarships for Younger Students—From Kindergarten to 11th Grade," for scholarships and awards you qualify for now.

Summer After Tenth Grade

- By now you should have begun to receive information from colleges as a result of already taking the PSAT or the SAT and participating in the Student Search Service. Keep this information in a file folder or electronic folder on your computer or a USB drive after you have read it carefully. Make special note of the literature that interests you. If you want more information, visit the college or university's website or respond to any special online invitations you might receive. On the

Internet you can take advantage of several other ways colleges and universities currently offer to get a feel for their campus and academic programs. This includes online chats and webinars, special apps for prospective students, virtual tours, or viewing YouTube videos through their websites.

- If you are late on the scene, meaning you took the tests late and haven't received any scholarship information, your local library could be an excellent resource. Libraries generally have tons of information on numerous colleges. If the library doesn't have enough information on the colleges you are interested in or on scholarship opportunities you may be eligible for, the Internet is an excellent resource to gathering information quickly. For more information on using the Internet in your scholarship search as well as loads of social media information, refer to chapter 3, "Using the Internet and Social Media in Your Scholarship Search."

Eleventh Grade

- Refer to chapter 5, "Financial Aid Forms and Help from the Government with College Expenses," for two major strategies in securing more financial aid when filing financial aid forms. For example, if you need to restructure your assets (student) by using some of them to pay off debt and thus increasing your eligibility for financial aid, you should do it now. By December of this year, make sure you and your parents have positioned your assets correctly and legally to get the maximum financial aid possible to help cover your college costs. One book devoted primarily to helping you and your family do this is *Paying for College Without Going Broke*. This is an annual college financial aid guide, published by *Princeton Review*, with line-by-line instructions for completing the FAFSA and CSS—PROFILE aid forms. The guide also provides tips for maximizing financial aid eligibility.
- Go to http://www.commonapp.org to begin an online college application and get a feel for the electronic application process.
- Take the PSAT again, even if you took it last year or the year before. With the appropriate scores, this time it will qualify you for the National Merit/Achievement Scholarship Program. Your counselor should be able to tell you the date to register for scholarship consideration; it is usually October of your junior year. However, even if you don't qualify for the scholarship competition you will still get practice for the SAT. This year you should take the SAT at least twice to become familiar

with it. Make sure you take the time to read the information online about preparing for the test—don't wait until the last minute. You can also visit the test preparation websites discussed extensively in chapter 8. Again, after receiving your scores, note your weak areas. Some schools prefer the ACT and some students actually do much better on it, so take that in your junior year also.

- Begin to finalize college/university choices. Visit college and university websites for those you really like. Discuss your choices with your counselor to get his/her insight on the school, its reputation, and your chances for being accepted.

- Review application requirements and scholarships at your favorite colleges and universities. Consider using http://www.meritaid.com to review merit aid at various colleges and universities.

- Start to attend college fairs. Go to http://www.nacac.com for more information about upcoming college fairs in your area. Also contact your counselor or visit your school or county educational website for information about smaller, community-based college fairs.

- Visit a college or university close to your hometown to get a feel for academic life.

- In your English classes, make sure you master the basic five-paragraph essay format—this is most efficient and the most effective format for scholarship essays (see chapter 11, "Writing Scholarship Essays That Get Noticed").

- Don't forget, in your junior year it's still important to stay out of trouble and remain involved in various activities in your community and school. Also make sure you get involved in at least two volunteer activities.

- Keep entering contests; whether you win or lose, participation is important.

- Visit your counselor to make sure you will meet the college preparatory requirements with the classes you have taken or will take next year.

- Consider applying for scholarships as a junior. Read chapter 26, "Scholarships for Younger Students—From Kindergarten to 11th Grade," for scholarships and awards you qualify for now.

Summer after Eleventh Grade

- Go to the library and find books that list types of scholarships, grants, and monetary aid. Record the Web addresses and deadlines. Put the deadlines in a calendar so you can start getting organized. Many of them are catalogued according to academic majors, ethnic groups, military affiliations, and private scholarships. Unless you are certain about your major, don't pick scholarships geared toward a specific career. Try to focus on general scholarships and list those that apply specifically to your ethnic group and interests. Refer to chapter 2 for more information. For example, if you are Caucasian, born of military parents, and your future major is undecided, look for general scholarships that apply to almost anyone, such as the Coca-Cola Scholars Foundation, and for scholarships and state aid that may be for the children of military parents.

- Begin looking at current newspapers and magazines for upcoming scholarship opportunities. Also contact local organizations and radio and television stations to uncover local scholarship and award opportunities (see chapter 2). Do an advanced Internet search to find locally based scholarships and awards.

- Do a computerized scholarship search using a website such as http://www.fastweb.com. (See chapter 3, "Using the Internet and Social Media in Your Scholarship Search.") To stay abreast of new scholarships and other helpful information, sign up for The Scholarship Workshop newsletter at http://www.scholarshipworkshop.com; "like" us at http://www.facebook.com/scholarshipworkshop and follow us @ ScholarshipWork on Twitter.

- If you need to send a formal written request by mail (students who do not have Internet access), send the inquiry letter in chapter 2 to those institutions that require them.

- If you choose to use a computerized scholarship service that you must pay for to get additional information, you should apply now to ensure that you receive the information before your senior year of high school begins.

Twelfth Grade

- Take the SAT or ACT as soon as possible. If you can register online during the summer or the very first day that school opens, do so. Therefore, when you get your scores back you will have enough time to take the tests again if you aren't satisfied and will be able to send the later scores to the colleges of your choice.

- If necessary, send a letter to private organizations requesting information and applications for their scholarship programs (refer to chapter 2). This should be done as soon as your senior year begins or before September 15, if possible, to catch the earliest deadlines. Otherwise visit the program's Web page, Facebook page, or Twitter page to download and explore applications or the application process, read about previous winners and the organization's mission and goals, and note all deadlines.

- Complete a résumé of your activities and the awards you have won. Refer to chapter 9, "Writing Your Scholarship Résumé: How to Stand Out and Why Grades Don't Mean Everything."
- Make your recommendations list of teachers and administrators.
- Write two basic essays (future career goals and describing yourself) based on the five-paragraph format. Refer to chapter 11, "Writing Scholarship Essays That Get Noticed," or the publication *The Scholarship and College Essay Planning Kit*, available at http://www.scholar shipworkshop.com.
- Visit colleges or participate in college/university tours. Go to a local college/university fair.
- Apply for admission to the colleges and universities you have decided upon.
- Apply for scholarships from colleges and private organizations. If you have already received acceptance letters, e-mails, or some other type of notification from colleges you applied to earlier in the year, send copies of the notification (formal letters look better if you have them) along with your scholarship applications for private organizations. Deadline dates are usually December 1, December 15, January 1, January 15, February 1, February 15, March 1, April 1, and April 15. Some larger scholarship programs such as the Coca-Cola Scholars Foundation, whose application deadline is October 30 each year, have even earlier deadlines.
- Call radio and television stations to find out about various community organizations' scholarship competitions they may have announced.
- In December of your senior year, complete the financial aid form (FAFSA), which you can get from the Federal Student Aid information website, your counselor, and possibly the library. Do not submit it until after January 1 of the year you plan to enter college and after you and your parents have received their W-2s from the previous year, although you can complete a worksheet and forecast using the FAFSA4Caster at http://www.fafsa4caster.ed.gov. After your application is complete with the required documentation (some individuals

may be able to import tax information automatically), submit the FAFSA as soon as possible after January 1, along with the CSS—PROFILE if required.

- Wait. And review your priorities for considering a college or university if offered a scholarship from one.
- If you are really interested in a particular college or university and have received a financial aid package that includes loans, write a letter before June of your senior year requesting that the private outside scholarships you have won be used in place of a loan. See chapter 37.
- If you feel your financial aid package isn't sufficient, you may be able to request more by sending a letter describing your financial hardship and your very high interest in attending the college if you had enough money. See chapter 37.

Summer After Senior Year

- If you didn't get enough free college financial aid to cover your costs for four years, do another free computerized scholarship search. Also review chapter 18, "Scholarships for Current College Students and Transfer Students" or read *College Survival and Success Skills 101*.

Freshman Year in College

- Apply for private scholarships that you found in your search during the summer.
- In January of your freshman year in college, submit or renew your FAFSA for your sophomore financial aid.
- Contact the financial aid office at your school to find out about additional sources available to current undergraduates at the college.
- Contact the department in which you are planning to major to see if they offer scholarships to students in your field.

33

SCHOLARSHIP DO'S AND DON'TS: INSIDER TIPS FROM SCHOLARSHIP PROVIDERS

You can do anything if you have enthusiasm.
Enthusiasm is the yeast that makes your hopes rise
to the stars. With it, there is accomplishment.
Without it there are only alibis.

—Henry Ford

The scholarship tips in this chapter are based on responses to key questions and comments addressed to some of the largest scholarship programs in the United States as well as some of the smaller, community-based scholarship providers. The summary of their responses is designed to help you be successful in avoiding mistakes when it comes to scholarship applications. This survey encompassed both merit-based and need-based programs. It also included scholarship programs that have an online-only application process as well as programs that still have mostly paper-based components. Read on for insights to help you achieve success with your scholarship applications.

DO'S

- Do use an appropriate e-mail address. For example: firstnamelast name@xyz.com. Your address can give a negative or positive impression of you. It's amazing how much little things can matter. For example, an e-mail address such as imanidiot@aol.com, ilovemyboyfriend@xyz .com, or ihatewomen@gmail.com is certainly not appropriate.

- Do check your e-mail. Even if you have more than one e-mail address, have your e-mails forwarded to the account you check daily. Many providers still send letters in the mail but many now send e-mails for initial acceptance and notifications. One scholarship provider noted, "Many colleges now only issue acceptance/rejections via e-mail. Although we send physical mail too, we find more and more students each year do not check their e-mail and they miss important notifications. Some scholars have had scholarships re-awarded in the past because they did not check e-mail and then called and told us they don't check e-mail—only texts. As they get into college, this is an important habit for them to work on—they must check e-mail because this is how most businesses and organizations communicate now."
- Do use a professional username and password. Slang words or derogatory names as a username or password do not present a professional image. You should assume that any information you submit can be seen by anyone (this includes via Facebook, Twitter, and other social media). If you want something to stay private, do not submit or transmit it. This includes personal information. And always be aware of the words you post online and how they might appear to others, especially if you want them to contribute to funding your education. Naming you as a scholar or winner of their award means you are their representative. If they feel you will not present a positive image for their organization, they will not want to select you as a winner.
- Do capitalize proper nouns and names. One representative from a scholarship provider wrote the following: "So many students won't even capitalize their own names in an application. To many, it shows you don't have a sense of respect for yourself. Maybe that's harsh— but they have to learn that there are some things that the professional world will not acclimate themselves to just because the 'Millennials' decide they want to change the rules! And capitalization of their names, address, city, and state is one of those things. It just comes across as lazy and that is the wrong message to send."
- Do spell-check, grammar-check, and have someone else check your work so you can make the best first impression.
- Do have an understanding of global issues. According to one of the largest merit-based scholarship programs, "We do see a broader understanding of global issues/opportunities among the students who become scholars in our programs."
- Do understand that with many national programs, the application pool

has increased significantly. For one program, the application rate went from 80,000 to 110,000 due to the use of social media such as Twitter and Facebook as well as traditional advertising like billboards. What does this mean to you? Be competitive. Extracurricular activities, community service, and leadership are key. Read chapter 9, "Writing Your Scholarship Résumé: How to Stand Out and Why Grades Don't Mean Everything," for more information. And make sure to apply for local and regional scholarships as well, where you may be competing against fewer than a couple-dozen applicants.

- Do stay involved with community service and volunteering, even after you begin college. This can help you win additional scholarships once you become a college student and it's the right thing to do. According to one scholarship provider, "high school students are more involved with community service—mainly because it's a requirement for them to graduate or to get into college. I think it's more telling of the impact of community service once students finish college."

- Do understand the length of time your scholarship award will cover if you win, how much it pays per year, and whether it's renewable. "Students receive the bulk of their outside awards for the first year," stated one program when surveyed about students applying for additional scholarships. As you begin your first year of college, start making plans to finance the rest of your education with scholarships. See chapter 18, "Scholarships for Current College Students and Transfer Students." Of course, if you have a full ride, enjoy your experience to the fullest for two years, then start making plans to get accepted and get funding for graduate school. And if you get credit cards, manage your debt responsibly. See my book, *College Survival and Success Skills 101*, for more information about managing debt. The book focuses on helping students be successful with their college career and beyond. To me, college success includes graduating with little or no debt.

- Do consider the impact of loans. Although you may win multiple scholarships, there is a possibility that the full cost of your education may not be covered. Compare your offers and move away from your dream school (even though it hurts) if the cost of attending is too great for you and your parents. When asked to comment on the statement, "Students once they enroll in college are less prone to apply for additional scholarships even though they may need them to pay their entire cost to attend," one scholarship provider responded. "Very true—students feel more pressure to accept the 'dream' school offer even if they have to take out loans and many students have their parents take out loans the parents can't afford, to attend a school they want to go to. It's very unfortunate to see parents who earn yearly less than half the cost of a school's tuition per academic semester or quarter feel like they have no other option than to take out $20,000 to $30,000 a year in loans for their child to go to school."

- Do use your essays to tell the rest of your story that application questions don't address. Do not give a laundry list of activities that are revealed elsewhere in your applications. Expand upon your activities by answering the questions: Who? What? When? Where? How? and most important, Why? as it relates to an activity.

- Do choose someone to recommend you who will be able to answer questions about you from a personal *and* academic perspective.

- Do clean up your social media life. If your name and information is on a Facebook page, Twitter account, or YouTube video with derogatory, unflattering, or inflammatory remarks, clean it up. Although many outside scholarship programs may not have the time to look you up on social media, some programs might and many universities and colleges do, particularly if considering whether to award one of the most prestigious scholarships they have to offer to you.

DON'TS

- Do not rely solely on your counselor for information about scholarships and college funding opportunities. "Students are not necessarily more aware of available scholarships because counselors are inundated with other responsibilities. Most students find out about our scholarship through scholarship searches or word of mouth," stated one national scholarship provider.

- Do not e-mail your application to a scholarship program unless it is clearly indicated on the application that this is acceptable. If you have questions about whether e-mailed applications are acceptable, send an e-mail or call.

- Do not send your application registered mail or requiring signature confirmations. Many programs receive such a large volume of applications that this could actually delay your application being received.

In addition, some postal service areas will return your application to you if the signature is not available within a certain time frame.

- Do not answer questions on applications or in any written communication in the form of text language. Organizations are seeing this phenomenon get worse every year. In the words of one national scholarship provider that awards millions each year, "Students continue to write as though they are talking to their friends in text messages. No capitalization or punctuation; and spelling and grammatical errors are always a problem."

- Do not let your parents do all the work. As stated by one scholarship provider, "The parents are informing themselves to inform the students because the kids are too busy to look for scholarships on their own. It is sad because a lot of parents have taken over this process and even wind up applying for scholarships for their students, which is wrong—we can tell when a parent applied for a student."

- Do not wait until the last minute to start or complete an online application. According to most scholarship providers, online applications are the norm. However some online application programs can have technical issues when the system becomes overwhelmed near the deadline as masses of students apply. Apply at least a week before the deadline date if you can.

- Do not use abbreviations or slang in your answers. It can create an unprofessional impression of you and your achievements.

- Do not indicate anywhere in your essay that you are reusing the same essay you wrote for another competition, even if you are recycling an essay. Although many organizations understand that the scholarship search and win process can be exhausting and time consuming, they still prefer essay answers that are crafted specifically for their award or scholarship.

34

UNDERSTANDING AND MINIMIZING STUDENT LOANS IF YOU DON'T WIN ENOUGH SCHOLARSHIP MONEY INITIALLY

> What can be added to the happiness of a man
> who is in health, out of debt, and has a clear
> conscience?
>
> —Adam Smith

The cost of a college education continues to rise exponentially every year. So even though it is possible to win scholarships to cover all of your costs, it may not happen and you might decide to supplement with loans. That's okay, as long as you understand the financial implications and continue to apply for scholarships and other free money once you start college. See chapter 1, "College Costs," for more information. In fact, don't stop your scholarship search until you've won enough to pay for your entire education.

Unfortunately, since applying for a student loan can be much easier than researching and applying for scholarships, which typically involve a great deal of work and follow-up, most students turn immediately to loans to finance their education. Many do not research the loan companies, their repayment terms, or the interest rates. Also, students don't usually check to see if they qualify for a loan where the interest is subsidized by the federal government or even try to understand the difference between an unsubsidized and subsidized loan.

Currently, getting a loan with subsidized interest means that the government will pay the interest on your loan while you're in school and for the first six months after you leave school. The government will also pay the interest if you qualify to have your payments deferred for a period of time. On the other hand, with an unsubsidized loan the interest begins to accrue as soon as you obtain the loan. This interest, if unpaid, is added to the loan balance and will eventually increase the balance well beyond the original amount you borrowed. Unfortunately, many students are just glad to get the money they need and are happy to not worry about the ever-growing loan balance until later or absolutely necessary. This is a bad strategy.

BEFORE YOU BORROW

You should thoroughly explore other financial aid opportunities such as scholarships, grants, and community service awards before you begin borrowing for college. Although many students will borrow some amount to fund their education, the amounts borrowed are often too large. Some will borrow well over $100,000 to finance their education.

While you're in college and not currently facing a huge loan payment, the loan balance may not seem like much. However, when you graduate and start your first job after college, handling a huge student loan payment, a car payment, rent payment, food, clothing, gas, and other miscellaneous expenses can be overwhelming. So it's best to borrow only when absolutely necessary.

To determine if you could be borrowing too much, I suggest putting together a budget for life after college. The budget should be based on how much you expect your starting salary to be in your chosen field. If you want to determine the amount your future loan payment might be for a particular amount you plan to borrow, use loan repayment calculators from the lending organization. For example, Sallie Mae, a provider of student loans and administrator of college savings plans, has a loan repayment calculator for the different types of loans they offer. Visit http://www.sal liemae.com for more information.

You can find starting salaries in your field by visiting sites such as http://www.salary.com or http://www.bls.gov/oco/ or http://www.bls.gov/ooh to review the *Occupational Outlook Handbook*. If the amount borrowed to fund your education will result in monthly loan payments that consume a large percentage of your future salary, making your budget unrealistic despite any adjustments, then the amount you plan to borrow is too much.

Janel Janiczek, a University of Pittsburgh graduate with a Bachelor of

Science in Mathematics and a Master of Arts in Teaching, would agree. Janel said, "I only took out the minimum to pay off. I have friends who graduated with over $100,000 in loans. A starting salary of $32,000 with loan payments of over $800 a month doesn't leave much for other living expenses."

ALTERNATIVE WAYS OF PAYING OFF EDUCATION LOANS

In addition to devoting a significant portion of your paycheck to pay off loans after you graduate, a few other strategies can help you pay off your education loans:

- Join the Upromise.com savings program in which you earn back a certain percentage from purchases you make at hundreds of online retailers. The money you earn back is placed in an Upromise savings account. Money in this account can be used to help pay off your education loans. See chapter 30, "For Parents Only: Saving for College," and http://www.upromise.com for more information.
- You can volunteer or agree to work in an underrepresented area. Contact your state financial aid agency. Review chapter 5, "Financial Forms and Help from the Government with College Expenses," and chapter 14, "Scholarships and Awards for Community Service, Volunteering, and Work."
- Consider scholarships and grants based on service to an organization. Some organizations will help with outstanding loans if you agree to work with them for a period of time before, during, or after your college career. Also review the chapters referenced above.

WHY CREDIT CARDS ARE A BAD IDEA FOR FUNDING AN EDUCATION

If you're thinking of using a credit card to pay for any part of your college tuition, *don't*. Unless you have a 0 percent offer from your credit card company that will last until you can pay your debt off, the interest rate on an education loan is usually lower. Not only that, most education loans allow you to defer payment until you graduate or stop attending college. Credit cards generally do not.

35

MAJOR REASONS WHY SOME STUDENTS WIN SCHOLARSHIPS AND OTHERS DON'T

> Every hardship; every joy; every temptation is a
> challenge of the spirit; that the human soul may
> prove itself. The great chain of necessity wherewith
> we are bound has divine significance; and nothing
> happens which has not some service in working out
> the sublime destiny of the human soul.
>
> —Elias A. Ford

- Successful students always remember the five P's: Prior preparation prevents poor performance. Prepare for the scholarship search early. Do not wait until your senior year.
- Successful students do not rely on their parents to do all the work.
- Successful students do not make many mistakes on their essays and their applications. They always spell-check, proofread, and ask another person to proofread their applications and essay for errors.
- Successful students do not ignore scholarships that may be local or those for small amounts. Scholarship amounts, even as small as $50, can add up. My scholarship total of more than $400,000 included book scholarships as small as $50.
- Successful students do not rely on only one source such as the Internet for their scholarship search. They use many resources. Most scholarships on the Internet or in the free online scholarship searches are nationally known and are harder to win due to greater competition. Local and regional scholarships are not found as easily, and they may

be easier to win because the applicant pool is smaller. You have to use a combination of resources to find as many scholarships to apply for as possible.

- Successful students do not give up after receiving a rejection letter or e-mail or a letter stating that an organization has run out of funds or does not serve students in an area.

- Successful students market themselves well. In their applications, they highlight positive aspects about their lives, especially community involvement. They are not afraid to discuss obstacles or challenges they have overcome.

- Successful students do not apply to one or two scholarships and hope for the best. They apply for all scholarships they are eligible to win. They keep applying until the total they have won exceeds what they need to pay for their chosen college or until they graduate with a degree.

- Once they have been sent an inquiry letter or e-mail, successful students follow up with organizations if they have not heard from them within a reasonable amount of time.

- Successful students are organized. They keep track of deadlines and the materials required to complete an application.

- Successful students recycle essays. Parts and pieces of an essay can be used to create a slightly different one for another organization. Recycling can help you save time, especially when applying for many different scholarships.

- Successful students are well rounded. They participate in extracurricular and community activities. They write about these activities in their scholarship and college essays in a descriptive manner. They try to benefit others as well as themselves with the extracurricular and community activities in which they are involved.

- Successful students understand that SAT scores and grades alone do not win most scholarships. Scholarship programs look at many factors such as community service, leadership, presentation of your application package, special or unusual talents or skills, and so on.

- Successful students do not look for the easy way out. It is harder for them to believe in a scholarship scam that promises to do all the work for them. They understand that those things for which we work hardest often bring the greatest rewards. Hard work in the scholarship process as a high school student could result in an easy college life without work later, or a loan-free life *after* college.

36

TIPS FOR REDUCING YOUR COLLEGE EXPENSES AND INCREASING YOUR SCHOLARSHIP CHANCES

> No one can cheat you out of ultimate success but yourself.
>
> —Ralph Waldo Emerson

- Improve your writing skills. Many scholarships are based on essays alone. If you acquire and study each year's topic for these competitions and the winning entries, it will help increase your chances for not only scholarships based solely on the quality of your essay, but also the scholarships that require an essay as part of the application package. Even though you may not like to write, I strongly suggest entering competitions that are based solely or in part on writing ability. If you prepare, you can compete for and quite possibly win many of them.
- Begin to get involved in activities that involve speaking in public. Become an announcer for your school, participate in contests like the Optimist Oratorical Contest, or get involved with your debate team. I started speaking in public as a six-year-old. My sister, Stephanie, taught me how to read before I started first grade. Since I never went to kindergarten, my grandmother thought I was a child genius and wanted to show me off to her friends, so she started having me read from the Bible at her church, as did my aunt at her church. Starting to speak in public at such an early age prepared me to feel comfortable in front of an audience. I wasn't a child genius, but as far as the communicative arts of writing, reading, and speaking in public, I was

and still am very well prepared. Although you may not have started public speaking as early as I did, if you start participating in activities in front of an audience, no matter how large, and you learn how to prepare an engaging speech for that audience, you'll be ahead. Since several oratorical competitions have large scholarships attached to them, start participating in activities that put you in front of an audience as soon as possible.

- Consider going to college in the comfort of your own home through your computer. Review online degrees and programs from colleges and universities with excellent reputations. If you find a program that seems interesting, first verify that it is recognized by the Council for Higher Education Accreditation at http://www.chea.org. Confirm that the classes required to complete your degree are fully available online, and review graduation statistics and the percentage of students acquiring employment in their field after completing the program. Use Google or another Internet search tool to check out the program's credentials and its reputation. You can also refer to *U.S. News & World Report*'s yearly rankings for best online education programs.

- Consider majors in science, mathematics, technology, or engineering-related fields (STEM). These fields usually have more scholarship money available to them than others.

- Review "Countdown: The Scholarship Checklist," in chapter 32, and do everything suggested that is applicable to you.

- If you can do it without completely exhausting yourself, consider completing four years of undergraduate work in three. Or, make sure you finish in four years instead of five or six. Review the book *College Survival and Success Skills 101* for strategies to help you complete your degree on time and under budget.

- Consider taking SAT preparation courses. Although standardized test scores alone will not win the majority of scholarships, you may want to boost your score with preparation courses, which can help you as a scholarship applicant. Even though you can use test-taking services that counsel you on the best strategies for taking the test and help you to become familiar with the test itself, one of the best—and also free—strategies is to take the most challenging courses in high school and to read as much as possible, particularly for your verbal scores.

- To navigate the financial aid process and the various forms required, your family may want to hire a financial aid consultant. Financial aid consultants can help students match their interests and academic background to a particular college and discuss financial aid and payment options with you. Consultants who take their services further than the financial aid process can also help match a student's academic background to a particular college or university to find the best fit. They assist students and parents in determining priorities and completing applications, and some consultants can also oversee the entire college process, from taking standardized tests to making choices from acceptance letters received. They can also help you select challenging courses to help improve a transcript. For private or outside scholarships, the services of a financial aid consultant or similar professional are not really necessary. If your family has complicated finances and generally uses a tax professional to help make sense of IRS tax forms, then you may want to hire a professional to navigate the financial aid process as it applies to getting need-based aid from colleges and universities. Their services are billed on an hourly basis and vary widely. Visit the National Institute of Certified College Planners website at http://www.niccp.com for more information about Certified College Planners. Also read chapter 31, "For Parents Only: Saving for College," to get information about Certified College Planning Specialists who may also be able to help you in this area. If you decide to use the services of a consultant, particularly for financial aid, note the following:

- Ask for and call at least three references.
- Do not agree to a fee that is based on how much your son or daughter receives in aid.
- Review everything you sign, including all fine print. This is especially true for the FAFSA, which you should send yourself to be certain the task is done and for your own peace of mind. For the FAFSA, there is plenty of helpful information available at no cost, so if you only need to file the FAFSA, use the following sources to help you file for free. Visit http://www.fafsa.ed.gov, http://www.studentaid.gov, or http://www.fafsa4caster.ed.gov. In addition, you can get information about the FAFSA on YouTube at http://www.youtube.com/user/federalStudentAid or using Twitter. The Twitter handle for FAFSA is Federal Student Aid @FAFSA.
- Ask about refunds if any of your information filed by the consultant is returned due to errors or incomplete information that the consultant should have caught.

- Take advanced placement courses. If you take the AP exam and earn a score high enough to exempt you from an introductory college course, you can save thousands of dollars by not having to pay for the course and speeding up your path to graduation.
- If you are interested, become a teacher. Many states, colleges, and the federal government have loan forgiveness programs for students who become teachers. Consult chapter 5, "Financial Aid Forms and Help with College Expenses from the Government," to find the state financial aid agency to find aid for teachers on your state.
- If you're not particular about a specific school but want one with a good reputation and could be considered a bargain, or one that offers numerous merit scholarship opportunities, use Google or another Internet search tool to find the *U.S. News & World Report*'s best value college rankings. Currently the link for this list is http://colleges .usnews .rankingsandreviews.com/best-colleges/rankings/national-universities/best-value. You can also use http://www.meritaid.com to research colleges and universities that fit your needs and also offer merit aid.
- If necessary, discuss with your financial aid administrator the possibility of a more attractive aid package.
- Participate and get involved, especially in your community. This will significantly increase your chances for scholarship dollars.
- Become a leader in some extracurricular activity. This is also key in many scholarship competitions.
- Volunteer. Volunteer activities look very good on your résumé when applying to scholarship programs.
- Develop a good relationship with your high school principal, your counselor, other administrators, and especially your teachers. If recommendations are being made to organizations about you as a prospective applicant, you want them to be good ones. For awards that require nominations, you'll want to be one of the first students your teacher, counselor, or administrator thinks of.
- Look at institutions that have a matching grant system. In this system if a student who enrolls has an outside scholarship, the institution may match the amount of the outside scholarship up to a certain amount.
- Go to a community college for the first two years. This should cost significantly less than a four-year institution, particularly if you live at

home. Using this strategy could potentially get you a degree from an expensive and possibly prestigious institution at a fraction of the cost. If you decide to do this, make sure the courses you take during your first two years will transfer to the four-year school you want to attend and will count toward your bachelor's degree.

- Research and look at schools that value your interests. For example, if you are considering an unusual major for which a college or university is starting a new department, you may be able to get a scholarship or reduced tuition as they begin looking for students to enroll in their new program.

- If you're looking at the top-tier schools such as Harvard, Yale, or Princeton, consider putting second-tier schools on your prospective list as well. When it comes to financial aid, you may get more assistance from the second-tier schools that accept you.

- Look at universities and colleges where your grades and SAT scores will place you in the top 10 to 25 percent of prospective students. To find this information, consult a guide such as *Peterson's Undergraduate Guide to Four-Year Colleges* to find statistics for the freshman class and student body. If your grades and SAT scores are in the top tier of students the school tries to attract, you have a good chance of securing more aid from the school. Also visit http://www.petersons.com or the College Search on http://www.collegeboard.com to help find this type of information.

- Once you receive a financial aid award letter from a school you really want to attend, don't be afraid to appeal the aid decision if it is not enough. In your appeal include any extenuating circumstances such as a sibling or parent currently in college, reduced family income, disability, divorce, or excessive consumer debt that may be affecting your circumstances and your ability to afford the tuition and related costs of attendance. Many schools will reevaluate their decision. See chapter 37.

- If you have received scholarships or large amounts of non-need aid from another institution but you have your heart set on another school that has not offered you nearly as much, make sure that the institution you really want to attend is aware of the money the other school offered you. They may match the other offer.

- Consider participating in AmeriCorps (http://www.americorps.gov) or a similar program, which allows participants to earn education awards or scholarships in return for some type of service or employment during or after college. For more information about service scholarships review chapter 14, "Scholarships and Awards for Community Service, Volunteering, and Work."

- Studying abroad for a semester, quarter, or year may also be an option for lowering your costs because some colleges and universities in other countries may have tuition rates significantly lower than those in the U.S. As long as your academic work in the foreign country will be counted as credit toward your degree in the U.S., going abroad to save some dollars might work for you, particularly if you can speak the language.
- Consider the military as an option to reduce your costs. The U.S. Armed Forces offer several educational programs. For example:
  - If you are accepted to a military service academy you can essentially go to college for four years tuition-free while earning a commission.

    For more information:
    - U.S. Military Academy in West Point, New York: (800) 822-8762 or see www.usma.edu.
    - U.S. Naval Academy in Annapolis, Maryland: (800) 638-9156 or see www.usna.edu.
    - U.S. Air Force Academy in Colorado Springs, Colorado: (800) 443-9266 or see www.usfa.af.mil.
    - U.S. Coast Guard Academy in New London, Connecticut: (800) 883-8724 or see www.cga.edu.
    - U.S. Merchant Marine Academy in Kings Point, New York: (866) 546-4778 or see www.usma.edu.
  - Enroll in the Reserve Officers' Training Corps (ROTC) program while in college. ROTC will pay for your tuition, fees, and books, and provide you with a monthly allowance.

    For more information:
    - For the Army program call 1-80-USA-ROTC or visit www.armyrotc.com.
    - For the Navy program call 1-800-USA-NAVY or visit www.navyrotc.navy.mil.
    - For the Air Force program call 1-866-423-7682 or visit www.afrotc.com.
    - For the Marine program call 1-800-MARINES or visit www.marines.com.
    - The Coast Guard has a program called the College Student Pre-Commissioning Initiative (CSPI) that is similar to the ROTC program of the other Armed Forces. Visit www.gocoastguard for additional information.

- You can join the armed forces before you go to college and use the Montgomery GI Bill to help pay for college expenses once you've completed your military service.
- In some instances, you can earn college credit for certain military training. This could possibly reduce the number of classes you'll have to take in college.

To get additional information for the military options discussed above, refer to chapter 27, "Scholarship and College Funding for the Military and Their Family." You can also look at websites such as http://www.military.com or http://www.gibill.va.gov.

37

WHAT TO DO IF YOUR FINANCIAL AID PACKAGE IS NOT ENOUGH OR YOUR DREAM SCHOOL REDUCES YOUR AID PACKAGE DUE TO SCHOLARSHIPS YOU'VE WON

It's when things get rough and you don't quit that success comes.

—Unknown

If you've been accepted to your dream school and the financial aid you've been offered is not enough for you to attend, what can you or your parents do? After reviewing a financial aid award package from a school you're really interested in, you can appeal the decision or ask for a professional judgment review if the aid is not enough. In your appeal make sure to include any extenuating circumstances such as another sibling or a parent currently in college, reduced family income, disability, divorce, or excessive consumer debt that may be affecting your circumstances and your ability to afford the tuition and related costs of attendance. Some schools will reevaluate their decision.

In addition, if you have received scholarships or large amounts of non-need aid from another institution but you have your heart set on a school that has not offered you nearly as much, make sure that your first choice school is aware of the money the other school offers you. They may match the other offer, particularly if you outline specific reasons you want to attend their school and how you can contribute, either through your intent to get involved in campus-based activities or community service or your plan to start a new club or group that aligns with the institution's mission statement, excellent reputation, and long-term goals.

Also, if you are faced with a situation that has resulted in grants and scholarships being reduced due to the outside scholarships you've won, you should consider the following steps:

1. First, contact the outside scholarship program to let them know about the situation and determine if they are aware of the school's policies and if they might be able to assist you with an appeal.
2. Second, contact the school's financial aid office and request a meeting (over the phone or preferably in person) to discuss the matter. During the meeting, outline why you've selected their school as your top choice, and most important, outline any benefits your presence will bring to the school should you enroll.
3. Review the outside scholarships you've won, and the characteristics you have that resulted in them choosing you as a winner. Reiterate that you plan to use these positive characteristics to contribute to the school's reputation and success through your continued academic achievement and/or campus and community involvement and future career.
4. Last, outline reasons why keeping loans in place while taking away offers that do not require a future repayment commitment, such as school-based scholarships and awards, could negatively affect your family situation and/or future success.

If the institution still does not adjust their aid decision, and particularly if the loans you'll need to incur are significant, then consider another school on your list that meets your needs. Read chapter 34, "Understanding and Minimizing Student Loans If You Don't Win Enough Scholarship Money Initially."

After reading the above paragraphs, you may wonder, "Why should I even bother with scholarships?" Understand that the process of winning scholarships can have benefits that far outweigh the monetary awards. For example, being a scholarship winner, particularly for a prestigious and well-known merit-based scholarship (whether needed or not), can be a wonderful addition to your résumé. Many scholarship organizations also excel at providing ongoing support throughout a student's college life and beyond. Furthermore, these organizations can be great networking opportunities for future employment, graduate school, and even business ventures. And being prepared for and ready to engage in competitions throughout your life can be helpful for your future success.

STEPS FOR APPEALING A FINANCIAL AID DECISION

Step 1

Review your financial aid award carefully and consider the following:

- Has anything changed about your financial situation since you completed the financial aid form?
- Is there an impending change that will affect your finances (i.e., birth of a child, another dependent)?

Step 2

Gather any documents needed to support your claims, including income statements, expense records, and recurring or major bills. If you are interested in additional aid because another college is offering more money, obtain a copy of your award letter from the other school and include it with your supporting documentation. You should also support your appeal with clearly articulated reasons for why a school is your first choice and why you may have to accept the other school's offer because your family cannot afford your first choice with the current aid package offered.

Step 3

How should you contact the financial aid office? If possible, call and request an in-person appointment. If that is not possible, send a detailed letter via certified mail with documents to support why you believe your aid package should be adjusted. Make sure to alert the financial aid administrator, with whom you have already briefly outlined your situation that a letter will be coming to his/her attention. Don't just send your letter without prior notification.

Step 4

Even if your aid package is not adjusted initially, there may be an opportunity months or weeks after your appeal. For example, if you approach a school about work-study and nothing is available at the time, this does not mean they will not have work-study later. Or they may be able to steer you toward another on-campus position.

38

PARTING WORDS

Life is a journey, not a destination—we determine
our destiny by the direction we take.

—Anonymous

Wonderful! You have successfully completed your scholarship journey.
Many of the skills, such as research and interviewing techniques, that you
honed while using this book will aid you throughout life, especially in college. I hope the hours of research, writing essays, taking tests, interviewing, and the many other activities that went into your search have resulted
in multiple scholarships that will allow you to thoroughly enjoy your college experience.

College and graduate school can be one of the most exciting and reward-
ing experiences of your life. Not only is it possible to tap in to a wealth of
knowledge from a variety of people on campus, you'll also meet friends
that will last for a lifetime. The experience that can be gained only through
a college education is unparalleled.

As a student on a campus surrounded by professionals and intellectuals,
you can build a network of influence and knowledge to draw from as you
begin to search for a job, start your own business, or undertake other
ventures. Read my book, *College Survival and Success Skills 101*, available
through http://www.scholarshipworkshop.com, to learn more about how
you can do this.

The decision to enhance your education by attending college or graduate school is one of the best choices you can make. As our world careens
toward extremely technological societies, education beyond high school
becomes more important each and every day. An advanced education is

an important tool to fashion the lifestyles that many of us would like to enjoy. In fact, life itself is a continuous learning process. For those of us who choose to embrace education, learning everything we can, whenever we can, there are infinite opportunities that await us.

By choosing to pursue your education further and securing the scholarship funds to implement it, you are embarking on another exciting journey, much like the scholarship journey, that will reward you throughout your life. I wish you much success in all your endeavors. Most important, enjoy your life and strive to take advantage of every opportunity that comes along. I love to hear good news! If you have a success story you'd like to share with me, please send it to feedback@scholarshipworkshop.com or you can send it in the mail to Marianne Ragins, c/o The Scholarship Workshop LLC, P.O. Box 176, Centreville, VA 20122.

Appendix A

ABBREVIATED LIST OF SCHOLARSHIP PROGRAMS

The following is an abbreviated list of scholarship programs. Under no circumstances should this partial list take the place of individual research. Most of the programs are general in nature and should apply to most students nationally. You should make use of the research techniques discussed in chapters 2, 3, and 4 to find scholarships specific to your community and your regional area. You should also do your own research to be certain you have uncovered all opportunities available to you, including new programs that have been implemented since the printing of this edition of this book. Although every effort has been made to ensure the accuracy of the addresses and information listed in this section, some of them may be out of date. If you find an invalid Web address, use an Internet search engine such as Google to find the correct address for the program or scholarship. Or visit http://www.scholarshipworkshop.com to sign up for our newsletter to get updates and alerts. You can also follow us on Facebook (http://www.face book.com/scholarshipworkshop) or on Twitter @ScholarshipWork.

A Few Important Items to Remember

- Deadlines change frequently. It is best to visit the website for a listed scholarship program or award for the most current deadline. Or you can review *The Scholarship Monthly Planner* on our website at http://www .scholarshipworkshop.com, which has deadlines updated frequently. Also join us on Facebook (http://www.facebook.com/scholarshipworkshop) and follow us on Twitter (@ScholarshipWork) for frequent alerts on new scholarships and upcoming deadlines. Join our mailing list to get the latest updates about scholarships and other helpful information. Text "SCHOLARSHIP INFO" to 22828 or visit our website to join.

- Do not send blanket e-mails requesting an application from an organization. Many organizations have a large number of people interested in their programs and may not respond.
- Do not rely solely on the following scholarship list. It is best to use the strategies described in chapter 2, "The Scholarship Search: Discovering Hidden Treasures," chapter 3, "Using the Internet and Social Media in Your Scholarship Search," and chapter 4, "The Local Scholarship Search: Finding Scholarships in Your Backyard," to uncover the most opportunities available to you.
- Some programs change their application requirements and eligibility guidelines. Please review their websites carefully for any changes.
- If you've reviewed their website thoroughly and still have questions, use the e-mail address and/or telephone number, if provided.
- Programs can and do stop awarding scholarships or suspend their scholarship programs. Don't get discouraged. You can still find available scholarships. But please know that there are no guarantees about the availability of a given scholarship, or that you will win it.

SCHOLARSHIPS FOR HIGH SCHOOL SENIORS

AMERICAN LEGION NATIONAL HIGH SCHOOL ORATORICAL CONTEST

(317) 630-1200

E-mail: oratorical@legion.org

Website: http://www.legion.org (click on *Programs\Family and Youth\ Scholarships\National High School Oratorical Contest*)

Additional Information: Open to students in grades 9–12 who are less than 20 years of age (as of the national contest date) and are U.S. citizens or lawful permanent residents of the United States. You must be currently enrolled in a high school or junior high school (public, parochial, military, private or state-accredited homeschool) in which the curriculum of the high school is considered to be of high school level, commencing with grade 9 and terminating with grade 12 to participate in this contest. You must be able to prepare and deliver speeches in public to win these awards. In addition to the scholarships awarded by the national headquarters, several hundred scholarships may be awarded by intermediate organizations to participants at the post, district, county, and department levels of competition. Consult the website for more details and current deadlines. Award amounts range from $1,500 to $18,000.

AMERICAN MENSA EDUCATION AND RESEARCH FOUNDATION SCHOLARSHIPS

American Mensa, Ltd.
1229 Corporate Drive West
Arlington, TX 76006-6103
(817) 607-0060 or 1 (800) 66-MENSA
E-mail: Director@mensa.org
Website: http://www.mensafoundation.org
Additional Information: Open to citizens or permanent residents of the United States. You must be planning to enroll for the academic year following the award in a degree program in an accredited American institution of post-secondary education. Awards are based totally on essays written by applicants. This organization does not require applicants to be Mensa members nor do they consider grades, academic program, or financial need when selecting applicants. Selection is based solely on an essay describing your career, vocational, and/or academic goals. Essay should be fewer than 550 words and must be specific rather than general. The essays are judged on content, grammar, organization, and craftsmanship. To get an online application, visit the website. Awards can be used for all fields of study. The deadline is usually January 15. Applications become available online in September. Awards range from $300 to $1,000.

AXA ACHIEVEMENT SCHOLARSHIP IN ASSOCIATION WITH U.S. NEWS & WORLD REPORT

Website: http://www.axa-equitable.com/axa-foundation or http://www.axa-achievement.com
Additional Information: The AXA Achievement Scholarship, sponsored by the AXA Foundation in association with *U.S. News & World Report*, provides scholarship awards ranging from $10,000 to $25,000 to high school seniors who plan to enroll in a full-time undergraduate course of study at an accredited two- or four-year college or university. Each year, there is a winner in every state, nationwide. Applicants must be U.S. citizens or legal residents and must have demonstrated ambition and self-drive as evidenced by an outstanding achievement in a school, community, or workplace activity. Visit the website in September to get information for entering the competition. In recent years, there has been an application limit for this scholarship program which is prominently advertised in certain issues of

U.S. News & World Report. Apply early for this scholarship, which usually has a deadline in early December.

AXA ACHIEVEMENT COMMUNITY SCHOLARSHIP

Website: http://*www.axa-equitable.com/axa-foundation* or http://www .axa-achievement.com

Additional Information: The AXA Achievement Community Scholarship, sponsored by the AXA Foundation, is open to high school seniors who plan to enroll in a full-time undergraduate course of study at an accredited two- or four-year college or university. Applicants must be United States citizens or legal residents and must have demonstrated ambition and self-drive, which can be shown through an outstanding achievement in a school, community, or workplace activity. Scholarship awards are $2,000. You must live and attend school in an area with an AXA Advisors' branch office.

AYN RAND'S NOVEL THE FOUNTAINHEAD ESSAY CONTEST

E-mail: info@aynrandnovels.com

Website: http://www.aynrand.org/contests

Additional Information: Open to 11th- and 12th-grade high school students who submit an essay of 800 to 1,600 words. Awards range from $50 to $10,000. Deadline is usually in April of each year.

BEST BUY SCHOLARSHIP PROGRAM

Website: http://pr.bby.com (click on *Community Relations\Scholarship Programs*) or https://bestbuy.scholarshipamerica.org

Additional Information: The Best Buy Scholarship Program awards scholarships to 9th- to 12th-grade students in the United States or Puerto Rico. To be eligible you must plan to enter a full-time undergraduate course of study after you graduate from high school. Good students with strong participation in community service or work experience are strongly encouraged to apply for these $1,000 scholarships. Best Buy has awarded over $20 million in scholarships to more than 16,000 students since 1999. This program is administered for Best Buy by Scholarship Management Services, which is a division of Scholarship America. You may also be able to visit the Scholarship America website at http://www.scholarshipamerica.org for more information about this scholarship program and other open scholarships.

BUICK ACHIEVERS SCHOLARSHIP PROGRAM

(800) 537-4180
E-mail: buickachievers@scholarshipamerica.org
Website: http://www.buickachievers.com
Additional Information: See chapter 18.

BURGER KING SCHOLARS

(507) 931-1682
E-mail: burgerkingscholars@scholarshipamerica.org
Website: http://www.bkmclamorefoundation.org (click on *What We Do\
Scholars Program*)
Additional Information: This scholarship is open to all high school seniors.
All company and participating Burger King franchises as well as corporate
and field employees and children of employees are also eligible. Scholar-
ships range from $1,000 to $50,000, and are intended to help students offset
the cost of attending college or post-secondary vocational/technical school.
Awards are based on grade point average, work experience, extracurricu-
lar activities, and/or community service. The deadline is normally in early
January.

CARING AWARDS

The Caring Institute
228 7th Street SE
Washington, DC 20003
(202) 547-4273
E-mail address: info@caring.org
Website: http://www.caring-institute.org
Additional Information: If you haven't yet graduated from high school
or reached your eighteenth birthday, you can be nominated for a $2,000
Caring Award from the Caring Institute if you've been involved in activities that show your depth of caring for your community, state, region, the
world, or its inhabitants. Winners of this award are considered role models
with an extraordinary sense of public service. Many have founded organizations designed to serve others and/or have made a meaningful impact in
their high school, community, state, or beyond.

THE CHRISTOPHER REEVE AWARD

Heart of America Foundation
401 F Street NW, Suite 325
Washington, DC 20001
E-mail: scholarships@heartofamerica.org
Website: http://www.heartofamerica.org
Additional Information: The Heart of America Foundation recognizes outstanding students who are high school seniors or younger with the Christopher Reeve Award, a $1,000 scholarship from Merriam-Webster, Inc., to be used for your higher education. To be eligible for this award, you must have demonstrated tremendous compassion and caring in service to your community. You must also be nominated. See the website for additional details.

COCA-COLA SCHOLARS FOUNDATION

(800) 306-COKE (2653)
E-mail: scholars@coca-cola.com
Website: https://www.coca-colascholars.org
Additional Information: Scholarships are merit-based and selection of winners is based on consideration of the applicant's leadership, character, achievement, and commitment, both inside and outside the classroom. Scholarships can be used for any field of study. According to the organization, "The kind of students that become Coca-Cola Scholars are ones that belong to a diverse group of outstanding young people, characterized by their ability, commitment, perseverance, and determination. They share a 'special something else,' giving back in unselfish ways, embodying service over self, and are already finding ways to make a difference in society. By supporting these students, Coca-Cola, too, is giving back to the communities that have supported it for more than 100 years." To apply, you must be a current high school senior attending school (or homeschooled) in the United States, a U.S. citizen, permanent resident, temporary resident (legalization program), refugee; asylee, Cuban-Haitian entrant, or humanitarian parolee planning to pursue a degree at an accredited U.S. postsecondary institution. You must carry a minimum 3.00 GPA at the end of your junior year of high school. The initial application is available online. Selection of recipients for these scholarships occurs in three phases, beginning each fall and culminating the following spring with the announcement of the award recipients. Scholarships range from $10,000 to $20,000. The deadline is usually October 31 of each year.

- **Phase I:** The initial application, available online after Labor Day each year, seeks a record of your overall involvement in school and community affairs as well as academic success and employment. During this phase, 1,500 to 2,000 are chosen as semifinalists in December.
- **Phase II:** Semifinalists are notified and sent an expanded application in mid-December that requires detailed biographical data, an essay, a secondary school report, and personal recommendations. After this phase, 250 finalists are selected.
- **Phase III:** In the spring of each program year, the finalists attend the national competition in Atlanta, convened by the Foundation at its expense, to determine whether those finalists will receive the $20,000 National Scholarships or the $10,000 Regional Scholarships. All finalists receive an award.

NOTE: I won a Coca-Cola National Scholarship, and the competition was one of the best and most organized I entered. In chapter 11, "Writing Scholarship Essays That Get Noticed," I included the essay I submitted in my semifinalist materials. I also have letters from the organization when I became a semifinalist and a finalist in chapter 28. My résumé in chapter 9, as well as an example of my poetry, were also included with my semifinalist materials.

COLLEGE IS POWER SCHOLARSHIP

E-mail: service@collegeispower.com
Website: http://www.collegeispower.com/scholarship.cfm
Additional Information: See chapter 20.

COLLEGE JUMPSTART SCHOLARSHIP

College JumpStart Scholarship Fund
4546 B10 El Camino Real, 325
Los Altos, CA 94022
E-mail: admin@jumpstart-scholarship.net
Website: http://www.jumpstart-scholarship.net
Additional Information: This scholarship is open to high school grades 10 through 12, college students, and nontraditional students who are U.S. citizens or legal residents. You must be attending or planning to attend an accredited two-year, four-year, or vocational/trade school in the United States and be committed to using education to better your life and that of your family and/or community. Deadlines are normally in April and October.

THE COMCAST LEADERS AND ACHIEVERS SCHOLARSHIP PROGRAM

Website: http://corporate.comcast.com/our-values/community-investment/youth-education-leadership or see http://corporate.comcast.com (search for "Leaders and Achievers" or "Scholarship")

Additional Information: This scholarship rewards high school seniors for their leadership, community involvement, and academic achievement. To enter this competition, you must live in a community that is served by Comcast and be nominated by your high school principal or guidance counselor. Winners are recognized with one-time scholarship grants of $1,000 from the Comcast Foundation to pursue higher education, which can include vocational or technical school. See the website or consult your counselor for additional details. See chapter 13 for additional information about requesting nominations.

CREATE-A-GREETING CARD SCHOLARSHIP CONTEST

Website: http://www.gallerycollection.com/greetingcardscontests.htm or http://www.gallerycollection.com/greeting-cards-scholarship.htm
Additional Information: See chapter 18.

DAVIDSON FELLOWS SCHOLARSHIP

Davidson Institute for Talent Development
9665 Gateway Drive, Suite B
Reno, NV 89521
(775) 852-3483 ext. 435
E-mail: DavidsonFellows@davidsongifted.org
Website: http://www.davidsongifted.org/fellows or http://www.davidsonfellows.org
Social Media: Follow DavidsonGifted on Twitter, Facebook, and YouTube.
Additional Information: The Davidson Fellows scholarships range from $10,000 to $50,000 for students age 18 and under who have completed a significant piece of work. The program looks for students whose projects are at, or close to, the college-graduate level with a depth of knowledge in their particular area of study. The application categories are Science, Technology, Engineering, Mathematics, Literature, Music, Philosophy, and Outside the Box. To apply you must be a U.S. citizen or a permanent resident residing in the United States, or be stationed overseas due to active U.S.

military duty. There is no minimum age for eligibility. The deadline for pre-liminary submissions is in January. See website for specific details and guidelines for entering this competition.

DELL SCHOLARS PROGRAM

(800) 294-2039
E-mail: apply@dellscholars.org
Website: www.dellscholars.org
Social Media: DellScholars is on Facebook, Twitter, and YouTube.
Additional Information: The Dell Scholars Program is open to high school seniors with a 2.4 minimum GPA who have participated in a Michael & Susan Dell Foundation–approved college readiness program for a min-imum of two of the last three years. You must have a demonstrated need for financial assistance, be planning to enter a bachelor's degree program at an accredited higher education institution in the fall after your gradua-tion from high school, and be a U.S. citizen or have permanent residency. See the website for approved readiness programs. As an example, programs such as AVID, GEAR UP, and Upward Bound are considered college read-iness programs. The deadline is usually in January.

DOODLE 4 GOOGLE

E-mail: doodle4google-usteam@google.com.
Website: http://www.google.com/doodle4google
Additional Information: Doodle 4 Google is an annual program that encourages K–12 students in the United States to use their artistic talents to think big and redesign the Google home page logo for millions to see. Previous themes have been "My Best Day Ever" and "What I Want to Do Someday." Winning student artists will see their artwork appear on Google, receive a $30,000 college scholarship, and a $50,000 technology grant for their school, along with some other great prizes. Visit the website for com-plete eligibility guidelines, templates, and submission information.

THE DUPONT CHALLENGE

DuPont Office of Education
P.O. Box 80357
Wilmington, DE 19880-0030

E-mail: thechallenge@usa.dupont.com
Website: http://thechallenge.dupont.com
Additional Information: Open to high school students in grades 7–12 (candidate must be at least age 13) attending public or private high schools in the United States and its territories. Awards are given based on an original science essay of 700 to 1,000 words written by applicants and signed by their science teacher. Award selection is based on the scientific accuracy of the essay and the student's writing ability. To obtain an entry form which must accompany your essay and to get additional information and contest rules, visit the website. The deadline is normally in January or early February of each year. Prizes range from $1,000 to $5,000 in savings bonds.

ELKS NATIONAL FOUNDATION—MOST VALUABLE STUDENT SCHOLARSHIP AWARDS

Elks National Foundation
Programs Department
2750 N. Lakeview Avenue
Chicago, IL 60614-2256
(773) 755-4732
E-mail: ENFPrograms@elks.org
Website: http://www.elks.org (click on *Our Programs\Scholarships*)
Additional Information: Any high school senior planning to enroll full-time at an accredited U.S. college or university and is a citizen of the United States is eligible to apply. Resident alien status does not qualify. You do not need to be related to a member of the Elks. Applications must be submitted to your local Elks lodge by the deadline. To find an Elks lodge near you, look in your phone book or visit http://www.elks.org/lodges/default.cfm for an online list. Awards range from $4,000 to $60,000 payable over four years. The deadline is usually in December.

EXECUTIVE WOMEN INTERNATIONAL SCHOLARSHIP PROGRAM (EWISP)

3860 South 2300 East
Salt Lake City, UT 84109
(801) 355-2800
E-mail: ewi@ewiconnect.com

Website: http://www.ewiconnect.com
Additional Information: Available to high school seniors who live within the boundaries of a participating chapter. You must be nominated by your high school for this award, which currently ranges from $1,000 to $5,000. Competition starts at the Elks chapter level. Visit the website for additional information and deadlines.

FRAME MY FUTURE SCHOLARSHIP CONTEST

E-mail: churchhillclassics@diplomaframe.com (enter Frame My Future Scholarship Contest in the Subject line)
Website: http://www.diplomaframe.com (search for "Frame My Future")
Additional Information: See chapter 18.

FOSTER CARE TO SUCCESS (FC2S) SCHOLARSHIP PROGRAMS

21351 Gentry Drive, Suite 130
Sterling, VA 20166
(571) 203-0270; fax: (571) 203- 0273
E-mail: info@fc2success.org
Website: http://www.fc2success.org
Additional Information: Award is open those who have been in public or private foster care for the 12 consecutive months prior to their eighteenth birthday, or who have been adopted or placed into legal guardianship from foster care after age 16, or who have been orphaned for at least one year at the time of their eighteenth birthday. You must have been accepted into or expect to be accepted into an accredited, Pell-eligible college or other post-secondary school, and be under the age of 25 on the application deadline date if you have not previously received scholarship funding from FC2S. If you have been in foster care or orphaned while living in the United States, U.S. citizenship is not required. Visit the website for application and information. Scholarships can be used for all fields of study. Awards range from $1,500 to $1,600. The deadline is normally in March of each year.

GE-REAGAN FOUNDATION SCHOLARSHIP PROGRAM

(507) 931-1682
E-mail: ge-reagan@scholarshipamerica.org

Website: https://www.reaganfoundation.org/GE-RFScholarships.aspx or https://www.scholarshipamerica.org/ge-reagan

Social Media: This program is on Facebook.

Additional Information: To apply, you must be a U.S. citizen and current high school senior attending high school in the United States. You must also demonstrate financial need, and strong academic performance (minimum 3.0 grade point average/4.0 scale or equivalent). You should exemplify the attributes of leadership, drive, integrity, and citizenship—at school, in the workplace, and within the community. You must be planning to enroll in a full-time undergraduate course of study toward a bachelor's degree at an accredited four-year college or university in the United States for the entire upcoming academic year. Scholarships are $10,000, which can be renewed for up to an additional three years, up to $40,000 total. Awards are for undergraduate study only, and may be used for education-related expenses, including tuition, fees, books, supplies, and room and board.

GLORIA BARRON PRIZE FOR YOUNG HEROES

The Barron Prize
545 Pearl Street
Boulder, CO 80302

Additional Information: Each year, the Gloria Barron Prize for Young Heroes honors outstanding youth leaders ages 8 to 18 who have made a significant positive difference to people and our planet. Top winners in this program receive a $2,500 cash award to support their service work or higher education. You must be nominated for this prize. The deadline is usually in April. Visit the website for additional information about nominations, application requirements and other details.

GO DADDY .ME SCHOLARSHIP

E-mail: scholarship@godaddy.com.

Website: http://www.godaddy.com/scholarship/mescholarship.aspx or www.godaddy.com (search for scholarship)

Additional Information: See chapter 18.

HORATIO ALGER NATIONAL SCHOLARSHIP PROGRAM

(866) 763-9228

E-mail: horatioalger@act.org

Website: http://www.horatioalger.org

Additional Information: The Horatio Alger National Scholarship Program is designed to help high school students who have faced and overcome great obstacles. As a result, the program not only recognizes students who show academic achievement and leadership potential, but also are committed to use their college degrees in service to others. To be eligible for this scholarship you must be enrolled full-time as a high school senior, progressing normally toward graduation, and planning to enter college no later than the fall following graduation. You must also have a strong commitment to pursue a bachelor's degree at an accredited institution (you can start your studies at a two-year institution and then transfer to a four-year institution); have critical financial need; be involved in extracurricular and community activities; have a minimum 2.0 GPA; and be a citizen of the United States or in the process of becoming a U.S. citizen. Scholarships are for $20,000 (payable over four years) and winners receive an all-expense-paid trip to Washington, D.C., during the spring of their senior year to participate in the National Scholars Conference. The deadline is usually in October of each year. NOTE: Please allow plenty of time to apply for this scholarship. There are four required essays. One essay requires you to compare your life with that of a Horatio Alger Association member, which means you should research the association and its members to plan and write your essay. The other essays involve the adversity or obstacles you've faced and overcome.

JESSE BROWN MEMORIAL YOUTH SCHOLARSHIP PROGRAM

DAV (Disabled American Veterans)

Voluntary Services Department

P.O. Box 14301

Cincinnati, OH 45250-0301

Website: http://www.dav.org (click on *Volunteer Services\Jesse Brown Scholarship*) or http://www.dav.org/volunteers/Scholarship.aspx

Additional Information: The Jesse Brown Memorial Youth Scholarship Program was established to recognize youth volunteers age 21 or younger who have volunteered for a minimum of 100 hours at a VA medical center during the previous calendar year. You must be nominated for this program and write a 750-word essay titled "What Volunteering Has Meant to Me." You can also nominate yourself. See the website for additional eligibility criteria, current deadlines, and the nomination form. Scholarship amounts can be up to $20,000.

JOSTENS FOUNDATION RENAISSANCE SCHOLARSHIP PROGRAM

Scholarship Management Services
One Scholarship Way
Saint Peter, MN 56082
(507) 931-1682
Website: http://www.jostens.com (search "Jostens Renaissance Scholarship Program") or http://sms.scholarshipamerica.org/jostensrenaissance/contact.html
Additional Information: Open to high school seniors who have dramatically improved their GPA during their high school career. Applicants must be attending a high school with a Renaissance program. Contact your counselor or Renaissance coordinator to find out if your high school is a part of this program. The scholarship is awarded based on the following: the largest cumulative GPA increase from first semester freshman year through first semester senior year as certified by transcript; a 500- to 1,000-word essay describing how Renaissance has impacted your life; and a recommendation letter from your school's Renaissance coordinator. Awards range from $1,000 (non-renewable) to $2,500 renewable for three years. The deadline is in March.

KOHL'S CARES SCHOLARSHIP PROGRAM

(319) 341-2932 (indicate you need information for the Kohl's Cares Scholarship Program)
E-mail: kohls@act.org
Website: http://www.kohlskids.com or
http://www.kohlscorporation.com/CommunityRelations/scholarship/index.asp
Additional Information: If you are a student between the ages of 6 and 18 who has made a difference in your community, you can be nominated to win a $10,000 scholarship from Kohl's Corporation. They have been

awarding these scholarships since 2001 to recognize young students who have made amazing contributions in their communities. Since the program's inception, Kohl's has awarded more than $3.5 million in scholarships and prizes to youth. If you're interested in this program, see the website for details. The deadline is usually in mid-March of every year. To get nominated, review chapter 13, "The Art of Getting Good Recommendations and Requesting Nominations."

"LEADING THE FUTURE II" SCHOLARSHIP

The Scholarship Workshop
P.O. Box 176
Centreville, VA 20122
(703) 579-4245
E-mail: scholars@scholarshipworkshop.com
Website: http://www.scholarshipworkshop.com
Social Media: Follow this program on Facebook and Twitter.
Additional Information: The "Leading the Future II" Scholarship is designed to elevate students' consciousness about their future and their role in helping others once they receive a college degree and become established in a community. It is open to high school seniors or current college undergraduates who are U.S. residents. Go to http://www.scholarshipwork shop.com to download an application.

THE LEOPOLD SCHEPP FOUNDATION

551 Fifth Avenue
Suite 3000
New York, NY 10176-3201
(212) 692-0191
Website: http://www.scheppfoundation.org
Additional Information: This foundation was established by Leopold Schepp in 1925 to encourage youths to develop good character and to help them complete their high school education, an opportunity he never had. The foundation currently provides awards to high school seniors and full-time undergraduate and graduate students. Fellowships for post-doctoral students are also available but are limited due to available funding. High school seniors and college undergraduates younger than 30 years old, as well as graduate students younger than 40 years old, are eligible to apply.

You must have a minimum GPA of 3.2 and be enrolled or planning to enroll full-time. You must also be a U.S. citizen or permanent resident of the United States, and you must be willing to travel at your own expense for a personal interview in New York City. Visit the website for additional eligibility requirements and deadline.

LIFE LESSONS SCHOLARSHIP PROGRAM

LIFE Foundation
Website: http://www.lifehappens.org/life-lessons/
Additional Information: See chapter 15.

THE LOWE'S SCHOLARSHIP

Website: http://www.lowes.com (search "Scholarship") or
http://careers.lowes.com/college_recruiting_scholarship.aspx#1
Additional Information: The scholarship is available to high school seniors who intend to enroll full-time in an undergraduate course of study in the United States for the upcoming school year. Scholarship amount is $2,500. To be eligible you must have demonstrated a history of commitment to your community through leadership activities, community service, and/or work experience. Deadline is usually in January.

NATIONAL HONOR SOCIETY SCHOLARSHIP

1904 Association Drive
Reston, VA 22091
(703) 860-0200
E-mail: scholarship@nhs.us
Website: http://www.nhs.us
Additional Information: Open to high school seniors who are members of the National Honor Society (NHS). Contact your NHS advisor for information about obtaining applications. You must be nominated for this scholarship and will be required to answer an essay question as part of the nomination form, which is mailed to all active NHS chapters in early November. Chapters can nominate two seniors to compete for the national awards. Scholarship awards range from $1,000 to $13,000. Deadline is usually in January. Visit the website for current deadline and additional details.

NATIONAL MERIT AND NATIONAL ACHIEVEMENT SCHOLARSHIP PROGRAMS

1560 Sherman Avenue, Suite 200
Evanston, IL 60201
(847) 866-5100
Website: http://www.nationalmerit.org/merit.htm
Additional Information: Applicants must qualify for this competition by taking the PSAT in their junior year of high school. U.S. citizenship is required. Refer to chapter 8 for more detailed information about this competition. Scholarships can be used for all fields of study. Actual award amounts vary.

NATIONAL YOUNG ARTS FOUNDATION

Programs Department
2100 Biscayne Boulevard
Miami, FL 33137
(800) 970-ARTS or (305) 377-1140; fax: (305) 377-1149
E-mail: info@youngarts.org
Website: http://www.ARTSawards.org or http://www.nfaa.org
Additional Information: This talent search competition is open to high school students between the ages of 15 and 18 (or in grades 10 through 12) with talent in the arts such as dance, writing, music, theater, visual arts, and jazz. Awards can be used for any field of study. To apply, you must be a citizen or permanent resident of the United States or its official territories (e.g., Puerto Rico). The deadline for final submission is in October. There is an application fee for this program. See the website for details.

OPTIMIST INTERNATIONAL ORATORICAL CONTEST

Programs Manager
4494 Lindell Boulevard
St. Louis, MO 63108
(800) 500-8130 or (314) 371-6000
E-mail: programs@optimist.org
Website: http://www.optimist.org (click on *Home\Members\Scholarship Contests*)
Additional Information: This scholarship is based on your ability to

prepare and present a timed four- to five-minute speech on a specific topic. Contestants, who must be no more than 19 at the time of contest entry, must speak about the official oratorical contest subject, which changes each year. For example, one year's contest subject was "Why My Voice Is Important." Contest is open to citizens of the United States, Canada, and the Caribbean. You must enter the contest through your local Optimist Club. To locate your local Optimist club, use the e-mail address above. Students must compete in several levels. Visit the website for more details. Award amounts range up to $2,500.

NOTE: I competed in the Optimist International Oratorical Contest for several years at various levels beginning in the sixth grade, usually winning at each level but not the final level. Although I did not win the $1,500 award, I did gain invaluable experience in public speaking and in writing speeches, which also helped me to write essays. These are very important skills to have, especially if you want to win scholarships. The ability to speak well in public will help you both in interviews and in preparing essays.

OPTIMIST INTERNATIONAL ESSAY CONTEST

Programs Manager
4494 Lindell Boulevard
St. Louis, MO 63108
(800) 500-8130 or (314) 371-6000; fax: (314) 371-6006
E-mail: programs@optimist.org
Website: http://www.optimist.org (click on *Home\Members\Programs Scholarship Contests*)
Award Amount: $650–$5,000
Additional Information: This is a multilevel essay writing contest. Student winners at the district and international level win scholarships. Contestants must be no more than 19 at the time of contest entry. Contest is open to citizens of the United States, Canada, and the Caribbean. You must enter the contest through your local Optimist Club. To locate your local Optimist club, use the e-mail address above. Visit the website for more details.

THE PRUDENTIAL SPIRIT OF COMMUNITY AWARDS

Website: http://spirit.prudential.com
Additional Information: This program, sponsored by Prudential in

partnership with the National Association of Secondary School Principals (NASSP), recognizes students in grades 5–12 who have demonstrated exemplary community service. Local honorees are selected at participating schools and organizations in November, and from these winners, two state honorees are chosen from each state and the District of Columbia. State honorees receive an award of $1,000, an engraved silver medallion, and an all-expenses-paid trip to Washington, D.C. National honorees receive an additional award of $5,000, an engraved gold medallion, a crystal trophy for their school or organization, and a $5,000 grant from the Prudential Foundation to donate to a nonprofit, charitable organization of their choice. Although this program is not officially a scholarship, the funds you win, if you're an avid volunteer, could add nicely to the money in your college fund to pay for your educational expenses.

PROFILE IN COURAGE ESSAY CONTEST

Columbia Point
Boston, MA 02125
(617) 514-1600
E-mail: profiles@nara.gov
Website: http://www.jfkcontest.org
Additional Information: In recognition of one of President Kennedy's most important legacies, this contest is designed to promote the involvement of young people in the civic life of their country. High school students in grades 9–12 can participate in this essay contest, by writing a compelling 1,000 word (maximum) essay on the meaning of political courage, citing at least five sources, while also learning about and being inspired by America's elected officials, past or present, who have tried to make a difference in the world. Registration forms must be submitted with the essay and are available on the website. The first-place winner and the nominating teacher will be invited to receive awards at the Kennedy Library in Boston. Awards range from $500 to $10,000. The contest deadline is usually in early January of each year.

PROJECT YELLOW LIGHT SCHOLARSHIP/HUNTER GARNER SCHOLARSHIP

Julie Garner
One Shockoe Plaza

Richmond, VA 23219-4132
(804) 698-8203
Website: http://projectyellowlight.com
Additional Information: See chapter 18.

THE RAGINS/BRASWELL NATIONAL SCHOLARSHIP

The Scholarship Workshop
P.O. Box 176
Centreville, VA 20122
(703) 579-4245
E-mail: scholars@scholarshipworkshop.com
Website: http://www.scholarshipworkshop.com
Social Media: Follow this program on Facebook and Twitter.
Additional Information: The scholarship is available to high school seniors, undergraduates, and graduate students who attend The Scholarship Workshop presentation or an online class given by Marianne Ragins, winner of more than $400,000 in scholarships. Award is based on use of techniques taught in the workshop or class, application, essay, and extracurricular activities. Interested students should visit the website for more details and class information. The deadline is usually in April.

THURGOOD MARSHALL SCHOLARSHIP FUND

901 F Street NW, Suite 300
Washington, DC 20004
(202) 507-4851; fax: (202) 652-2934
E-mail: info@tmcfund.org
Website: http://www.thurgoodmarshallfund.net
Additional Information: Open to students attending or planning to attend a historically black public college or university (HBPCU) full-time. The scholarship may also be used at one of the member law schools. Students must be U.S. citizens with at least a 3.0 GPA and must be admitted to a qualifying institution before applying for the scholarship and be recommended by the faculty or staff member at their current school. To see a list of institutions, current scholarships, and deadlines as well as scholarship amounts, visit the website. Award amounts vary.

THE SCHOLASTIC ART AND WRITING AWARDS

557 Broadway
New York, NY 10012
E-mail: info@artandwriting.org
Website: http://www.scholastic.com/artandwriting or http://www.artand
writing.org
Additional Information: These awards are designed to recognize out-
standing talent among students in the visual arts and creative writing.
Students submit individual works as well as art and writing portfolios.
Check the website for entry details in the fall. Awards range from $500 to
$10,000. You can begin submitting for one of these awards in the fall, usu-
ally September.

SIEMENS COMPETITION IN MATH, SCIENCE AND TECHNOLOGY

Siemens Foundation
170 Wood Ave South
Iselin, NJ 08830
(877) 822-5233
E-mail: foundation.us@siemens.com
Additional Information: This program is available to high school seniors
who want to enter individual research projects and to all high school students (from grades 9–12) who wish to enter projects as part of a two- to
three-member team. The Siemens Competition is designed to recognize
remarkable talent early and foster individual growth in students who are
willing to challenge themselves through science research. Students can
achieve national recognition for science research projects that they complete in high school and earn up to $100,000 in scholarships for their work.
The competition deadline is normally in September.

SODEXO FOUNDATION

Stephen J. Brady STOP Hunger Scholarships
9801 Washingtonian Blvd.
Gaithersburg, MD 20878
(615) 320 3149 (indicate your call is about the Sodexo Foundation STOP
Hunger Scholarships)
E-mail: STOPHunger@applyists.com

Website: http://www.sodexofoundation.org (see *Scholarships*)
Additional Information: See chapter 14.

SONS OF THE AMERICAN REVOLUTION JOSEPH S. RUMBAUGH HISTORICAL ORATION CONTEST

Chairman, Joseph S. Rumbaugh Historical Oration Contest
NSSAR Headquarters
1000 South Fourth Street
Louisville, KY 40203-3208
Website: http://www.sar.org/Youth/Oration_Contest or http://www.sar.org (see *Education*)
Additional information: Oration competition for high school freshmen, sophomores, juniors, and seniors who submit an original five- to six-minute oration on a personality, event, or document of the American Revolutionary War and how it relates to the United States today. Oration must be delivered from memory without props or charts. For more information and complete rules, visit the website. Awards range from $200 to $3,000.

U.S. SENATE YOUTH PROGRAM

William Randolph Hearst Foundation
90 New Montgomery Street, Suite 1212
San Francisco, CA 94105-4504
(800) 841-7048 or (415) 908-4540; fax: (415) 243-0760
E-mail: ussyp@hearstfdn.org
Website: http://www.ussenateyouth.org
Additional Information: Open to high school juniors or seniors holding student office: student body president, vice president, secretary, or treasurer; class president, vice president, secretary, or treasurer; student council representative; student representative to district, regional, or state-level civic organization. For an application contact your high school principal or state-level education administrator. Visit the website page to find more information about your state-level education administrator and the program details. The organization's advice to interested students is to apply in your junior year so that you will have two years of eligibility rather than one if you apply as a senior. Award is a $5,000 college scholarship and an all-expense-paid trip to Washington to experience national government in action. The deadline is usually in early fall. Visit the website at the beginning of your junior or senior year for additional details and current deadlines.

VEGETARIAN RESOURCE GROUP SCHOLARSHIPS

P.O. Box 1463
Baltimore, MD 21203
(410) 366-8343
E-mail: vrg@vrg.org
Website: http://www.vrg.org
Additional Information: See chapter 15.

VOICE OF DEMOCRACY ANNUAL AUDIO ESSAY CONTEST

Veterans of Foreign Wars of the United States
(816) 968-1117
E-mail: kharmer@vfw.org
Website: http://www.vfw.org (click on *Community\Programs*)
Additional Information: This is a scholarship contest open to students in grades 9–12. Students write and record a three- to five-minute essay addressing the assigned theme for the year. Previous themes have been "I'm Optimistic About Our Nation's Future," "Freedom's Obligation," "Reaching Out to America's Future," and "What Price Freedom?" To participate in this contest, visit the website for more information, speak with your high school counselor, or contact your local VFW post. Scholarship awards range from $1,000 to $30,000. The deadline is usually November 1. Submissions should go to your local VFW post. E-mail or see the website to find your local post.

Specific Scholarships

Additional information for the following scholarships is included in other chapters of this book because they are specific to certain situations. Visit the chapters referenced to obtain more details about each scholarship or award program.

Scholarships for the Disabled

Please refer to chapter 22, "Scholarships for Disabled Students," for additional information including websites, addresses, and telephone numbers for each of these awards.

Scholarships for Minorities

Please refer to chapter 17, "Scholarships for Minorities—What's the Difference in a Minority Scholarship Hunt?" for additional information including websites, addresses, and telephone numbers for each of these resources, scholarships, fellowships, or awards. The chapter includes sections on General Minority Scholarship and Fellowship Opportunities, African American Minority Scholarship and Fellowship Opportunities, Hispanic/Latino Minority Scholarship and Fellowship Opportunities, and Native American/Indian Scholarship and Fellowship Opportunities.

Scholarships for Current College and Transfer Students

Please refer to chapter 18, "Scholarships for Current College Students and Transfer Students," for additional information including websites, addresses, and telephone numbers for each of these resources, scholarships, prizes, or awards.

Unusual Scholarships

Please refer to chapter 15, "Unusual Scholarship Opportunities," for additional information including websites, addresses, and telephone numbers for each of these resources, scholarships, prizes, or awards.

Scholarships Available for Texting, Blogging, and Using Social Media Platforms

Please refer to the section "Scholarship Programs Incorporating Social Media, Texting, and Blogging into the Selection Process" in chapter 2 for more information.

Scholarships for Nontraditional Students

Please refer to chapter 20, "Scholarships for Nontraditional Students—Distance Learners and Adults Returning to College," for additional information including websites, addresses, and telephone numbers for each of these resources, scholarships, prizes, or awards.

Scholarships for International Students, International Study, and Study Abroad

Please refer to chapter 21, "Scholarships for International Students and Study Abroad Funding for U.S. Students," for additional information including websites, addresses, and telephone numbers for each of these resources, scholarships, prizes, or awards.

Scholarships for the Military and Their Dependents

Please refer to chapter 27, "Scholarships and College Funding for the Military and Their Family," for additional information including websites, addresses, and telephone numbers for each of these resources, scholarships, prizes, or awards.

Scholarships for Students in the 11th and Lower Grades

Please refer to chapter 26, "Scholarships for Younger Students—From Kindergarten to 11th Grade," for additional information including websites, addresses, and telephone numbers for each of these resources, scholarships, prizes, or awards.

Scholarships for Graduate Students

Please refer to chapter 19, "Going Beyond the Undergraduate Degree—Paying for Graduate School," for additional information, including websites, physical addresses, and telephone numbers for each of these resources, scholarships, prizes, or awards.

Appendix B

OTHER RESOURCES FROM MARIANNE RAGINS

BOOKS AND PUBLICATIONS

The Scholarship and College Essay Planning Kit
> If you have trouble getting beyond a blank page when it comes to writing an essay, this resource is for you. This resource is updated yearly.

Get Money for College—An Audio Series
> If you don't have time to read a book or attend a class but you do have time to listen, this audio series can help you learn how to find and win scholarships for college.

10 Steps for Using the Internet in Your Scholarship Search
> This is a resource designed to be used at your computer to walk you step by step through your scholarship search on the Internet. It keeps you from being overwhelmed by the massive amount of sometimes misleading information found on the Web. This resource is updated yearly.

The Scholarship Monthly Planning Calendar
> This convenient and easy-to-use monthly planning calendar will help you with time management, getting organized, and staying on track with activities to meet major scholarship and award deadlines. This resource is updated yearly.

College Survival and Success Skills 101
> This invaluable guide, rich with anecdotes from students across the nation, is essential for any student who wants to improve time management and study skills, boost a college GPA, get along with roommates, stay on track to graduate, become a world traveler with opportunities such as study abroad, and find scholarships and awards to shrink the tuition bill.

Last-Minute College Financing Guide

> If you've got the acceptance letter but are still wondering how to pay the tuition bill because you haven't yet started searching for college money, this resource is for you.

WORKSHOPS AND BOOT CAMPS

The Scholarship Workshop Presentation

> The Scholarship Workshop presentation is a 1-, 2-, or 3-hour interactive seminar in which speaker Marianne Ragins proves that it is not always the student with the best grades or the highest SAT scores who wins scholarships. Instead she shows students of all ages that most scholarships are awarded to students who exhibit the best preparation. By attending The Scholarship Workshop, a student will be well prepared to meet the challenge of finding and winning scholarships. The presentation is designed to help students conduct a successful scholarship search, from the research involved in finding scholarship money to scholarship essays, scholarship interview tips, and strategies involved in winning them. This presentation is usually sponsored by an organization and individuals usually attend at no cost. Attendees become eligible for the Ragins/Braswell National scholarship sponsored by Marianne. If you or your organization is interested in sponsoring a workshop or motivational presentation with Marianne Ragins, visit http://www.scholarshipworkshop.com.

The Scholarship Workshop Weekend Boot Camp

> This is an expanded version of The Scholarship Workshop presentation, a full day and a half of activities designed to help students and parents leave with scholarship essays, résumés, and applications completed and ready to go. The weekend boot camp is usually sponsored by an organization and individuals usually attend at no cost. Attendees become eligible for the Ragins/Braswell National scholarship sponsored by Marianne. If you or your organization is interested in sponsoring a workshop or motivational presentation with Marianne Ragins, visit http://www.scholarshipworkshop.com.

WEBINARS/ONLINE CLASSES

The Scholarship Class for High School Students and Their Parents and *Scholarship, Fellowship and Grant Information Session for Students Already in College, Returning to College, and Pursuing Graduate School*

The above classes are webinar versions of The Scholarship Workshop presentation. They are offered to those who do not live in an area where a workshop is being sponsored. Attendees of either class become eligible for the Ragins/Braswell National Scholarship.

Writing Scholarship and College Essays for the Uneasy Student Writer; Turbocharge Your Résumé—Résumé Writing Skills to Help You Stand Out from the Crowd; Preparation Skills for Scholarship and College Interviews; Minimizing College Costs and Student Loans For more information about these webinars, visit http://www.scholar shipworkshop.com/online-classes.

EBOOKS

Marianne Ragins has numerous eBooks available for Nook, Kindle, and iPad. Go to http://www.scholarshipworkshop.com/ebooks for the latest.

You can find information and additional resources from Marianne Ragins by visiting the following:

http://www.scholarshipworkshop.com
http://www.facebook.com/scholarshipworkshop
http://www.twitter.com/ScholarshipWork
http://www.shop.scholarshipworkshop.com

 Scan this QR code to join our mailing list for scholarship updates and information or text "SCHOLARSHIP INFO" to 22828.

ACKNOWLEDGMENTS

First, I would like to acknowledge the former principal of Northeast High School, David Dillard, for his dedication to both the school and its students. He called the first reporter when my scholarship totals reached more than $258,000 in funds because he was determined that I receive recognition for my achievements. Without him, my achievements may not have been recognized as widely, or possibly at all. I acknowledge my mother, Laura Ragins, and my entire family for the support they have given me throughout my life. Furthermore, I acknowledge all of my teachers from elementary, middle, and high school who contributed to my education. Most important, I thank God for nurturing my family and myself, and for the blessings He has bestowed upon us.

To my wonderful husband, Ivan McGee, thanks for being my partner in so many endeavors. You have been an awesome help with this fourth edition of *Winning Scholarships for College*. And to my kids, Aria and Cameron, thanks for supporting Mommy just by being my "beautiful and fun lumps of sugar."

Thank you Rose, Nett, Greg, and Dutch for helping so much with the first and second editions.

Stephanie, your covers for the first and second edition were beautiful.

To the editors for this current and previous editions, thanks for your time and patience.

To Tracy Sherrod, my first editor at Henry Holt for *Winning Scholarships for College*, thanks for all your suggestions for the third edition. They were a major improvement.

To Allison Adler, editor for this fourth edition, many thanks for championing this edition and for your very careful comments, suggestions, and clarifications. Wow! I don't think you missed a thing.

Also thanks to the entire Henry Holt editing and design staff who worked on this edition. It looks incredible and reads wonderfully.

I would also like to thank the members of Stubbs Chapel Baptist Church, especially my Aunt Sister and Uncle Sammie, for the support they have given me over the years.

Thanks to all my friends and family members, especially Mom and anyone else who listened to all my frustrations in finishing this book and trying to make it even better than before.

A hearty thanks to Cheron Reed for helping to type all my old-fashioned notebooks, written by hand, into my computer word-processor for the third edition.

To the scholarship judges and program administrators who chose me as a scholarship recipient, thank you very much for giving not only me but many others the chance to further our education. I hope there will be many other winners to follow.

Thanks to Patti Ross, J. Mark Davis, and the entire Coca-Cola Scholars Foundation staff for keeping such good records from many years ago and allowing me to reprint my original essay from the 1991 Coca-Cola Scholars competition. And for their insightful comments in response to my questions, I thank you. A hearty note of appreciation to Stephanie Gargiulo for your assistance as well.

Thanks to the many scholarship programs and organizations that provided information on their various awards, scholarships, and requirements. Your response to my inquiries helped tremendously.

To Marie Brown, thanks for helping to get *Winning Scholarships for College* initially published by Henry Holt.

INDEX

Page numbers in *italics* refer to illustrations.

ABOUT THE AUTHOR

As publisher of the website http://www.scholarshipworkshop.com, author of the highly successful *Winning Scholarships for College*, and the winner of more than $400,000 in scholarship money, Marianne Ragins has worked with students, parents, and educators as a motivational speaker and education professional dedicated to student success for over twenty years. As perhaps the first student ever to amass nearly half a million dollars in scholarship money, she has been featured in many publications, including *USA Today*, *People*, *Newsweek*, *Money*, *Essence*, and on the cover of *Parade*. She has also made hundreds of radio and television appearances.

Ragins is not only the author of *Winning Scholarships for College: An Insider's Guide*, *College Survival and Success Skills 101*, and many other publications, she is also the president of The Scholarship Workshop LLC and sponsor of the Leading the Future II and Ragins/Braswell National Scholarships. Ragins is an experienced inspirational speaker and lecturer who has traveled nationally and internationally conducting The Scholarship Workshop presentation and giving other motivational seminars and speeches. She has presented at Georgetown University, Spelman College, Morehouse College, the University of the Virgin Islands, the National Black MBA Association National Convention, and the American Institute of Architects National Convention. She is a member of the National Speakers Association.

Marianne received an MBA from George Washington University and graduated summa cum laude with a Bachelor of Science from Florida A&M University. Both her degrees were entirely funded by scholarships and other free aid.